The

ERNEST HOLMES
PAPERS

The

ERNEST HOLMES PAPERS

A COLLECTION OF
THREE INSPIRATIONAL CLASSICS

ERNEST HOLMES

Compiled by

GEORGE P. BENDALL

JEREMY P. TARCHER/PENGUIN
a member of Penguin Group (USA)
New York

JEREMY P. TARCHER/PENGUIN
Published by the Penguin Group
Penguin Group (USA) LLC
375 Hudson Street
New York, New York 10014

USA • Canada • UK • Ireland • Australia
New Zealand • India • South Africa • China

penguin.com
A Penguin Random House Company

The Philosophy of Ernest Holmes © 1996 by Ann Bendall
The Anatomy of Healing Prayer © 1991 by George P. Bendall
Ideas of Power © 1992 by George P. Bendall
First omnibus edition published by Jeremy P. Tarcher/Penguin in 2014
Foreword © 2014 by Kenn Gordon

Most Tarcher/Penguin books are available at special quantity discounts for bulk purchase
for sales promotions, premiums, fund-raising, and educational needs. Special books or book excerpts
also can be created to fit specific needs. For details, write: Special.Markets@us.penguingroup.com.

ISBN 978-0-399-17055-3

Printed in the United States of America
1 3 5 7 9 10 8 6 4 2

Book design by Meighan Cavanaugh

CONTENTS

Volume One

THE PHILOSOPHY OF ERNEST HOLMES

Volume Two

THE ANATOMY OF HEALING PRAYER

Volume Three

IDEAS OF POWER

A NOTE FROM THE SCIENCE OF MIND
ARCHIVES & LIBRARY FOUNDATION

George P. Bendall was a close friend and associate of Dr. Ernest Holmes. After Dr. Holmes's wife, Hazel, passed away, Mr. Bendall lived in Dr. Holmes's home. Because of this close association, Bendall was privy to the internal life of Dr. Holmes in his later years. Bendall revealed his understanding of Holmes's inner life in the introductory sections of each volume of the original Holmes Papers, which are included in this anthology.

The material included in this anthology is derived from spontaneous, intimate talks delivered in private with close personal friends and associates during the last year or two of Dr. Holmes's life. Material also comes from the Tuesday Invitational Group at the Institute of Religious Science in Los Angeles, as well as with Holmes's private practitioner's class. Also included is a transcription of Holmes's dedication of the Whittier Church of Religious Science on February 12, 1959, which included Holmes's "cosmic consciousness" experience that is of special note to Science of Mind students. All of the material is presented as close to verbatim as possible, with only minimal changes to improve clarity and comprehension.

FOREWORD

This compendium of Ernest Holmes's public talks, compiled by his long-time associate George Bendall and edited by Arthur Vegara, brings into the public venue not only the brilliant mind of the man Holmes, but also the character and soul of one of America's greatest philosophers. Ernest Shurtleff Holmes was born in 1887 in Maine and died April 7, 1960, in Los Angeles. In that seventy-three years he formulated, applied, and founded the Religious Science organization—now known as Centers for Spiritual Living—wrote over twenty books, initiated, published, and wrote both *The Science of Mind* and *Creative Thought* magazines, and spoke most every week at one or more of the churches and centers he led around the world. His pivotal teaching, "The Science of Mind," is a spiritual philosophy that is known as a leader in today's New Thought movement as a working cosmology that provides a positive and supportive approach to daily living and to connection with a higher power. It focuses on humankind's relationship with what is often referred to as "Spirit," and provides both an immanent approach to life and a transcendent understanding of the individual and society's place in the Universe.

This compilation of *The Ernest Holmes Papers* is a revised version of three books put together by George Bendall: *The Philosophy of Ernest Holmes*, *The Anatomy of Healing Prayer*, and *Ideas of Power*. It is a collection of Ernest Holmes's public lectures over the last years of his life and sets about, in a most human and personal manner, bringing to life not only thirty-eight of

Ernest Holmes's best lectures but also Ernest Holmes himself. It covers the A-to-Z of his spiritual philosophy from "The History of New Thought" to "God and Your Personality." In between, it delivers a perspective on Ernest Holmes's personal evolution, as well as insight into who he was as a human and how he applied this marvelous teaching not only in his own life but to the lives of others. Above all else, it touches your soul.

My personal feeling—after a lifetime of studying this man and his teaching—is that it brings a powerful and productive touch to the study of the Science of Mind. For me, it has a way of bypassing the intellect and delving deep into my soul and the soul of Ernest's work. Reading the spoken word somehow circumvents the intellect and reaches deep into my own personal resonant knowing. His charisma and life energy flow clearly, even in the written word, and awe me with an understanding of the power and might he must have commanded when he stood in front of thousands of people and eloquently described the beauty and simplicity of life in person. As the biblical phrase goes, "it restoreth my soul." It brings his personality to the forefront so that one might feel the faith and passion he had for life and in life. It awakens something deep that lies in repose awaiting a stirring to magnify it and birth it back into conscious recognition. And it does more. It provides practical and applicable means, motivation, and pathways to change one's life and, in so doing, change the world. It captures the gift of Ernest and rises above the veil of opinion and personal interpretation that one might experience when being taught by another. It focuses on the teachers of Science of Mind and, in so doing, dissolves the preconceived notions of others and lands the reader solidly on their own two feet in the midst of their own and Ernest's greatness. It awakens and cleanses what some consider to be the greatest distillation of the greatest teachings that exist in the world.

This is a book not only for students of the Science of Mind, but also for anyone who desires to become awake and apply spirituality in their life and the life of the world. The spiritual organization that Holmes spent his life creating—which is now known as Centers for Spiritual Living— holds as a purpose, "the awakening of humanity to its spiritual magnificence" and is drawn by its vision, which is Holmes's vision, to "a world that works for all."

As such, this is an awakening collection.

Whether you are a minister, a practitioner, a student, or a novice, even if you have never heard of Ernest Holmes and the Science of Mind, I guarantee you one thing—after you read this, you will be more awake to the beauty and power of life than you ever were before. Ernest Holmes was a gift to this world and this collection brings to life exactly what that gift is. He writes, "I think we should feel we are on a mission. Not a mission of sadness to save souls—they are not lost; if they were you wouldn't know where to look for them—but a mission that glorifies the soul. Not to find we are here for salvation, but for glorification—the beauty, the wonder, the delight of that Something that sings and sings and sings in the soul of man." Ernest Holmes, like all other great avatars, saw into the future and, in so doing, he saw the potential of this life. He said, "There is no question in my mind but what we are is the next greatest religion of the future—because the religion of the future will be a combination; it will come from science, from philosophy, and from religion. It will come, as science becomes less and less materialistic, which it is now doing; when philosophy stops being dualistic, as though there were a material and spiritual universe—or just a material; and when theology gets over its superstition."

This is the recipe for peace and joy, this is the "to-do list" of a practical and functional world, and this is Ernest Holmes. This book brings it all together, brings it to life and brings it to a logical application. It's time to wake up, and this collection—by touching mind, body, and soul—motivates and activates what is needed within and what is required to do for every one of us here, which of course, is you. Enjoy!

—*Rev. Dr. Kenn Gordon, Spiritual Leader for*
Centers for Spiritual Living

Volume One

THE PHILOSOPHY OF ERNEST HOLMES

INTRODUCTION

U se what I gave you!" I heard from my subconscious in that all-too-familiar New-England-accented voice—Ernest S. Holmes speaking to me in November 1988, twenty-eight years following the death in April 1960 of this great man and originator of the Science of Mind.

I had spent a week thinking what a great potential for the world the teaching and practice of the Science of Mind offered. To my mind, the movement had fallen into the morbidity that follows over-organization: worship of effects, lack of zeal and interest in retaining the purity and greatness of the teaching. The obvious present weakness was a reversal of what had once been a great strength in the field churches throughout the world: a strong element of individuality, but with the retention of a unity that was represented by the principle of "one for all and all for one." Wordsworth puts it so aptly: "The world is too much late and soon./ In getting and spending we lay waste our powers." The movement suffered from the loss of belief and the sacrifice of the teaching's uniqueness to whatever would financially benefit and otherwise suit those involved in the resultant complacency.

One night I put this into prayer, unconsciously blaming Ernest, and then went to sleep. In the middle of the night the sentence "Use what I gave you!" surfaced from God knows where. I went to my office and began rummaging through some of the works and personal memorabilia given to me by Ernest in the last two years of his life when I lived with him. No inner chord of response was struck. Then I remembered I always attended every talk of his wherever it was given. I could not get enough of his wisdom. He recognized that and would take me with him.

I got in the car one night with a notebook and he asked, "What's that for?" I replied, "I don't want to miss anything important as you talk." Ernest said, "I'll take care of that. I'll have Helen [his secretary] type a copy of all the talks for you."

I thought that was a nice gesture—even if he had no intention of doing it. To my joy and surprise, several days later Helen Heichert presented me with a copy of the talk we had had that night. Ernest's gift of his shared wisdom continued throughout the rest of his life in this expression—some two years. I treasured these papers; but in the moving in and out of different households and offices in the ensuing twenty-eight to thirty years, they were scattered to the winds—some in my library, some in files unnoticed, some at home, some interspersed in things to remember, and, sadly, some lost forever. I proceeded to rediscover them and arrange them in their proper page sequence, stapled them together, and began rereading them. I knew this was what was meant by "Use what I gave you!"

Only a fraction of these papers are presented in this first volume, which is dedicated to the philosophy of Ernest S. Holmes, my friend and mentor. I've called the entire collection, for want of something better, *The Ernest Holmes Papers*.

George P. Bendall

1.

HISTORY OF THE
NEW THOUGHT MOVEMENT

In the first three chapters we see emphasized what Dr. Holmes expressed to me many times. "George, I have talked or written about only three things":

1. There is one God, common to all, in and through all things.
2. There is a Universe that responds with mechanical regularity to the spontaneity of our thoughts.
3. The 11th Commandment of theology—"Thou shalt love one another, as I have loved you."

In this chapter and the next he emphasizes that "We are Christian and more."

The Rev. Dr. Barclay Johnson,* introducing Dr. Holmes, said in part: "All of you in later years will count these hours as among your most precious recollections, for you will be able to say that you heard the story of Religious Science from the one who gave it to the world, who tonight shares with us his vision."

DR. HOLMES

I have always contended that before we can know what is a normal human mind [referring to the MMPI test that Dr. Johnson announced was to be

---

*Religious Science minister.

given] we shall have to stop estimating it by our mental and emotional disturbances, which we all have. In all these things they look for the abnormal, so of all people in the world, the psychiatrist—and this is nothing against him, because I believe in what he does—but of all people in the world, unless he is very careful, he might know less about the human mind than any other person. Because in studying that which is emotionally unstable and devoting one's whole time to that, you are liable to lose the perspective of what might be stable. In the *exhaustive* analysis, you would have to analyze, if one out of ten is unstable, the nine who are more or less stable, as well as the one who is unstable, to get your law of averages, or it wouldn't be fair, would it? That is the way it is: it ain't fair!

I wish to start with the history of the New Thought movement because there would be no Religious Science movement had there not at first been a New Thought movement. We are one of the New Thought groups of America, which have come up in the last sixty years and influenced the thought of the world and this country more than any other one single element in it—that is, spiritually, religiously, theologically, psychologically too. But the New Thought movement itself, which originated in America, had its roots in a very deep antiquity. We would have to go back, because it has drawn its knowledge from all sources; it is not just a Christian philosophy, although it is a Christian denomination.

It draws many of its sources from India. Now India did not have any one outstanding prophet or revelator as most of the religions have had, such as Buddhism or Christianity or Judaism. India never had a great prophet or a great savior—never claimed any. Rather, their teaching is an accumulation of generations—thousands of years, probably—of wise people (they didn't even call them saints, but *sages*).

In looking over these generations of the teachings of India, we find a very great concept of the unity of all life. They believed in one God and only One. They didn't call it God; they called it the Absolute, or Brahma; but it doesn't matter what you call it. They believed in one Presence and one Power, and only One in the Universe. They believed (which later came out as a theosophical teaching) in the mind that sleeps in the mineral, waves in the grass, wakes to simple consciousness in the animal, to self-consciousness in the human, and to cosmic consciousness in what they call the upper hierarchies, or an ascending scale of evolution, ad infinitum.

They believed in the theory of involution and evolution, "the spark that ignites the mundane clod," or the divine idea which exists in everything—*everything*—a Something that all things are impregnated with. It is called involution, or the passing of Spirit into substance prior to the passing of substance into definite form to begin an endless round of evolution or unfoldment, cycle after cycle (if they believe in reincarnation, as they do), over and over here, until they have learned what there is here, and then on and on and on.

I personally happen to believe in the upper hierarchies. For all we know, planets are individuals; we don't know that they are not. As intelligent a man as Dean Inge,* who was the greatest living exponent of Platonism, and who probably understood Platonism better than anyone else in his day (he just passed on recently while still active in the Anglican church in England), said it didn't seem strange; it was rather rational to accept that all planetary bodies are individuals. Now, whether they are or not doesn't make any difference; I don't know; that is part of their teaching. If you would like to take the time to read the best single volume on what real Hinduism is, the ancient teachings of the Bhagavad Gita, the Upanishads, and the Vedas, you will find it in one volume of about 900 pages—we have it, and you can probably get it out of the library, called *The Life Divine*, by Aurobindo.† He was considered by both Tagore‡ and Mahatma Gandhi§ as the greatest intellect and exponent of real Hinduism of modern times.

This is one of the sources of the New Thought movement, because the New Thought movement, while it is a Christian denomination, is very much more than that. You do not have to belittle the concept of Christianity to say the Hebrews were nice people and a few of the Greeks had quite a bit

---

*William Inge (1860–1954), English prelate, educator, writer, and Dean of St. Paul's cathedral.
†Sri Aurobindo Ghose (1872–1950), Indian seer, philosopher, and nationalist.
‡Sir Rabindranath Tagore (1861–1941), Indian Bengali poet.
§Mohandas Gandhi (1869–1948), Indian nationalist and spiritual leader.

of intelligence, since the philosophy of Christianity itself is a combination of the Judaic and the Grecian philosophies—that is what it is.

Stace,* in a book called *The Destiny of Western Man*—a professor at Princeton, I believe—said the philosophy of Christianity is a combination of what he called Palestinian impositionalism (which means "Thus saith the God from *up here*," as the Hebraic prophets said) and what he called Grecian immanentism ("Thus saith the God from *in here*")—while Dean Inge said that the philosophy of Christianity is 25 percent from Judaism and 75 percent from the Greeks. You see, the Hebrews were the greatest line of emotional prophets the world has ever known. They were terrific people. They believed that God is One: "Hear O Israel, the Eternal, the Lord thy God is One God"—*but One*. Absolute monotheists.

The ancient Hebrews (and still today; they haven't changed in their doctrine) and the ancient Hindus (they haven't changed) were, together with certain phases of ancient Egypt which I wish to mention, the first people to perceive a unitary Cause. Whatever it is, it is one and not two ultimates. If they were alike, they would destroy each other. If they were unlike, they would coalesce, amalgamate, and come together and be one; there can't be two finalities. The Truth is one, undivided, and indivisible.

But 1,500 years prior to the time of Moses we find the Hermetic doctrine—Hermes Trismegistus (Thrice-Great Hermes). In this teaching we find a great deal that Moses taught (because Moses was educated in the Egyptian court, in the Egyptian temples. He was brought up by the Egyptian priests, the hierarchy of nobility), and he was a "top guy," as history has shown.

We find in the Greeks a rehearsal of the Hermetic teaching, particularly in their concept of what Emerson[†] called the Law of Parallels and Swedenborg[‡] called the Law of Correspondences, because the Hermetic teaching had said, "As above, so beneath; as beneath, so above." What is true on one

---

*Walter T. Stace, educator and writer.
†Ralph Waldo Emerson (1803–1882), American essayist and poet.
‡Emanuel Swedenborg (1688–1772), Swedish scientist, philosopher, and religious writer.

plane is true on all—which really means (and this is where we got the idea) that for every visible thing there is an invisible pattern to which the visible is attached.

One of the latest words in modern physics I read within the last two or three years is a book on an explanation of Einstein and Eddington* by a very prominent man (accepted by both of these people), in which he said, "Modern physics has become metaphysics"; and the view of the physical universe (which we used to call the material universe) in modern physics is that what we see is not a thing in itself. Whether it is a mountain or a planet or a wart on our finger, it is more like shadow cast by an invisible substance. Isn't that interesting? The Bible says, "We see now as through a glass darkly." It says, "The things that are seen are not made of the things which do appear, . . . he shall count the things that are as though they were not."

This Law of Parallels which Emerson said he believed in—for he said, "Nature has but two laws, but she plays the familiar tune over and over again"—is Hermetic. That would be in line with concepts of Swedenborg where he said, "There is the celestial correspondent to every terrestrial thing." And the Bible says, "How is it that the dead are raised up and with what body do they come? . . . There are bodies celestial and bodies terrestrial. . . . so also is the resurrection of the dead. . . . The body is sown in weakness, it is raised in power; it is sown a natural body, it is raised a spiritual body. For there is both a natural body and a spiritual body."

And Plotinus,† whom Inge called "the king of the intellectual mystics of the ages," said that every organ in the physical body is attached to a cosmic pattern. Now, you see: the pattern is generic, the organ is individualized. A generic pattern means a universal pattern. There is a pattern of man—not the individual but the generic or the universal. This is what is meant by "Christ" and by "Buddha" and by the "illumined," the "one Son," whom, Eckhart‡ said, "God is forever begetting, and He is begetting him in me now."

---

*Sir Arthur Eddington (1882–1944), English astronomer.
†A.D. 205–270, Roman (Egypt.-born) philosopher.
‡Johannes Eckhart (1260?–1327), German mystic.

Every organ, Plotinus said, is attached to its pattern, and when by reason of any fact it seems to become detached, it gets in pain and longs to get back. Augustine,* speaking of it in a different way and with a different motivation, said, "Thou hast made us, Thine we are, and our hearts are restless till they find repose in Thee."

Probably 50 percent of the best philosophy in the Catholic church came from Augustine, and he was continuously referring, as Eckhart did, to whom they called "the pagan philosophers," by whom they meant the Greeks—because the Greeks produced the greatest line of intellectual thinkers the world has ever known. The Hebrews produced the greatest line of emotional prophets the world has ever known. And it is an interesting thing that the philosophy of Christianity is a combination of the two, isn't it? Observe Greek art and see how perfect it is. You will not find a piece of Greek sculpture, unless it is something running, where it doesn't have to overcome the gravitational balance and attraction; but if you could draw a line right straight through the center, you would find it is in absolute balance, as is all their architecture—but it is an intellectual concept, it is kind of cold; yet it is beautiful.

Then look at Roman art: it is all warmth and color but grotesque in form, isn't it? You know, all these guys who painted the pictures of the little Madonna and Jesus—Jesus looks like a strange creature, to say the least. Four times as big as a baby ought to be, and legs as big as an elephant's.

We have to put all these things together—art, science, philosophy, and religion—to find out what makes it tick. No one system, no one teacher, no one person has given the world what it knows. It is very significant, because this is what Religious Science stands for.

So we have Buddhism, which plays an important role in the New Thought movement. Just as Christianity is a combination of the Hebrews and Greeks—drawing much through Egypt, because Hermes was an Egyptian—so Buddhism stems from Hinduism. It is rather an interesting thing, you know, Buddha's history—it was a heretical teaching in India. He was a

---

*St. Augustine of Hippo (354–430), Church Father and bishop of Hippo.

Hindu. He was born a prince, and his father would never let him go out in the world to see the horrors, poverty, and death. But one day he got out and saw them, and then he went out to try and find out what it was all about— and that is how he got started. He was supposed to have discovered the Law of Cause and Effect. Whether he did or not I don't know and don't care. All I want to know is, does it work and can we get it or use it? There is a utilitarianism; we must be practical. I say we are practical idealists and realistic transcendentalists. I think of us as that.

He, sitting there at the Banyan tree or whatever tree it was, had tried both paths. He found asceticism didn't work, because he became emaciated and fell over almost dead, and someone had to take care of him. He followed what he called the Middle Path; as he sat in contemplation, there was supposed to have been revealed to him the Law of Cause and Effect. The Law, Annie Besant* says, binds the ignorant but frees the wise. There was supposed to have been revealed to him the endless chain of cause and effect, karma, the karmic law, which means the fruit of action, which Jesus referred to when he said, "As a man sows, so shall he also reap," and Moses too when he said, "An eye for an eye and a tooth for a tooth"—cause and effect, the sequence; that is what karma means. And Moses said, "The word is in thine own mouth that thou shouldst know it and do it." Annie Besant said, "It is a law that binds the ignorant but frees the wise." From our viewpoint, it means that bondage is freedom used *as* bondage. There is no final negation.

So we get this sequence of cause and effect from both the Buddhist and Mosaic teaching. Moses said, "The sins of the fathers are visited on the children to the third and fourth generation of them that hate God." There was much also in Zoroastrianism.

The greatest contributions toward the New Thought came from Hinduism, Buddhism, the Old Testament, Judaism, the New Testament (of course), and the Greeks. The philosophy of Emerson is a combination, a compilation, a unification, a putting together of all these things, because he had studied them all his life. You find continual references, if you know

---

*(1847–1933), English theosophist.

where to find them and know what they mean. He had studied all these things and that is why he was so great. And then he had added to that which he had learned and synthesized it. Eliot* classed him as one of the ten greatest thinkers who have ever lived. There has not been such another intellect since the time of Plato, in my estimation.

So we find these ancient sources coming down, stemming from things before them, and in their turn contributing to what followed after them, gradually formulating certain concepts which do not necessarily agree with each other in detail but which, in the main, agree. We shall find, out of them, a synthesis—the best the world knows spiritually, I would say.

I leave Mohammedanism out. While it is one of the great major religions and very tolerant in many ways, it did not have the influence on Christianity and the New Thought movement that others do. The New Thought stems out of Christianity.

You will find the greatest tolerance in ancient Hinduism, less maligning of others than in any other system of thought up until the New Thought movement. They were very broad-minded people. They believed everything is in a state of evolution, a divine spark which, Browning† said, "a man may desecrate but never quite lose," and to which Wordsworth referred in "The Vision of Sir Lancelot," where he said, "What is so rare as a day in June/ When, if ever, come the perfect days;/ Then heaven tries earth, if it be in tune,/ And over it softly her warm care lays./ Whether we look or whether we listen,/ Hear a life murmur, or see it glisten,/ Every clod feels a stir of might,/ An instinct within it that reaches and towers,/ And groping blindly above it for light,/ Climbs to a soul in the grass and the flowers." That is no different from the theosophical concept of the mind that sleeps in the mineral, waves in the grass, wakes to simple consciousness in the animals, self-consciousness in man, and cosmic consciousness in a few men and the upper hierarchies.

Jesus said, "I came not to destroy the Law but to fulfill it." Moses said

---

*Charles William Eliot (1834–1926), American educator.
†Robert Browning (1812–1889), English poet.

this also, and Jesus said Moses was right. I say this, and I am right too. What did Jesus do? He added to the great impersonal laws of Moses the personal touch—to the great automatic laws of karma the concept that they can be broken at any split second, which is exactly what the Zen Buddhist believes and seeks to discover today; and he is right.

The past need no longer be married to the future; the future need no longer be the child of the past, inexorably carrying on the sequence of a chain of cause and effect that binds us to rebirth or to whatnot. If it is re-birth, I don't happen to believe in that. Half the world believes in it, but I shall be surprised if they are right. But I can't help it if they are; and if they are right, I am wrong and shall have to accept it. You and I don't make truth; we are only lucky if we come to believe in it and understand it. It is impersonal. Truth will be triumphant.

Buddha discovered—he was almost contemporary with Plato—the sequence of the chain of cause and effect, and he said it all has to do with the ego. Therefore get rid of the ego and you won't have cause and effect. Aurobindo calls Buddhism nihilism. Buddhism did not flourish in India the way it did in China, Japan, and the Malay states. Why? Because the Hindus had a purer teaching and it had to be the one that stuck. Buddhism added much to it but never replaced that essential, fundamental concept of a system of a unitary wholeness, an evolution which is a part of its process, and the certainty that Browning had when he said, "I shall arrive,/ As birds pursue their trackless paths;/ Some time, some day,/ In God's good way,/ I shall arrive." Which is a nice way of saying everybody is Hell-bent for Heaven and will get there.

Truth is candid. It is a cannonball—Truth as such itself. Emerson said it is a cold fact which we must accept. What did Jesus contribute to Judaism and—if we wish to include a little larger territory, and I am very happy to— Buddhism? Much which in theology has been called the remission of sins, forgiveness. He forgave people.

His opponents thought they had him caught. Today the two most highly trained people in the world are the Jesuits in the Catholic church and the rabbis in the Jewish church. They study more and work harder; they are wise people. Now Jesus forgave somebody, and they said, "You don't have a right to do this." He said, "Is it easier to say I forgive a man or tell him to get up and walk?" Now, whether or not you call it the remission of sins, theology has done terrible things with it.

Jesus introduced this, and it was his great contribution to Christianity, to the religions of the world, to the spiritual philosophy of the ages, and to the New Thought movement more than any other movement. Zen Buddhism teaches the same thing but with a more cumbersome method. Jesus knew there is a split second, now an unborn hour, in which the future need no longer be bound to the past, to repeat itself, as Freud said, "as a neurotic thought pattern does with monotonous regularity" throughout life. And Jesus was right. Can you step in the same river twice? Impossible. It is impossible that anything shall be repeated the way it was in nature—*anything*; because all nature is in flux and a flow. Everything.

And therefore the logic of what we know coincides with the inspiration of Jesus when he said, "Your sins are forgiven you; you don't have to worry over the past." But he didn't say, "Keep on doing it"; he said, "Don't do it any more lest a worse thing come upon you." It wasn't saying you can make a mistake and get away with it—you can have your cake and eat it—but it is a great consolation to know that "all of the yesterdays," as Isaiah said, "shall be remembered no more against you forever." One of the most beautiful things.

I have just finished making a tape recording of the highlights of Isaiah—which I called *The Song of Isaiah*; it is a transcendent thing—and of the Psalms, and of Proverbs (which I called *The Wisdom of Solomon*)—the most beautiful Bible readings I have ever seen, because I took only the affirmative and forgot the rest; the rest is of no consequence.* We do not care why it *doesn't* work—we only care why it *does* work. We no longer care why it is that two and two are *not* seven—'t'ain't so!

So we have these great contributions, taken down through the ages. We

---

*These readings became Part 2 of Holmes's posthumously published *You Will Live Forever* (1960).

don't have to go into the Reformation or Renaissance. You all know about them—all contributed something: Spinoza,* the great Jewish philosopher—prophet, perhaps; one of the greatest of the great, Jakob Böhme.† Swedenborg was called the man with the seven-storied brain. Emerson—the greatest intellect this country has had in modern times, I think. You see, Emerson delivered a baccalaureate sermon at Harvard and wasn't allowed to speak there for 30 years afterwards. It took them 30 years to discover what he had been talking about. Then they decided it was good.

Eckhart was excommunicated 200 years after he died, because it took them that long to find out what he was talking about and that it was bad. Among the things he said was, "God never had but one Son; but," he said, "the Eternal is forever begetting His only-begotten, and He is begetting him in me now." That is blasphemy, you see. Meister Eckhart is the most classical example of pure mysticism in the simplest form that has ever been presented, because he is as deep as Plato and as simple as Jesus. He was a great student of both.

The philosophy of Plotinus is the most classical example, for one who approaches it academically, of mysticism. I like Eckhart better. It is so simple. It is kind of sweet and beautiful, like the aroma of beautiful roses, fresh breezes, or morning sun or evening sunset. It has great beauty. He must have been a great artist in his mind.

You all know the philosophy and history of Christianity as well as I do, and probably better, until a little over a hundred years ago, when Mesmer began his experiments in Europe, which were brought over here and witnessed by a man by the name of Quimby, Phineas P. Quimby,‡ a watchmaker in Belfast, Maine—a mechanic, but a natural philosopher. He was a natural thinker, one of the most startling men who have ever lived. *The Quimby Manuscripts*, in my estimation, constitutes a compilation of the most original sayings in one book that were ever uttered by the mind of man. I

---

*Benedict de Spinoza (1632–1677), Dutch philosopher.
†(1575–1624), German mystic.
‡7(1802–1866).

studied it for nearly 30 years. It is almost impossible to get it, but it can be had.[*] Everyone should read it. We have excerpts from it at the book desk. It was upon his teaching that the philosophy of the New Thought movement was based—I mean its practical application.

I do not think Quimby knew about the philosophers I have been talking about. Some people think he probably had read Swedenborg, but I doubt it. One of his immediate followers was a Swedenborgian[†] who understood the Law of Celestial Correspondences, which merely means or says that in the invisible there is a prototype of the visible, all up and down the line.

At any rate, someone[‡] came to this country and lectured, and this guy in Maine saw it and thought it was very interesting. He got a subject named Lucius Burkmar, a young boy of 19, and he would mesmerize (partially hypnotize) him. Then this boy would become very clairvoyant and diagnose disease. He could see at a distance like psychics can. It is all real. Quimby had been suffering from a kidney complaint, and one day he mesmerized Lucius. He said, "Go in there and see what is wrong." Lucius did. He said, "One of your kidneys is practically detached."[§]

This is rather interesting. Remember, Plotinus said that when the organ appears to become *detached from its pattern*, it gets in pain and longs to get back to its pattern, that it shall be whole; and Quimby said he knew it was right, because this was what he had been told. He had been examined and he felt he had to suffer; but Lucius said, "Don't worry, I'll fix it up." He goes in and does his stuff, and it is done; and Quimby never had any more trouble from it. Lucius *attached it to its pattern*.

There *is* such a pattern—there must be, or we wouldn't be here; because no artist has ever seen beauty, no biologist has ever seen life, no psychologist has ever seen the mind, no physicist has ever seen energy, no philosopher

---

*See *Phineas Parkhurst Quimby: The Complete Writings* (DeVorss).
†Warren Felt Evans (1817–1889), first published New Thought writer and systematic formulator of the teaching. It is probably a mistake to consider him a "follower" of Quimby; however Dr. Holmes was reliant on a largely hearsay version of New Thought history.
‡Quimby heard both Charles Poyen and Robert Collyer.
§See Quimby, *Complete Writings*, III: 174–178.

has ever seen reality, and no theologian has ever seen God. All we see is the tail end of an effect, a shadow cast by an invisible substance. But the Celestial Visitor we *converse* with. That is interesting, isn't it? He doesn't seem to quite *inhabit* this house but He does seem to *use* it. He seems almost sometimes to withdraw and then come back again; and if ever the silver cord is broken, as Isaiah said—that is, the psychic thread that binds the psychic or mental to the physical—if it is severed, then that is it!

Quimby started his experiments. He soon found he could dispense with the services of Lucius and discovered what he announced as the principle, in which he said, "Mind is matter in solution, and matter is mind in form." Together they constitute what he called the matter of a superior intelligence or wisdom, which he called Christ. The use of it he called the Science of Christ. He used the term Christian Science in some places, which doesn't matter, because we are noncontroversial and I don't care where anything came from or who got what from whom. All I want is the *is*ness of things.

Out of this and out of his practice stemmed the law and method which probably has been used in 90 percent of all of the modern New Thought practice. There came along during this time, for healing, Mrs. Eddy.[*] She acknowledged she was healed. She changed the system, she said. Probably she did, and I don't know or care. And there came another man and his wife[†] (I think it was his wife) by name of Dresser who were healed, and they stayed with Quimby and were his very close friends and helpers. Quimby dies practically in this man's arms.

Julius Dresser was the father of David Seabury,[‡] our psychologist. The one who wrote the first history of the New Thought Movement, Horatio Dresser Jr.,[§] was a brother of David Seabury. (Seabury took his mother's name so there wouldn't be confusion.) Seabury believes in this cause; he knows it is true.

Quimby passed on in 1866. About ten years later we have the first edi-

---

[*]Mary Baker Eddy (1821–1910), founder of Christian Science.
[†]Julius Dresser (1838–1893); Annetta Seabury Dresser (1840?–1895).
[‡](1885–1960), associated with *Science of Mind* magazine.
[§](1866–1954), philosophical and metaphysical writer.

tion of *Science and Health*.* It has been revised many times. About this time the modern theosophical movement in America started.

I believe Annie Besant and Madame Tingley,† the two great apostles of Blavatsky‡ (who originated the modern theosophical movement and wrote *The Secret Doctrine* and other books), were responsible for the occultism and the swamis. There was a great group of people along with modern traveling psychologists all stirring up thought and modern spiritualism. The Rochester rapping§ came about the time of the advent of theosophy and Christian Science in America. Now of course there was a great deal of weirdness and peculiarity in all of this, but *something* was happening. Always there is a weird fringe when things start; of course it certainly looks weird to people who aren't accustomed to it, doesn't it? It is no wonder they called Quimby an infidel; and Mrs. Eddy, they said, was a witch, because they didn't understand what they were talking about a hundred years ago.

If you translate the universe in terms that now science accepts and upon which the atom bomb was made possible—the equation of Einstein where he said that energy and mass are equal, identical, and interchangeable—that is no different, scientifically, than it would be, philosophically, for Quimby to say matter is mind in form and mind is matter in solution. Not one bit. Or for Spinoza to say, "I don't say mind is one thing and matter is another. I say they are the same thing." It is no different when Einstein said, "There is probably one law in physics that coordinates and synthesizes all laws," than it was for Emerson to say, "There is one mind common to all individual men," or the Jews to say, "Hear, O Israel: the Eternal, the Lord thy God, is one Lord," or the ancient Hindus to say, "He is One." Whatever you name it, it can't be that, because He isn't limited to that name. He is one undivided and indivisible intelligence, consciousness, awareness, law and order, and action and reaction—the polarity.

Out of all this stemmed the modern New Thought movement of Amer-

---

*By Mary Baker Eddy (1875).
†Katherine Tingley (1847–1929), American theosophist.
‡Helena Blavatsky (1831–1891), American theosophist.
§Table-rapping phenomena in spiritistic sessions held in Rochester, N.Y., in 1848.

ica. Along came a woman by the name of Emma Curtis Hopkins. We have her lessons on mysticism.* I was fortunate enough to have taken them 35 years ago when she must have been 80. She was, at least for a brief time, contemporary with the founder of Christian Science. She edited some of the first publications.

However, I don't think we would ever class her as a Christian Scientist. I don't think she got what she learned from there.† She had studied all these things and probably this too, but she became what was called the teacher of teachers. The Fillmores‡ went to her, who founded the Unity movement. People who founded the Home of Truth,§ one of the early New Thought movements, and the Church of Truth¶ were all students of hers. I was a student of hers, insofar as she had students.

You went there and took the 12 lessons—just 12 hours of talks; but she had a transcendence about her that you could feel. It was really there. She had quite a good deal of illumination I could feel. It is strange language to begin with, and you won't understand it. I gave her book to Adela Rogers St. Johns** several years ago and she said, "I don't know what she is talking about." Then she studied and studied and caught on to it and said, "This is terrific when you begin to find out what it is all about." And it is.

You have to get accustomed to the language to find the meaning back of it. Emilie Cady,†† who wrote *Lessons in Truth*, took her courses; so did George Burnell,‡‡ if you ever heard of him; he wrote the *Axioms and Aphorisms* and was one of the great teachers. I would say that two-thirds of the greatest teachers who were responsible for the New Thought movement went to her.

---

*(1849–1925), American New Thought teacher. The reference is to her book *High Mysticism*.
†Some contemporary scholarship disagrees. See "Who Was the *Real* Emma Curtis Hopkins?" in *Creative Thought* magazine, August 1996.
‡Charles (1854–1948) and Myrtle (1845–1931).
§Annie Rix Militz (1856–1924) and Sadie Gorie († ca. 1891).
¶Albert Grier (1864–1941). Influenced by the ministry of a Hopkins student, among others.
**(1894–1988), American journalist and popular social historian.
††(1848–1941), homeopathic physician and metaphysical writer, a mentor of the Unity movement.
‡‡(1863–1948), New Thought teacher and writer.

I don't know whether Ralph Waldo Trine* did or not. He wrote *In Tune with the Infinite*, which was one of the first books along this line to sell over a million copies—one of the biggest sales of any book ever printed. Christian D. Larson†—you have heard of him; he is still living and lectures. The first thing I ever read by him was *The Idea Made Real*, up in the Maine woods where we used to spend our summer.

In later years, naturally the thing broke down into groups. The Unity movement was formed, the Divine Science church, our own church, the Church of Truth, and, many of them—all of them stemming out of the teachings of Quimby. Many of the teachers were influenced by him; he was the greatest mystic of modern times, the greatest spiritual genius I ever contacted—because you could feel it; it was all behind the scenes, I think. That is the New Thought movement of America. That is where it came from. We came out of it.

It is estimated that between 15 and 20 million people (this was 20 years ago) in America belonged to this movement. They don't all belong, as you might belong, to one of our churches, but they read the literature, they study. There are a couple of million periodicals a month in the different avenues going out; over 100,000 clergymen, for instance, subscribe to the Unity literature.

How this must have influenced the pulpit as well as the pews, gradually working like leavening and making possible people like Liebman,‡ who wrote *Peace of Mind*—! There is *The Power of Positive Thinking* and *Guideposts* (with a circulation of about 750,000) by Norman Vincent Peale,§ a very great man. And then along came all the modern psychologists, as I said before.

I want to mention too one of the most remarkable women who ever appeared in the New Thought movement—she passed on a few years ago—

---

*(1866–1958), New Thought writer.
†(1874–1962), New Thought writer.
‡Joshua Roth Liebman, clergyman, author of *Peace of Mind*.
§(1898–1993), clergyman, author *The Power of Positive Thinking*.

Julia Seton.* She spoke to theaters packed, jammed, and running over in the English-speaking towns around the world: South Africa, England, across this country, New Zealand, and Australia.

We owe a great deal to spiritualism, whether we believe they are talking to spirits or not. I sometimes think they do and sometimes think they do not. But those are things that Rhine[†] has dealt with. He used a friend of mine, the most famous medium in the world—Eileen Garrett[‡]—and he has used Arthur Ford,[§] who was also a friend of mine, in extrasensory-perception experiments at Duke, and now at Redlands University. They all have stemmed out of this New Thought or modern metaphysical movement, which is the most terrific thing, spiritually, that has ever happened to the spiritual life of the United States. We stemmed out of that.

That is a very brief and very sketchy history, but it is comprehensive enough to show, as we go back and back and back until the teaching in its abstraction is lost in obscure and unknown antiquity, that somewhere down along the line there have always been bringers of the truth—but never before in recorded history. Whether there may have been civilizations destroyed (which I do not doubt might have happened—as this one might be, to start over again) I don't know, and it doesn't matter. The soul of man is eternal and indestructible.

---

*Physician and New Thought leader, lecturer, and author.
[†]J. B. Rhine (1895–1980), American psychologist.
[‡]English psychic.
[§]American clergyman and psychic.

2

HISTORY OF RELIGIOUS SCIENCE

Ernest tired of people writing of his life and the Religious Science movement in an over-imaginative manner. When I asked why he permitted this to continually occur, he replied, "If it makes them happy, let them do it." However, in April 1958, at a lecture to a group of students, he took the opportunity to express the truth.

In this chapter we see expressed and reflected his constant belief: "We are a teaching and practicing order." Ernest had expressed to me his feeling that we are "the only religion or teaching that includes all and excludes none."

I neglected to mention the writings of Judge Troward,* which are fundamental to the New Thought movement. They didn't come along until about 1909, I believe, starting with *The Edinburgh Lectures*. There are all of them plus a compilation on the Psalms, which came out after his death. They are fundamental books, and everyone in our field should understand them, because I would say 25 percent of our philosophy came from Troward. It all came from somewhere; I didn't make it up. The thing that is original about us is that we don't claim any originality, and that is the most original thing in the world. We rang the bell just that way.

You will find much in reading Troward, particularly *The Creative Process in the Individual*. And you should read the book I suggested on Hinduism; it is just one volume by Aurobindo.† His section on the Gnostic Being is a more complete elaboration than *The Creative Process in the Individual*, but it

---

*Thomas Troward (1847–1916), English colonial administrator, jurist, and metaphysical writer.
†*The Life Divine*.

is the same thing. Troward's chapter "The Dénouement of the Creative Process" is the same as a section in Aurobindo's book on the Gnostic Being. Of course, Troward did not get it from Aurobindo, because Troward died before Aurobindo's book was written—about 1914–1915 I think.* But they teach the same thing, which shows the source was the same. It derives from Hindu philosophy.†

Now we come to our own movement. Our movement is also in a certain sense a Christian denomination. It would be classed as that, but it is very much more than a Christian denomination, remembering again that the philosophy of Christianity is a combination of the Jews and Greeks. "The God without and the God within," the mystics said, "the highest God and the innermost God, is One God." I changed that a little and said, God as man in man *is* man. It is more simple, more direct, and means the same.

I have to make certain personal references. I don't like talking about myself. Anyone who thinks about himself hasn't very much to think about. It is like someone who thinks he owns something. If he does, and cares very much for it, it will own him. Emerson said, "Cast your good on the four winds of heaven. Only that can increase and multiply which is scattered." I don't think I own anything. These are our playthings here. We exist for the delight of God and we will play with other things somewhere else. And no thing and no era in history is of any value other than as it expresses some ceaseless, incessant Urge which presses against everything, that It shall express Itself for the joy of Its own being, the delight of Its own being, to sing a song: *creativity*. That is what everything exists for.

I have to refer to myself because I happen to have been there when it happened—but I consider Religious Science a thing of destiny or I wouldn't be here. I have given my life to it. I never even made a living out of it, because it doesn't interest me in that way. I think it is a thing of destiny. I

---

*d. 1916.
†Troward in fact relied almost wholly on the work of Thomson Jay Hudson for the specifically mental-science element of his teaching.

believe that the evolutionary process, periodically in history, pushes something forward as a new emergent to meet a new demand.

Now that is not original with me. It is held in all philosophy, and every school of philosophy, that the principle of emergent evolution meets the demand made upon it, in terms of the demand made. I think that is the way everything happens. It is the way we got our fingernails: we had to scratch, so we developed something to scratch with. It is the way we got our feet: we had to walk, so we developed feet and stood up, etc.—things to grasp with, things to think with, etc.

So it had to be, it seems—as though out of all these things I have been talking about, history might be ready for a new emergent. Now I don't consider I had anything to do with it; I happened to be here. Maybe I was willing to devote the time to synthesize it. It has taken a lifetime; I have been doing it for 50 years, and I don't think we are any more than just started. Something had to happen.

They said, "You believe Jesus lived?" I say we have an authentic record of Jesus, so I accept the fact. But I always say, it does not make any difference to me whether Jesus lived or not, because something had to be done; and if he hadn't done it, somebody else would. It is like they say, "Who wrote Shakespeare?" and I say, "What difference does it make whether William Shakespeare wrote it or *another* guy by the name of Shakespeare? *Somebody* wrote it! Who cares?" It is beautiful; nothing is greater than the sonnets of Shakespeare. Whoever did it had experienced Cosmic Consciousness.

People are always trying to hang a halo on you or embarrass you by tying onto you something that doesn't belong. I am writing a story of this movement, with the help of a real writer, only because a couple of years ago one of our own ministers, in a sermon, told the story of my life and very proudly brought it to me, transcribed, and there wasn't a single truth in it—not a single "fact" that was true. And it was broadcast, by some public-spirited fool, that when I first started, my mother had been a medium. I had just as soon she had been, but she wasn't. I wouldn't have cared what she had been. There is just one race, the human race, and one religion, and that is somebody's belief in God—and everybody's belief in God. Some belief is better than others; that would be the only better religion there is.

But I did get born in Maine and didn't go to school, because I didn't like it—hated it—and quit when I was about 15. I didn't go back except to study public speaking. That is one of the troubles with this movement. There are certain liabilities without proper training and certain liabilities with too much training. I said to the head of the Department of Philosophy at USC one day, after he asked, "Why don't more people come to these public lectures on philosophy?"—I said, "They don't get anything." He asked, "Why not? These are the best in the world!" I said, "Let me tell you something. You get somebody who actually knows what Plato taught and tell him to throw all his textbooks out and forget what Plato said, and tell us what he thinks Platonism means in his language; and if he is good, you won't have a hall big enough to get them in, because he will speak from his heart; it won't be out of a book."

At any rate, I rebelled against authority and didn't want to be taken care of, so I went to work when I was a kid. What I have gathered has been from reading, studying and thinking, working—it is a long, laborious, tough method, but it pays off. I don't believe there is a real *other* method. Whatever you are going to learn after you take these classes—which is the best we have to offer—or in any good reading you can get: what you will really learn will be what you tell yourself, in a language you understand, that you accept—giving yourself a reason that is rational enough to accept, reasonable enough to agree to, inspirational enough to listen to with feeling, profound enough to sink deep, and light enough in it to break away the clouds. Because there is a place where the sun never has stopped shining in everyone's mind, and there is ever a song somewhere and we all have to learn to sing it.

Well, I didn't see things or have hallucinations; I wasn't strange in any particular way. When I was a kid, I began to study Emerson. I was from the beginning a nonconformist, asking so many questions my relatives hated me—every time I visited them I drove them crazy. I was, fortunately, brought up in a family by a mother who refused to have fear taught in her family. She was an old New Englander—born a hundred years ago—and New England, theologically, was pretty strict. However, she was a smart woman and she determined we should never be taught there was anything to be afraid of. I had to grow up and be almost a man before I knew that people actually believed in Hell. I don't know now what they believe or how they think; I only know this: that anyone who does, if he will ever get to the place where there is complete forgiveness for himself and heal his own unconscious sense of rejection, will never believe in Hell and never condemn anybody else. You can only project *yourself.*

So I studied Emerson, and this was like drinking water to me. I have studied Emerson all my life. Then I went to Boston to a school* to study speech for a couple of years, while working to pay my way through this very wonderful school. The people were Christian Scientists and very good ones; the head of it was a reader† in the Mother Church. Here, naturally, I heard wonderful things. Some of my own classmates were Christian Scientists, and I asked if what they believed was true and they said yes, and then I said, "I can do it." Anything anyone has ever done, *anybody* can do—there can be no secrets in nature. This I have always held to. There is no special providence; there is no God who says—to Mary or Ernie or Josie, or anybody else—"I am going to tell *you* what I didn't tell the other guy." There is no such being.

So coming out here to L.A. 45 years ago or whenever it was,‡ I came in contact with New Thought students. Here is where everything was taught—everything; more here in the earlier days than now. They used to say everyone here was a screwball, but they weren't; they were very remarkable people. When you get someone who gets up and moves to another place, tears up all their background, you at least have a progressive person. He has at least found courage to move out of some rut, if it is just to move across the country to live, and leave everything that has tied him there. This will be the most progressive place on earth.

---

*The Leland Powers School of Public Expression.
†One of two who read aloud selected texts in a Christian Science service.
‡1912.

Well, here was occultism and theosophy; they had their schools—much more than they have now. The New Thought movements were flourishing. Julia Seton was here, and I became acquainted with her. She was one of the early New Thought teachers. Many of them came here to lecture, and I often lectured with them after a few years, and I began to read and study everything I could get hold of—no one thing. I started from the very beginning with the thought that I didn't want to take one bondage away from myself and create another. I have always been very careful about that. When the history of our movement is written and understood, they will know how careful I have been. Some day people will applaud that; but it is too soon now, because it is too close. But it will happen.

We happen to have the most liberal spiritual movement the world has ever seen, and yet it is synthesized and tied together by the authority of the ages and the highlights of the spiritual evolution of the human race, all of which I have been familiar with, since I have spent 50 years studying it and thinking about it.

I was always studying; and since I had to make a living, I took a job as purchasing agent for a business house.* A street superintendent asked me what all the books were I had around my office, and I said they were books on philosophy and metaphysics, the occult, New Thought—everything you can think of. He said, "They look interesting to me." I said, "You are an engineer and wouldn't be interested"; but he thought he might. He borrowed some of them and after a while he said, "How would you like to come over to my house and I will invite a few people one evening and you can just talk to us—?" I said that would be fine—and we did.

These were the first talks I ever gave, in two homes. During one of these evenings a lady came to me and said she was at the Metaphysical Library (we used to have a big metaphysical library at 3rd and Broadway, and I used to get books out of it) and she said, "I told the librarian you would come up next Thursday and talk." I said, "Talk on what?" And she said, "Like you talk to us! You are really better than the people we hear up there."

---

*In fact, for the City of Venice.

I went, and the librarian said, "You have a class this afternoon at 3 p.m." I said, "I wouldn't know how to teach a class." She informed me I could pay a dollar for the room and charge twenty-five cents a person to come. I decided to teach Troward. I had read *The Edinburgh Lectures*. I believe I had 13 in the class and got home with a five-dollar gold piece above my rent. Within two years I was speaking to thousands of people a week and never put a notice in the paper. They just came.

This went on for a number of years, and I thought I would like to see how it worked in other places; and for several years I went to Eastern cities and around and discovered that wherever there were people, they wanted it and were ready for it. I had already started on what I consider our great synthesis, putting the thing together.

It has always been my idea that the greatest life is the one that includes the most—that we have to study what everybody has to say, we have to be the judge principally of what we think is right or wrong, good or bad, or true or false. There is nothing else, and we must not live by authority. We must have no more prophets or saviors. Now I say this guardedly, and not out of disrespect to the saviors of the world. The Gita says, "The self must raise the self by the self." Shakespeare said, "To thine own self be true and it shall follow as the night the day, thou canst not then be false to any man."

This is true. You learn from yourself in doing. So I decided that to kite around the country wasn't good for me; I didn't care for it. I had a beautiful home here and had made many friends, so I came back to L.A. after several years' being out of this local field. In 1925 we took the little theater which used to be in the Ambassador. It seated 625 people. We put an ad in the paper and started on a Sunday morning. Within a year the people couldn't get in. Then we took the Ebell Theatre and within a year were turning people away from there. It seated 1,295 people.

Then Bob Bitzer* came from Boston where I had met him. I started him in Hollywood; he was very young. I said we would take the Women's Club

---

*(1896–1994), founder and presiding minister of the Hollywood Church of Religious Science, 1930–1994.

on a Sunday afternoon; we invited everybody to come. We had about 800 people. I told them we were going to start their own church over there and Dr. Bitzer was to be the head of it. That is the way that church started.

Then, because we needed the space, I took the Wiltern Theater, where Dr. Hornaday* now speaks—and we turned away many, many hundreds every Sunday. This was during the time of the Depression, and probably many people were looking for help even more than ordinarily. I had a big radio program too, which was a big help.

I want to go back before this happened. I came back here in 1925, and in 1926 some friends of mine said, "You should organize this." But I said, "No, I don't want to do that; I don't want to start a new religion or be responsible for it; I don't want to tell anyone what to do. I don't know what to do myself, so how can I tell anyone else?" But they argued that this was something they thought valuable and the greatest thing in the world, and they finally convinced me—and we became incorporated 31 years ago last February as a nonprofit religious and educational organization. The Institute of Religious Science and School of Philosophy, it was called.

Finally I said, "This can't be done this way. If we are going to have a church and there are more people, let's have more churches." So I asked everyone in Pasadena to come to the Arroyo Seco Hotel on Sunday nights and everyone who went to Glendale to come Tuesday nights there. I carried this on for about six months and started churches. I did the same thing in Long Beach and in Huntington Park and Santa Monica and Redondo Beach and other places. That is how our churches got started; they were surpluses from Wiltern services. We started classes, trained them, and so on. This is merely the way the movement originated. It grew up; it wasn't a planned thing.

It wasn't until it had many, many, many branches that I really thought to myself, Something is going on here, this really is a thing of destiny; it is really going to become the next spiritual impulsion of the world—and I

---

*William H. D. Hornaday (1910–1992), later pastor of Founder's Church of Religious Science.

believe it. I finally came to see that it had to be organized so it wouldn't fall apart. We have a very wonderful organization, democratic; we are governed by a top board of 19 members, seven of whom are elected by the field.

This is a new spiritual impulsion in the world; it has certain objectives in the world, has certain purposes: to teach and to practice, and nothing else; teach and practice, practice and teach—that is all we have; that is all we are good for; that is all we ever ought to do.

We must bear witness to a spiritual truth which has come down to us through the ages; and if there is any truth, this is it. It is a compilation, a synthesis—a putting together of all the great thoughts. When they ask me how I know I am right—I *don't* know I am right; I don't *have* to be right. If I thought I was "right," I wouldn't be here. But if you skim off the top thought of the ages and it is wrong, you have no criterion to judge by at all. That is the only way we can do.

If you simply take the best all the great teachers have given us, the essence of all great religions of the world and put it into one; take the hellishness out of it; take the rudeness and crudeness and vulgarization out of what was, perhaps, almost a revelation to suit the whims and fancies of people or the emotional emergency of a group or individual—you still won't get anywhere. But if you take the deep thoughts of the ages—Plato and Moses and Jesus, Buddha, Socrates, Aristotle and Emerson and Plotinus, all of them— you will *have* to have the greatest teaching the world has. It must almost be done by one or a very few people, not because one person is a genius as against others. It must be done by few enough minds at first so they will know *what to take out* and *what to keep*; what is *this* one thought and *that*, and *where* they dovetail.

It's very difficult to get a synthesis like this that we have and try to get it out of too many minds. It is merely that you have to say, What is the relationship between, for example, Einstein saying that energy and mass are equal, identical, and interchangeable and the Jews saying God is One, or Emerson saying there is One Mind common to all individual men—? What is the difference between psychic phenomena as they have appeared throughout the ages and experiences you know? What synthesizes them without their becoming ridiculous and a superstitious belief that someone is perched on your sleeve all the time telling you what happened? It is ridiculous.

It is a terrific thing to synthesize the wisdom of the ages. I don't claim to have done it, but we have come nearer doing it than ever has happened before in the history of the world. Therefore, we are beneficiaries of innumerable sources. Those sources we gladly recognize, and we feel very proud and happy we have had sense enough to use them. They must be brought into line—the great philosophic and spiritual truths must be brought into line with the modern metaphysical knowledge of the Law of Mind in action, which the ancients did not understand at all. If they did, they didn't practice it or, as far as I know, teach it. They taught the broad, generalized principles that underlie it and which will explain it—*but not in action.**

Then we have to put together that which synthesizes modern psychiatry and psychology—and this vast group of people are still teaching as though you and I had an individual psyche, *and we haven't at all.* There is no such thing as *your* subconscious mind and no such thing as *your* subliminal mind or Christ Mind; this is all a fantasy. The only mind you will ever know is the mind you are using right now.

The reaction to it is what we call your subconscious, which, instead of being an entity, is a subjective state of thought in a universal medium of mental and creative reaction. This is one of the great truths; because if you had a mind separate from mine, you and I wouldn't know each other is here.

It is Kant,† who was called the Father of Logic, who said we are able to perceive an apparently external object because it awakens an intuition within us. I know you, and you know me, because the God in us knows Himself—not as each other, separate and divided, but *Itself as us.* This is the only way we can know anything.

So the Christ Mind, the subliminal mind, the subconscious, and the un-

---

*By "in action" is meant *how it works* and *how to use it.* The elucidation of this, based on the work of Thomson Jay Hudson and Thomas Troward, was Holmes's great contribution to New Thought. Prior to this, "law" in New Thought (Malinda Cramer's breakthrough Law of Expression apart) was "the broad, generalized principles" Holmes refers to here.
†Immanuel Kant (1724–1804), German philosopher.

conscious are all only names we give to the possibility of that without which we would have no conscious awareness of existence on this plane—just the down-to-earth practical old mind that we have been using since we were weaned. Isn't that remarkable—that we should go all around and around and come back as ignorant as in we went! Until, finally, we arrive at the simple conclusion: I must take myself for better or for worse. Here I am; this is what I think with; this is what I know with; this is what I understand with. Should I ever be illumined, this is the thing that will be illumined. Have I a subconsciousness? It is what trails out behind me as a result of this; therefore, only this can change it. Have I a subliminal possibility beyond this? This shall perceive it. And that is why Lowell* said, "I behold in thee the image of Him who died on the tree."

That is what Religious Science is. Its background is the *impulsion* of love. It is intelligent. I would debate with any team on earth to uphold that which I believe, and I would lick them. It is an irrefutable fact, now proved in science, logic, and reason, that the only revelation there is is intuition. We have launched a movement which is destined—I won't live to see it and don't want to—in the next hundred years to be the great new religious impulsion of our day and of modern times, far exceeding in its capacity to envelop the world anything that has happened since Mohammedanism started.

I don't count any of the others: they are too caught and bound by their littleness. Several of the other modern religions have another revelation, another "thus far and no farther," another authority, God bless them. But we can have no part of it. We have to be open. People come along and know so much more than we do that it is just funny. But it will come out of this little we know—what we have as stemming out of Christianity, and Christianity out of Judaism and the Greeks, and back and back. I am convinced our movement is a thing of destiny.

Now what do we teach? It is very simple: God is all there is. There isn't anything else; there never was and never will be. That is what I am. There is nothing else I can be; I am compelled to be That. I have nothing to do

---

*James Russell Lowell (1819–1891), American poet, essayist, and diplomat.

with it. I have no virtue great enough to make It and no vice bad enough to destroy It. When the psychological reaction of condemnation is done away with in the world, Hell will have cooled off; the Devil will be out of business; present-day evangelism will have been rolled up like a scroll and numbered with the things that were once thought to be real.

Something new and grand will have appeared. We are the forerunners of a new race of people; we are the arbiters of the fate of unborn generations; we are the custodians of the chalice of truth. But we are not hung on a cross. We have a song to sing; we have a joy to bring to the world, and love and peace and happiness.

I am ready to introduce new thoughts and new ideas into our movement, starting the first of the year, which I think will be transcendent. But I believe we are just starting. I believe that we can do something to ourselves psychologically that will yield the same faith and conviction in our science and our truth that the electrician has when he wires a building: when we press a button, we will get a light. Did you ever stop to think of that?

Faith is an attitude of mind accepted and no longer rejected. No one can accept it but himself. No one can accept it for him; no one can reject it for him. We have to have the same faith in what we teach and preach and practice that science has or the gardener has. And when that terrific and great simplicity shall have plumbed and penetrated this density of ours, this human stolidness and stupidity, this blindness which we seem to be born with, this drunkenness, this debauchery of the intellect and the soul—then something new and wonderful will happen. It is the only thing that will keep the world from destroying itself.

I think we should feel as though we are on a mission. Not a mission of sadness to save souls—they are not lost; if they were, you wouldn't know where to look for them—but a mission that glorifies the soul. Not to find we are here for salvation, but for glorification—the beauty, the wonder, the delight of that Something that sings and sings and sings in the soul of man. "Build thee more stately mansions O my soul,/ As the swift seasons roll!/ Leave thy low-vaulted past!/ Let each new temple, nobler than the last,/ Shut thee from heaven with a dome more vast,/ Till thou at length art free."

3.

THE SOURCE OF
THE POWER: ONENESS

In this talk, given before the Tuesday Invitational Group on May 19, 1959, three months following his Cosmic Consciousness experience,* Dr. Holmes stresses the cornerstone of our teaching: "Total unity: we all are unique individualizations of the same Thing." Reflecting the impact of his recent experience, he also said, "We have the concept of a united conclusion of the deepest thinkers who ever lived."

Many scholars have decided that:

1. Ernest probably based the teaching on the works of Ralph Waldo Emerson, because his father was a Unitarian minister, and they had heard that he had helped his mother to prepare lectures based on Emerson's essays for his father before Ernest was 12 years of age.
2. Ernest based the teachings on Christian Science. Ernest had studied Christian Science in Boston with Emma Curtis Hopkins. He dropped the study of Christian Science in Boston when he was told that only licensed practitioners could pray in public. This followed a public prayer by Ernest in the absence of his Christian Science teacher.
3. Ernest based the teaching on the writings of Judge Thomas Troward— this probably because of the use of much of Judge Troward's terminology and some of his basic logic.

Ernest often commented about people's opinion: "If it makes them happy, let them believe it."

---

*See *The Anatomy of Healing Prayer*, vol. 2 of *The Ernest Holmes Papers*, pp. 235–40.

More completely perhaps than of any other system of thought, Emerson believed he was beneficiary of this antiquity [of teaching], as did the Hebrews to a degree. Emerson said, "There is one mind common to all men." Now, according to our concept and according to the greatest teachings I know of throughout the ages, the spiritual philosophy and realization of the ancient Hindu system, the Hermetic teaching, and the spiritual teaching of the Egyptians were the same—all covered up with apparent dualism and multiplied deities; but back of them all you found there was just One. We have the concept of a united conclusion of the deepest thinkers who ever lived.

I am not talking about academic psychology or philosophy, which may or may not be right; I am talking about the deepest spiritual perceptions the human mind has ever gained. I have no doubt at all but they are correct in essence even though we do not understand the full meaning of them. No one understands the meaning of a unity in which there is infinite variation; no one completely comprehends infinite variation in which there is a constant unity; they are figures of speech. But real unity cannot exclude anything.

Throughout the ages there have been those who have seen how real unity can include everything, and there have been those who, unable to perceive it, have denied most of that which they thought denied the true unity. Even Gandhi attempted this system. In his story of himself he says that when he started out, he said God is truth. He then discovered the error of it, the reason being that we all *assume* what God is and then say *that* is truth.

Therefore, everything is according to the nature of our assumption. This has been the error of the ages—trying to explain what God is. So he said he reversed his opinion and said, "truth is God"—because there can be no God higher than truth. The Bible speaks of the Lord God of Truth—and that means we judge the divine nature by what goes on that we can understand. Many modern metaphysicians say God is all there is, there is One Mind, that Mind is God, that Mind is my mind—and then proceed to use it as though their finite mind knows what is contained within the Infinite Mind.

In order to make the whole thing come together, they begin to deny that which they think is contrary to the nature of God. Unfortunately, it is so easy for one to coerce his own consciousness; psychologically, where there is an emotional bias there will be an intellectual blind spot. They are very liable to run around denying everything they do not like, affirming everything they do, declaring this is the nature of God. That is contrary to reason and judgment: prejudice. It is the way we arrive at most of our theologies.

There was an ancient culture in India that developed probably the longest successive and deepest single line of thinkers who ever lived. The Greek philosophers developed perhaps the greatest line of intellectual thinkers. Their system is very difficult to follow; Emerson said that probably not over 12 people at any one time ever understood Plato, but the works of Plato were brought to those 12 as though God brought it to them. I think that is a very interesting saying.

The Hindu system didn't have prophets, never had saints or saviors—never had people who claimed a special revelation or a special dispensation. However, over a period of several thousand years cumulatively, each concept of one was added to the concept of the other, and that is why there are so many writers. Through the Gita, the Upanishads, even though they are different things, you find a succession of writers who have thought deeply, abstractly, and who probably gave the world the most comprehensive sense of the meaning of the unity of all life that any system has ever taught.

The Christian philosophy or theology is supposed to be based on unity that came from the Hebrew concept that God is One. There was a terrible lamentation among the ancient Hebrew prophets. In spite of the One, there was an awful lot that contradicted it and a great sense of rejection. A true system of unity will have to include all there is. The Christian theology and philosophy is about 90 percent materialistic and almost 100 percent dualistic. Therefore we may thank the God that is, that the God that is believed in, *isn't*. Then we may as well go to Hell and call it a day.

The philosophy of Jesus was based on a unitary wholeness. There is nothing wrong with that. However, the theology of Christianity is a combination of dualism, pluralism, and materialism, all mixed in with confusion. They have not arrived at the comprehension of a necessary unity which must of itself include all varieties, and a necessary variety which must of necessity include the essence of all unity. At the center of every variety or variation is the undivided and indivisible totality in essence, while the only difference could be in *degree*. (That doesn't seem very clear!)

If anything is to be at all, there has to be an absolute unity of all life, no matter whether we like it or don't like it. This will include war, pestilence, famine, tigers fighting in the jungle, exalted love, and the most debased passion. We are not going to be able to deny one experience without denying the validity of all of them.

By getting into confusion trying to decide which is right and which is wrong, we set up theological courts of injustice to decide, and false edicts to announce, creating dogmas that are very much at variance with the truth. While we have all these differences in our theologies (they are all good, all part of the unity too), we have to start with the necessary base of fundamental unity in all things, over all things, through all things, and which *is* all things. *Brahma is all.*

"There is no God save Allah"; "I am the beginning and end"; "My name is I AM"; "I am that I am, beside which there is no other"—it runs through all religions. The basic teaching runs through all religions; it is the interpretation that gives us confusion. We are confronted with fear, pestilence, war, famine, poverty, decay, and death. We shall either have to deny all these things as real to the ultimate Reality, even while we affirm them as necessary experiences (this is a very difficult thing to do without getting a split personality; it is like a guy going down the street and trying to walk two ways at once—it can't be done; something will have to give), or else say there is no such thing as unity, there is nothing but duality—which isn't tenable, because you cannot have two absolutes, two infinites, two ultimates.

Jesus said, "If I do this by Beelzebub, it would be a house divided against itself." Jesus understood unity and lived on the basis that there was no difference between himself and God in essence. "Who hath seen me hath seen the Father." Emerson said, "Who in his integrity worships God becomes God."

You find this in all the great, great philosophies; but they brought it down from an Absolute to a spirit, to a soul, to a mind, to a body. Plotinus had these five divisions, but as one was hid in the other, the other was itself concealed. That is, mind, as we understand it, would be concealed in soul; soul would be concealed in spirit; and so on.

According to the ancient system of gradations of consciousness from the lowest to the highest—from the mind that sleeps in the mineral, waves in the grass, to simple consciousness in the animal, self-consciousness in man, and God-consciousness in the upper reaches—you would have a gradation upward from that which is unconscious of itself, as such, but has an element of intelligence and a purposiveness instinctive within it, involuted in it, or put there in the beginning—no particular beginning, but all beginnings. Beginnings are endless, and endings are endless. Evolution goes on eternally in manifestation and creation, world without end. It has to be that way; there cannot be an inactive creator.

That would mean: in the mind in the mineral sleeps the mind that is going to wave in the grass; in the mind that is in the grass sleeps the mind that is going to awake in simple consciousness in the animal; in this mind (even physically) is the mind that ultimately is going to wake up into the human or self-consciousness; in the self-consciousness is the mind that is going to awaken in the Super-consciousness.

The Super Mind is hidden in the Mind; the Spirit is hidden in the Super Mind, the Absolute is hidden in the Spirit.* I hope this is clear. According to the Hermetic teachings: as above, so below; as below, so above—what is true on one plane is true on all. It is Swedenborg's Law of Correspondences, or Emerson saying he believed in the Law of Parallels of the Hermetic teaching; Emerson saying Nature has but a very few laws, but she repeats the process over and over and over again. That is the simple thing. The mind that is in a state of complete unconsciousness (to us) must contain the further push of its own evolution or the evolution of its instrumentality. The Absolute, I suppose, doesn't evolve until it takes another round of ex-

---

*The relation of terms in each pair is *greater: lesser*; here the sense of "hidden" seems to be equivalent to "implicit."

perience. This must push on to another: "Ever as the spiral grew,/ He left the old house for the new." "In my Father's house are many mansions," etc.

But there would have had to be, for this *e*voluting process, a prior and continuing *in*voluting process. I am not telling you what I think; I am telling you what the great minds of the ages have taught. I am talking about the great, not the near-great—the ones who have given the world the most inspired and exalted thought it has ever had. It is a very interesting thing: we are about to witness the reemergence of this teaching and a more complete acceptance of it, having gotten rid of all the occultism and the weird part that has gone with it up until now.

Now we have to have, along with the evolution, the irresistible unfoldment of an infinite variety from an infinite unity. Unity, in passing into variety, never falls into illusion itself (or disunion or separation or otherness) but must always contain within itself that seed which, Browning said, many may desecrate but never quite lose—"that spark," he calls it. It is in our own Bible where it talks, in Genesis, about the time when the plant was created before it was in the ground.

It is so darned simple, but the implications are so terrific and the possibility of their utility might be so immediate. Remember, we are not saying, "God is truth." That is arbitrary, because we don't know God this way. We haven't met Him this way yet—and that is very interesting. We have to *observe*. We must not arbitrarily say, "God said this," and "Thus saith God"—we have to say, "Truth is God." This means that, instead of trying to explain the nature of truth (which is inexplicable), when the intellect and that which *is* explicable reaches the ultimate of its explicability (if there is such a word), we have to say that *it is the nature of Reality to be thus-and-so.* If anyone can carry his mind to this point of perception, he should stop saying, "Thus saith God," and ask, *"What does Nature teach?"* because its cause will be like that.

And the Bible says, "The invisible things of God from the foundation of the world are made manifest by the visible." What you see comes out of what you don't see; what you do see interprets what you don't see; what you do see is what you don't see in the form of what you do see. It cannot be something else. The Universe has to be an undivided and indivisible total-ity, whose whole essence appears at any and every point within it simultane-ously and evenly distributed.

Theoretically, at the point of a pencil is all that was, is, or ever will be, in essence. It has to be there, or there couldn't be a Universe. Now, that doesn't mean God doesn't make something new—"Behold, I make all things new"—but that the newness will always conform to the nature of the reality which brings it about. We have to say this is the nature of life—we are justi-fied in supposing this—and the greatest intellects and the greatest spiritu-ally enlightened people that have ever lived have told us so. I think we are justified in accepting it; what other criterion have we got? People very fre-quently say to me, sometimes snootily, "How do you know you are right?" I don't have to be right. It doesn't mean a thing to me whether I am right. If I cannot accept the most profound conclusions, the most exalted thoughts the ages have given to me, then there *is* no criterion.

Evelyn Underhill* said that the only news we have of the Kingdom of Heaven has come through the consciousness of man. The Bible says, "No man hath seen the Father at any time, only the Son hath revealed him." But Jesus boldly said, "I and the Father are one," and "Who hath seen me hath seen the Father"; but "the Father is greater than I." Troward says, and rightly, that the *degree* is the difference; the *essence* is identical.

We have to just *suppose*—because that appears to be the nature of the thing, until we can think of something better than facts, which are the final arbiter of fate, and its conclusion. Remember, when I say *facts*, I am not necessarily referring to physical facts. We now take into consideration psy-chosomatic facts, psychic facts—more potent than physical.

Some day, we shall take into consideration the necessity of spiritual facts more potent than the psychic—because as the essence of the psyche is hid in the physical, the essence of the spiritual is hid in the psychic.† The an-cient Chinese taught that man has three bodies, and you have to get them

---

*(1875–1941), English writer; noted lecturer on mysticism and religious life.
†See footnote, p. 38.

circulating, all three together, or nothing good is going to happen. We have proved this in the first two instances: circulation physically and psychosomatically (emotionally), where there is no stagnation, congestion, or backing up of the libidic stream, which demands expression or it goes back to destroy itself.

So we have to assume it is the nature of Reality that a cosmic will, force, power, imagination, purpose (not as we understand purpose, but only to fulfill a desire) is continuously pressing forward *into* everything, *through* everything, to express that which It feels and knows Itself to be and for the sole and only purpose of Its own delight. That is saying a lot.

It has nothing to do with sin and salvation, nothing to do with the fall of man and his redemption. These are by-products of life having no significance other than that somebody said so; they have no ultimate cosmic significance, nothing to do with destiny or humanity—nor does Heaven or Hell, as theology understands it. They are too morbid and the one great mistake.

So we have to *suppose* this is the nature of Reality, and not even the will of God. God has no will as you and I understand will. Dean Inge in his *Philosophy of Plotinus* said that to suppose an infinite purpose is a contradiction of logic, reason, mathematics, and everything else; but to suppose limitless purposiveness for self-expression is different.

We must suppose that hid in everything is the "secret" of that thing—the intelligence, will, volition, self-choice, creative imagination backed by a power, energy, and force *of* itself, *within* itself, which will project itself. Now, this is why Troward wrote *The Law and the Word*; he understood this. Jesus understood it when he said, "Heaven and earth shall pass away, but my words shall not pass away." Troward placed the sequence of the creative order in absolute Intelligence—its movement upon itself, the law of that movement, and the form that the law takes there. This is the "secret."

Now we have to suppose an eternal and everlasting descent of the Spirit,* in what we call or miscall matter, into form—and an eternal transformation of matter in form back into Spirit. This is the meaning of Jacob's ladder, I

---

*See Metaphysical Charts II-A and III in *The Science of Mind*, pp. 569, 571.

think; don't quote me on this—I don't know; I wasn't there. Remember, this is where all our Bible interpretations come from: somebody makes it up just as I made that up, and someone else says it has to be so.

We make up all our theologies. The angels were ascending and descending: this would comply with the descent and the ascent of Spirit, wouldn't it? The eternal impregnation of the mundane clod with the original creative Spirit; the eternal and everlasting unfoldment of that into the much and the more, going through all processes of evolution—to arrive at what? Here again, we cannot place words in God's mouth, you know, and say, "This is why God did it." These are human thoughts we put in the mind of God; these are words of limitation we put into the mouth of God and then we say, "Oh, my God hath spoken!" and every worshipper sees behind the idol's face what he believes he sees behind it.

Mrs. Eddy said that mortal mind sees what it believes as truly as it believes what it sees. Emerson said that we see what we animate, and we animate what we see. Jesus, with the profundity of simplicity unsurpassed in the annals of all teaching, said, "It is done unto you as you believe." If you will analyze that to a fare-thee-well and think about nothing else, you will arrive at something which Troward called the reciprocal action between the Universal and the individual. It is one of the great teachings of the ages.

We have to suppose the involution not as a time when God began to create; "In the beginning, God" does not mean *in the beginning of Creation*, but *in the beginning of any creative series*. That is different. "In the beginning" of this particular cabbage that we are making into cole slaw, there was nothing but God; and God poked the seed of a cabbage into a creative medium [soil] which had no choice but to make cabbage. So it is in the eternal beginning of things, in the creation of a wart or a cancer, in the creation of a headache— in the creation of anything.

In the beginning of this creation there is an involutionary thrust. It is the time when "the plant was in the seed before the seed was in the ground," the oak tree was in the acorn, the chicken in the egg. And the answer to prayer is *in* the prayer when it is prayed rightly (it would *have* to be, or the universe would blow up and burst right open) and not because it is the petition of somebody who needs bread and butter—this has nothing to do with it. The Infinite has no need other than the necessity to express Itself.

Now we can't put words in God's mouth and say, "This is why God did it." There is no reason, according to the greatest thinkers of the ages, why God "did it," other than for the delight. I think the nearest way we can think of it is the creative urge in everyone. In modern psychology there is an emotional craving for self-expression back of all things, the repression of which leads to psychoneurosis. Jesus said, "The Spirit seeketh such"; "the wind bloweth where it listeth, and thou canst not tell whence it cometh, and whither it goeth; so is everyone that is born of the Spirit." What I am trying to say makes sense; that way I am saying it may not. The thoughts are so kind of big and abstract: a continual descent of Spirit, a continual corresponding ascent of Spirit for the purpose of the expression. The ancients said, "The delight of the Supreme—the delight of God."

Why do we create? Unless we live creatively, we die, because there is an irresistible desire to express life. "I am come that ye might have life and have it more abundantly." Tennyson* says, "It is life and more life for which we pray./ Our little systems have their day;/ They have their day and cease to be;/ They are but broken lights of thee,/ And thou, O Lord, art more than they." Augustine said, "Thou hast made us, thine we are, and our hearts are restless till they find repose in Thee."

There is an incessant demand; we may call it the libido; it doesn't matter what we call it—an emotional feeling, instinctive desire which *must* come out, and *comes* out in every form, whether you and I call it constructive or destructive. There can be no difference in the energy back of varying emotions. The energy is identical and cosmic. It is what the energy is attached to as emotion and identified with that makes it what we call constructive or destructive.

But there is no ultimate destruction. They† had a system of the builder and destroyer where everything was constantly being torn up to be reas-

---

*Alfred, Lord Tennyson (1809–1892), English poet laureate.
†Presumably "the greatest thinkers of the ages" (see p. 41).

sembled until the day of deliverance of the ignorant—which is what in our theology we call the Fall. I like the idea of the ignorance better.

Then there will be an irresistible urge from the lowest to the highest. The Id: this is the one who is awake at the center of the one who sleeps— something like that. "Awake thou that sleepest, and arise from the dead." At the center of the one who sleeps is the instinctive urge, the impulsion of the whole evolutionary process, the spark that Browning says "disturbs our clod."

In our theology it is Lucifer thrown out of Heaven. This is also an attempt to tell the same story—but look how it was vulgarized by having a terrible fight in Heaven and God rise up and throw this guy out. This is the same devil who was heaved over the embankments of Heaven that Browning was talking about when he said, "a spark disturbs our clod." All the poets have spoken and written about it.

There is Wordsworth in "The Vision of Sir Lancelot," speaking of a day in June ("Every clod feels the stir of might," etc.); Emerson, who goes out into the fields and writes the "Ode to a Rhododendron"; and someone else, who said, "It blooms to waste its sweetness on the desert air." Emerson thought it through and ended his poem by saying, "Beauty is its own excuse." Let us say that God has desires; the ancients said God is pure desire. There is so much in this that modern psychology is attempting to prove, using emotional drives. Modern science goes in the back doorway of ancient intuition almost invariably.

Now we have the involution of things, the involuted—but it isn't static. It is alive, awake, and aware. This is the burning bush that spoke to Moses— but it is really any bush we commune with. This urge makes the involution *evolve*. It can't help it. It is the nature of Reality that this drive shall be there. It is the nature of Reality that, during this process, ignorance, even backed by intelligence, dominates the spark, which Browning said "many may desecrate but never quite lose." The great poets have been intuitive perceivers of that which science gradually will verify—the language of the soul. Like music, like mathematics, it proclaims that which is beyond the possibility of intellectual embodiment. The intellect may drag itself by a laborious path up to perception, where it falls exhausted, close to the apex—and being exhausted, must go to sleep.

Hid within the problem is its own solution. This is the perception of the self-existence of all life; hid within the apparent evil is the good; hid within the hell is the heaven; hid within the devil is the god; hid within the disease is its own healing. Any doctor will tell you it is the nature of any disease to heal itself. Any psychologist will tell you it is the nature of every mental disturbance to heal itself. At the center of everything, Whitman* said, "nestles the seed of perfection."

Now let's come to the beginning of the evolutionary process and skip over a lot of it, to *now*. We know evolution is an eternal process. Anyone inclined to affirm the nature of God and the reality of truth who will deny evolution is a stupid person; he is a person who thinks the only way to arrive at faith is through the denial of fact. It is exactly the wrong way; nothing can lead us into a greater error. We must not try to find facts to fit our theories; we may only, intelligently, try to find an adequate theory that will fit all facts that are known. Having found it, we must accept it as a reality as far as we understand it. Every deep thinker who has ever lived has done this.

We do not arbitrarily say God is Love. We *believe* it. We might like to announce it arbitrarily, but we don't. Some great psychologist will say, "Love or perish." They discover that love is the greatest healing power. Without love there is nothing worthwhile. They discover that love is the most salutary thing. By and by, so much evidence will be piled up that the thoughtful mind will say: What's back of it must be all love. Intuition is the self-pronouncement of Reality. Induction is the gradual acquiring of the evidence to prove this pronouncement is true. The great intuitive perceivers, deep abstractors of thought, merely have announced, by intuition, that which, by laborious intellect, will take a lifetime to try to discover.

But here we may assume God is Love. There is an urge to express, therefore there is involuted in us whatever God is. Whatever process that evolutionary Thing took to get us where we are, we may assume; it is an as-

---

*Walt Whitman (1819–1892), American poet.

sumption, but it looks as though it were true—that Its whole intent and purpose is evolved instinctively according to Its own nature by a power, force, energy, creativity inherent within the constitution of Its own being.

Nothing is brought there, nothing is willed there or purposed there or created there. This is very important. *Reality is not something God made.* God did not make God, or else the God we are talking about is not the one we are trying to talk about. The human mind must assume the Reality that *is, was,* and *will remain,* no matter what anybody thinks. It *has* to be that way. We may assume it is the nature of Reality—not the presence of God, not even the will of God, but the *nature*—that implies the purpose and will, and the energy, force, and creativity to execute the purpose. It is all involuted in that indivisible Invisibility which is everywhere present.

In you and me is the idea of whatever we are going to evolve into. I don't know what it is. I think there are beings beyond us as we are beyond tadpoles, because I cannot conceive an unfoldment that stops anywhere. I can conceive, however, that there are leaps from certain steps here to steps out there without going through all the various processes. We have plenty of evidence of it and a name for it in science: epigenesis.

We don't have to say, "God is *this* way." We say, "*This* way is God," which is infinitely preferable for people like Jesus. It will account for the fact that there must be a deep beyond our deep, height beyond our height, an utmost of our concepts at the end of any creative series. The ending marks the beginning of the next.

We must suppose that the undivided Will, undivided Purpose, undivided Law, undivided Energy, undivided Force, and undivided Delight (which I think is most important) exists at the center of all of us—"The undivided light,/ The light of being and undivided need/ That everything shall reunite," Tennyson said; "It will make one grand music as before." He knew what he was talking *about* but didn't know *by what* he was talking. He said to a friend, "There are times when I, as I know myself, seem to disappear and this other thing happens." He was still himself, without loss of consciousness.

This is the struggle of life, the drama of life, the play of life upon itself.

At the center of our being is the delight and bliss and need to reunite with all things. Why? Because that Thing hid within us was never disunited from itself. "Before Abraham, I was—destroy this body and that which I AM will raise up another like unto it." Even in the multiplicity, the apparent duality, the infinite variation, all is necessary for the delight, the bliss, and the self-expression of this Thing, whatever we choose to call It, which is God or Reality.

There is that which we cannot resist, that which is stronger than all our denials. Shakespeare said, "There's a Divinity that shapes our ends, rough-hew them how we will." This is what he was talking about. There is an urge that makes the chrysalis open so something will fly out. It is even the meaning of death and birth, integration and disintegration, apparently all for the purpose of expressing that inevitability, that necessity, that Thing which even God did not create: it *is* God. And so we say that the life that refuses to create stagnates and dies.

Next week I want to speak on what that would mean to us in practical application, in what we call treatment—because our treatment, rightly understood, is not a willpower which we throw upon the wind of chance. It is not a concentration of the Absolute and Ineffable, which has never been divided against Itself—so how, in the name of God, *can* It be concentrated? It just can't, any more than you can shuffle the principle of mathematics into a corner and sit on it. It will elude you.

Rather, we are constrained not to *believe*, not to *hope*, not to *long for*, not to *pray for*, but to *accept* that it seems to be the nature of all thought to be creative. Some thought is less creative than others; and by the very token of this self-evident fact, there will have to be some thought that is all-creative. Jesus said to capture this mystery; *how*, it does not matter.

This is what we seek to do, and if we can't do it by pure faith—which I guess is belief; most people don't have it—we can do it by pure reason and logic, if we will take logic and reason as far as they will go, without deserting them, and shove them into the background to accept a super logic and super reason. We can do it by induction, through the laborious scientific methods of deduction—or by the flight of fantasy, of the imagination.

Evelyn Underhill referred to "the doorway of that little gate, up here somewhere, through which intuition passes." We may do it as certain groups of people over a period of thousands of years did it—by combining all methods until at last it is essential that we accept certain self-evident facts and need no longer even have faith in them, but rather pass to the faith *of* the fact, rather than the faith *in* it.

Let's try that—and know we are one with the eternal and ineffable Presence, divine Spirit. We are one with all the love and beauty and peace and presence and power that there is in the Universe. It is what we are: "Thou hast made us; Thine we are"; and "we are that which Thou art, and Thou art that which we are." There is one Life, that Life is God, that Life is our life, that Life is perfect—infinite and eternal peace, ineffable beauty, stillness, silence, tranquility—the peace of That which everywhere is but does not move, but all movement takes place in It, the limitless strength of that Force and Energy that supports the Universe, upholding Its own creation in cosmic harmony—the Love which eternally gives of Itself through the outpouring of Its own spirit, to the delight of Its own soul and the expression of Its own will and the joy of beholding. With all this we identify ourselves; with all this we align ourselves in simplicity. Nor shall the mind contradict. That which affirms itself shall be united.

4.

THE POWER OF THE INDIVIDUAL

Ernest emphasizes here* that we all have the unlimited potential of God; for "God in us, as us, *is* us." By this awareness, we can affect all areas of our life for the better.

Recognition of a universal God and a universal Mind, which we express, so that we are living, loving, worthy expressions of God: this confirms to all of us the personalness of God and the Universe in which we live.

This chapter emphasizes the divine pattern underlying all Creation.

The Hindu says we are saved by works—that every man is, as Browning said, "a god though in the germ." Through the process of involution, the divine creative spark has impregnated the mundane clod which now has the impulsion, ad infinitum, to evolve—the mind that sleeps in the mineral, waves in the grass, wakes to simple consciousness in animals, to self-consciousness in man, and to God-consciousness in the upper hierarchies, all of which I believe.

Dean Inge, the greatest of modern Platonists and the greatest expositor of the philosophy of Plotinus who ever lived, said that there is no such thing as an infinite purpose—it would be a contradiction of logic and mathematics; that there can be no eternity snipped off at either end; and that it doesn't seem at all strange that the planets might be people.

Now what has all this to do with being saved by grace? It has everything to do with it. We cannot take an arbitrary viewpoint; we have to put it to-

*April 23, 1958.

gether to find out the reality, so far as I can see, in these two great streams of consciousness. It is something that Jesus did: he put them together and never denied them.* He said, "I came not to destroy but . . . to fulfill." He added, to the impersonality of Moses and the Hindus and the Buddhists, a concept of the immediacy of a Personalness in the Universe.

Arthur Compton,[†] in a little book called *Freedom of Man*, said that modern physics has found nothing to deny the concept of a universal mind, which is, in a sense, the parent mind of the human. St. Augustine said, "Thou hast made us, thine we are, and our hearts are restless till they find repose in Thee." He gave the Catholic church the major part of its greatest philosophy, which itself was derived from the Greeks, the Hebrews, and the ancient Hermetic teachings. You will find it running down through the teaching of the Old Testament and the Greeks.

Here is a philosophy of "the mind that sleeps in the mineral, waves in the grass" from India and from Buddhism. Buddhism was an offshoot of Hinduism; it moved over into China, although it never flourished there as it did in other places. It was not as grand a concept as ancient Hinduism. It had a certain element of nihilism in it, which, Aurobindo says, makes it a nihilistic philosophy entirely. We have the concept of the Divine impregnating the mundane clod, which in our Bible is referred to as Lucifer thrown from Heaven, falling like a flaming sword. Browning says, "a spark disturbs our clod."

Now this teaching means—and this is true Hinduism and true Buddhism—that everything is impregnated by That which is alive and awake and aware of everything, from a grain of sand to an archangel, from an ant hill to a planet; that everything we call individual is not individual by separation, but *individuated* as a self-expression of the totality of all things. That is why Jesus said, "Who hath seen me hath seen the Father" and Emerson said, "Who in his integrity worships God becomes God."

---

*The two are presumably the Law and the Presence, the impersonal and the personal; also evolution and involution.
†(1892–1962), American physicist.

This is the reciprocal action between the Universal and the individual. Troward said that since we are It in manifestation, and It is all there is (these are not his exact words), when I see It, it is It seeing me, at the level of my seeing It. This can go on and on without ever reaching a point of saturation, world without end—probably the greatest single spiritual teaching the world has ever had. Troward did not give it to us, but he clarified it. Jesus said, "Who hath seen me hath seen the Father."

Now, we have this idea of a universe that is alive, awake, and aware, not a dead universe, not a material universe. Mrs. Eddy would not have used the Scientific Statement of Being* had she been living today; she was a smart woman. "There is no life, truth, intelligence or substance in matter": there isn't any physicist living who believes in a material universe any more. But the sum total of it, the meaning, would be just the same. The practical application would be just the same in everything which responds—in everything an individuation of the totality of all things, being infinite variations of individuation without there ever being any such thing as an individual anything in the Universe.

I hope that is clear; there is all the difference in the world. If you have an *individual* in the Universe, it will be separated from everything else. If you have an *individuation* of all things, in all things, behind everything is the potential of all things. Therefore, the evolution is anything that is the potential of all things; it will be forever upward, outward, spiral, ever more and never less itself; there would never be any limit.

You couldn't do that if all things were individual. If all things were individual, we could not talk to each other, we could not know each other was here. We are able to talk to each other, as Kant said, because *we have an intuitive perception in a field of unitary wholeness.* In other words, I can see the mountains because they exist in the Mind which is me. We can know each other because we are *individuations* of the one Mind.

Now, a principle does not evolve but is that which is back of our evolution. Our evolution is merely catching up with that which is involuted—becoming

*In her *Science & Health*, p. 468.

aware of itself and catching up with the principle in the presence of its own being. By experience, it extends itself further and further out into a cosmic territory, which is without limit and which must contain all things.

Each individuation has back of it the whole works; all of God is potential in everybody. "Who in his integrity worships God will become God." "Act as though I am and I will be." The Talmud says, "God will doubly guide the already guided." Isn't that interesting! Jesus said the same thing—probably got it from the ancient teaching; it doesn't matter. He said, "To him who hath shall be given; from who hath not, shall be taken away even that which he hath." That is a tough statement: if you have, the Universe will give you more; if you haven't anything, it will kick your teeth out. Tennyson said, speaking of the evolutionary process, "so careful of the type it seems, so careless of the single life."

The theory is, then, that the single life is the monad—the original thing that impregnates the mundane clod, putting into it the seed of self-existence, self-evolution, perpetual life, eternal unfoldment, limitless expansion. Browning said, "a god though in the germ": "Therefore I summon age/ To grand youth's heritage;/ For having served its term,/ Thence shall I pass, approved,/ A man; for I removed,/ From the developed brute,/ A god though in the germ." It is from *Rabbi Ben Ezra*.

This seems a lot of not much in particular. It really has a point somewhere, if I can expose it. It is from the standpoint of one of the oldest and most perfect systems of thought the world has ever known, one of the most comprehensive. We have the concept that we are saved by works. Why? Because here is the thing: it doesn't say work out your salvation with fear and trembling, as our Bible does. (Whoever wrote that was feeling badly.)

So here is the possibility of all things, neatly wrapped up in a little package, laid down in a hunk of clay, and let alone to discover itself. It may be an arbitrary propulsion and impulsion to be compelled to arrive at a certain stage of evolution, which would stop in its impulsion toward evolution as soon as the evolving instrumentality knew it was not its environment; or knew itself separate from it; or knew itself, recognized "I am here"; knew *something*, looking at things, and was not lost in its landscape.

Now, from that time on, nothing has happened to the evolving seed of perfection. Wigan* says of these original genes—those things which are handed from generation to generation, as though God brought them in the Ark of the Covenant—that nothing can destroy them; they are Life itself. Genesis says that the plant was in the seed before the seed was in the earth. All of this means: within us is self-existence, self-perpetuation, self-energy, self-knowing. "The self must raise the self by the self." "Behold I stand at the door and knock; I wait." "Whosoever will, may come." There is nothing there, then, that would force that evolution beyond the point of self-perception. Therefore they rightly say, "The self must raise the self by the self."

Now the Christian philosophy says we are saved by grace. *Grace* means the givingness of God. *Works* means that which is earned. *Faith* means that which is given. "By Moses came the law; by Christ came grace." Then someone says, "Is the law of no avail? God forbid." This person understood there must be both law and grace—both givingness and usingness (if there is such a word). Every individual must have within himself the ability to work out his own salvation. Life itself has imparted itself to him by giving-ness, which theologically interpreted is grace. It is all right. What they meant is: *it is all right.*

I think we combine both, undoubtedly; we did not make our life; we don't even make our own liver or anything else. We, in certain sense, do not create anything. God is the thing He creates. "I am . . . beside which there is none other." Therefore there is, within us, that germ of life which is inde-structible, uncreated—that still creates. There would have to be. Only the uncreated can create, it seems to me; only the unmanifest can manifest; only that which is not spoken can be said. Now that sounds screwy, but you know what I mean. I believe it is true.

Kettering† said, "Every invention is an intuition, and the continuation of the techniques and furtherance of it is just a series of intuitions." Now, there

---

*Arthur L. Wigan, American neurophysicist.
†Charles Kettering (1876–1958), American electrical engineer.

is within each one of us, then, not only a presentation of the Infinite—"Who hath seen me hath seen the Father, yet the Father is greater than I"; there is also that which perpetuates; there is that which extends itself; there is that which the Self knows. "The self must raise the self by the self"; and it is the gift of life—we didn't make it. By grace, then, or by divine giving-ness, we receive life; by works, we use it. We shall combine the two, because they are two great perceptions of our relationship to reality.

But there is, within each one of us, a divine pattern. I do not know what it looks like; I do not know what anything perfect looks like, nor does any-one else. As I suggested last week, it is my conviction; I have been spending hours thinking about this one thing. I try to put every fact I know together—synthesize it and see what comes up out of the pot. It seems to me that is the way we learn things—even truths that are self-evident; they *would* be self-apparent if we saw them; but we see as through a glass darkly.

I suggested last week that I have been trying to figure out what is illu-sion, what is real; what is so, what isn't so. God is not laboring under an illusion; "God is not mocked," nor is reality profaned; truth never suffers shocks; "truth crushed to earth will rise again." No one has ever sinned against God. It is impossible. Did you know the teachers in the Catholic church do not believe God sees or knows evil?

There is, in us, that thing which belongs to the Universe. "At the center of everything nestles the seed of perfection," Whitman said. Browning said: "in loosening this imprisoned splendor"; Emerson said, "We are beneficia-ries of the divine fact." The Bible says, "God made man perfect, but he has sought out many inventions." Now, we are already perfect; we don't look it or act it; we don't seem to be; we don't understand how we could be or that we are; this we do not know. This is the ignorance.

I like Aurobindo's concept of the great ignorance rather than sin and salvation, the fall and redemption—which is pretty finite stuff, and which comes up out of the Christian theology. Ignorance has a broader sweep to it. Here are ignorance and its consequences; "there is no sin but a mistake and no punishment but a consequence." Emerson said ignorance is the only sin there is, enlightenment the only salvation. "The self must raise the self by

the self." But the self is there; we didn't put it there. That is your grace—
that is your givingness. But by the very nature of reality, we cannot understand it until we see it as it is, and we cannot see it as it is until we understand
it. Isn't that terrible!

"Beloved, now are we the sons of God"—that is a statement of being—
"and it doth not yet appear what we shall be; but we know that, when he
shall appear, we shall be like him; for we shall see him as he is. And every
man that hath this hope in him purifieth himself, even as he is pure."* Now,
this is not referring to Jesus. It is referring to what the Hebrews called the
Messiah, the Buddhists called the Buddha, the Hindus called the Atman,
and we call the Christ—"Christ in us, the hope of glory."

It refers to the spiritual principle and presence of "the spark that ignites
our clod," or the pattern which is given (this is "the Lamb slain from the
foundation of the world"). "And the veil of the temple was rent at the least
breath of the outgoing soul": now, this is a symbol—the symbol of when
that which is human completely gives way to the divine. There is the temple: "Know ye not that ye are the temple of God?" The veil that stands between the face of Reality and what we have seen (which is too unreal) is
rent, and we "see him as he is." "We do not know what we shall be; but when
he appears, we shall be like him."

"When he shall appear . . . we shall see him as he is": we cannot see him
as he is until he appears; he can't appear until we see him. We are between
the Devil and deep blue sea. Everything is, of course, the result of the self-
combustion of the Universe; it has to be. This is our greatest trouble as
metaphysicians: that we are still dealing in our minds with a material universe or with a universe separated from a fluidity. Or as Emerson said, "We
see it as a solid fact, God as liquid law." That is our great trouble. We think
we are spiritualizing matter or materializing spirit and that mind is influencing or controlling something that is not mind.

Now, if we would follow Einstein's equation, we would not do that: we
would merely apply it through a law of parallels of the kind where he says

---

*John 3:2, 3.

energy and mass are equal, identical, and interchangeable—they are the same thing. Mrs. Eddy said, "All is Mind and Its infinite manifestation, and God is All-in-all." Spinoza said, "I do not say mind is one thing and matter is another; I say they are the same thing." Quimby said, "Mind is matter in solution, matter is mind in form." The Bible says, "the invisible things of God, from the foundation of the universe, are made manifest or known by the visible."

All it means is that what you see comes out of what you don't see; what you don't see must have* the pattern of what you do see; if you should [truly] see what you do see, then what you don't see you would see, and it would be what you do see.† Then "when he shall appear, we shall be like him; for we shall see him as he is." But he cannot appear until we see him as he is.

Our vision is cast at a lower level; it is beclouded, as through a glass darkly, by some kind of psychological projection we hang up—the pattern of what we think—in front of the Universe we *think* it is. And looking at the Universe it *is*, we see only the Universe we *think*—which is a projection. Our thinking doesn't change reality at all. Some people think it does; but it never flattened the world when they thought it was flat—it only flattened their experience on a round one. When someone knew it was round, he could navigate it.

Now there must be in here (symbolically at the center of man's being) a pattern which is perfect. What we see has to be attached to a pattern which is perfect or there wouldn't be anything to vitalize it, just as the gene is indestructible, handed from generation to generation. I don't consider truth a matter of my opinion at all; truth isn't what I think. I am fortunate if what I think is in line with truth. It would be terrible if truth had to be what I think. I did not put the mountains up there. The mountains, as I look at them, are to me what I am to the mountains.

"As thou seest, that thou be'est. As thou beholdest man, that to become

---

*= hold.
†"Don't see" relates to substance, reality; "do see" relates to immediate appearance.

thou must: God if thou seest God, dust if thou seest dust." We tend to become like what we look at. The mountains are here, but I hang a veil in front of the mountains, in a sense. We don't see each other and everything as it is, do we? We know enough about psychology, projection, emotional bias, and intellectual blind spots to know that we have a veil between ourselves—all of our experiences and everyone we meet veiled by a projection, by an emotional bias.

There is no way in the world to figure how the wisest, the most erudite, the most scholastic people on earth—the Jesuits—would still believe in Hell except there is an emotional bias in them that will not let them analyze it. If they ever got to that analysis, Hell would cool off. We are looking at a real Universe but are not seeing it.

Now when the veil is rent, the veil of the temple: the temple is this body. It isn't "over there"; it isn't a church or mosque or synagogue. We call it such, but the temple is this: "Know ye not that ye are the temple of God? . . . whose temple ye are." And so the veil of the temple is rent; the dead walk, and the graves give up their dead. It is all a symbol—something that happens in some degree in our own experience if the veil of the temple is rent. The darned thing won't tear (if that is what a rent veil is; it is one that is torn, isn't it?) until we see it as it is. Then when we see it, it can't help ripping itself apart, because it was held together only by our own imagination. (It is a curtain of concealment, someone said.)

This does not mean that when we look into the perfect, the corn-popper is already there, the threshing machine, the sewing machine, and the breadmixer—it doesn't mean that at all; because the Universe isn't static. Emerson said, "The Ancient of Days is in the latest invention." It means that That which is self-perpetuated, self-imagining, self-executing, self-everything is there. But now, out of It shall come a new creativity. Since It never presents Itself, even in Its entirety, to two persons alike, then out of this, through each one of us, shall come a unique creativity.

That is why Emerson said imitation is suicide. No two persons are ever alike or need be or could be if they tried. If there were two people alike, one would be unnecessary in the creative process and wouldn't be here at all.

Therefore Emerson said that there is a place where everyone may let out his reins to the full extent—but he is afraid to do it.

So there is unique presentation in each one of us, if we would listen to it. Emerson said, "Listen greatly to yourself; keep up this lowly listening," etc. Our Bible says, "Be still and know." It all means the same thing. There is, then, within each one of us "a god though in the germ." I don't think this is an opinion; to me it isn't just a poetical something—it is beautiful, inspiring; it is God-given. Life has made it this way, and you and I can't change it. We may only accept what it is. Though we appear to reject it and throw it out the front door, it will come in the back door; it will always be there by a persistency that is completely irresistible, by a nonresistance that nothing can resist and a nonviolence that nothing can violate.

Therefore it is certain that any individual, in such degree as he will see reality, will experience it. It will automatically manifest. If all the world said, "No, all the thoughts of the ages have nothing to do with the fact that two and two are four" (referring to the old shibboleth which we have in our field and others have, that what a guy thinks has something to do with what he knows), it still would not be so—or else what you know isn't so. If when Jesus—it is my belief—said to Lazarus, "Come forth," Lazarus had not come forth, I think Jesus would have dropped dead. The frustration would have been so great it would have killed him.

I find nothing in the Universe that says No to reality; there is nothing in any of us that can. Therefore there must be a transcendency of our own thought that is possible, that has immediate precedence over everything that has ever gone before, everything that everybody ever believed or thought, or that all people believed. "The great are great only because we are on our knees. Let us arise."

You will discover no greatness outside yourself; that which appears to be greatness in another is merely as much as you have projected from yourself to the other. As that hidden thing is removed, you and I will see, in the other, the more perfect image. We have disclosed it; but we couldn't disclose it until we saw it as it is. And we can't see it as it is until we *are* as it is—and there isn't any more *is*-er than that!

Now we may, to be brief, play a game with our intellect, our emotions, our religions, and our philosophies; we may sit around with our saviors and saints; but they will all have to go out the window when God comes in. They will all have to go out in such degree as the Truth comes in, and we shall no longer live by proxy. Jesus knew this when he said, "Why callest thou me good? There is none good save God." They tried to make him king, and he had no desire to be that; he was a teacher; he was following the law of Moses and adding to it the personal equation "I came not to destroy, but to fulfill." It makes a perfect thing—a Universe of Law and order, Presence and person; and that is exactly what it is. It may be that there is an action and reaction which governs everything.

Jesus said, "It is expedient that I go away, in order that the Spirit shall understand what I am talking about." This is *you.* "I have come to reveal the self to the self"—that is the only revelation there is. That is why Shakespeare said, "To thine own self be true, and it shall follow as the night the day thou canst not then be false to any man." But we are afraid of the real self.

First of all, we think we have to be so spiritual. *We don't know what it means to be spiritual.* We do not listen to children praying—that is our trouble; we forget the spontaneity of it. We think it must be something so profound we can't understand it. We don't know it is so simple that every time we deny it, we are affirming it! Our trouble is we don't *expect* enough. Yet since grace is given, the gift is made, or the Lamb is slain "from the foundation of the world." "The self must raise the self by the self."

When the little boy was in the pigpen, papa didn't come and say, "Come home." If he had dragged him home, then the little boy would have been an automaton, a cosmic robot. Everything in the Universe is alive, awake, and aware with spontaneous self-combustion. You and I or somebody else might (whether we do or not) draw some kind of a picture that was never drawn before. So let's do it.

Know that originality is within us; we are very humble, and there is nothing arrogant about this, neither is there anything self-effacing. Even if this is the only thing we ever know, all things must forevermore remain in relationship to it—no matter how glorious they are. The Universe has decreed it and we cannot change it. We shall recognize that effort, that power, that depth of feeling, that glory of creativity, that warmth and color of love, that song that is celestial. We shall know that here and now God Himself goes forth anew into creation through us. We have accepted the gift of Life and are now playing with it on the shores of time, where the waters of the Infinite wash our feet. Yet all eternity seems in our hearts. We are embraced—held in the soft embrace of That which is pure Love and perfect Peace.

And so it is.

5

THE DEFINITION OF
RELIGIOUS SCIENCE

Shortly after the previous talk, Ernest had a group of us at his house for a "command dinner." In attendance were Dr. and Mrs. Reg Armor,* Thornton Kinney and his wife, Dr. Mabel Kinney (member of the California State Board of Education), Mr. and Mrs. William Lynn,† Dr. William H. D. Hornaday, Dr. Barclay Johnson, and myself.

Dr. Holmes announced to us that the Governor of California, Goodwin Knight (holder of a doctorate in Humanities conferred by the Institute of Religious Science), had requested that Dr. Kinney obtain from Dr. Holmes a 25-word definition of Religious Science. For an hour or two, we all contributed ideas; but when Ernest announced the definition, it didn't seem much to resemble what we had talked about.

A couple of weeks later, on May 27, 1958, he addressed this before the Tuesday Invitational Group. Attendance was only by those receiving his personal invitation. Guests flew in from Arizona, New Mexico, Illinois, and Texas. Before this group Dr. Holmes sat in a chair and expressed freely his thoughts and ideas. I felt a great sense of humility as the only minister on the permanent invitational list.

I had a very interesting experience yesterday: I spoke to 50 Christian ministers—I mean ministers of the Christian Church, which is rather liberal in a way. One of them said to me, in a very sweet way, "In reference to what you said about such-and-such a thing . . ." and I stopped him and

---

*Reginald Armor (1903–1977), the earliest of Dr. Holmes's associates besides his brother Fenwicke.

†William Lynn was, as a young man, a "protégé" of Dr. Holmes. He later served the United Church of Religious Science and in retirement is executor of Dr. Holmes's estate.

said, "I didn't say anything about that subject," and he said, "You implied it," and I said, "No, you inferred it." I said, "This is in your mind and is a psychological projection—but unconscious—and has nothing to do with what I said." There was nothing mean or bad about it, and I thought how our reactions to life are that way.

They are a nice group; all have churches and are pretty broadly gauged. They have had ministers from all faiths—even a Catholic priest and a rabbi. Someone asked the priest, "How about the Reformation?" and he said, "I don't know anything about any reformation; I have not heard of any reformation in our church." He said the Catholic church has never had a reformation; they are just as they always were. Now isn't that a clever answer? I thought it was.

In talking with Mabel Kinney the other evening (she is a member of the State Board which has charge of our scholastic work—schools, colleges, etc.), she said that one of the members of the Board—and they are all college professors or educators—said, "Will you please write out for me in 25 words what Religious Science is?" That is something, isn't it? So I sat down and wrote it, and it said: Religious Science is a synthesis of laws of science, opinions of philosophy, and revelations of religion applied to human needs and the aspirations of man. Isn't that good? *Religious Science is a synthesis of laws of science, opinions of philosophy, and revelations of religion applied to human needs and the aspirations of man.* I think it is wonderful!

Nearly 2,000 years ago, Plotinus, who was the greatest of the Neoplatonists and whom Dean Inge called the king of intellectual mystics of the ages, said that the only avenues of learning we have, have come from science, philosophy, and illumination. By illumination he meant what we mean by religion, intuition. We believe revelation is intuition perceived by the conscious intelligence, and therefore to us *religion* wouldn't be quite as broad a term as *intuition*. But to cover the need of the world, I thought we better put it that way, because the only avenues through which knowledge may come to the human mind are science, philosophy, and religion.

Science is defined as a system of laws, causes in nature, and techniques for the use and application of them to human needs; philosophy is anybody's opinion about anything. Most people mistakenly think philosophy means Plato and Aristotle and Socrates. It means them only because these people wrote or because what they said was recorded. Therefore we refer to them as "the philosophers" merely because they were the ones whose words were taken down and recorded. There have been thousands of others just as good that we never heard of.

I repeat: philosophy is anybody's opinion about anything, and revelation means intuition (which we all have) brought to the surface and perceived by the conscious intelligence. It is back of the psychic. Now, the revelations which have come through the psychic are distorted by the psychic. That is why, when you read so many of these "revelations," you will find them a combination of intuition and projected opinions. This is where Hell came from. (There is no Hell.)

One time, a very good friend of mine who belongs to AA came to my house and said, "I want to tell you what an alcoholic goes through and why only an alcoholic can understand one." For two hours he recited things that happened to him in this state. That was the most gruesome recital, the most realistic and damnedest thing I ever listened to. When I asked if that was the way it was, he said, "That is the way it is." He said he would finally wake up by breaking everything in the room, tearing the pictures down, breaking out the windows. I thought, then, that this isn't so different from the poet Dante. Maybe *he* was drunk when he painted his pictures of hell! It comes from the same source—a grotesqueness.

The prolific imagination, bordering on morbidity, that projects itself from the psychic into the intellect is not to be discerned. It has nothing to do with intuition, which is a direct perception of truth without processes of reasoning. That is why you can always tell whether someone is writing from intuition or the psychic. Most people think a hunch is an intuition. It may or may not be. We live in these three worlds of spiritual absolute, human psychic reactions, and physical manifestation.

3,500 hundred years ago, Pantanjali* was compiling the knowledge of

*(2d century B.C.), Indian scholar and grammarian.

Ancient India at that time. Have you read *The Sutras of Patanjali*? It is one of the greatest little books of the ages. It very definitely shows how you have to get through what we call the psychic. The Bible says, "Try the spirits and see whether or not they are of God." Now this psychic field is what Mrs. Eddy called the mortal mind or sum total of human thought and what the Bible calls the carnal mind, "which is enmity against God." It is what Carl Jung* calls the collective unconscious, which means the sum total of all the thoughts and actions of the ages, operating on a psychic level and a psychic field that impinges upon everyone—just as it is now definitely known that there is an inertia to human thought patterns.

Joseph Jastrow† said that in counseling and analysis in psychiatry, one of the principal things they have to overcome is what he calls the inertia of thought patterns. Now there is one of our prominent psychologists talking, and he said they act exactly as though they were entities. Mrs. Eddy called this "the argument of error," if you are familiar with her sayings. Quimby said, "We go around surrounded by our opinions. I represent the man of wisdom; I enter the man of opinions; I explain that they are only opinions." Jesus said, "Know the truth, and the truth shall make you free."

We are surrounded by a psychic realm which contains the thoughts and opinions; and that is what we are hearing a lot of now in "regression" through hypnotism. People get caught in a psychic trap which is omnipresent and can be picked up by anyone at any time. If they are clairvoyant, they will see the action; if they are clairaudient, they will hear the voice. This same field impinges upon all of us, and I think in some degree we are all hypnotized from cradle to grave.

Why does everybody say, "You can't do it"? Why does everyone say, "There will always be war," "There will always be poverty"? Only because there *has* been! There is no logic in it. The logic of experience is no criterion of judgment, of what could be now or ought to be in the future. Every new advance in science can be an advance only because it arbitrarily contradicts

---

*(1875–1961), Swiss psychologist and psychiatrist.
†(1863–1944), American psychologist.

much that, up until then, was considered to be true. That is why Tennyson said, "New truth makes ancient good uncouth./ Our little systems have their day;/ They have their day and cease to be:/ They are but broken lights of Thee,/ And Thou, O Lord, art more than they."

I said to some ministers yesterday something I said to you last week: I think that the time will come when religion will get free from its superstition. It is inevitable that it will come, but I don't know when. Philosophy will get rid of its dualism, because most philosophy is materialistic and dualistic. Science, because of its findings, will merge into more or less of a mystical state relative to the nature of the Universe, which many scientists are now doing. When those three things combine, you will have the next and new religion of the world, which will ultimately immerse all religions and finally dominate. Why? *We have it.* That is what Religious Science is supposed to do, and that is why I made that definition with that in mind. Why? Because we do not consider that there is an isolated fact in the Universe, a separate entity, or an apartness from the sum total of all things.

We consider the whole universal system to be a unitary wholeness, undivided and indivisible. Therefore its entirety is at the point of our perception, always. But our perception is somewhat influenced by the psychic background of the world. I mean, these regressions pick up the experiences of the ages. I have read and seen so much of this stuff all my life—because it has been a part of what we know about; and I know this is what happens. Anybody can remember anything that ever happened to anybody who ever lived—if he happens to tune into it.

Some day there will be a physical instrument perfected that will tune into it and record the words of Jesus, John the Baptist, or Caesar. Right now, one who can practice psychometry and really objectify it would take a brick (if Caesar lived in a brick house) and hold it in his hand, and it would be entirely possible for him to describe the house, the rooms, the furniture (if they had any), what they ate, who was there, and to hear them talk and say what they said 2,000 years ago. Already in the annals of the British and American societies of psychic research there is irrefutable evidence of this. While it might be the world will say 't'ain't so, it *is*.

I really wanted to discuss the concept that we have suggested many times for us to think about during the summer. This fall we are going to do some very special things. We exist to prove our position as far as the world is concerned. I even had the nerve yesterday to say—it was a question about salvation—"Well, that has to do with salvation, the problem of evil, which you people know more about than I do." It was mean of me to say that. I had the nerve to say that "If anyone was lost, I wouldn't know where to look for him." They looked strange.* I said, "Neither would you."

Logic and reason compel us to accept that the Universe is a unitary wholeness, but we do not stop to think what this means—that it is a *unitary wholeness.* That which is one, naturally, is undivided and indivisible. Therefore all of it appears at any and every point within it; the totality of infinity is whatever you are thinking. All of God is right where you are. The entirety of the universal laws of nature exists between your two fingers when you put them as close together as you can; all action and reaction exists in the possibility of the quiver of an eyelash. It is impossible to shove a grain of sand across the width of your thumbnail without shifting the entire weight of the sidereal universe—that means all the universe that is in manifestation, anywhere. That wouldn't be possible if it weren't for this unitary wholeness. The fact that you and I can talk to each other is proof enough that we exist in a medium which, Emerson said, "is common to all individual men."[†]

Immanuel Kant, in *The Critique of Pure Reason*—he is called the Father of Logic as Socrates is called the Father of Philosophy and Homer the Father of Literature—stated: "It is impossible for us to recognize each other. The only way we can is that it awakens an intuition within us in a common medium." Now, this is his way of saying, "I know you when you know me, because the mind in you that knows me is the mind in me that knows you." *There is one mind common to all men.*

This unitary wholeness we must accept, whether we understand it or not. We must always remember that we may *believe* what is *not;* so we can

---

*i.e., the ministers referred to on pp. 61 and 68.
†"There is one mind common to all individual men."

know only what *is so*, even though that which is not so (which we believe in) may bind us—because we believe in it. All bondage is ignorance. That is why Emerson said there is no sin but ignorance and no salvation but enlightenment.

That is also why the Hindus say man is saved by works rather than grace; the Christians say he is saved by grace rather than works; and, in our system, we put them both together and say: the possibility of salvation—not the salvation of the soul, but salvation from the lesser to the greater—lies *in works, through grace.* Don't you think that is better? I tried to synthesize it and put it together. *Grace* means that which is given; *works* means that which is earned. Since everything is given, we will have to earn the right to use it—to even know that it is there—by perception and through action. So there is a difference between believing and knowing. Someone said, "The devils also believe, and tremble."* Of course, we don't believe in devils. I think he was merely making a point.

If the whole thing is everywhere present, which it is, then all of God is between our fingers. The infinitesimal and the magnitudinous (I don't know whether there is such a word; if there isn't, I just made it up), the big and the little: Emerson said, "There is no great and no small to the Soul that maketh all." We know this theoretically, but we do not know what it means practically. For instance, it is well accepted in medicine that a person has a wart; yet someone says, "You haven't got it," and nine times out of ten it will disappear. I used to take warts off the boys when I had a Boy Scout troop. This we accept; but the moment we try to erase a cancer, what happens? All the thought of pain, of anguish, of incurability, or else fear in the whole race mind, backs up our negation and flows through it, making it very difficult to affirm its opposite. This is the only difference, if what you and I believe is true. The difference would not be in the thing but in our reaction to it.

Infinity presses against finiteness, absoluteness becomes relativity—but finiteness hasn't learned how to give itself back to infinity, nor relativity

*James 2:19.

back to absoluteness. Therefore it considers itself *apart* and *separate* and *other than*—and not *one with*. We say we are one *with* God and one *in* God. This is a mistake; we are one *of* whatever the nature of God is. Whatever it is, it is *one*. All the great have said it; I didn't make it up. The Hindus say, "He is all"; the Hebrews say, "God is One." It is all the same thing.

Now, you see, that which the intellect may perceive, logic may accept, and rationalization (that which is rational) cannot deny. Like an axiom, it is a self-evident truth that rationality and sanity cannot deny—but they *do* deny its implication. We think it is much more difficult to heal a cancer than a wart; we think a million dollars is a lot of money and a dime isn't very much money; and we are right. But if we didn't know the one from the other and had never been told the difference, we shouldn't know. So the causation is right here.

I saw a cartoon one time of a Sunday School teacher asking the class about Daniel in the lions' den. The lions are there, like a bunch of kittens, very docile, and she asked the class, "Why didn't the lions attack Daniel?" Now, most of the kids answered that Daniel was taken care of by God; but one little kid said, "They were not afraid of him." She was the only one who had the right answer.

Have I told you about the young Episcopal clergyman who was told to take a shot of brandy? He was speaking for the first time, and his bishop was there. He finished and he rushed down, and the bishop said he did fine. He said, "You have the looks, you are young and handsome, your diction is perfect; but you haven't quite enough oomph. Even in our church you have to have a little pep. I will not object to your taking just a little glass of brandy before you go into the pulpit—for a little while, until you get warmed up to the situation."

The next week he had evidently followed the suggestion—and probably had not measured the glass very accurately: he was pretty pepped up! After the service, he came down to the bishop again and asked how he did. The bishop said, "You did wonderful; I *knew* it was in you. But I have to warn you about something: don't carry anything too far. Where you were telling the story about Daniel in the lions' den, you should have said, 'and by the grace of God, the lions were subdued.' You should not have said, 'and Daniel kicked the living hell out of them.'" You can see he entered into the spirit of it, anyway.

The Universe has the funniest way of putting the ridiculous and sublime together—else how can you account for our being here? It is impossible. There is an answer to this. Most people in our thought,* as in other religions, put on a long face and say, "Look at me and drop dead." Why is this? Because we seek to divide the indivisible. We arbitrarily place a limitation on everything we do. We think it is imposed on us by the Universe or by destiny.

Now, it isn't our fault! This is our bondage, our ignorance; this is our fall; and this is our sin—if we have one. But let us consider, next, that the entire Universe—all that God is, all that destiny may ever become, all that evolution shall ever produce—exists in its entirety at the standpoint of every manifestation within it, whether you and I call it big or little; good, bad, or indifferent; consequential or inconsequential—it doesn't matter. It doesn't know about these things. Remember, it doesn't know a mountain is bigger than a marble; it doesn't know our assumptions, else they would be true. Therefore infinity presses against the point of finiteness, and absoluteness against the point of relativity; and infinity is the finite. The finite is not the infinite, but the infinite is the finite.

Relativity is not absoluteness, absolutely; but absoluteness is relativity at the level of relativity, with nothing between the much and the more on the one hand, and what appears as the smaller and the lesser on the other. There are no mediators, Christs, saviors, avatars, Buddhas—all have to go by the wayside. They are no longer necessary to the evolution of the soul. How many know that they are *wayshowers* and not saviors? There is no such thing as a savior; don't ever tell anyone I said so, but it is true just the same.

It is a startling thing—Emerson said it is a cannonball. It is not always tender and gentle; it doesn't always appear even to be kind, because it is so impersonal.

---

*= teaching.

Even having accepted its logic—which we must, if we think—we still do not quite catch its meaning, do we? Here, say, is a thing. The nature of its meaning may be explained; its essence can only be felt. Would that have any meaning? They have a saying in the theater about young actors and actresses—the director will say, "I didn't believe him. It wasn't real." "My words fly up, my thoughts remain below: words without thoughts, never to heaven go."

The logic of it is not difficult to understand; the mathematics of it is not difficult to understand: infinity undivided is omnipresent; and omnipresence is pressed against every point, flowing to that point in its entirety, and at that point existing only at that point, and for no other point. And that is the next thing I want to establish: individuation in the Universe. This is deep stuff for us to think about this summer.

How do we know this? Because no two thumbprints are alike; no two blades of grass are alike; no two snowflakes are alike; not any of you can jump in the same river twice; no moment coalesces, or combines, with any other moment. That is why Dean Inge said, "Time is a sequence of events in a unitary wholeness"; Augustine said, "It is anticipation, recollection, and memory." To more simplify these things, I just said, "Time is any measure of any experience but has no existence in and of itself. It is not an entity." The Zen Buddhist seeks to find that moment here, when *here* is no longer bound to *there* by a sequence of cause and effect. This is the reason why Jesus forgave people. He was right scientifically, logically, inspirationally, and in essence. *And it worked.*

To get back to the thought that, because of the uniqueness of every individual, it is necessary to say, "I hope it is; I would like to believe it is. Lead me to some prophet who will tell me, or some religion which will announce it, or some authority": there are no such things. "There are no prophets other than the wise." "The great are great to us only because we are on our knees; let us arise." The only greatness they have is that which we have loaned them from the inexhaustible magnitude of our own magnificence, as humble as we may be.

Emerson said, "There is a place in every man's life where the lines may run out full length." Genius is something that has not to be caught, but used; everyone has it. Now, it may be blocked by accident at birth. Physiologically, psychologically it may be blocked; but it still exists there, back of insanity, back of everything that looks crazy. It is why Browning said, "a god though in the germ." Well, we are screwy; but we are not crazy.

Genius—the possibility of everything, all that God is, all that the Universe has—exists solely that this rose shall bloom, that this man may paint this picture, that this girl may now go out and sing, that a child may make a mud cake and a mother nurse her baby—all of these. Isn't this a magnificent concept! The trivial is not incidental; it is merely the mode of manifestation of all things. The laughter of a child is as important to the Universe as the creation of a planet. A friend of mine* built the Golden Gate Bridge; it was the greatest engineering feat accomplished up until then, and possibly since then—I don't know—and the most difficult. He was the most childlike of persons.

A child builds a little house and kicks it over. The Golden Gate Bridge will someday fall down, rust out, be torn down, because something better will happen. Change is the only thing that is permanent. The only thing we can say of anything that looks static is: This too shall pass away. If it were not so, the Infinite would get caught in its own mold—God would be stopped by His own creation, and creativity would be absorbed in its creation.

I believe in pantheism to the extent that the soul of the Universe is in everything, but apart from it. That is why I said God is in His creation but not absorbed by it. This creation is necessary, and without it there would be no cause. It is impossible there should be a cause without creation. You would have an intelligence that is not intelligent of anything. A consciousness that is not aware of anything is not conscious—therefore it hasn't any existence; consequently it isn't and 't'ain't so. Therefore there is an infinite consciousness.

Now, this was what Bishop Berkeley† said—that "All things have to be in

---

*Joseph Strauss (1870–1938), American bridge engineer.
†George Berkeley (1685–1753), Irish philosopher. "To be is to be perceived."

some mind." All things, he thought, were not in his intellect, therefore he supposed there is a Mind in which all things are real, but a Mind to which he has a relationship. Emerson said the same thing when he said, "Every man is an inlet to the same and to all of the same."

But now let's get back. We have the logic, we have the reason, we have the conviction; we believe these things, you and I, and perhaps most of the world does. They would if they understood them, I am sure. But to this intellectual concept, to this mathematical understanding, something else must be added. One is the Spirit, and the other the letter of the Law. A Universe without Law could never take form; a Universe without consciousness could never be creative. It is always a combination of the two: the thought and the feeling. Words, of themselves, are just words, are merely molds. There is no effective word without a meaning. You all have molds you use with your salads, etc.—you put something liquid in it and it takes form. But the mold is not the form of the *essence*.

There is, to the testimony of the intellect, the mind, the intelligence, the logic, and the reason, another and a higher testimony, which cannot be explained. For we may kill the nightingale and not capture the song; we may break an egg and not find the chicken. The mystery of life is just as much a mystery to God as it is to us, except God isn't *mystified* by it. I didn't used to know that.

There is no God which can explain God; if there were, then that thing we call *God* would be itself a secondary cause, subject to something beyond it. Therefore all inquiry into the Truth has to start where the Truth is. The thing *is* this way; life *is*. I live, therefore I am. You and I may just as well accept that infinity exists for the expression of everything, from a blade of grass to an archangel to a drop of water of the ocean.

The whole Universe is reflected in each speck of its own indivisibility, but the contemplation of that which permits the flow of its essence lies beyond the intellect and cannot be explained. It isn't beyond reason or rationality; it is beyond explanation and reasoning. Is that clear? We go through a process of reasoning to arrive at that which does not reason, but which if it did reason would always be reasonable. Jesus bore testimony to it in the same way when he said, "I judge no man; but if I judged, my judgment would be right." This is why Jesus, like the other great mystics, never explained anything. He said it is *like* this and *like* that—like grains of mustard seeds, and like whatever. That is why the poets never explained. It is an intuitive expression, a language that is beyond processes but which contains them.

Browning said, "All that is at all/ Lasts ever past recall." He doesn't go through an explanation and say life can't get dead, therefore it is going to live. He just says *that is the way it is.* They said to him, "What does it mean?" and he said, "I knew when I wrote it, but I don't know now." And that is true of all of us. Therefore there is a feeling; and there is an artistry. The art is mechanical; it is mathematical. Some warmth, some color, some feeling is breathed upon it through the artist by the original great Creativity; that thing about which Longfellow* in *The Song of Hiawatha* said: "He is gone, the sweet musician;/ He, the sweetest of all singers,/ Is gone from us for-ever./ He has gone a little nearer/ To the maker of all music,/ To the master of all singing."

So as we try to put these things together, the intellect is absolutely necessary: rationality, logic—all are necessary. But back of them all, and flowing through them all, there is something *beyond* them all—a feeling, an intuition. That is what religion is; that is what revelation is. That is why every great thinker who ever lived has told us that God does not argue; He contemplates. The barriers that we have to break down are the relativities—big and little, good and bad, right and wrong, Heaven and Hell. It is very difficult to do.

The experience of the race bears so much evidence that is negative, and it seems irrational to refute it. I do not know that we necessarily have to *refute,* as much as we have to *contemplate its opposite.* Without trying to bring opposites together, we will arrive at that viewpoint the poet must have had in mind when he said he viewed the world as one vast plane and one bound-

---

*Henry Wadsworth Longfellow (1807–1882), American poet.

less reach of sky. Then would be brought to bear our simplest affirmation, the mandate of the Universe. If Lazarus hadn't come out when Jesus said, "Come forth," Jesus would have gone in and lain down with him.

We know that we are the offspring of Life, the manifestation of Light. We know that all the presence and all the power and all the love and all the wisdom and all the peace and joy and all the friendship and togetherness exist in this totality which we are, in which we embrace each other in love, in joy, and in peace. And it is our desire that there shall be unfolded to us— all of us—during this brief interval of our own contemplation a power so dynamic, a beauty so terrific, a peace so deep and a joy so flowing that Heaven and earth shall meet and make one vast music as before.

And so it is.

And God bless you.

6.

MONEY IS A SPIRITUAL IDEA

Ernest always had a high concept of an abundant Universe. In evening treatment (prayer work) in late 1958 and early 1959 he was cognizant of the need of money for the completion of Dr. Hornaday's church.* I always felt one shouldn't specify an amount as such, but rather pray for the need to be met. He believed differently and many times proved his consciousness by demonstrating the exact amount needed. To get me to understand his belief, he gave me three reprints from the magazine *The Uplift* of 1917 and 1918, which he had edited. They tell the story.

Jesus painted the tragedy of the unused talent. Natural gifts entail obligation to the giver. The greater the endowment, the greater is the responsibility. Every good and perfect gift cometh from God. We stand debtor to Him. We discharge the debt by using what He gives us. Among all those marvelous powers bestowed upon us by a gracious God, none stands higher than the faculty of thought. It is indeed supreme, for through it we employ every other faculty. Without it, all else is nothing. With it, even the meanest objects of nature are clothed in the uncounted wealth of things. Yet some people refuse to think! It is pitiful, tragic, incomprehensible. The thinker can but stand amazed before the thoughtless who contentedly mumble, "Ignorance is bliss." His astonishment increases when he stops to think that the thoughtless did not think out this thought. They accepted it. They were too indolent to challenge it, too lazy to think there was anything in it to challenge.

They follow in mental life the maxim of efficient industry, "Never do for yourself what you can get another to do." So someone else does their think-

---

*Founder's Church of Religious Science.

ing. Not that they delegate anyone to do it—that would require thinking. They just let them do it. Like dried leaves in the current, they float into the channel that the winds and eddies of chance select. They accept what chance brings them.

In civic life, someone does their political thinking. They remain loyal to the party, even though they do not know its principle. In social life, they belong to their set. In professional life, they drift into a vocation. In religious life, they acknowledge the supreme authority of "the Church of their Fathers" and are unaware whether their religion is ancient enough to be "old time," or new enough to be "ragtime."

"Behold, the kingdom of God is within," and one who is to find it must look where it is to be found. "Speak to him, thou, for he hears,/ And Spirit with Spirit shall meet./ Closer is he than breathing,/ Nearer than hands and feet."

As we begin to get some grasp of this great indwelling power, we begin to see how it is that man is made but little lower than the angels. We begin to see that the first thing to do is to seek this inner kingdom, this spirit of God working through us, and we see how it is that from this seeking all else follows. This spirit is power, the only power, in the universe, the power of God. Can we imagine this power as ever falling short of its mark, as ever having to be told anything, as ever having to be helped to do anything? No, this is not *a* power; it is THE POWER, and we do well to let it guide and direct our way.

Not all the combined power and intelligence of the human race could produce a single rosebud, except it first comply with the Law. Money cannot buy this power, position cannot command it; it is not for trade.* And yet in the heart of the most humble as in the most exalted, this power forever dwells as the Spirit of the Most High. Is it, then, that as the Spirit of God dwells in man, it follows that he is God? No! As the child is not its father, so man is not God. He is in union with the Father. And as he more and more comes to realize this divine union of the Father and himself, he begins

---

*= commerce.

to see how it is that Jesus, who always lived from the spiritual standpoint, could say, "What the Son seeth the Father do, that doeth the Son also." Is this claiming too much from God? No! Are we not His image and likeness, and shall He not become glorified in us as we more and more put on this likeness and use it for the benefit of the world?

Let us, then, begin without fear to claim from the Spirit the things of the Spirit; this is the gift of the Infinite to His finite reflection, the gift of God to man. And as a gift, let us take it and make use of it. We must daily come to this indwelling Spirit to be made clean from our contact with the world. "Not by might nor by power, but by thy Spirit"* is our motto. Happy is the man who has found out this the greatest of all truths. Happy is he who dwells in this kingdom, and who draws from it his strength and his inspiration. He no longer listens to the voice of the world; he no longer becomes confused at the sight of outside appearances, for he knows that within is the power to change all and make all things work together for the good of all. Dwelling in the "secret place of the most High," he abides under the power of the Almighty. A peace that is more than all else comes to him and he is at home in the kingdom of God. "Then go not thou in search of him, / But to thyself repair; / Wait thou within the silence dim,/ And thou shalt find him there." Peace comes from within.

THE RICH MENTALITY

With what vastness of power we may ally ourselves! What mighty energy is His who hurled the stars into ordered space! What infinite wisdom in their stately workings! What exquisiteness of beauty in the creative Mind that paints sunsets and adorns rainbows! What melody in His soul who teaches birds to sing! What depth of tenderness in Him who gave the mother-heart its love!

This energy, wisdom, beauty, and love—dynamic and creative—belong

---

*See Zechariah 4:6.

to the man whose simple, seamless fabric of faith is the deep abiding consciousness of the indwelling Presence, and who dares to draw forth the God within him. He shall have health, for he thinks it; wealth, for he creates it; joy, for he gives it.

It is the simple, rich mentality of him who is in unity with the Spirit. Majestic is his power, satisfied is his soul, who, in the midst of the storm, despite the raging of men, in the chaos of material thinking, can enter into the silence and declare the absoluteness of his own being!

When we reach this high consciousness, we need only to speak the creative word, and it shall be done unto us even as we will. Herein is the secret of the perfect power of demonstration. The healer who can realize in his own consciousness the perfectness of being need do no more for his patient. Such consciousness is universal; and when it is true in his mind, it is true in all minds at all times and in all places. For God is present in His entirety at every point.

Nothing is more tragic than the blunders of the unthinking in any of these fields. Jesus was murdered because the mob didn't think and the leaders wouldn't. The history of the world, too, throngs with martyrdom of the great thinkers by petty ones. So Chrysostom* was expatriated and destroyed. Savonarola† was hanged, and Hus‡ was burned. Today, many men and women whose only offense is that they are thinking for the good of the people are being crucified by a mob of the unthinking, led by those who only half think—*their* half. They are martyrs to freedom of the press, honesty in government, and truth in religion.

My friends, the hardest thing in the world is to think, and the easiest thing in the world is to raise a hue and cry against the thinker. You have a mind, or at least God gave you one; is it your own or another's now? What governs YOUR actions? Do not answer "NEVER—MIND!"

---

*St. John Chrysostom (c. 347–407), Church Father and patriarch of Constantinople.
†Girolamo Savonarola (1452–1498), Italian reformer.
‡Jan Hus (1372 or 1373–1415), Bohemian religious reformer.

Money a Spiritual Idea

Every time I talk on this subject I begin with this: I have no gold brick to sell. This is no get-rich-quick scheme. I have nothing at all to sell to you. There are no secret doctrines that will tell you how to make a million in a month.

While there is an exact science of gaining wealth, yet I will say, in beginning, that possibly none of you will ever prove it. Nevertheless, I will say that it is an exact LAW, a scientific and unfailing LAW. There IS a law of perfect supply.

To begin with, we must come to see that the supreme Intelligence must, in creating man, have also made a way by which he could be provided for in harmony and in peace and without robbing anyone of that which belongs to him. Now this way must be a natural way; it must be a natural law. Nature is always natural.

Now, we are talking about money, as that is the evidence of supply. Money is the highest medium of exchange that the race has as yet been able to produce. Jesus knew this, and he told his students to render unto Caesar the things that are Caesar's. He knew that money was an idea and a necessary one to the needs of human life. So there is a law of success, and all who will can prove it.

Success Isn't Dependent on Location

To begin with, does money depend upon location? Can it be made only in certain places? Let us see. In all places people make money; in all places there are some who are rich and some who are poor. Go to the smallest town, as well as to the largest city, and it is just the same—some are rich and some are poor. Success, then, does not depend on location.

Is it the kind of business? No. There may be two men in the same kind of business, equally well situated. One will make money, and frequently the other will lose. Does it depend on education? No. Some very ignorant men make money. Does it depend on a man's circumstances? On a man's bringing up? No. Some of the wealthiest men in the world began with nothing.

Success Depends on Law

Upon what does it depend? It must depend on a certain, definite way of doing things. The man who succeeds must have succeeded through a certain method. The man who failed must have done entirely different. It must be a certain way of looking at it. There we get back into the spiritual realm.

There is a way which the Father hath provided by which we may demonstrate success. The way is there. I cannot go on the way for you; God cannot do that for you. You must walk the way yourself.

Now, as Browning said, "All's love, yet all's law." We are dealing with law—a mental and spiritual law. Now, law is not God; it is an attribute of God. So this law of success is not God, but it is an attribute of God. Man is given dominion over all laws, and when he comes to understand a law, he becomes the master of it. Jesus always referred to the Law and always complied with it. He so perfectly understood the Law that he could, with a word, make it work for him. Now the difference between Jesus and you and me is this: he could concentrate creation with his word. We do the same thing, only it takes us longer because of our unbelief. To illustrate: I once worked with a man who could add up several columns of figures at once and get a correct answer. I had to take the slower but nonetheless as-sure method of adding each column up separately. We both got the same answer, and we both did the same thing in getting it. One got it at once, the other got it by a slower method. Both were correct. One man can figure in his thought, the other has to use paper. But it is the same process.

We plant corn and let it grow, and then harvest it and make bread from it. Jesus said the word, and bread was made for him at once. Both methods are the same, in one respect, for both are natural. Now, then, what is this natural law that we can use? Is it something that we can come to understand

and be sure of? Let us see if we can state it in simple and understandable words so that all may understand.

There is a mental atmosphere all around us; it is Mind and it is Intelligence; it knows, feels, hears, sees, and understands everything. It is universal—that is, it is ever present, it is always where we are. It is receptive—that is, it receives our thought; it has power to do anything, to produce anything, to create anything.

It is a great divine, natural medium and law. I am not going to try to convince you today that this Mind is a reality, for we have so often studied it. If you are spiritually developed enough, you will accept the fact and act upon it, and by so doing you will most surely reap the benefit of one who believes. If you cannot as yet accept the fact, you will be the loser. It matters not who takes it for a fact and who does not take it for a fact, the Law is there just the same. Happy is the man who can take it, for he shall reap the reward of the true son of his Father.

We ARE surrounded by this Mind, and we can use it just as we use any other natural law. You ask can we see, feel, hear, touch, taste or smell it? I answer "No." I ask about the law of gravitation: can you touch, taste, hear, see, feel, or smell it? You answer "No." We both must confess to a limited understanding of what the law really is, yet we both know that it exists. The things of the Spirit and Mind are not seen. The most sensible thing to do is to take all natural law for granted and instead of arguing over it, find out how to use it and how to reap the benefits of our knowledge.

We must have some faith if we are to live, so why not have a little more faith and live just that much more? Now, while this Mind is and works for all who will work it, to deal only with it as Mind is to deal only in mental law. This means limitation, and it is our endeavor to overcome limitation, and this can only be done through the Spirit. This mental law is an attribute of the Spirit, and we will get the best results only as we operate upon it in the Spirit. Jesus simply said, "Have faith in God." He knew that that would produce the required results.

But if a thing is true, there is a way in which it is true, and this is the way: this Mind is there to be used; it is Mind—and the only instrument of Mind, the only tools of mind, are thoughts. Therefore we must look to thought to get our answer to the problem of success. The man who is a success is the man who, whether he knows it or not, is using natural law. I say "whether he knows it or not," for all are using this Law all of the time. Every time we think, we are "starting something," so to speak; that is, we are thinking into this Mind and it is doing the thing for us. Our word is our thought, so our word shall accomplish.

MAN NOT THE CREATOR

Now this word which we send out is going out into creative Mind. I say "creative Mind," for man does not create, he simply uses creation; and creative Mind is going to take it up and is going to bring back to us the thing that we have thought of. "I will send out my word and it will not return void." Now we are using Law, and Law is Mind in action, so we are putting Mind in action through the avenue of thought. Mental Law is thought going out to produce a certain definite result. The Bible says, "The Word [or thought] became flesh and dwelt among us": that is, the word or the thought became manifest to us. Thousands of people are today proving this to be true. Money, then, the same as all other things, is a spiritual idea.

7

RELIGIOUS SCIENCE AND
MAN'S GREAT IDEAS

Dr. Holmes always, when he went to bed, read until he was tired. He wore a green plastic visor and would underline passages that impressed him. The last book he read before his transition was Aurobindo's *The Life Divine*. He suggested I should read it. I asked him how many pages it contained. When he told me it contained over 1,000 pages, I suggested that when he finished it he tell me about it. He didn't like that and shook his head sadly. In October 1958, in a talk to a class of students, he emphasized reading as necessary for growth. This talk actually covered the relationship of humanity's great thoughts to Religious Science.

Good evening. I see I am surrounded by a great bunch of highbrows! We are embarked on an unknown voyage, which will be theoretical, speculative, mystical, and/or intuitive—which will be, or should be, logical and philosophical, and some of which is to be psychologically practical in applying what very little is known of the Principle of Mind to the persistent problems of life.

We happen to be a group of people who claim no infallibility whatsoever, and we never issue encyclicals or edicts. Those few of us here who have the privilege of talking to you happen to be here because we have the nerve to talk to you and you haven't any better sense than to listen to us. But that isn't *our* problem at all. So we should feel we are on pretty much of an equal basis, always remembering that the great are great to us only because we are on our knees. "There are no prophets but the wise."

There is no God in the Universe who ever tapped anybody on the shoulder and said, "I will deliver something to you that I have not given to anyone else." The last word will never be spoken, or God will pass out of existence.

So we happen to be in a certain place in the evolution of the human mind where we are able to stand up and look about us and survey our environment and recognize that, in a certain sense, we are separate and distinct from it; we are *other* than it. As the poet said, "A fire-mist and a planet,/ A crystal and a cell,/ A jellyfish and a saurian,/ And caves where cave-men dwell;/ Then a sense of law and beauty,/ And a face turned from the clod—/ Some call it Evolution,/ And others call it God."*

I happen to believe we are all on the pathway of an endless evolution, that the impulsion back of the evolution is a divinely created spark which has impregnated us with "a Divinity that shapes our ends, rough-hew them how we will." I believe that every man is an incarnation of the one living Spirit; this one living Spirit is undivided and indivisible, and must, therefore, remain a total unit whose center is everywhere and whose circumference is nowhere. At any and every point in it is infinity. Theoretically, there must exist all that it is, and not in fragments.

There is a certain process of reasoning that is called *axiomatic*, which means self-evident truths, things that the human mind could not deny. It is very apparent that we and all physical manifestation are in a process of some kind of evolution, from a lower to a higher form of life, of consciousness, of intelligence, and of awareness. It is equally self-evident that you cannot get out of a bag what is not in it; that which evolves must primarily, and first of all, have been involved.

Have you read *Bible Mystery and Bible Meaning*†? If you haven't, you should; it is a great book—the most intelligent book ever written on the Bible that I have ever read—one of the few books written on the Bible that I consider has very much intelligence. Most books on the Bible are just somebody's reaction to what they think the thing means. That is why we have so many different interpretations of it. They couldn't all be right—that is self-evident.

---

*William Herbert Carruth, "Each in His Own Tongue."
†By Thomas Troward. It examines the Bible in the light of involution and evolution—i.e., in the light of the Law of Mind in action.

Now we are considering tonight the impact of the great thought of the ages upon our belief—our system of thought—which we happen to call Religious Science. Religious Science is not a revelation that I had. It is well that it is so—that we are this way and remain rational human beings, not overly influenced by anything nor coerced by our own desires until they project a false image of the self to appease the ego. We should be able, dispassionately but with feeling, to study the great thoughts of the ages. It is only through the great thinkers of the ages that we may learn what the human mind has discovered about its relationship to God. Neither will you find it in any one teaching, given by any one teacher or one system of religion or philosophy, nor will you find it comprehended in any one age.

I am reading three volumes on the writings of Hermes, who lived (it isn't definitely known whether he is a mythological person or not) 1,500 years before Moses. I am reading practically everything that is of cosmic significance in our Bible and in the philosophy of Plotinus and Plato. You will find it in the Upanishads and the Vedas. You will find it in *The Book of the Dead* of the Egyptians; in the Bhagavad Gita. You will find it in every great religion that the world has ever had, and in every great system of thought, and in most of the great poets, and in all of the great mysteries and great mystery religions. We have to separate, somewhat, the wheat from the chaff.

Evelyn Underhill said, "The only news we have of the Kingdom of Heaven has come through the consciousness of man." We should swing between a contemplation of the mind and an action outwardly. I can only tell you what I believe, and you don't have to believe what I believe. We haven't got any set of beliefs or dogmas or anything like that. I believe something; you might believe something different. For instance, a number of our leaders believe in reincarnation, and to me it is ridiculous; but I won't argue with them.

I discovered a long time ago: life would be very simple if everyone would agree with me. But I also discovered that they didn't. So I said, "Well, let's let everybody believe what he wants to. If what he believes is true, we can't help it; if what he believes is not true, it can't hurt anything." I think it's important to maintain a good-natured flexibility in all our studies, to real-

ize that no matter how much we study each day's accumulation of knowledge and facts, be they physical, psychic, or spiritual, they but give us a fresh
starting point for something else. "Ever as the spiral grew, / He left the old
house for the new." I believe things today that would have scared me to
death 30 years ago if I had ever thought about them or that they might be
true. You will find the same experience.

As knowledge increases and contemplation broadens its base that it may
deepen its perspective, it will at the same time heighten the apex of its receptivity. Values will change. While living in the same Universe, we will
discover that we are living in a different one, but that it is attached to the
same one.

We have to look to the great thoughts of the ages to discover what the
world has found out is true. If we look to only one of the great thinkers—
there are no exceptions to this—we will not discover as much truth as we
would if we looked to all of them. When we look to all of them, unless we
have a good ability to synthesize, we might very easily become confused. It
is a very difficult problem and proposition to have liberality of mind and not
to read everyone's thought. I do it continuously. I have a half-dozen books I
am reading all the time. I pick them up and read them so I won't get caught
too much in any one and get shifted onto a different track. (It just happens
to be my method.) I find what Lowell called "that thread of the all-sustaining beauty that runs through all and doth all unite."

In my own mind, I am more teachable and more flexible today than I was
40 years ago. At that time, being new, young, crude, and raw, I thought I
knew it all. Someone said, "I used to think I knew I knew,/ But now I must
confess/ The more I know I know,/ I know I know the less."

Count Keyserling,* who taught 30 or 35 years ago, would not take anyone
in his classes until they had reached the age of 40. He said they were too
immature; they hadn't developed the ability to think. And now they don't
let people take professions after they are 40 for fear they are too old. How

---

*Hermann Alexander Keyserling (1880–1946), German social philosopher whose philosophy
centered on the theme of spiritual regeneration.

strange and inconsistent! We have to turn to the thoughts of the ages and analyze them one by one; then, as we analyze, we must synthesize, or put together.

Now, if you read *Cosmic Consciousness* by Bucke (and if you haven't, you will),* you will find a man who had a very deep knowledge of the difference between spiritual illumination and psychic hallucination. He cites about 60 cases, as I remember, of those who undoubtedly have had illumination or been cosmically illumined. They had a deeper perspective, understanding, appreciation of, feeling toward, and knowledge of the spiritual nature of man and of reality. He shows, by an analysis, certain fundamental things that they all believed in and that we are justified in accepting.

These are things that do not contradict each other, if, indeed, we are justified at all—which I believe we are—in believing that the human mind has revealed anything. We have no source to go to other than the sources which we call *human*—no matter how divine they may have been. These are the only sources; we have no other knowledge of reality.

Bucke showed a half-dozen main things, including a consistent belief in immortality; a consciousness of the absolute unity of all things; a realization that everything is in a process of evolution; and a consciousness that there is no fundamental, basic, essential entity of evil in the Universe. Now, that was his synthesis after carefully analyzing—with the ability to analyze the difference between psychic hallucination and spiritual realization and cosmic illumination. He found certain persistent facts running through the lives of these outstanding persons from all walks of life, facts which we may accept as valid and real. We have every reason to believe that it is so.

We have to look to the spiritual realization of the ages to discover this spiritual truth, whether it is in Jesus or Buddha; or the philosophic, whether it is in Emerson or Plato. We have to look to scientific research. In our system, we believe that the Universe is one system, and *but* one. Every apparent part and every apparent segment of it reveals the nature of all of its other parts—*all* of them. For instance, attraction and repulsion, demonstrated in

---

*Richard Maurice Bucke (1837–1902), Canadian psychoanalyst and author.

physics and the Universe, is one system. We should expect to find the same attraction, repulsion, adhesion, cohesion, and polarity in the mind: the Universe is fundamentally a thing of intelligence. As Emerson said, "The mind that wrote history is the mind that reads it." Human history is a record of the doings of that Mind on this planet.

We start with the supposition *God is all there is*—all life, truth, reality. Life, God, Spirit, or Reality is incarnated in each one of us, equally and evenly distributed to all. As Jesus said, "He causes his sun and rain to come alike on the just and on the unjust."

We have to start with the proposition, then, that there is that in me which can understand what anyone has ever said or known or taught or done. I shall be interpreting the action and reaction of that which is identical with myself, in myself, for which I have an affinity. Kant said, "We are able to recognize an apparently external object because it awakens an intuition within us in a field of common denominators." That sounds awesome and gruesome; that is the way these guys talk. All he meant was this: I look up here and see the mountain. I didn't put the mountain there, but I can recognize the mountain, because the Mind that put the mountain there is the Mind that put me here.

"There is one mind," as Emerson said, "common to all individual men." Therefore it awakens an intuition or a perception—I know you only because the Mind which you are and the Mind which I am is recognizing itself in each other. That is the discovery Lowell made or caused to be made in *The Vision of Sir Launfal*, that finally comes out, "I behold in thee the image of him who dies on the tree."

Now, people in our field are always trying, or should be, to develop their consciousness—to expand, deepen, and broaden and heighten their awareness of life. For instance, I happen to be reading for the third time one of the most remarkable books I have ever read. The man believed in reincarnation; he spends about a hundred pages out of 900 explaining why it is so. I haven't the slightest idea it *is* so, but he had. Outside of that, we get along beautifully. Maybe he is right and I am wrong. If he is right, I can't help it; if I am right, he can't help it.

We may *believe* what is, is not so; we can only *know* what *is* so. Knowledge is of reality; belief is of theoretical supposition, which may or may not be true. That is what is the matter with a great deal of our philosophy: it gets nowhere because it starts nowhere. Its premise being wrong (although its logic may be perfect), its conclusion will be completely in error.

The other night, I read a statement in *The Life Divine*—one of the great books of modern times; you must read it; Gandhi and Tagore considered Aurobindo the greatest spiritually enlightened intellect of modern India, so you know he must have been somebody; he only passed on a few years ago. He said that the transcendence, by which he means the Absolute (we would call it the Reality, the Finality, God, or Truth), does not *reconcile*; it *transmutes*. I said to myself, "This is one of the greatest things I have ever heard." Now, I have read it several times before, several years ago. Then I loaned the book to Barclay Johnson and he read the same thing and was struck by it. *The transcendence does not reconcile—it transmutes.* I said to myself, "This is a great saying," and I laid the book down (I do all my reading after I go to bed), and I said, Just what does the guy mean? And so I thought for about a half-hour before I went on. Then I put it in my own words.

I find myself in reading the great thoughts. We should continually read them. It is like talking to a great mind, holding conversation with a heavenly guest. It is terrific. It is something we can't afford to be without—just as we cannot afford not to be surrounded by beauty. No one can afford to be without love, beauty, happiness, and action. Love is the only protection and the only security there is in the Universe. Beauty unveils the invisible to us. Action is the only thing that releases the tension of the accumulated emotions (psychologically) and realizations (spiritually) that seem to be pressing against everything. When it does not move into the explosion of self-expression spontaneously, it is repressed into the unconscious, and this is the cause back of all neurosis—not some of it, but *all* of it.

I thought, Now what is Aurobindo saying? What does he mean when he says this? I always try to find out: What does this person mean? If it seems a little involved, I put the book down and make up my mind what the fellow meant when he said it. I think of everything that is related to it that comes to my mind and synthesize it with what other people have said. It just flows through my mind like this, rather quickly; because if I have ever made any contribution, this is it. I am not an original thinker—but it *is* original to know you are not.

I say in my own language, to myself, "This is what he meant; this is what it means to me." I have transformed a language with which I am not familiar into a terminology which I understand because it is my own. Have you ever tried that? You will be surprised how it helps to hold a thing in consciousness. So I said, "Now, this is a great saying." Then I thought: the Bible said, "Be still, and know that I am God." Lao-tzu* said, "All things are possible to him who can perfectly practice inaction." Long since, I came to know the only thing in the Universe that cannot be resisted is nonresistance; and as one after the other of sayings of great people with whom I was familiar came to my mind to coincide with this, I said, "Now what does it mean to me?"

I no longer cared what it meant to Plato or Socrates or Aristotle or Jesus—because they came and they went, even as words written on the sands of time, to be blown away by the wind. Nothing is permanent but your self; nothing is unshakable. I said in something I wrote, "Hid within all things evolved/ In silence: beauty, wisdom, will,/ Is that which makes the cycle move:/ Unmoved, immovable, and still." It was inspired by reading the Gita, so it isn't entirely original, but a way of saying that at the center of every person there is that which doesn't move, and everything moves around it. That is you—that is myself—a unique representation of the infinite and ineffable One and Only, beside which there is none other.

I said to myself, "The transcendence does not reconcile"; and I remembered Jesus said, "You cannot serve God and mammon. . . . Judge not according to appearances but judge righteously." And I remembered that the Gita said, "You cannot enter into bliss while you deal with pairs of opposites." Do you begin to see what it means? *The transcendence transmutes*—it does not reconcile opposites; they clash. And I said, "This is what it means

---

*6th century B.C. Chinese philosopher; traditionally, author of *Tao-te Ching*.

to me: the rays of the sun will melt an iceberg, even two icebergs floating side by side that could easily crush the Empire State Building should they clash from both sides of it." Emerson said, "The physical universe is spirit reduced to its thinness, oh so thin." This is what great reading will do for you: it brings to you the wisdom of the ages. Automatically, your own consciousness coordinates, synthesizes, as the intellect analyzes. Something inside of you synthesizes, and you never forget it.

Emerson also said, "We see the universe as a solid fact, God sees it as liquid law." And then I thought: Quimby said, "Mind is matter in solution; matter is mind in form." His dual unity of one whatever-it-may-be is as the matter of a superior wisdom which governs it.* I thought about what Plotinus said: "If I were to impersonate the Infinite, God, I would say, 'I do not argue; I do not contend; I contemplate.' And as I contemplate, the images of my thought form into what is called this great indetermination of nature, which is more than nothing and less than something, having no mind of its own, but being moved upon by that which is a superior thing to it." And I said, "All right!"

Now, then: that is what it means to me philosophically. I got very elated and lit up. Now I said to myself, "This is what it means philosophically; it is right. If the Universe is one system, there is a transcendence which governs everything, there is an Intelligence which controls everything, since it is One-and-Only-and-All and has not an adversary." "I will contend with him that contendeth with thee, saith the Lord." And that flashed through. You see how things come together? I said, "What does it mean in practice? *You have no adversary; you have no enemy; you have in that transcendence nothing to heal as though it were an entity, or change as though it were a confusion. You do have practicality.*"

You are not dealing with a pair of opposites, or good or evil, or God or mammon; we have been warned by all the great thinkers not to—and now I know why. I only wish that my heart knew what my intellect proclaimed

---

*i.e., to which it is plastic. For a reliable and brief exposition of Quimby's thought, see Ervin Seale, *Mingling Minds* (DeVorss).

in those 30 minutes; but it doesn't, because it still gets sad, because we are human. We just get to look through the veil temporarily, as some great mind lifts the veil from before the face of Isis; we see the form, the beauty, the warmth, and the color of that which is a part of Reality, closer to us perhaps than our very breath. The Talmud says, "nearer to us than our neck vein."

It is something, as one of the great poets said, "To see clear-eyed the future as we see the past,/ From doubt and fear and hope's illusion free"—said Sill.* (I didn't know, when I started to say it, who wrote it.) "To see clear-eyed the future as we see the past,/ From doubt and fear and hope's illusion free": first time I ever knew of hope being referred to as an illusion—and it is an illusion.† It is an illusion to a greater thing; it is transcendent of a lesser one. It is a salutary attitude, but there is one beyond it, which is one of certainty.

I said, "What does this mean to me?" It means that in treatment, if I can get my mind still, "Look unto me, and be ye saved, all the ends of the earth." Look to the One-Only. Plotinus said our work is done better when our face is turned toward the One, even though our back is turned to our work.

That is no different from saying, "Be still, and know that I am God"; "Look unto me, and be ye saved, all the ends of the earth." So I said, "Here is a transcendence that does not deal with opposites; therefore it doesn't resist, and consequently it conquers them." "And the light shines in the darkness, and the darkness comprehendeth it not." And so forever more it is set in my mind and it will never leave it. It will never leave me. I took 30 minutes, maybe an hour, just to think about this one thought: the *transcendence does not reconcile—it transmutes.*

And I likened it even to what is called sublimation in psychology, which is defined as deflecting the energy of the Id into socially useful purposes. Now, if I say, "sublimation is a deflecting of the energy of the Id into socially useful purposes," I am saying exactly the same thing—but there aren't any psychologists who would know you were saying the same thing. What

---

*The reference may be to Milton Sills, co-author, with Holmes, of *Values* (1932).
†He himself refers to it thus in *The Science of Mind* ("Hope a Subtle Illusion"), p. 49.

they mean is this: if the neurosis is resolved, it is not resolved by bringing another contention with which to combat it, but by actually translating, transmuting. They call it sublimation: deflecting, transmuting, a lower form of energy into a higher, without contention. That is the exact meaning of psychological sublimation. In our language we would call it *transmutation*. It is the meaning of the alchemist: to transmute a lower or base metal into pure gold or a higher one. (But they have back of it symbolism.)

Remember, this external act and endeavor of the alchemist was stimulated by the intuition of an inner knowing, beyond processes of reasoning, that everything in the Universe is made of one stuff. While every separate thing has its formula, if the formula is changed, the form will translate itself into something else—and it takes so little to change it.

This is what great reading does for us. It does another thing, in my estimation, which is psychological, or psychic, or subjective. I believe it puts our consciousness in rapport with the consciousness of the writer—not necessarily where he now is, but in the state of consciousness that he was in when he was here. Maybe it goes beyond this—I am not arguing about that; I do not know. In this way, we read between the lines. This is why we read great poetry. This is why, when you read thoughts, always you are getting something that "wasn't there before"; but it *was* always there.

I definitely believe that these thoughts exist in the Universe. I think they are indestructible. And I believe we get in vibration or rapport with them. This is what happens in psychism (this is known and scientifically demonstrated). Now why, then, should it not follow: if we go the whole limit, we should enter into thoughts of others beyond anything they expressed—while what they expressed was merely like a more objective psychometric reading.

By holding a physical object, you are contemplating a thought that someone had: it doesn't seem strange to me that that should happen in psychometry. They will take the physical object, like this watch, and you know what happens: they enter into the subjective state of it—another dimension of it; but it is real. It is a terrific illusion and delusion, but the thing is real. We must not be afraid to play with things merely because there is a certain danger. Emerson said he had no patience with a man who, having read that somebody committed suicide by cutting his throat with a razor, would never use a razor again.

I told Barclay* the other day, "I have coined a new expression for what we are; and if somebody asks me now what we are, I am going to say: we are practical idealists and transcendental realists." I think that is good. Because, in order to be ideal we are not going to desert the real; in order to be transcendental we are not going to desert what is so. We do not say we are trying to heal people of what does not ail them. That is ridiculous.† I have noticed that people who do this are very liable to fall into the error of coercing their own consciousness until finally they are running around denying everything they don't like and affirming everything they do. That is a very great danger. "Keep faith with reason, for she will convert thy soul." "There are no prophets but the wise."

I believe it brings a psychological or psychic as well as a spiritually illumined state of consciousness. We cannot afford not to read people like Emerson, Plato, Jesus, Buddha, Socrates, Mary Baker Eddy; I love them, and they are all great people; and truth belongs to no one. If it was their great privilege to reveal something beyond the ordinary, still, that which they revealed belongs to the ordinary. Jesus said, "I came that ye might have life and that ye might have it more abundantly," and when they confused him with the life he came to reveal he said, "It is expedient that I go away that the Spirit of truth shall bear witness—that you shall awake within yourself." As Paul said, "Awake thou that sleepest, and arise from the dead, and Christ shall give thee light."

Now, we may start out with the proposition that we can learn only from the great; but all science, all knowledge is built up a little here and a little there. We are beneficiaries of the ages. Truth belongs to no one, no group of people, no class of people—never did and never will. You and I too, fortunately—if we *are* so fortunate—might add something not to the sum

---

*Barclay Johnson.
†I.e., we do not deny their experience of an ailment.

total of truth itself, but to the sum total of the accumulating knowledge that men have.

I always like to ask a practitioner, when I see he or she has done some outstanding thing or work, "How did you feel inside yourself when you treated this person?" I don't care what words they said, "My words fly up, my thoughts remain below:/ Words without thoughts, never to heaven go." Jesus could stand in front of Lazarus and tell him to get up and come out. If I were having a funeral and I told the corpse to arise and the corpse got out of the casket, the people would jump right through the wall.

We are four-dimensional people living in a three-dimensional world. But there ever more are echoes from beyond the shores of time which are singing of the timeless. There are always impingements upon our intuition and even our physical being, I believe; a gentle urging and pushing. "There is a spirit in man," Job said, "and the inspiration of the Almighty giveth them understanding." Jesus said, "The wind bloweth where it listeth, and thou . . . canst not tell whence it cometh, and whither it goeth: and so is everyone who is born of the Spirit." "God is Spirit and seeketh such."

Emerson said, "We should set up a lowly listening." We are also told to beware, to be careful that this listening is done with intelligence. I would rather speak ten words with my understanding than a thousand without it. It is a very fine thing to think straight, but we have the guidance of the greatest thinkers of the ages. We have scientific research, if we can put it together with psychology and metaphysics, which will spell to us the synthesis of an animating principle that repeats the same thoughts over and over and over again.

The Hermetic teaching said, "What is true on one plane is true on all: as above, so beneath." Which merely means this: physical, spiritual, and mental laws coincide. They are the same laws. They are not three sets of different laws: they are but one set of laws functioning on different levels, be it physical, mental, or spiritual. That is why we say, "We translate the physical symbol into its metaphysical meaning." Start out with that, and it would change the nature of the physical. There is no one thing that we can do that is more valuable to us than repeatedly to read the thoughts of great people. The thoughts of the great people remind us—and the lives of great men all remind us—that "We can make our lives sublime,/ And, departing, leave behind us/ Footprints on the sands of time, / Footprints that perhaps another, / Walking o'er life's solemn main, / A forlorn and friendless brother, / Seeing, may take heart again"—Longfellow.

We "never forget"—but we don't always remember! True, isn't it? Then, from these thoughts we are led to formulate our own thinking. Great thoughts induce in us a chain of thinking—a sequence of thinking that stimulates our own consciousness not only to a new endeavor, but also to the discovery of new pathways; they open up a new possibility for the expansion of our own minds. That is probably the greatest thing that they do; nothing that comes to us can do anything more than awaken an intuition on the level of that which comes to us. Is that clear? It was already there potentially; this drags it out. We couldn't perceive it if it weren't there so we could see it; but it does stimulate that greater possibility—it bores a hole down, as it were, in our own consciousness and lets up a new gusher, a new freedom, a new expansion. We cannot afford not to companion with the great and the good and the wise of the ages. Now, this takes time—but it is worthy of our effort. It takes thought and thinking and is the most difficult task on earth. It takes analysis and synthesis, which calls for bringing intelligence to bear, that we may discover that which we have inherited from the ages. That is the legacy of every sane and intelligent person. As Emerson said, "Only a few people in each age can understand, or do understand, Plato—but to every age the works of Plato are brought and placed in the hands of these few as though God himself had brought it."

There is a natural affinity of thought, since like attracts like and birds of a feather flock together. I believe that as we companion with the great thoughts of the ages, we draw not only from the great thinkers we might be perusing now, but from other thoughts that more or less are in harmony with them. There is, it seems to me, in the psychic storehouse of our world the accumulated knowledge of the ages. Now the occult has called this the

Akashic records; if you ever heard of it, that is what it means. I think Jung calls it *the collective unconscious*, and I think that is true enough.

We shall keep it very simple and say: there is a repository of all the thoughts of the ages. Just as you and I have a memory, some little incident will bring things to mind, just like the verse I just read—I had forgotten who wrote it or where it was from.* There is a world mind and memory which Jung was the first one to speak of as the individual and collective unconscious—and we all draw upon it. It is a source of much inspiration because there is somewhere, if we can get a handle on it, this accumulated knowledge that flows through every instrumentality that is more or less open to it.

Stimulating our own thoughts is like an exercise. We should not just skim over the pages lightly and say, "What a great guy!" Take time to let the meaning sink deep until, finally, whatever it means to that man, it now means to you. We have captured his wit, his will, and his imagination and made it our own. We don't do it by stealing it from him, but because here it is, and it belongs to everyone. And more and more we shall find our reading expands our consciousness—if we contemplate its meaning; if we think about it.

Great thoughts begin to awaken in us, and you will be surprised how right Emerson was when he said, "Sometimes the muse too strong for the bard sits astride his neck and writes through his hand." Every man may write beyond his intellectual comprehension; every man may speak, at times, a language the meaning of which he does not comprehend. I am not talking about psychic confusion—I am talking about something beyond that. Every man is a revelator of the whole thing.

That is why Emerson said, "Watch that spark that flashes across your own consciousness; it is the one and only solid fact that you possess." It is all that you brought with you; it is a cinch it is all you will ever take away with you. This is a pearl of great price, for which a man will sell all that he

---

*See p. 92.

has in order that he may possess it, the wonder of it, the beauty of it, and the thrill. (You know there is a little ham in every preacher or nobody would come to listen to him. I am willing to admit it; and if I haven't got it, I would like to have it!)

Every man may speak, think, act, and write beyond his own comprehension. If he doesn't do it and think beyond the day of yesterday, tomorrow will find the old monotonous pattern, as Freud* said, repeating itself over and over again and playing its tune over and over and over again. We live under the hypnosis of the ages. Try to originate thought out of this greatness; feel yourself to be unique and great without being conceited. It isn't any of your business that God Almighty put his spirit into your soul and animated your being with His life; it is none of your business, and don't *let* it be any of your business. You must not confuse this with the little peewee who occasionally wakes up, squeaks, and soon sinks back into the slumber from which he had only become half awake.

Very deep in you and in me is the source, the reason, the essential cause, the destiny, the evolution, Heaven and Hell, God, man, and the Devil, the possibility of all things—if we will listen simply, sincerely, almost impersonally. Never confuse the little we know with the much that might be gathered as by a child joyfully, enthusiastically clapping its hands. This is why Jesus said, "Verily I say unto you, their angels do always behold the face of my Father which is in heaven."

---

*Sigmund Freud (1856–1939), Austrian neurologist and founder of psychoanalysis.

8.

OUR MISSION TO THE WORLD

Ernest always felt that the strength of Religious Science was in the member churches. He had great personal interest in all the ministers; one in particular was Dr. John Hefferlin* from Long Beach. Ernest had shared with me that people at national headquarters didn't think that John should be a minister. But Ernest recognized something in him and overruled them. He always said that you can teach ministers comparative religion, the Bible, and many things, but until you put them in a pulpit, you would never know.

On the evening of January 8, 1959, at a church banquet concluding a week-long meeting of representatives and ministers from all the churches, he expressed his feeling to the people. He was introduced following a talk of acceptance from Dr. Hefferlin, and it was fitting that the last lines of John's talk reflected Dr. Holmes's continuing beliefs. It emphasized Ernest Holmes's great humility, as you can sense from Donald Curtis's† introduction, which followed.

JOHN HEFFERLIN
(LAST PART OF HIS SPEECH)

We have learned the power of imagination, but there is one other power. We may have all the treatment in the world, we may have all the feeling, all the imagination, but I tell you this one thing: without a spiritual awakening, without a spiritual awareness beyond the imagination and beyond the intellect, we will remain as grasshoppers. But with the awakened soul, with the awakening of the spirit within us, we too become giants, not only

---

*(1903–1987), Religious Science minister.
†At the time, Religious Science minister.

of the present, but on into the future of mankind. Thank you and God bless you.

DONALD CURTIS

Tonight, in line with the request of our beloved dean, founder, and leader— Dr. Holmes—as he comes to the podium to speak, he has asked that you do not rise, and I would suggest we tender him that great tribute too of perhaps withholding our applause, because this might well be the greatest applause of all—because we know this will be the climax in consciousness and guidance for us to sustain this spiritual refilling throughout the year to come.

I wish all of you here at the banquet could have been at the opening session of the convention this year when Dr. Holmes spoke. But we have possibly, if it *were* possible, even a greater treat in store now. I can't help but compare the level of consciousness in Dr. Holmes to the modern parable which is told of the old minister and the new minister.

There was a testimonial dinner given for a founding minister in a church. He had over the years turned out a great many great people, leaders in society, in the ministry. They sent for the most famous of them, a man who had made his mark as a great orator; he was known throughout the world. They brought him to give the testimonial speech, and he talked on the 23rd Psalm. He expounded, he explained, and he sat down after reciting it, and the applause was deafening. Then the beloved founder got up, and he simply recited the 23rd Psalm. There was no mistaking the silence and the depth of the response.

As he was traveling back to the airport, the great man, known throughout the world, was a little chagrined and piqued. He asked his companion, "Didn't I give a good talk? What was wrong with my rendition of the 23rd Psalm?" His friend said, "Well, it was this way: you knew the 23rd Psalm; but the old minister, our founder—he knows the Good Shepherd." Ladies and gentlemen, Dr. Holmes.

ERNEST HOLMES

Thank you, Don; it was very sweet and very deeply appreciated.

I would like to explain the real reason why I asked that you didn't stand up. It is that it isn't a good habit before the world. I love it and appreciate it passionately; but we have a principle that we practice, and we teach something that is the common denominator of every man, and it is only because of your great generosity, and my liking it so much, that we kind of formed this habit. I do appreciate it—have always—but we have overdone it, I think, and you will understand that. I love it. I would like to take each one of you in my lap and rock you to sleep. But instead of that, I will have to try to wake you up, I guess.

But you know, in the eyes of the world, who know not very much about Religious Science, we are a small group compared to the population of this city or the world. It might give a false impression. We do not deny or decry the personality of man; it is the only evidence we have of his divinity. But we do proclaim that inward Man, which is the common denominator of all human beings. In my belief, one man is neither better nor worse than another man. In my belief, every person is on the pathway of an eternal evolution.

I hold with the ancient Hindu teaching of the divine incarnation, from which the Christian concept of theology came in very inadequate form and was surrounded by superstition and ignorance. Until now the central flame has practically died out in the consciousness and in the awareness of those who would interpret the meaning of the incarnation. For all men are divine or no men are divine; every man is an incarnation of God or no man is; every man is immortal or no man is immortal.

There is nothing good enough that you and I can do to earn the privilege to live, and there is nothing evil enough we can do to destroy it. Browning said, "Fool! All that is, at all, / Lasts forever, past recall; / Earth changes, but thy soul and God stand sure:/ What entered into thee/ That was, is, and shall be:/ Time's wheel runs back or stops: Potter and clay endure."

We have the most wonderful time together. I have never seen in so large a body of people so much love, so much affection, so much understanding. There has been no discordant note, no criticism—it has been almost beyond belief, the experience we have all passed through these last four days. I shall never forget it. It is an experience that can come only from a group of people who are happily, normally, and sanely dedicated to an idea, without walking around thinking they look like a bunch of saints, which I would detest. We have no saints, we have no saviors, we have no prophets, we have no priests. We have a very deep simplicity in our philosophy, a very simple approach to reality. It is as profound as Plato, and I have studied Plato all my life— although I don't claim to understand him. There is no philosophy that has ever been given to the world more profound than ours, nor has one ever been given that is more simple.

I have naturally been gratified that John Hefferlin and his wonderful church have united with us.* He is like a son to me, and Mrs. Hefferlin is like a daughter and a very beautiful one, don't you think? And I am so happy Don Curtis is with us on our board and is a representative from John Hefferlin's church. Last year, Fred Bailes† came to me and said he would like to find someone to take over his very great and flourishing church, and that there would be no other organization in the entire New Thought or metaphysical movement from which he felt he could choose a leader other than ours. That is a great tribute to us.‡ However, it is true—like the little boy whose mother said, "You think you are pretty good don't you?" and he said, "No, mother, I don't think I am good at all, because I know I am a lot better than I think I am." Now, we are better than we know—very much better, indeed.

---

*In 1954, 19 member organizations (churches) of a total of approximately 65 enrolled in the International Association of Religious Science Churches declined to enter into the new organizational arrangements proposed by the Institute of Religious Science. The 19 included Hefferlin and his Long Beach church. In December 1958 Hefferlin, who had found Holmes "very shocked and grieved" by the split, returned with his church to the Institute (now the United Church of Religious Science). See Marian Hefferlin, *A Time to Remember* (Los Angeles, 1991), pp. 261–63, 270–71, 279.

†(1889–1970), minister and teacher of the Science of Mind and sometime collaborator with Ernest Holmes.

‡Donald Curtis became Bailes's successor upon the latter's retirement in 1959.

The keynote of our convention has been *togetherness*—the unity of our thought and purpose and plan and action for the extension of our work and for the deepening of our own consciousness in that field of divinity "that shapes our ends, rough-hew them how we will." I have never felt so much affection, personally and collectively—and it is the greatest thing in the world. I have learned in the last year and a half* that no one does anything for himself—it is absolutely impossible. *We live unto others.*

Now that isn't just a sweet saying. We live unto others because that which is myself is yourself; that which is yourself is myself; that which is ourself collectively and ourselves individually is the one and only self there is—there is no other self. I believe we are living in a spiritual Universe right now, surrounded by perfect situations, by perfect people, and by perfect events. Such intellectual training as I have, any such capacity of reasoning or rationality I might possess, would deliver that to me axiomatically: it is self-evident.

The intellect can arrive at an intelligent profundity which is far beyond our inward understanding and our embodiment. God is all there is; there isn't anything else—there never was and never will be. Even that which appears not to be God is God in disguise. As Emerson said, "We are on a drunk that seems as though somebody or something gave us something too strong to drink when we entered this world and we are in a perpetual sleep; but once in a while someone wakes up." Now, we are trying to wake up to something within us and something cryptic, hidden in the Universe, always ready to be revealed.

I believe the divine pattern of perfection—not a plan, but a pattern—is resident in everything. That energy, force, intelligence, will, consciousness, desire, feeling—call it what you will—that came with the early dawn contained within it the pattern not only of perfection but of the whole evolution of man; and everything that has happened in evolution is but the unfoldment of that pattern through the thought, feeling, intellect and action of man. That pattern contains what is beyond our present perception. This is the secret that Jesus had.

---

*This coincides with the period following his wife's death in May 1957.

This is what Buddha discovered when he found out what the Psalmist meant when he said, "Thou hast led captivity captive." He was called the Man of the Heart.* We belong to the Christian philosophy; we are a Christian denomination;† it is what we mean by the Christ. Christ does not mean Jesus; Jesus embodied the Christ. It is what the Buddhists mean by the "Enlightened One," what the Hindus mean by Atman, or the universal and divine incarnation of the Absolute.

There is, in you and in me, a unique presentation of this—that by the very nature of the process of our evolution we should finally spring full-orbed into our divine nature and consciously cooperate with it. There is that which must wait until slumber passes from our eyes and the inertia from our minds; the Spirit within us proclaims it to us. I do not believe that we as individuals or the race evolve spiritually, other than through our own consent—otherwise we would not be individuals. But if that is true, then there is that within us that we should get together with.

Now, we have been talking about getting together organizationally. It is all necessary—personally, that is all necessary. We love each other; and I trust it shall be increasingly said that this is a group of people who love each other—who are at least making a bold effort to turn every negation into an affirmation, every denial into an acceptance, every no into a yes, every evil into a good, every lack, every want, into an abundance.

The Universe imposes nothing on us but a freedom so great that we tie the cords of that freedom around us in our ignorance and believe that *they* are imposed upon us. There is nothing in the Universe that can will us other than freedom. The Universe has a certain nature; God has a certain nature; and we shall spring forth full-orbed. We shall come into the divine inheritance of that which the Infinite has bequeathed to us only on its own terms—not on ours. We shall not do it in exclusion; we shall not do it in hate; we shall not do it through unloveliness. There is something poetic about it.

---

*Refers to the divine Ideal and not to the Buddha. See p. 105.
†But see vol. 2, *The Anatomy of Healing Prayer*, p. 277.

You see, everything in the Universe springs from an absolute silence equally distributed everywhere, and this so moves that everything in movement will contain number and color and tone. We shall not do it, then—as John has said, and rightly so—just through the intellect.* We need the intellect, God knows, and we could use a lot more of it than we have; but there is another Man inside us that we shall have to get together with. I think this is a secret we all share with God; it is a secret we share with ourselves; and I have of late years become increasingly aware of this whatever-it-may-be, call it what you will.

As Wordsworth said, "The experience we have with it in the silence of our own soul is still, be it what it may, the light of all our day." And it is not an illusion; it is not a hallucination. There is that which is within us which is first cause and the only cause and the last cause and the present cause and the active cause. Now, very few people understand the philosophy of metaphysics. As I explained this morning, we are not spiritualizing matter, we are not materializing Spirit: we are living in a spiritual Universe right now.

We are merely experiencing the Universe in which we live. We free ourselves from the thraldom of our own superstition, ignorance, fear, and sense of isolation from the central flame. We call it the Man of the Heart; Jesus called it "the light that lighteth every man's path."† As we go on, let us seek, individually and collectively, more and more to develop a very intimate relationship with the indwelling whatever-you-want-to-call-it. I believe that God is an overdwelling Presence, a universal Presence; but I believe this universal Presence is, within each one of us, the person that we are. I think this is the secret of life: *the overdwelling Presence is the indwelling Person.* Therefore even the Infinite is personal to me in a unique way.

I have a Secret Place, you have a Secret Place, where the Universe presents itself to us fresh and new and lovely, and in transcendent beauty, and in a light so bright that we cannot conceive it—but it is a light different from the light of the sun. "There is in the Universe around us that which re-

---

*Perhaps referring to John 1:13.
†Perhaps John 12:35.

sponds to us, in the rock and the brook, from the tree and the wind and the wave." Let us identify it. This was the genius of Walt Whitman.

There is that within us which is the eternal Presence as its own Son; it was this with which Meister Eckhart identified himself. There is that within us which is God as His Son and the Son of God as God. It was with this supreme Reality that Jesus identified himself. If it happens to be true— and I believe it is—that there has to be a constant cooperation on our part before this divine consummation can transpire in our individual and collective experience, then it will be our consent through our efforts, through our attention, through our listening—but without sadness and without tears and without weight and without burden. In those transcendent moments everything becomes weightless.

This is real—not a word picture; and so let us get together with the interior Reality of ourselves. Very few people realize it. Religious Science teaches and gives to the world—and it will someday know it—the most transcendent concept of the personalness of God in the life of the individual that has ever been put into print since time began. We do not teach that God is a principle (we teach that electricity is a principle and that there is a Law of Mind in action which is another principle): we teach a transcendent Presence and an immanent Presence and a very close, warm, colorful relationship not between the two but the interplay of the One in, around, and upon Itself. And in those moments of transcendence you will see everything bathed in Its light. You will hear that which is behind all music; you will feel that "whatever-it-may-be"; there is no name for it, but you will feel a force playing around you on its level and on its plane, as real as the wind in your face, and you will see all of the celestial substance. It seems forever to be falling, not *on things*, but *through everything*—until everything becomes saturated with it. But you will be more consciously alive than you ever were before.

Being one who has but heard the slightest echo of this, caught the slightest gleam of it (Jesus referred to it as the "pearl of great price"), you will not be satisfied until it comes more fully orbed. In many experiences I have had, and know that others may have had, there is nothing weird, nothing queer. There is nothing peculiar about it. It is just another extension of what we now are. It takes in more territory; it encompasses and embodies the center of your own being. It is another kind of an awareness, another kind of a get-together-ness.

I think what we have done this week, what we are doing now, is a prelude to it. I think the time has come in evolution when many people will step from the pages of history who will be like the great masters and sages and saviors. I think we are a product of that evolution which pushes itself irresistibly forward, urges itself forward, but never insists. It waits. It has all eternity to wait in.

If we listen, if we stay still long enough, if we accept enough, something will happen to us. That which the good, the great, and the wise proclaimed, and all great religious systems have been built on, will no longer be heralded by the saviors. *You* will be that savior; *you* will become that Christ; *you* will be that Buddha; *you* will be that Atman. If the theory I have is correct—and I believe it is—each must give his own consent first.

Emerson said, "God will not make Himself manifest through power." I don't think there is any renunciation in it; there is no renunciation in my religion, no denunciation, no lamentation. The whole miserable mess of sin and salvation (two ends of one morbid mistake) will have to be swept from the face of the earth; we will have to get it out of our own consciousness. There is no such thing as the fallen man; there is no such thing as the human apart from the divine. There is no God you and I will ever meet outside that thing, which is in us now, as the immediate Person that we are, the divine Presence we seek to embody. And always, always, there is a voice. It may not be a physical voice—but it comes.

I am the most surprised person among you at what happens in our movement; and I am most delighted. I don't feel I had anything in the world to do with it other than to enjoy and appreciate it, and to companion with you. Let us remember this: the world—our world—has yet to meet the man who has no fear, no morbidity, no denial, no negation in him. Whitman said, "No one has ever worshiped enough; no one has ever adored enough; no one has ever loved enough; no one has ever communed enough." He said that when that divine moment came it "unstopped" him; this thing entered and possessed (but did not obsess) him: he knew of the divinity of all men; he knew that God inhabits everything, flows through everything, and *is* everything.

The message of Jesus is our message to the world. It has never been done before. There is no egotism in it; there is no harshness in it; there is no dogmatism in it: let us keep our movement forever free. We are giving birth to the next great spiritual impulsion of the world—and for the first time in history: free from dogma, fear, superstition, materialism, and all that is built on ignorance and the denial of God. The Universe in which we live is a spiritual system *now*; we are spiritual beings *now*. In such degree as any one of us bears witness in his mind to the "divine fact," the tomb is open and the dead come forth.

This is our mission to the world, this is our message. Never forget it. The world is waiting. Waiting, longing, hoping causes the mind of every living soul to sing the same song. There is something listening to and striving toward that which it knows exists, and it is our office in joy, in peace, in communion, and in the sweetness of friendship to so live, to so love, to so aspire, and to so realize. The transformation takes place *here*. You don't have to wonder if it will take place *out there*; the world will come when enough of us see through the night into that celestial light "that shineth more and more, unto the perfect day."

We are the children of that light. God is real, personal to you and to me, to be communed with. "Speak to Him, then, for he hears./ And spirit with Spirit shall meet./ Closer is He than breathing,/ Nearer than hands and feet." We shall have to speak to Him in each other and embrace Him in each other and love Him in each other—in the child at play and the baby drinking from the fountain of nature and the young man and the chorus of angels in one grand accord—that the Eternal may itself go forth through us anew into its own creation.

I wouldn't dare to try to tell you how much I think of you, because I am too sentimental. I love you very much and appreciate very much your love. It is the thing to me that is worthwhile.

Now let us turn deep, deep within, to your God and my God—to our

Father in our Heaven—that infinite and ineffable Beauty that paints the rose and spreads its glory across the hilltops as the sun rises to bathe the valley in the warmth and color and radiance of a new day; that inhabits the soft twilight shadows in the rose at hues of evening and the song of the lark and the laughter of children and the peace of the night—eternal and forever blessed. We are that which Thou art, and Thou art that which we are.*

Amen.

---

*See *The Science of Mind* 423:3 for Holmes's use of this expression from the opposite perspective.

9.

PRACTICAL TRANSCENDENTALISM

This talk, given to the Tuesday Invitational group on May 26, 1959, was intended to be the last talk of the year. Ernest was now excited about the imminent completion of Founder's Church. He referred to it as "the symbol of the national movement."

I had mixed emotions as I listened to him. Not too long before this talk he had told his spiritual daughter, Peggy Lee,* in a trip to Palm Springs, that there were only three things he had to do and then he was ready to join his wife, Hazel†:

1. Complete the new church.
2. Dedicate the new organ to Hazel Holmes's memory.
3. Correct the thinking of several people in the Religious Science movement.

He completed the first two of these self-imposed goals. Regrettably, he never got to the third. I have always wondered: if he had, where would Religious Science be in the world of religion today?

Last week, I talked about the general theory back of all of the greatest spiritual perceptions the world has ever had. I had to abbreviate it very much. There was a man here who is a student of philosophy; he is majoring in it to teach it. He asked if you people knew what I was talking about. I said, "Of course. Why else would they be there?" and then he said, "I didn't

---

*The popular singer. She gives a warm account of her relationship with Dr. Holmes and Dr. Bendall in her autobiography, *Miss Peggy Lee*.
†d. 1957.

know there was any group of laymen in the world who could be talked to the way you talked to them." Of course, he would not find them anywhere else except in a university.

Few people know how to think abstractly, and having thought abstractly, they do not know how to apply the abstraction to that which is concrete. Troward said that the broader we generalize, the more completely we can specialize. Emerson said, "The possibility of the elevation of the apex is determined by the base of the structure."

We came to the conclusion that if there is any truth that is known—or if we may accept, with validity, truth that is known—we would have to accept, in philosophy, spiritual things, and, in the general concept of life, that those people who have so accepted are few. In Ouspensky's* *Tertium Organum*, at the end, he tells us that Dr. Bucke, who wrote *Cosmic Consciousness*, said that there was a certain group of spiritual and intellectual elders who appeared throughout the ages, and all of them (from standpoint of number) could be put "in a modern drawing-room."

They have so completely influenced the thought of the world that the highest and best in religion, philosophy, and education has come through this group, who appeared over a period of thousands of years. I think that most interesting. Moses would have been one; Lao-tzu would have been another—as would Buddha, Emerson, Kant, Spinoza, and probably Troward. But Bucke was remarking on the fact that a few people had made such a large contribution and exerted so much influence, directly or indirectly, and that the teachings of those few had spread out through larger groups, and so on.

We know that, in the New Thought movement, Emma Curtis Hopkins taught practically all the greatest leaders of the last 50 years. She taught the people who started the Divine Science church and those who started the

---

*P. D. Ouspensky (1878–1947), Russian philosopher and writer on abstract mathematical theory.

Unity movement.* Practically all of the leaders of the New Thought movement came under the influence of this one person, and I think that is a very interesting thing. She was an illumined soul, and everything she taught is in the book *High Mysticism*. You have to get used to the language, because her whole theme, discourse, was really: where is your vision set? Jesus asked, "What went ye forth for to see?"

It is an interesting thing that Bucke should say a drawing-room would contain the number of people who have thus influenced the world—not necessarily by a direct teaching, but by teaching people who went out and taught what they taught—and that it is all traceable back to these very few people. Consequently, if we find out what these very few people were talking about (which is what we talked about last week—and we do know what they were talking about), then we have the essence of the spiritual wisdom of the world. But we do not necessarily understand the implications of its meaning.

I remember an old man coming up to speak to me after I had talked to Rabbi Trattner's[†] group one day about the Ark of the Covenant. He asked me where I had gotten the information and things I said, particularly when I told him I was not a Jew. I said, out of many books—because I was interested in that sort of thing. Dr. Trattner said the man was the greatest Jewish scholar on the Pacific Coast. This came into my experience to show that way back there were these great thinkers of the ages who transmitted their thoughts to their people—no matter what denomination you call them (and God doesn't know the difference between any of them).

We will have to go to these original sources to find out what is known to the human mind that translates its experience into transcendent terms—an ever-ascending scope and greater possibility. There would be no group of people on earth who have ever lived, other than these few, as original

---

*Mrs. Hopkins taught neither the founder of Divine Science—Malinda Elliott Cramer (San Francisco)—nor the co-founders of the affiliated activity in Denver (the Brooks sisters). Dr. Holmes was reliant on the hearsay that has long constituted much of New Thought history.
[†]Ernest R. Trattner, rabbi of Westwood Temple, Los Angeles, and friend of Ernest Holmes.

sources—who Bucke said have influenced the thought of the world more than everything else put together.

Steinmetz* said, before he passed on, that the next hundred years' investigation into what he called psychic (mental and subjective) and spiritual truths would produce more progress in evolution than the last 7,000 years in human history—and that is quite a statement from a man of his day. He is right, because there is something that opens up; there are certain things that happen in consciousness that you cannot talk to just everybody about. You can talk *at* them, but not *to* them—because there is no communication. You know this is true.

Let's briefly recapitulate what we have talked about, because I would like to speak about its application. Although a transcendent theory is not necessarily the best thing for us, it *is* necessary, in my estimation. I don't believe anyone speaks with authority or with power on any subject unless he knows the subject, and unless there is so much more in the background that he can say, that the people heed what he says and get what he knows by proximity.

Did you read Vincent Sheean's book *Lead Kindly Light*, on the life of Gandhi? He speaks about the thing between Gandhi and the audience, which they called *darshan*, which is a third thing that is established as a result of the contact of the consciousness of the audience and whoever is speaking to them. Unless that happens to some degree—I think it happens in a political talk or any talk that is good—then nothing happens to the audience; but when it happens, something happens to the audience and to the speaker which is transcendent of anything either one of them would independently experience.

It is what people got from Jesus; what one got from Emma Curtis Hopkins. Sometimes I felt it very definitely as a breeze in my face—I am psychic and know the difference between what we call a breeze in a seance and what I am talking about now. This is warm and colorful; it is an entirely different thing. It emanates from a different thing, a different state of mind, of con-

---

*Charles Steinmetz (1865–1923), American (German-born) electrical engineer.

sciousness, and looses a different kind of energy. Nor is all subjective energy necessarily good to experience.

They all have taught the one thing. It doesn't matter whether it is the Jewish Bible, our Bible (of course, the Jewish Bible is our Bible up to the New Testament); they have all taught in one way or another the incarnation—what we call the divine incarnation—except in Christianity they got it all confused and thought it only had to do with Jesus. The divine incarnation didn't have anything more to do with Jesus than the amount of it he permitted to take place consciously—which probably was a great deal of it.

Eckhart said, "God never had but one Son; but," he added, "the Eternal is forever begetting His only-begotten, and He is begetting him in me now." This is heresy, according to some religions. God never had but one Son: if there is only one Father, there can only be one Son; but the Son can appear in many ways. There is only one sonship, generic man, Atman, Buddha, or Christ: "God never had but one Son; but the eternal is forever begetting His only-begotten, and He is begetting him in me now."

This is in line with the teaching of the ages, which we call progressive evolution. "Ever as the spiral grew, / He left the old house for the new." But a progressive evolution is merely that which mathematically and irresistibly follows what was once a spontaneous involution. You can only get out of the bag what is in it. Nothing will ever evolute that isn't first involuted. But since there is a continual process of involution, there is a corresponding and continual process of evolution.

This is the esoteric meaning of the Tree of Life, which was described as a tree rooted in the ground growing up into the heavens and an inverted tree rooted in Heaven growing down until its branches mingle with the first; and what it meant was this: that as there is something involuted in generic man—man as universal—which *pushes* him up, there is something continually descending into him which *lifts* him up.

I think Lloyd Douglas,* who wrote *White Banners*, must have understood this, because somewhere in it toward the end, the question is asked, "Which

---

*(1877–1951), American Congregational clergyman and novelist.

is the greater, the push or the pull?" And he said, "They are equal." I think he had to have a pretty good understanding to have said that. In other words, this is Jacob's ladder ascending and descending; there is that always flowing into us which forever tends to flow back into itself. And as Troward said, since you are dealing with an infinite, the point of saturation is never reached.

There are beings beyond us as we are beyond tadpoles. In a progressive evolution, there would have to be. But a progressive evolution is the result of the *conscious* (this is meaning of divine incarnation); it has nothing to do with our theology, the Virgin Birth, the Immaculate Conception—which don't mean anything to anyone who has any sense—and don't worry about it: every conception is immaculate; everything is a virgin birth, whether it is a potato or Topsy.

But there is a truth—an esoteric or hidden truth—back of all these fables and allegories, back of all the teachings and bibles of the world. There is a terrific truth, but it is put in this form to conceal the truth from the average person, thinking that when he was ready, he would get it—which is probably true; but it wouldn't be true in our day and age. We seek all the knowledge and wisdom and learning we can get, because we need it so badly.

The whole teaching is that this is known as the descent of the Spirit into matter, and in our theology it would be Lucifer thrown over the embankments of Heaven and landing like a flaming sword on the earth. This is a word picture, telling us that the mundane clod is impregnated with a cosmic spark. That is all it means. There wasn't any devil, or big row, and they didn't throw him overboard—he has no existence, therefore he didn't land anywhere. This is merely a story, like the allegory of Eden. There wasn't any Adam and there wasn't any Eve, but the story depicts a process through which people go in their ignorance, having to learn by experience to return to the state of Eden.

Now, self-conscious individuation no longer is subject to the law of chance and change and the vicissitudes of fortune—like Jesus, who definitely and deliberately said, "I know where I came from; how I got here; why I am here; where I am going; and how to get there. And there isn't anything you have to do about it." He sort of scorned the thought that they could do anything. He said, "You can only do with me what I will." In my estimation, he could have caused his physical body to disappear and they couldn't have found him; and he might have caused theirs to, but he wasn't vicious.

What would happen to any person where the divine spark was completely loosed into action? Would it carry with it not only the Essence and Presence, but the power that is back of everything, and the force that is induced? All words will have some power; some words will have all power, in my estimation. Now, the power is already resident; there would be no creation, because there is only one of whatever there is. It has to include what you and I call Spirit, Soul, Body, Mind, matter—everything. It is not alien to anything: there is no place where God is not; there is no such thing as something which is not already impregnated with the divine Life. This is the meaning of the burning bush. Moses was aware of That in Nature which speaks. This is beyond illusion; you cannot explain it to anyone; because unless they have had it, they don't know what you are talking about. But it is real.

We go back, then, to the divine spark in everything and in everyone; and this spark is God. It is more than a spark, although we call It a spark. Because of the indivisibility of the whole, It is circumferenced nowhere and centered everywhere. It has to be. All of It is present in Its entirety wherever our thought rests. Now, this is a stupendous concept; it is logically and mathematically true, and one of the great teachings of the ages. "I behold in thee the image of him who died on the tree," Lowell said. That is what he found after his search for the Holy Grail.* It is what Jesus understood: "Who hath seen me hath seen the Father. The Father and I are one, yet the Father is greater than I."

It is this divine spark in us, this universal Life in us, this God in us, this Atman—whatever you want to call it. The Truth or Reality automatically had to contain, by the very nature of its being, everything that was going to happen in the processes of evolution to the time when "the divine spark first

---

*In *The Vision of Sir Launfal.*

ignited the mundane clod," from which there evolved that which became man, who finally stood up and looked about him and said, "I am not my environment." The poetry of each in his own tongue is so beautiful.

This is why Jesus said, 'The Father worketh until now, but now I work." What he is trying to explain is what they have all taught: the passage of the divine into whatever you want to call it, containing, as Whitman said, "the seed of perfection at the center of everything"—till what we call the "fall" in Christian theology, which I don't like, because man didn't fall, since there wasn't anywhere for him to fall to, and he won't rise, because there isn't anything for him to rise to. Let's say he fell asleep and will awake—isn't that better? The harshness of the theological connotation of the hellishness that people believe in is too crude for a gentle soul to accept. It has no element of beauty; it has no atmosphere of mysticism. It is cold and brittle and harsh and mean; and don't accept it—because it isn't true.

There is a great beauty; and, as Plotinus said, its beauty is terrific. Emerson said, "Ineffable is its beauty," transcendent; but that which was involuted, that which was planted—the seed, the genesis of all creation—had to contain that which pushed, compelled, impelled arbitrarily, automatically, the instrumentality evoluting to the point of its self-conscious life. It had to do it; it couldn't help it, because it is an irresistible force backed up by an immutable will existing in the consciousness of an infinite Something that knows nothing but itself. It cannot be frustrated—God will never have a neurosis; and neither will people when they know God. I think all psychiatrists should be spiritual people. I wouldn't send anyone to a psychiatrist who was a materialist: he would do them more harm than good. You can only become whole when you get to what is whole. Now, I belive in psychiatry. I believe in anything that works. Anything that will work is good.

But what we are discussing had to contain that which automatically, mechanically, arbitrarily pushed the evolving instrumentality—and that is man—through the period of ignorance, let us say, until there emerged that which now consciously cooperates with the Principle and Presence of its own being. "The Father worketh until now, but now I work." And that is what it means.

Now in all probability, in time (as we measure time—which has no existence other than as the measurement of a sequence of events in a unitary wholeness) when the "face" is turned from the "clod" (the arbitrary and mechanical impulses of the evolutionary principle, other than those things, we will say, like the automatic stuff in the body that keeps the blood circulating and heart going, and things we don't think about—and if we don't think about them, we are better off), the clod would keep going, but the will and volition and choice and return of affection—let us say, the "communication"—would not be there until the evolving instrumentality became aware of itself. That is why in the East it is called self-realization—the self must raise the self by the self, which is true, and Christian theology says we are saved by grace. They are probably both right. I would put the two together, because grace is the givingness of life, and *that* certainly is given automatically; but we are only saved by using it. The self must raise the self by the self, because the self is God.

Now, if in the background of the cosmic process of involution and evolution there was that which shoved man in his evolution—no one man but all men in all creation—to a point of differentiation of self-perception in a unified field which is equally and evenly distributed everywhere, whose center is everywhere and whose circumference is nowhere, then there is that in us which is still going to further evolution. I mean it is already here. That is why everything is from within, out—that which brought life to the point where man could get up and say, "I am not a dog or a cat; I don't know *what* I am, but I am *something*." And we are still saying that.

That which made us reach that point must have infinite variations and limitless reaches of other points to which it will ultimately bring us. "Eye hath not seen nor ear heard, neither have entered into the heart"—much less the intellect. But there will have to be that within us, right now, already, which is the future evolution of our own soul.

But the next important thing never to forget is that this has all gone through the process of endless eons of time—Emerson said, "So careful of the type it seems, so careless of the single life." It has gone through an endless process of time, because it was subject to the ignorance of time, birth, decay, and death. There is no logic which would lead us to suppose that in a timeless Universe the element of time is anything other than what it took to get where we were going, which we called a place.

What I am trying to say is that from now on—and this is the next great teaching of the ages (what Troward called "entering into the fourth kingdom" or fifth)—future evolution is *conscious cooperation*. If there is already something in us which can turn the water into wine, there is that in us right now which has been awakened in some people like Jesus, Buddha, and others. But it awakened out of *what they were*, not what was in store for them "up there" by a divine providence or a special gift or dispensation. None of these things exist.

God did not pat Mary Baker Eddy on the shoulder. (He did and he didn't.) He is patting *everybody* on the shoulder—but maybe *Mary* listened. He didn't drag Joseph Smith out to look under a rock and dig out something.* (He did and he didn't.) He didn't come to Jesus and say, "You are a nice little Jewish boy and I am going to show you stuff I haven't shown the rest of them—even Isaiah." (He did and he didn't.) He didn't come to Steinmetz and say, "I am going to show you something I didn't show the rest." (But he did.) He didn't tell Einstein, "I am going to tell you things about numbers nobody else ever knew, not even Pythagoras."† But he did tell him—because the Universe is forever imparting itself to its creation; "the Spirit seeketh such"—it can't help it. There is a pressure against everything, whether we call it the libido or divine Urge or Cosmos.

It is the same thing as an irresistible expression of pressure. But since we have come to a point of self-determination, the pressure is an *impulsion*. There is always a witness; there is always something saying, "There is more; behold!" There is always something saying, "You can, I can, we can"—always. There is always the thing in us that is transcendent and triumphant. "My head, though bloodied, is unbowed." There is always that which is

---

*(1805–1844), founder of the Mormon church, who claimed to have excavated a book (*The Book of Mormon*) written on golden plates.
†(ca. 580–ca. 500 B.C.), Greek philosopher and mathematician.

prophetic of the future—prophetic physically, psychically, and spiritually—always. It is always there.

Therefore it is written in the Book of Life in our own soul what we are going to be*; and since we know this, our evolution by conscious cooperation should be much more rapid. In a timeless Universe there is no reason, theoretically, why you and I should not know now; but something in us *does* know what is going to happen to us a million years from now. I don't know whether it is valuable to know; I am not anxious even to try to find out. But the theory of the thing is correct, like a mathematic progression; but we would arrive at it and not understand its meaning.

It would be perfectly normal for a person to understand how to dematerialize his body and appear in New York and materialize it; it wouldn't be strange; it isn't crazy or silly; it has been done in our generation, regardless whether anybody did it exactly that way. I have had experiences where things passed through a wall. I don't know *how* they got through—*but it happened*; and nothing happens outside the realm of law and order. Our reaction to it may be that it is crazy, but that isn't so: it has to do with something in ourself that is there, but we don't understand it; we don't realize it.

There is no reason why we shouldn't take part in our conscious evolution. This is the practical application of the wisdom of the ages, which the ages did not realize until the present age—the last 100 years.† Something new then happened, not *to* the process of evolution—nothing can ever happen *to* it—but *in* the process of evolution which loosed a different kind of cosmic power. It had to happen sometime. It happens to have happened in the last 125 years,‡ and as a result of it, we have all these metaphysical movements—and they are still very much disturbed for fear one is stealing from the other, etc. What a lack of grandeur of concept!

Someone called me and wanted to quote something I had said, and I said, "All right"; and they said they would give me credit—and then I said,

---

*Perhaps a reference to 1 John 3:2.
†Beginning with the full maturity and closing years of P. P. Quimby.
‡Beginning ca. 1838 with Quimby's serious investigation of the phenomena of mesmerism.

"No, don't quote it: if it is true, it doesn't belong to me; and if it isn't, you shouldn't be repeating it." How can truth belong to anyone? Who owns beauty? It just can't be done; and it is only the one who gives all that gets all.

Now, the practical application of the cosmic reality is something new in the world. Remember this. It is something in our psychology. People like David Seabury know about it, and I have met a number* who do; but psychology as such knows nothing about it and doesn't believe in it. It is something that even medicine—which I think is much nearer to divine Reality than theology—does not. And I am a great admirer of medicine, because what can be better than something that relieves people from suffering? Anyone in our field who criticizes it is silly.

Every truth belongs to *all* truth. It is something only the idealistic philosophers, and only the top grade of them, can understand. They *will* understand it if they ever understand the philosophic and spiritual implications of Einstein's theory that energy and mass are the same thing. Our whole theory is based on the assumption that we are living in a spiritual Universe right now, governed by laws of intelligence. Intelligence, moving, acts as law. The Universe contains not only a will, but a force, an energy, an action. It is its nature to continuously express itself in form. There is no barrier. There is nothing but it. God is everything.

Our whole practice rests on the theory that mind and matter are equal, identical, and interchangeable, just like Einstein's concept that energy and mass are equal, identical, and interchangeable—because a thought or a mental or spiritual treatment could not reach that which is alien to its own field, could it? It could only reach that which is like itself. This is why Quimby said, "Mind is matter in solution, matter is mind in form" and that there is a superior wisdom, of which these two are as the matter of Spirit, and that use of this is the Science of Christ. It is true, and this is where we get that expression.

Therefore our whole theory is based on the assumption that everything is a mental formation in the Universe—the planets, everything. We don't deny

---

*i.e., of psychologists.

their reality. We don't say people don't have the mumps and measles; but *what are they*? We don't say it isn't good to do anything that will relieve them; but we say we have a specialized field. Yet we are interested in all the fields. We believe in them and in anything that works. Certainly there should be no derision—nothing that even contains the slightest degree of condemnation of something we know nothing about. Modern medicine is a great thing, as are modern surgery and psychiatry. We admire them and admit it, if we have to. We do not hesitate to use them. They are all right; nothing wrong with them. But we have the equal privilege, prerogative, opportunity—and, I think, *necessity* for our own evolution—to recognize that there is something else.

The Universe is not limited to what we call matter or physical form, or to the mind that molds it. There is something in us that can think differently. It certainly is not limited to what it has done or to what it seemed or appeared to have been. And who shall set any limit to the transcendency or to the possibility, mathematically and logically, of that greater Thing? And who shall say to you or to me, "You couldn't do it"? No one. This is where we do not desert our tolerance. We should not entertain the *in*tolerance of that which denies our prerogative—because we are lost if we do.

We are working in a transcendent field. We are working in the field of That which makes things out of Itself by Itself becoming what It makes by a process instinctive and inherent in the constitution and nature of Its own being. It doesn't borrow from anywhere. A spontaneous proclamation of Itself into form, an eternal creativity, implies the necessity of an eternal creation.

All creation is the logical and inevitable necessity of a creator. You will find that in the statement of convictions I wrote one time. It is self-evident, and the great minds of all the ages have known it. It has to be that way.

Now, we must not deny ourselves the privilege of working in a transcendent field, to which the visible is subject by the law of that transcendency. There wouldn't be any question in it whether it would be or not. We wouldn't argue with any given fact—as though it had the right to argue back and tell us whether it "would" or "wouldn't." It has nothing to say about it; it exists by proxy; it exists as a shadow of substance. In and of itself it is neither person, place, nor thing; neither law, cause, nor effect.

Plotinus spoke this of all nature. He said, "Nature is the great no thing, but it isn't nothing; it is less than something and more than nothing. Its business is to receive the form of the contemplation of the thought of the Spirit." If you could talk to the First Cause and say, "How do you create?" it would say, "I create by self-contemplation, and as I think or know or meditate, I let fall the forms of my thought into this whatever-they-call-it."

Lao-tzu said, "All things are possible to him who can perfectly practice inaction." But he is talking about an action whose intensity is infinite compared to our highest concept of movement. He is talking about the inaction in which all action takes place—"Be still, and know that I am God"; "Look unto me, and be ye saved, all the ends of the earth"; "I will look up unto the hills from whence cometh my help."

So we seek the direct, personal, and collective application of a universal Principle backed by a universal Presence. The Principle is a universal power whose nature it is forever to take form and forever to dissolve the form it has taken. Nothing is permanent. If it were, everyone would get caught in a trap, and evolution would cease then and there.

Someone said to me the other day, "Probably when you were a boy things were more stable and didn't change so much." And I said, "Yes, but never forget: you haven't an atom in your body you had a year ago." Everything out here is like a river flowing; you can't jump in the same river twice. You can never return to the same point in mind where you were. There is no such person as in the photograph that was taken ten years ago. It's a picture in loving memory, but there isn't such a person.

If you go back to the old swimming hole where you swam as a kid, you'll find nothing is the same but the hole; what you swam in rushed on long ago to meet the undifferentiated sea or ocean of its own being, to be caught up again and be precipitated in another hole. There is no permanency but change, and if there were, we would all be caught in the traps of the inexorable and the immutable. So we don't need to be afraid of change. It is just a question of the direction in which the change is taking us: to a greater liberation or toward a bondage (which will only be temporary).

There is no such thing as good and evil in the Universe, no such thing as right and wrong, no such thing as God and man, no such thing as a manifest Universe separate from what manifests it—the manifestation is the Manifester in the manifestation. It is not strange to me that Moses talked to a burning bush. Everything has a soul and responds. You can talk to a plant and have it spring into newness.

You and I are practicing in a transcendent field. We understand it. We are not going to argue with anyone who knows nothing about it, as to whether or not it is true. Who cares what anyone thinks about what I believe? I used to have a motto which said, "The great are great to us only because we are on our knees. Let us arise." You are the only great person you will ever meet; you are the only soul you will ever know; within you is the only God you will ever contact. Out of this thing which the Universe has seen fit to manifest because of Its own nature, with which you and I have nothing to do, comes the future of your evolution—and from nowhere else.

So now let us know, as we break for the summer in joy and gladness, grateful for the privilege of this communion of spirit, soul, and mind, this closeness of even that which is physical: there shall be warmth and color that emanate and embrace us all on all the planes of existence. They are all real, good, and wonderful; they all belong or they wouldn't be here; we *do* belong to the Universe. And as we give back to That which has endowed us with it, It shall again give back on the same circuit that which will still further accentuate the essence of our own being, until finally, looking up, we see God only.

So it is.

10

THE SOUL OF ERNEST HOLMES

Dr. Holmes loved poetry of all kinds. He avidly read it and quoted it in his talks. He recited it to us in the intimacy of his own home. When he and his brother Dr. Fenwicke Holmes got together, at the urging of Fenwicke, to write *The Voice Celestial*, he was overjoyed. However, Fenwicke was in San Francisco and Ernest in Los Angeles. Ernest would send his contribution to Fenwicke, and much of Ernest's simple sensibility would be lost in the process.

Ernest had an idea and wrote something that he retained for Fenwicke's next visit to see if it could be included in the book. He read it to the Tuesday Invitational meeting of February 4, 1959, when he talked about basic prayer work.* Fenwicke didn't want it, and not too many of the Tuesday group responded enthusiastically, so he gave the original copy to me, saying, "You like it, and I like it, so you can have it."

It is fitting that this first volume of *The Ernest Holmes Papers*, reflecting the philosophy of Ernest Holmes, include this, which he called "A Fable."

⇀ *A Fable* ↽

Time stretched in the arms of Eternity and yawned—longing for
    liberation from its bondage—it was tired of doing nothing.
Eternity embraced both Time and the Timeless—holding them fondly to
    itself lest it be without offspring;
But all three of them—Time, Eternity and the Timeless—were weary
    with the monotony of inaction;

---

*See "Basic Treatment Work," in *The Anatomy of Healing Prayer*, vol. 2 of *The Ernest Holmes Papers*, pp. 269–276.

And so they held a conference to see if they might not find some way to come to a solution of their desires.

Not knowing just how to proceed, since they had but little mind of their own, they decided to consult the Old Man of the Mountains—the Self-Existent One—who possessed the Apple of Wisdom.

So they journeyed into the Mountains where the Old Man lived and laid their problem before him.

The Old Man received them graciously and promised them to do whatever was in his power to help; together they held long conferences, but it was difficult for them to come to any conclusion.

Eternity was not particularly concerned, having been around for a long while, and being used to his own company and not lonesome—except for those periods when he wondered if he were not dreaming the eons away;

But Time and the Timeless were most impatient indeed—they just couldn't wait; for, you see, neither of them were beings in themselves; they both lived by a sort of reflected glory from Eternity—while Eternity depended on the Old Man of the Mountains for its life.

Now of course this was why they were having a conference.

The Old Man looked across space and down on Chaos and Old Night and said: My beloved children, I just want to make you happy; I can understand you do not wish to be waiting around for countless ages with nothing to do, so I have decided to grant you some powers which until now you have not enjoyed.

But first I must move upon the Face of the Deep and disturb Chaos and Old Night. Heaven knows they have been asleep long enough—I had almost forgotten them—they really are a strange pair, sort of lawless at that—almost, but not quite, beings—*things* they are, with no minds of their own. I suppose I will have to breathe some kind of law into them so when they get stirred up they will not destroy themselves; but I will put some kind of order in them so they can be playthings for Eternity; then he will not be bothering me with his ideas about creating things—he just can't seem to sit still and enjoy himself.

To which the Timeless answered by saying he felt almost as Eternity did;
he couldn't see any sense at all in waiting and waiting and waiting and
having nothing to do.

To which little Time peeped up with a very small voice indeed, saying he
too had waited for something to happen—he almost wished he had a
mind of his own and was not compelled to live on the Timeless.

The Timeless responded by saying that in many ways he was in a worse
condition than Time, because he was so much bigger and more
important—which of course he would have to be since he furnished
the background for Time to play in—and Eternity, who felt himself to
be the Father of both Time and the Timeless, said he would go along
with the idea.

So it was agreed between Time and the Timeless that they would work
together—Time as the child of the Timeless—and Time was given
power to be unhindered, almost but not quite, because the Timeless
never would wish to be in the position of being bound by Time, who
was prone to get into all sorts of trouble and might get caught up
in what he was doing, and then nothing but confusion would follow—
which it almost did, but not quite.

And it was agreed that the Timeless would cooperate with Eternity,
because all three of them—Time, Eternity and the Timeless—were
one family, really, and would have to work together.

So Eternity agreed to free the Timeless from its bondage, and the
Timeless agreed to free Time so it might act somewhat on its own.

Now all these discussions took place in the Mountains where the Old
Man lived who possessed the Apple of Wisdom.

The Old Man said he was quite happy where he was and never did wish
to limit himself to anything in particular; but he did agree that he
would find a lot of pleasure in watching the actions of Eternity, Time
and the Timeless.

But he cautioned Eternity and its offspring, Time and the Timeless,
telling them they must never do anything that would destroy his
peace, because the Old Man didn't wish to be bothered.

Eternity agreed to keep faith with the Old Man: he merely wanted to partake of his wisdom; he didn't expect to act entirely on his own.

The Old Man agreed to give Eternity as much freedom as was necessary for it to set Time in motion, and Eternity agreed to pass on some of the power the Old Man bestowed on him to the Timeless, that it might activate Time.

Time, Eternity and the Timeless were very impatient to get started—but the Old Man motioned them to wait while he meditated—and the Old Man sat in thoughtful silence for a long time, once in a while eating from the Apple of Wisdom, which was never consumed, and in his meditations every once in a while he would smile and nod to himself, as though he were very satisfied with what was taking place in his mind— and finally he said: My children, I have an idea to put before you:

Let us create Beings and a place where they can function and live in happiness and freedom, but bound to us with enduring ties that can never be loosed.

Time, Eternity and the Timeless laughed with delight and danced around the Old Man, clapping their hands with joy.

Eternity said: I will gladly give birth to such Beings for you and will guard them very carefully, holding them always in my embrace, just as I have Time and the Timeless—and bowing before the Old Man, he thanked him for his wisdom.

But the Timeless was not quite so certain, while Time was really quite impatient with the whole affair, which he always had been from the beginning.

But after much discussion, they decided to try the experiment and see what would happen. But just how to begin, Eternity, Time and the Timeless did not quite know—which they couldn't, because they themselves were always subject to the will of the Old Man.

And again the Old Man ate from the Apple of Wisdom, which never diminished, and after a long while he unfolded a plan to them which he thought would work.

The Old Man said: In creating such Beings as these I have in mind, it

will be necessary for me to impart some of my own life to them—
which was reasonable enough, since the Old Man didn't have
anything to make them out of but himself.

And so he explained to Eternity, Time and the Timeless that these
Beings he was about to create would have to be a little different from
them, since they had no real life of their own, and no mind with
which to create ideas, and no power except it were borrowed from
him—for after all, they were but reactions of the Old Man's thoughts
and ideas, enjoying freedom only in certain limits.

But the Beings the Old Man was about to create—he explained to
them—would have within themselves certain qualities which the Old
Man possessed. But he would hide these qualities so deep in their
beings that they would at first be quite unconscious of them, for they
had a long journey ahead of them before they could ever return to the
Old Man and consciously cooperate with him.

Now here was something indeed difficult—or it would be difficult for
finite Beings—but the Old Man, eating again from the Apple of
Wisdom which never seemed to be consumed, continued his
meditations and finally said: Lest the Beings I am about to create
would immaturely try to act on their own, I must create some kind of
a cloud between them and myself so they will not be able to see me
exactly as I am, because I am going to endow them with my own
being—they will always have a curiosity and an urge to return again
to me, because they can never really be whole until they do this—but
should they seize the power I am going to endow them with before
they know how to use it, they might fall into all kinds of confusion—
which they certainly did.

So the Old Man reaffirmed that while he was going to impart his own
nature to these Beings he was about to create, he would sort of let
them alone to discover themselves and gradually to come under the
Eternal Laws of his being—but the time of this would not be known
to them—but of course the Old Man knew, since he knew everything,
because he possessed the Apple of Wisdom.

He said he would move upon Chaos and Old Night and breathe some kind of law into them which would reflect back to the Beings he was about to create the images of their own thinking, like a mirror; and since their own thinking would be pretty chaotic to start with—and for a long time to come—they would look at these images—which were really reflections of their own minds—and mistake them for realities. But always there would be thoughts and ideas of the Old Man moving down through the cloud he would create to almost separate himself from these beings—but not quite; there would always be thoughts and ideas of the Old Man showing something through the cloud; and because he was endowing these Beings with certain qualities of his own nature, they would always be looking up as though they expected to discover something that would make them more complete and happy.

And so, you see, above these Beings would be the cloud through which the thoughts of the Old Man would be reflected down toward them, and they would feel these thoughts and ideas—because they were also within them; and because the Old Man would put some of his being into them, they too would have a certain kind of creativity which would reflect itself on the lower side of the cloud and all around them—because all the earth then would act like a mirror.

Then the Old Man explained to Eternity, Time and the Timeless that there might be quite a period of confusion down there, but it was the only way he knew to create beings that finally could act on their own but still in cooperation with him.

And the long time of their confusion would be called the Period of Ignorance—and gradually as the confusion cleared away and they looked up through the cloud that almost but not quite separated the Old Man from them, they would become more and more like him, and this process of becoming more like him would be called their Enlightenment; and finally as this Enlightenment grew, the cloud would disappear entirely and they would no longer reflect confusion into the great mirror of life, and the mirror would reflect to them only the nature of the Old Man's Being.

The Old Man explained to Time, Eternity and the Timeless that in creating this cloud of unknowing and the mirror of false appearing* he was creating a medium which in a sense would bind the Beings he was creating for a period of time, because they would be looking mostly at their own creations and mistaking them for realities, in that way becoming subject to them.

This would be part of the illusion through which they would pass in the Period of Ignorance.

And the Old Man said he would breathe on Chaos and Old Night and endow them with certain qualities that Time, Eternity and the Timeless did not and never could possess because they had no initiative of their own.

So the Old Man breathed two principles into Chaos and Old Night and endowed them with a certain amount of creativity: one of the principles would be reflected back to them, and in their experiences and conditions that would be like their own thoughts and ideas—and for a long while they might suffer some results of their own ignorance because of this; and the time of this period would be known as "evolution," or unfoldment of the life he was going to breathe into them—from complete ignorance, as far as the Beings were concerned, to gradually awakening to a realization of their own natures.

In other words, the Old Man said: The speck of my own life with which I am going to endow these Beings will lie dormant, but it will always be stirring and stirring and causing these Beings gradually to awaken to a realization of who and what they are.

And during this period the two principles which he breathed into Chaos and Old Night would be reacting to them in accordance with their own thoughts, and these Beings unwittingly, in complete ignorance of their own natures, would be reflecting into this mirror that surrounds them the thoughts and imaginations which some time would prove to be their own undoing—but only for a brief period of time.

---

*See, for example, Metaphysical Chart No. VI in *The Science of Mind*, p. 574.

And there would come up among them those who, because of a more
penetrating gaze, had looked through the cloud and mist and, receiving
more intelligence, would look again into the mirror that is around
them and become conscious that it was a mirror only, and it would be
called a Mirror of the Mind, and the forms it created would be called
the Mirror of Matter*—but neither one would be real in itself.

But these Beings would be subject to their own creations until their time
of emancipation—and the Old Man explained, because he possessed
the Apple of Wisdom and knew all things, that during this period,
not because of the spark he was going to breathe into these Beings,
which would cause them almost to look up, but because of the inertia
of the images around them in the Mirror of Mind and Nature,
considerable confusion would follow.

For the spark with which the Old Man would endow them would always
be groping its way through the cloud, and its very Presence would
endow these Beings with hope and faith and an inward assurance that
they would never become extinct. But because of the confusion around
them, they would always be trying to reconcile that which they
inwardly felt to what they were experiencing, as a result of the action
and reactions in the mirror.

And he said all sorts of different beliefs would arrive among these Beings
and distribute their arguments as they tried to adjust themselves to an
inward seeming that knew but little about these outward things which
would appear to contradict these inward feelings. And these Beings,
following an inward knowing with which he was going to endow
them, would, without knowing why they did it, announce there was
some power that could make them whole. But everywhere they
looked, it would seem as though what they said would contradict this.
And only those who continuously looked upward through the cloud
would really see things as they were, while the rest would be looking
at them as they appeared to be.

---

*These terms are discussed in *The Science of Mind*, p. 612.

And great systems of belief would arise, and much discussion and
argument and dispute would follow, and these Beings would feel
themselves alone and isolated but always speak of the knowledge to be
theirs; and as it grew in brilliance and they reached up through the
clouds that seemed to obscure their confusion and difficulties, these
things would gradually disappear, and with them their fears,
uncertainties and doubts.

The Old Man explained that because the life with which he
would endow these Beings would have to be some part of himself,
they would be eternal, and something in them would always
know this.

But here too great arguments would arise: the Beings' confusion would
create all kinds of strange beliefs about their destiny, and many of
them would be very weird indeed; but this ignorance too would
clear away.

The Old Man explained to Time, Eternity and the Timeless that
this whole action would take place within them, and that since
Eternity was forever, and never could be exhausted or its energies used
up, it would not be disturbed very much by the process; and since the
Timeless, which itself lived on Eternity, was by Eternity furnished a
background for Time, it too would not be greatly disturbed. But little
Time would fall into a lot of confusion, because the Beings he was
going to create would often mistake Time for Eternity and the
Timeless and, being caught in Time, would be bound to its
limitations, but only for a period.

And he explained to Time this was why he had told them in the
beginning that Time must never really be caught nor the Timeless
confined, else Eternity would be bound. He said, You see, Time and
the Timeless will be the action and reaction in Eternity; and Eternity
itself is merely a reaction to the mind of Beings.

Having carefully explained all these things to Eternity, Time and the
Timeless, the Old Man said: Now, my children, it is time for you to
return to your homes. But remember this: I have breathed law and

order into Chaos and Old Night, and you will never be permitted to do anything that can violate my Beings.

But Eternity was permitted to play with the Timeless, and the Timeless was permitted to play with Time; but none of them would ever be permitted to get caught even in their own actions.

So Time, Eternity and the Timeless, having thanked the Old Man for his generosity, hand in hand left the mountain and journeyed back again, happy with themselves and content with the power the Old Man had bestowed upon them. And having reached the Valley where they lived, and being fatigued because of their long journey, they all felt the need of resting for a while; and so all three of them fell asleep, not quite realizing what the Old Man had done to them.

And sleeping, they dreamed. Time dreamed it was Lord of all creation; the Timeless that it was Lord over all; and Eternity that it was the Father of all. The dream was pleasant enough; but like all dreams, it must come to an end, to be followed by an awakening.

And the waking from this dream is the story of man's evolution.

Volume Two

THE ANATOMY OF
HEALING PRAYER

INTRODUCTION

THE PHILOSOPHY OF ERNEST HOLMES:
THE ANATOMY OF HEALING PRAYER

D r. Holmes was founder of the Church of Religious Science, and author of the book *The Science of Mind.* He was a brilliant lecturer, a keen student of logic, an avid reader, and a student of Emerson, Plato, Troward, Aurobindo, the Bible, and all other greats of the past and present.

Overlooked in his accomplishments was his extreme dedication to healing—including research into, and study of, all areas of healing. He did this by developing mental techniques and exposing principles that were immutable and that could be used. He believed in medicine, although he told me he never took a pill or medication of any kind until his late sixties. I believe he felt that from his understanding of Mary Baker Eddy's line in *Science and Health, with Key to the Scriptures,* to the effect that when all else fails, get what help is necessary and then examine your own consciousness. He expressed to me one evening, out of our many talks together, that we should prove by examination and diagnosis that a healing was taking place or had taken place.

He encouraged practitioners of spiritual mind healing, and some even said he favored them above other people. One incident he shared with me involved the practitioner Ivy Crane Shellhamer. She lectured in the old meditation chapel in the original Institute building. People would line up in the street to gain admission to her special hour. Many individuals claimed they had physical, mental, and emotional healings.

The other practitioners complained to Dr. Holmes that her grammar and speech were bad, and that this reflected on the Institute. They urged him to remove her from her lecture time. Ernest in his wisdom said, "When you attract as many people, and heal as many, as she does, then I'll dismiss her."

He spoke to me of studying the writings of a medical doctor in England or upstate New York, who was fifty years before his time. Several months ago the writings of a Dr. J. H. Dewey of Buffalo, New York, 1888, came into my possession. On the assumption this is whom he suggested to me, I am including from Dr. Dewey's text the following writing.

"That 'all manner of disease and all manner of sickness,' even in their apparently most hopeless forms and phases, were healed by a purely mental or spiritual influence or action, under the ministry of Christ and his Apostles, is believed by thousands. According to the record, these experiences of healing were not exceptional but were a matter of common and daily occurrence. In the majority, if not all cases, the restoration was immediate; not progressive or gradual.

"That many cases of disease in its various forms pronounced utterly hopeless by good medical authority, have been cured in our own times by a purely mental or spiritual process, thousands of reliable witnesses are ready to testify, amongst which are plenty of those thus restored. Some have been immediate and apparently miraculous, while a much larger per cent, have been gradual, some slow and others remarkably rapid, yet all absolutely healed. Some of these were healed apparently in direct answer to prayer, others at the shrine of some canonized saint, or the touch of some saintly relic, or from the water of a blessed and sacred spring, etc., and come under the head of prayer and faith cure; and others still by a direct process of what is very properly called mental treatment, under the various schools of 'Mental Healers.' Numerous failures occur under the efforts of all these various branches of modern Faith and Mental Healing. As no tabulated reports are given of the proportion of success and failure, the relative success of the different methods cannot be accurately given.

"So far as our own observation extends, these seem to be about equally divided. There are certainly remarkable successes as well as failures with them all. One fact, however, is established beyond dispute, a fact of great significance and importance. Cases absolutely beyond the reach of medical skill, and pronounced incurable by the highest medical authority, have been cured under these various methods, and in so short a period as to have all the appearance of the miraculous. These modern instances confirm the probable truth of the record of the Christ and Apostolic Healing. They certainly demonstrate the action of a law and principle, by which such perfect results are possible through a perfect understanding and application of the law and principle involved.

"That the religious opinions held by the healer or the healed have nothing whatever to do with the result, save so far as they serve to stimulate faith, is demonstrated by the fact that equally good illustrations occur under nearly every form of religious belief; and some under no religious belief at all.

"That these remarkable results are effected through the operation of some law of mental action as universal as the existence of the human mind, whether this law be understood or not, is obvious to all rational thinking. Jesus, whose success was absolute, never failing in his effort, so far as the record goes, recognized this by ascribing the marvellous cures wrought under his hands to the exercise of faith. 'Thy faith hath made thee whole,' was a common remark to the one healed. He doubtless understood this law, the secret of which is found in his doctrine of Faith.

"The majority of those healed by the 'Prayer Cure,' or 'Faith Cure,' believe it to have been the result of a miraculous interposition of divine grace, though some believe it to be the result of a powerful impression of the mind upon the vital processes under the influence of faith awakened by a religious experience. . . .

"The founder of the modern school of 'Metaphysical Healing,' Dr. P. P. Quimby, of Portland, Me., a remarkably successful practitioner, believed that he had discovered the true secret and law of all mental healing. This secret was the 'non-reality' of disease itself. He believed that he had discovered and demonstrated (by his success based on this discovery) that what men called disease was wholly a delusion of the mind; that in the nature of things there could be no disease; hence, that to discover the fact of this delusion in one's self, or to awaken another to the recognition of it, is to utterly banish disease or error from life. This is essentially the working basis of the purely 'Metaphysical' method.

"Whether disease be a delusion of the mind or a fact of actual experience, that it is often cured by a certain positive attitude of mind, induced by an acceptance of this doctrine, is itself a demonstration of the power of mind to overcome and banish the apparent disease from the body.

"Whether this doctrine be a satisfactory explanation of the law on which the results are based, each must decide for himself. One thing is certain—it is the attitude of mind and not the doctrine, that secures the result, though the doctrine, when accepted, may bring about the attitude of mind which Jesus termed Faith, and emphasized so fully. As this doctrine cannot readily be brought into universal acceptance, if a more satisfactory basis can be presented which can be very generally accepted, and by which this attitude of mind can be more widely and generally induced, will it not be wise and prudent to adopt and apply it, until at least something still more comprehensive and perfect is presented? . . .

"Without discussing the reality or non-reality of the physical world, it has, at least, the appearance of a past and present reality; and in this chapter we will accept the appearance for the fact.

"Disease we will define as a disturbed or deranged condition of vital action, to which all physical organisms, whether of plant, animal or man, are liable under abnormal conditions, and which in animals and men, often causes great suffering and distress. To remove the disturbance and restore the balance of harmony in the vital processes, is to remove the disease and restore the health of the sufferer.

"There is an inherent tendency in the principle of life in all organisms, whether of plant, animal or man, to spontaneously react against the disturbance, recover the lost balance, and in case of injury to the organs or tissues, either from disease or accident, to heal and restore the injured parts. This takes place in plants, the same precisely as in animals and man, and therefore is independent of mental action one way or the other. It is the spontaneous and automatic action of the healing function of life itself.

"In plant and animal the process of healing and recuperation is always gradual; never immediate nor instantaneous, yet may be hastened or hindered by external conditions. The influence of external conditions is the same also upon the healing processes in man. But the active influence of mental states upon the vital processes, and especially upon the healing function of life, is very great and may be made almost absolute. Fear which engenders distrust and despondency, is the one demoralizing mental state, and faith, which gives assurance, confidence and trusting expectancy, is the one restoring and sustaining mental state. The problem of mental influence on health and disease is involved in these two opposing states.

"The functions of life as manifest in the processes of growth, repair, and reproduction, are spontaneous and automatic, and exist and operate independent of thought and mental influence, the same in man as in the plant; but where mind exists and is active, as in man, with free powers of choice and volition, it becomes the most direct and potent power to disturb the vital processes and induce disease, or to sustain them in their highest vigor, and so prevent or cure disease. It is through this direct influence of mental states over the vital processes, that immediate healing occurs so often in man, while it is always gradual in animals and plants.

"It has been demonstrated, however, that the human mind is capable of affecting the vital processes and the springs of life in animals and plants, by the concentration of attention in desire and faith upon them also to this end. . . .

"The 'Metaphysical' theory starts out with the assumption that all supposed bodily conditions, whether of health or disease, are wholly the reflection of mental states, and therefore that the mind, and not the body, is the only proper subject of consideration and treatment.

"While the mind is capable of inducing nearly if not quite all forms of disease, it obviously cannot produce a sliver in the flesh, or other external catastrophe; neither do all bodily derangements originate in mind any more than do injuries, however, from external and physical causes, the mind is just as potent in quickening the restoration and healing action of life, as though the disease itself originated in mental disturbance.

"With these explanations we may proceed to consider the physical as well as the spiritual basis of healing through mental action and supremacy, without being misunderstood. Our object is not to discuss theories as such, pro or con, but to consider the one law operating under all these theories; for as Spirit and Life are one, there can be but one law of health and healing though many conditions may be involved.

"There is but one power of healing, and that is lodged in the life of the individual; the same in plants and animals as in man. This power may be disturbed and its normal action prevented by various influences and conditions, and by the operation of the same law it may be quickened and reinforced by the appropriate influences and conditions.

"On the recognition of this principle all medical and hygienic measures are based, whether they be wise or foolish. Mental or Faith healing is but the substitution of mental therapeutics for the external measures of the other schools, medical and hygienic.

"If, as we think, it has been fully demonstrated in experience, that the mind itself in its various states and moods, is the most potent agent known in its direct influence upon vital processes of the organism in which it is manifest, either to exalt or depress, derange or restore; then the mental therapeutists are destined sooner or later to supplant all other schools.

"Every honest experimental effort in this direction should be encouraged; not opposed and ridiculed, as is too apt to be the case, from the stand-point of time-honored traditional bigotry and error, set with a flint-like prejudice against all advancing innovations.

"It is hardly possible to introduce an error under the head of mental therapeutics, so absurd in its nature, or disastrous in its result, as many which have been taught in the name of science, and indorsed and cherished by all the most popular medical colleges of the world.

"The one strong feature of the 'Metaphysical' school is its full recognition and positive affirmation of the absolute supremacy of mind over all supposed physical laws and conditions. This is practically true, and hence a truth of supreme importance. But the mind even in this supremacy, must operate in obedience to certain established laws and conditions. Through ignorance it is itself brought into bondage even to physical conditions, and is liberated only through enlightenment. It can assert and maintain its freedom only as it understands and obeys the law of its freedom and supremacy.

"Faith is the attitude of mind which crowns it with supreme power, but there must be a rational and demonstrable basis for the exercise of this faith. Faith is not credulity nor a blind adherence to creed and dogma, nor acceptance of any arbitrary authority whatever. This is superstition. True faith is perfect confidence and trust in the unvarying operation of recognized and established laws."

George P. Bendall

Part I

1.

CONSCIOUSNESS OF UNITY

I knew that someplace there was a talk given by Dr. Holmes on Unity that I had to make a part of this work. I searched and finally after Treatment a good friend, Betty Williams, gave me a copy of a talk given by Dr. Holmes to the Practitioners Group on May 23, 1955.

Ernest always believed that the biggest danger to the practice of the teaching was the practice of dualism. The basis of all healing is the complete conviction of one undivided spiritual system—"God in and through all things."

Therefore what is known at one point is known at all points:

"I am one with God"
(Implying a separation, so that we had to glue ourselves back to God.)
"Positive and Negative Thinking"
(Implying two kinds of creative thought.)
"I have to overcome this condition"
(Implying the condition is a god.)

He constantly stressed One-One-One-One. This talk emphasizes his deep conviction.

Now we are talking about Cosmic Consciousness and what it should mean to us. As you know, we have built up a concept starting with the idea of consciousness, and starting with the concept particularly that the Infinite never expresses itself in fragments. There is no such a thing as a part of God. In an indivisible unity, all of everything is present everywhere all the time. Science has told us within the last few years that, strange as it may seem, we are on the verge of having to accustom our thinking to the concept that every physical concept which seems so confined to its particular place is present everywhere.

Now we discussed that consciousness starts by involution, and consciousness, or pure Spirit, impregnates everything. This is the principle of involution and then it is hidden in all things everywhere. But if the consciousness of God—and this is what we are talking about—or the Presence of God, or the Spirit is in everything, and if it is unbroken, and if it is undivided and does not express itself in fragments but in a totality, it is all everywhere— then all of it is incarnated in everything, as far as its potential is concerned; but in each thing it must be incarnated as the idea and the potentiality of that thing in which it is incarnated, in which it is involved, invoking in this involution everything that is going to follow in the process of evolution. It is very important that we realize that involved, incarnated, encircled within us must be the potential of everything that we shall ever evolve into. In other words, it's certain that we will never become God, the Absolute, and exhaust the potential possibility of our own evolution because if we did and we were destined to be eternal, it would be an eternal hell—if we could ever exhaust the potential possibility; but if that which is the Cause of the potential possibility, that which is the Absolute and the final and ultimate Reality is involved in us or incarnate in us, then there isn't a *part* of it incarnated in us; *all* of it is there. The search for Divine Unity, the realization of Unity, necessitates the acceptance that there is no dividing line—that we shall expand, progress, evolve, ad infinitum, in a sequence, from where we are to any stage that we shall ever become. Out of eternal being comes everlasting becoming.

There have to be people beyond us as we are beyond tadpoles. You and I don't know what such a future evolution as we may undergo may mean. The potential of our future evolution is already inherent, latent, and, let us say, to us, asleep; or we're asleep to it. One or the other is true.

I think that theory is good enough about evolving from the lowest to the highest; but always hidden in this thing keeping evolving is the whole of it, therefore, since it is what we are, it is the potential of what we may become. Consequently, hidden within in us is everything we shall ever evolve into

and everything that it is, but evolving in a sequence and in a logical and
mathematical sequence ever spiraling upward. That which perpetuates itself
is this self; that which extends and expresses itself is itself. It is no longer
another self or a greater self descending into a lesser self. I think this is very
important because we shall always go in search after it where we think it
may be found, that thing which we think we do not have; and wisdom,
Spiritual wisdom, starts the day that we know from now on every discovery
is either a discovery of the self or related to the self in the Cosmic Mind.
The self must raise the self by the self.

It is for us to realize then, that evolution is the evolving of something
which is completely, entirely, and absolutely already involved. There is nothing you and I can ever know outside that within us which knows. There is
nothing we can know outside the Mind principle in us which is in all things
and which relates everything in harmony to itself because it is unbroken and
unbreakable. Unity merely dips into that thing, and because we see it externally and detached, we create it in disharmony. That is why it is said the
transcendence doesn't reconcile, it transmutes. There are sharp lines of apparent separation and apparent division in order that that which is unsepa-
rated and undivided may come to fruition and fulfillment; and believe me,
that's what is back of psychological frustration. All psychological frustration
is occasioned by the stoppage of a cosmic flow coming from the subterra-
nean river of our own consciousness and flowing out into our self-expression,
so that the energy tending the emotion shall find release by expansion and
explosion.

Now you might say, I want to know how to use this thing and I want to
be practical, and I don't want to soar only a little but a little more than a lot.
Remember this, we pray through the articulation of consciousness and in no
other way. We don't hypnotize people, we don't mesmerize, we don't send
out thoughts to hit them in the liver or rearrange their brain cells, could
they be located. That isn't what we do at all. We are not trying to reintegrate
or disintegrate anything; we are trying to find that which is not disinte-
grated, that its substance will cast a new shadow on the pathway of this
experience from the center of its own being, which is eternal harmony, eter-

nal peace, but an eternal and dynamic need to express itself, else God Himself would long since have died of ennui.

There is such a thing as hidden splendor, and all of it is here, waiting to come alive. Eddington* tells us that intelligence is law acting as law. Now, we want to know what relationship all of this has, because all of our work is consciousness acting through our word. The word without the consciousness is like the prayer without the thought.

No treatment is complete until the thought and the thing are synchronized and are one; and when they are one, they are not two; and when they are one, the word will become flesh and dwell among us. Therefore, we study consciousness—the cosmic perception of those who have arrived at least to a state in their evolution where their vision more completely penetrated the mystery of the vision. Where they looked farther and deeper into reality than most people—and going down the pages of history as is recorded in the ancient writings and teachings in Bucke's *Cosmic Consciousness, Men Who Have Walked with God* by Cheney, and *The Perennial Philosophy* of Huxley—you will discover what these great spiritually perceiving minds have told us about the nature of the universe in which we live.

Now if the evidence of every one of them contradicts the evidence of every other one of them, we should have every reason to doubt the validity of their testimony; but as Evelyn Underhill† has said, "The only knowledge we have of the kingdom of God or of heaven must come through the consciousness of man. The mind should swing between meditation and action." But these are the few who have known. You may be sure, since they all talked about the same thing but maybe used a different language, different terminology, they all knew of the Divine incarnation. We all have flashes of this, you know. We all see beyond the present situation and hear beyond the horizon of our present experience. Everything is built on everything else. Everything is a continuation of everything else. All of these . . . things which reproduce the energies and actions of the physical man and reproduce

---

*Sir Arthur Eddington, English astronomer.
†Evelyn Underhill, English religious writer.

them without the need of using the organs of the senses to do it are merely the extensions of those organs. They are already here within us and within everybody.

Now what have these people taught us that we should know? They have taught, of course, as we have said, the unity of all life, the indivisibility of all life, therefore the omnipresence of all life. Life does not come in fragments to anybody. That is why when we treat a lawsuit we say there is no plaintiff, no defendant; we are dealing with the One Mind and One Spirit, and nothing can lie to it. In other words, it is only such degree as we carry the apparent divisibility into the citadel of unity; but you cannot carry the divisibility into that which is undivided. This is proven by the fact that Science knows no energy that will destroy itself. There may be disintegrating forces in nature but no destructive. We work only with the tools of thought backed by a consciousness of the meaning of the words we speak, which flows through the word, which is a mere mold—and molds without meaning have no substance in them, and without substance they have no action. There is a state of consciousness that can do anything, and it is not hard for it to do anything; we merely have to arrive at it by argument or meditation. In other words, we too must not try to divide the indivisible. The Pentecostal Gospel reaches very high metaphysical points in its frenzy. How do you and I know but that the fight of two tigers in the jungle reaches a very high point? Do we know that it doesn't?

There is only one of whatever it is, but in the ascension even that which appears destructive will gradually recede in order that the higher principle may take over. But this means that each interpretation of the I AM might find an echo even in our limitation, that its action must be justified by some kind of an outgoing; and for all you and I know, a cancer may be the encircling within ourselves of something that wasn't expressed in any other way and had to take some form because of its inherent urge.

The moment I begin to deny facts, I begin to feel unsafe in my own mind for fear I should discard the wrong facts. It is just because the same law that made us sick can make us well—or we won't ever be able to get well or we won't ever have been sick. Now then, we have to extend our own consciousness inward and upward if we are going to extend it outward, because it will only cast a shadow equal to its own height and breadth. This is a natural phenomenon. All of God is everything. Evolution is an eternal process; there is no ultimate evil. Therefore if we could attach our consent through identification to the idea that "the Infinite is my supply—the Lord is my shepherd, I shall not want," we would probably be better able to demonstrate what we call *things*. I believe in treating for what we have need of.

The possibility of everything is in our own consciousness, and so the great and good and wise have told us. There will come with the idea everything that is necessary to project the idea. This must be back of our consciousness of the creative agency flowing through our word. It knows how to bring means to ends because it accepts the end in the beginning, and the sequence of evolution between those is already instinctive in that which impregnates the Divine fertility with the seed of an idea. Here's the mother principle which all have recognized and which should mean a great deal to us then. They have told us that this thing is love, it is beauty, it is of course power; it is peace, it is joy, it is eternal bliss—but it is not eternal inertia; it is eternal action, but an action with such complete harmony that to us it doesn't seem like action.

Within every action there is the possibility of another kind of action more swift in its speed, revolving at the center, which would dissipate the crudeness of the external action, and this is why it is that people who have arrived at any consciousness—whether it be peace, joy, faith—influence everything around them without doing anything about it. How far that little candle sheds its light! And everything that is in the nature of evil, of disillusionment, of pain, of fear, of death—everything that is of the nature of the ignorance of the Truth of the Reality—is still the Reality showing us the only face that we have learned to look at.

Everything that is of the nature of limitation is but the Limitless flowing through us at the level of our acceptance of life. Therefore we are not fighting the evil with the good, or the less with the more, or the wrong with the right; we are merely establishing at a higher level the action of that which is eternal and perfect. They have all taught us that there is no need to fear for our own soul in the Cosmos. Browning said, "I shall arrive as birds pursue their trackless path; / The destiny is certain, the goal is sure." The past is set, but now our individualization steps in.

We find every reason in the world why we cannot enjoy life. Don't we, all the time? It is so very difficult for us to accept our good each day. We have this morbid example of all the tragedy that the world has gone through in its evolution—creative mind, mortal mind, carnal mind, it doesn't matter what you call it. Then we have the psychic impressions that press hard against our unconscious, insinuating themselves as cosmic realities, until even the revelation from the eternal God has to be strained through the hallucination of the very temporal man, the very finite man. It doesn't penetrate that cosmic reality which some of these great minds have. If we can gradually learn to drop the morbid by reaching back into the substance of that which is beyond all shadows and abiding in it—this is the secret place of the Most High.

So if you say, What's this got to do with practice?: There is a physical healing; there is a psychological healing. There is a physical cure; there is a psychological cure. There is only one kind of healing and that's spiritual, and so the spiritual may attend the mental and physical that it may be permanent. It is inevitable some day the spiritual awareness will consciously accompany physical and mental healing. What we practice is spiritual mind healing. You cannot divorce spiritual awareness from the kind of mind healing that we practice any more than you can take heat out of fire. It is only as we blend, as best we know how, our highest mental equivalent of what we think is the greatest good that we look back deeply enough to draw that good out by identification, and every identification will bring the utility of progression. The mind of a spiritual practitioner, as it were, does swing between the meditation of the wholeness and the application of that which at that moment comes to it with the announcement of its word, which is identified by the thing that it is working for; and in this way alone can it bring heaven to earth.

2.

THE HEALING LIGHT

In June 1958, eight months before the memorable experience of Cosmic Consciousness at Whittier, Ernest Holmes talked to a group of students about the light. Dr. Holmes felt we all were aware of light as a result of deep meditation, if only for an instant. "Let there be light, and there was light."

His method as we shared together in our talks was to have a mental equivalent of a healthy organ, tissue, nerve, or blood cell radiating a vibrant energy of light. His logic was that, the human form being a perfect creation of God's Body, it would manifest the light of Pure, Divine Energy. We prayed to recognize that light beneath the darkness of apparent symptoms of disease or disorder.

I would like to talk a little about the concept of light in the universe. In the temple over the altar a light always shone. This light of course always is a symbol of the life that is never extinguished. Ye are the candle of the Lord—ye are the light of the world—let your light so shine that men seeing your good works shall glorify your Father which is in heaven. All these references to light which we find in sacred scriptures—you will find it in many of the Catholic Saints, like St. Teresa. She said the light was so strong that it was complete darkness. In other words, she is describing a light which makes everything look dark in comparison. There was a light around Jesus. When Moses came down from the mountain—this is a symbol, you know; probably Moses didn't go up into a mountain, and it doesn't matter whether he did or didn't—but there was a light around him, and they could not look upon him; and it was the same way with Jesus.

Now this light is real. There is such a light at the center of everything and you might, someday in ordinary affairs, not realizing it, look up and see that light—you might see it everywhere in all things. There is a light at the center of everyone, but it does seem that while, by reason of any fact, this light is never obliterated, it is obscured. Jesus said you don't put your light under a bushel. There is a light in every organ of the physical body. If any organ would be restored to the vibration of that light, it would become healed, because that light is the pattern of that thing. You see, everything individualized is universalized.

For instance, I have a friend who practices this thing with a certain electrical mechanics, and it seems that whatever has a liver—a bird or animal, or man or fish—there is only one rate of vibration of the liver. This shows the universality of the pattern, doesn't it? If that rate of vibration—if anybody's liver physically were tuned into the natural vibration, even if the physical liver is in a so-called diseased condition—if this were tuned into the rate of vibration which is the rate of liver, whatever that is, it would be healed. If it were caused by some mental state, you might get a bad liver again. But this is manifestation meeting manifestation externally. But it is enough to know it tends to demonstrate the universality of all things that become, we think, individual—but in reality they only become individualized.

You see, if you have an "individual" something, you will have it separate from the rest, as we discussed a few minutes ago. You can have an individuation of anything and of all things, so that each individuation merely comes to a point of universality, like that, flowing down into this point. Therefore, all of the universality of that thing is epitomized and pressing against this particular point in its infinity, which differentiates the universality without destroying its unity. It individualizes it without destroying the universality back of this individuation. It is necessary for us to conceive this because back of what you are and back of what I am is all that there is, surging to express what you are and what I am, and for us and to us nothing else.

Well, at first this might sound like a conceited concept and we say, "Does God spend all his time thinking about me?" Yes, God spends all his time thinking about me. But since God is undivided and indivisible and infinite, God spends all of his time thinking about you. Now somehow or other, we have to tune in to this universal, which is now individualized in us, because in it is our pattern, in it is our perfection. Augustine, whether he rationalized it or reasoned it, said, "Thou hast made us, thine we are, and our hearts are restless til they find repose in thee."

The search of every man is the discovery of himself. He doesn't know it. The search of every man is something that will make him whole. Of course, by intuition, instinctively, almost blindly, he gropes—as Tennyson said: "For what was I, an infant crying in the night, an infant crying for the light, and with no language but a cry." And as he develops his theme in "In Memoriam" he finally says: "But the feeble hands and helpless groping blindly in the darkness, touched God's right hand in that darkness, and are lifted up and strengthened." You will find the same thing in Wordsworth: "Not in loneliness but in trailing clouds in glory do we come from heaven which is our home."

You will find it in "Saul," one of the great poems of Browning, where David sings to Saul, and he begins by singing to him of the objective things—the cool silver shock of a plunge into cold water. He is playing, and Saul is in a state of melancholy; he is practically unconscious. David sits there and sings, first comparing the physical things, awakening him on that plane, and by and by, as the theme develops, David says, "O Saul, a hand like this hand shall open the gates of new life to thee, see the Christ stand." And now Browning says of Saul, "He slowly resumes his old motions and attitudes kingly, he is Saul ye remember in glory; error had bent the broad brow from the daily communion." David is singing to Saul of the divine pattern of himself; he is awakening him, not to something that is not, but to something that is. He is awakening Saul to himself. And out of the inspiration of his song came the illumination which revealed that light which lighteth every man's path.

So the light is over the altar. We are the altar. This is a symbol that the light is within ourselves. Some day you may be looking up and you will see the tree give us light, as Moses did. It was not an illusion. This is a reality. And you will see there is a light around everything, and it can, to some degree now, be photographed in the human body; but it gets kind of murky at times, because the light doesn't shine. It shines; but we have covered it up with a bushel.

The only reason, medically or in any of the therapeutic sciences—osteopathy or chiropractic (all of which I believe in; I believe in anything that will work)—is not to put something there that wasn't there, but to reveal something that was there and make the mechanics, so that what was there may flow—that is all anybody can do. In other words all that any human ingenuity can gain is to restore us to our pattern—it is a cinch we didn't make it. You and I can't lay an egg. But the chicken is in the egg. And so as in Genesis it says: This is the generation of the time when the plant was in the seed before the seed was in the ground.

How many of you have read Troward's *The Law and the Word*? It is written to show that the whole mathematics of the creative sequence starts with the word. "In the beginning was the word, and the word was with God and the word was God, and all things were made by the word, and without the word was not anything made that was made. And the word became flesh and dwelt among us, and we beheld it." "I am the light of the world."

Now, Jesus said he came to bear witness or testimony to the truth, the truth that is in you and in me. Jesus was not the great exception but the great example. He came to witness the fact that it is necessary in the universe that such a thing as truth exists. It is equally necessary that the perception of truth is no different from its manifestation mathematically; that the mathematics will take care of themselves, if the perception is right. We go through the mathematics merely to correct the instrumentality, for the perception of that vision which is beyond those mathematics, but which still uses them because it can't help it. I mean they are still a part of the universe. The light that lighteth every man's path. And this light is at the center of everything and everyone. Someday you might be looking at someone, and you might see it, and you would see them suddenly enveloped in a light. Now, they are suddenly enveloped in a light to *you*, but they are not suddenly enveloped in a light. If they were, it was merely that you looked up suddenly and saw it. It is there, it is real.

And so we must think a lot about light symbolically; everything must become light—everything must. I don't know how to put it in words; I don't know how to say it. I know how to think it; I know it is true. There isn't anything outside this light. There isn't anything in which the light does not exist. Now, although it appears not to exist, it is there just the same. If you should see a person's aura, that is psychic. It will change in color. There will be a movement in it. According to his emotional state it will vary greatly; according to his habitual emotional and mental states it will always take a set form or pattern. But if you look deeper into this, you will begin to see a light—and the pattern will clear up.

Now, our whole work is based on the concept Perfect God, Perfect Man, and Perfect Being. Our whole practice is based on the concept that God is where we are and what we are, and that there isn't anything else. Our whole concept is partially based on the theory that whatever appears to be wrong is not wrong in itself but is the wrong arrangement of what is right. There is no dualism in the universe, as I have always said. There is not God and something else; there is no such thing as good or evil in itself. There is only what is, which automatically and mechanically reports from itself or interprets itself to us the way we look at it. "As thou seest that thou beest." Now, we may change the way we look at it—it will not change; it will not lessen its potentiality to suit us. So Troward wrote that whole book to show that the word is the beginning of everything—first intelligence, word, law, fact.

Intelligence conceives by the word; the word acting as law becomes the thing. The thing is an effect; the use of the law is an effect; the word is an effect; but the intelligence is cause. Therefore it can reformulate its word, it can speak a different word. Our whole theory of practice is based on the assumption that truth known is, or will become, demonstrated by the law of its own being reacting to the word at the level of our perception when we speak that word—and that is why it is some people's treatments are better than others'. It isn't because we are more spiritual sometimes than other times. We will never be any more spiritual than we are right now. We can't be. It is merely because at some time, some periods of time, for some reason—whatever it may be—we see more clearly, we think more clearly, we understand more definitely, the thing is more real to us: then is when you can do your best work. All the preparation we take for prayer or treatment—we call it treatment—is the preparation of seeing within ourselves that which is real and no longer comparing and making it less.

I was saying to a friend of mine—I have just returned from being up in Yosemite and Lake Tahoe, and we were discussing this—I was saying, "I have 1,000 dollars; you have 1,000 dollars. At least we know what 1,000 dollars is, and we can take it out and spend it; we don't feel we are broke. We are all right, we are safe as we measure safety. Now 1,000,000 dollars is a thousand 1,000 dollars as people measure money." (This doesn't seem to have much to do with light, but it has a lot to do with enlightenment.) He said, "Yes." I said, "All right, then why don't you say, 'I will treat you for a million dollars,' and I say, 'I will treat you for a million dollars.' I don't want a million dollars; neither one of us has any need of it, nor does anybody else. It is just a theory I have." And I said, "What is wrong with us?"

We got to thinking, and this thought came to me: There was another party with us who liked to garden, and I said to her, "Suppose tomorrow morning when you go home, you get yourself a little flowerpot and you have a shovel and a lot of dirt around there, and you go out and take a shovelful of dirt and put it in your little pot—and you have a potful of dirt, with as much dirt as the shovel held in the pot." I said, "The shovel didn't know it, and the pot didn't know it, and the dirt didn't know it. Who knew it? *You* knew it. Now you have need of a little potful of dirt, because you want to put a plant in it that God may make it grow. Just suppose for the fun of it that after you had filled your little pot from your little shovel—and the pot didn't know about it, and the shovel didn't know about it, and the dirt didn't know about it—you had a potful of dirt, which is fine—that is a demonstration.

"Now suppose you take your little shovel and say, 'Just for the fun of it, I'll dig up ten more shovelfuls and throw them over in the corner': you'll have ten more shovelfuls over in the corner—and the dirt won't know it, and the shovel won't know it, and you'll be the only one who knows it." Do you see the point? We are not doing that. We say we've got a potful of dirt; we do not realize that merely is a symbol of the level of our acceptance, a symbol of the receptacle within us which contains that acceptance, a symbol of its projection in our experience. We have a little pot. There is a lot of dirt, but we only got a potful of dirt. We didn't know there were ten other pots full, because that was all the dirt there was.

Now Jesus knew this. That is how he multiplied the loaves and fishes and turned water into wine, brought the boat immediately to the shore, and raised the dead. It was a divinely natural thing for a man at his level of understanding. It wasn't any effort. Now there is a light in us that knows these things—and that is intuition. There is a voice in us that speaks this language and was never taught it. No one ever told God what to be. That is beyond our human equivalent. I believe in the law of mental equivalents only as I believe that my gas tank will hold twenty gallons of gas—in no other sense. If it were a bigger tank, it would hold more.

But you see, if there were not another language beyond the words we use, we could never step the words we use up from their present capacity. Beyond all human mental equivalents, beyond all human experience, breaking down every precedent, there is a light that you and I have to follow. Otherwise we shall merely be going round and round and round in a vicious circle, caught in a beautiful cage, trapped in a beautiful trap, living still pretty much under the law of illusion or delusion, whichever it may be. But there has to be a word—while I believe in our mental equivalents as "the now": automatic reactions through polarity in the law of cause and effect. Remember, it was the genius of Jesus and Buddha not to have broken that law, but to have transcended it—and that is what you and I have to do, otherwise we should endlessly repeat our previous experiences on the old time track where they were born monotonously over and over and over again. I've counted my seven times over and over; seven times one is seven.

And so it is necessary that you and I in our practice shall break down whether they are what Troward* said: a neurotic thought pattern will repeat itself with monotonous regularity throughout life; or whether we say we are endlessly repeating the history of the world, which I think we are psycho-

---

*Thomas Troward, English jurist and writer on mental science.

logically, therefore physiologically, therefore economically and sociologically. But you see, if there were not a transcendent pattern, if there were not a light beyond our darkness, if this thing were merely an illusion, if it were merely a fanciful imagination, like one might have if he were intoxicated—but that isn't true at all. There is such a light; there is such a transcendence in every living thing—and if there were not, the seed would not burst its encasement and send down roots and send up shoots; if there were not, the bird would not nest, the child would not play, the butterfly would not come out of its chrysalis and spread its wings for its celestial flight. Remember this: don't be afraid of letting your imagination go. So long as you know it is lucid, there is a difference. I am not talking about people who are confused. I am talking about the only absolutely, completely clear thinkers the world has ever known. Jesus was the only normal man, in what he did, who ever lived. Shakespeare's imagination was the only normal imagination, or more nearly normal than anybody else's. The deductions of Einstein were the only normal things in that category the world has ever known.

Spiritual genius is normality, but we must not mistake psychic hallucination for spiritual genius, or a hunch for an intuition, or a word we hear for divine guidance. This is where we have to be very careful. But there is a divine imagination; there is a light that lighteth every man's path. Every great creator has had it, every great composer has had it—or it's had him. Emerson said, "Sometimes the muse too strong for the bard sits astride his neck and writes through his hands." That is creative writing, as over against mechanical writing; and that is the only great writing there is. All great writing, all great poetry, great music—all great acting, all great everything—is done under the inspiration of that thing which is the only final dancer, the only writer, the only thinker and the only doer there is.

Now, next will come the question: am I then but a puppet? am I then but marionette? am I pawn on the checkerboard? Here is a valid, extremely intelligent expression; for I have said God wrote every poem that was ever written. I was invited to hear a certain singer sing the other night, and she said, "Because you are coming, I want to give the best show I have ever given." I said, "You will, but not because I am coming." And it is very interesting: Her manager and people who work with her called me up the next day and said, "That is the best show she ever gave in her life." Well, I treated her because I knew she had a very great desire to do it because I was going to be there. I said, Well what is to stop God from singing? She is going to sing; God is going to sing. Now you see, I said God sings all the songs, dances all the dances, paints all the pictures, creates all art, writes every book, plays every game. Then we will ask, "Where do we come in? Are we then but puppets?"

Now we would be if we accepted the old theology and old philosophy of life. We wouldn't have any more meaning than as if God had spit into the cosmos and let the wind blow it. That is a terrible expression, isn't it? Guess I better change it and say *if he whistled.* Sounds a little better. This is the light that the world knows nothing about. They don't believe it; but don't try to force it on them, but be aware of it. This is God singing. It isn't an imitation of God; it doesn't obliterate her individuality—it is the only thing that accentuates it, it is the only thing that permits it. That is why Emerson said imitation is suicide. There is a place in every man's life where the reins run out the full length; there is spiritual genius hid in the commonplace. If God is omnipresent, there is the entirety of the creative urge, which pushes against everything, whether we call it the Divine Urge or the libido—it is all the same thing. The libido of psychology is the Divine Urge of metaphysics; it cannot be something else. Jesus said the Father seeketh such. The wind bloweth whence it listeth and no man knoweth from whence it cometh nor whither it goeth, and so is everyone who is born of the kingdom.

There is this Universal Artist devoting His or Its whole time to what I am saying right now, as though He had nothing else to do. As Emerson said, if I could get my bloated nothingness out of the way, if I could possess nothing and have nothing but IT, without possession or obsession, I should give full reign to Its genius at the level of my present state of evolution. But there is something beyond that, and that, and that. "Ever as the spiral grew/ he left the old house for the new."

There is a light that lighteth every man's path. Now, don't be afraid to experiment with this light; don't think you are silly if you believe in it. I have seen it many times. It is real. It is not illusionary—it is a light. So we cannot say since God dances every dance and sings every song and plays every play and writes every book . . . As Emerson said, "The mind that wrote history is the mind that reads it, and interprets it, and it can be understood or interpreted only from this basis, because human history is a record of the doings of that mind on this planet." That is the way he opens up his great essay, the greatest series of intellectual essays the world has ever known.

And so, to surrender to this genius is not conceit, because you don't surrender to it while you are conceited. That is putting a blinder on it. There has to be in everyone a light—there has to be in everyone a divinity that shapes his ends, "rough hew them though he may." There has to be behind everyone an urge and a push, and in front of him a pull that is irresistible, immutable, absolute. There has to be a word or a state of consciousness that exercises its authority to the level of our present perception. There has to be, or we wouldn't be here.

I do not believe what I believe because I believe what I want to believe—because I know that all the belief in the world will not change reality, and all the unbelief will not change it either; that your opinion and my opinion haven't a thing in the world to do with it—we are only fortunate. That is why I believe that treatment is independent of the one who gives it. It is now an entity in a field of law and will perform its office for which it was created, and nothing can stop it—unless the one who gave it denies it. He is the only one who can neutralize it. This idea that other people influence us is all nonsense. Why? Because no two things exist at the same rate of vibration and in a universe of infinity, the manifestation has to be equal to the infinity of the Manifester. You and I may not comprehend but a little of that infinity, but logically and mathematically we know it goes on and on and there is never any confinement. That is why the Talmud said, "God will doubly guide the already guided." It is why Jesus said "to him that hath shall be given."

It sounds like a pretty cold fact, but it is the truth. But the light shines in the darkness and the darkness comprehendeth it not. And Jesus is one of the chief accusers. He said, "You would be followers of the dark; you would be worshipers of the dark. Light has come into the world and you fail to receive it. You live in darkness." He wasn't condemning them; he wasn't saying, "You are going to hell." His name wasn't Billy. It was Jesus the Christ, the Illumined. There is only one of whatever it is, not two. That one is what you are. You had nothing to do with it; it is none of your business; you can't help it; you can't avoid it; and there is no use putting it off. "If ye know these things," the Bible says, "happy are ye if you do them."

Let us individually, then, in the silence of our own contemplation, take time to feel that light and see it. Very frequently—I did it last night, after I got home from having a class—I sit down all alone for two hours and just listen to the silence, and it speaks, I look into the darkness and it turns light, and it is there—and there isn't any question about it. Back of you, the Infinite searches into manifestation through you, as you, what you are—it is you. We don't have to be ashamed of it. You don't have to say, "I despise my personality; I hate this body; I am a worm of the dust," and think you are surrendering to God. This is a denial of God. All we have to say is, "There is nothing in me but God."

What we surrender to is not a foreign agent, but we acquiesce consciously in a divine host, a celestial visitor, a universal individualization, and if it is true that that exists in us and it was put there not by our will but by *the* will, who are we to deny it? If it is that way and we have reached a place in evolution where acquiescence and consent alone can reunite our present experience with that which ceased to exist when all compulsory problems of evolution ceased—"Long since, fire or mist or planet, a crystal or a cell,/ a saurian and jellyfish, then caves where caveman dwell,/ then a sense of law and order and a face turned from the clod,/ some call it evolution, others call it God." When that day arrived in prehistoric times, that the evolutionary push had done all that could be done by compulsion, it left only the automatic reactions of the physical body to keep it going to the place of self-discovery. And from then till now and forevermore, it will be only the conscious cooperation at first between what appears to be the one and the other, and gradually the other as the one, and finally the one as the only.

We are not in it or of it or with it—*we are it*. If that is true, our future evolution will be only as we perceive that light in the darkness, until the darkness isn't there—only as we accept that divine individuation: that there is that within me which is already complete. This is where the soul makes its great claim on God; this is where the Spirit that went out in search of us discovered itself; this is where the prodigal returns to the Father's house; this is where we unite with that light that lighteth everything and that light in which there is no darkness.

And for those of us who believe in these things, and without any pretense of throwing ourselves around—that has nothing to do with it—I wouldn't walk across the street to impress anyone living—that means nothing—I would walk around the world to find someone who is enlightened; that is a different thing; I would crawl on my hands and knees. It is here. Everything we go in search after, we shall overlook; looking at, shall not see; or seeing somewhat, shall interpret only in the light of that which we reflect into it from the glory which is ours. Now this is not conceit; this is a humility so terrific, so great—a humility that does not obliterate but accentuates by acquiescence. For who are we to throw a lie into the face of the Almighty and deny what the Omnipotent has decreed?

Let us then believe in that life; let us seek to see it everywhere and feel it and announce it and pronounce it, because that greatness which we recognize in Jesus and Moses and Buddha and Emerson is wonderful—if they have awakened us to a higher level of perception within ourselves. But if they have, we may know that that perception now—as we look upon them no matter how great (there are no prophets but the wise; there is no God higher than truth; there is no universe we can get out of)—if they have awakened us to that, they have merely awakened us to a self-perception of something which already existed within us. That is why Emerson said, "I go to hear a great man talk, and I don't realize that I have already given him all the greatness he has." You are great and I am great—not in conceit, not in our isolation or separation, not as though we say to others, "Look at me and die," because you and I cannot announce our greatness without including the greatness of everything that lives. Something forevermore blinds our eyes to the perception of the self unless it interprets itself everywhere. This is one of the things we fail to realize: I can claim nothing for myself with validity, realize nothing in myself, unless I find it and see it in you—because I can see only with my own eyes. Here is where there is no danger; here is where there is no conceit; here is where the spirit has no arrogance.

And I think another thing, which seems very important to me, and that is to regain in our own consciousness that spontaneity we had as a child. Someone may say, "Oh, that is nonsense and silly." That is all right. Who cares if we are silly? I would just as soon be a fool, because I know all the world is fooled; I had just as soon be wrong, because all the world is wrong; I had just as soon be a sinner (I would like it to be done artistically—because I love beauty). But we may know this: This spontaneous manifestation of life everywhere that bursts forth out of nothing into full bloom is the nature and the order of the universe. The child who is in us, before we learn to be so sophisticated and fight and deny it and quarrel with everybody and be sore at everything, is not dead; he is not asleep; we have just crowded so much experience, so much negation, that not he, but we, have forgot that celestial palace from whence we came.

Each one of us should seek that beam of light—it is there—follow it to the greater light. Light is in everything; light surrounds everything; light lights our path. But if all the arbitrary and compulsory processes of evolution have long since stopped—which I believe they have, or we would not be evolving into individuations of infinity, which we are—then our acquiescence must come of God, who can no longer pronounce himself through us or pronounce himself in us and personalize himself as us. This is the surrender. It is not the surrender of our pleasure; it is not the surrender of that which is happy; it is the surrender of that which has isolated us, or that which has clouded our vision and dumbed our memory and stifled our imagination and paralyzed our action until we are immobile and inert, walking as dead men in a city of Gods.

And we must awaken ourselves—rediscover that lost paradise, that child who was not afraid of the Universe in which he lived, that child who did not deny himself or his God, that child who had not listened to the dull, monotonous tune of condemnation, until he had isolated himself in fear from the Universe in guilt and, being antisocial, became antispiritual, and finally, for his own self-protection in the world which hurts so much, must regret until nature relieves him, which it always will—because limitation and want and lack and pain belong only to the lower order of perception. There is a place on the side of the mountain we are ascending where, like the burden of the pilgrim, there is an ascent which, having gone beyond the peaks that obstructed the light around us, reaches an apex where no longer any shadows are cast. This is the light that is spoken of that lighteth every man's path; and as you believe that you live, believe you are that light. As you believe in the possibility of your own soul, believe it is God. As you believe in God, believe in yourself.

3.

HEALING AWARENESS

Jesus the great teacher said, "Physician, heal thyself." He accepted the idea that thought was a movement of consciousness and would manifest in the world of people, places, and things. Ernest Holmes disagreed with the concept of prayer of supplication to a distant God. He felt it was true that "All that the father hath is thine." Therefore we had to in effect give ourselves a "treatment for incorrect thinking."

As defined by Dr. Holmes, treatment—prayer in its proper content— is the time, process, and method necessary to the changing and redirecting of our thought, clearing the thinking of negation, doubt, and fear, causing us to perceive the ever-presence of God. Ernest suggested to his followers that when they spoke or thought of prayer it should be in this understanding. This had seemed difficult for many coming from backgrounds of restrictive prayer technique. He emphasized this in a talk to the Tuesday Invitation group on November 25, 1958.

We want to become aware of our own consciousness and its absolute oneness and fusion with all that is, so there can be nothing separate from what we ourselves are or apart from it, so that we know every word we speak is the presence and power and activity of the One and Only in us as us, so that we realize the transcendence of what we are doing, that the heart and mind and intellect and the will and consciousness completely accept it and that nothing within us can reject it.

We are aware of this—that our word is the presence and power and action of love, the living Spirit almighty, and of perfection and of peace and joy and wholeness, oneness—we are aware of the infinite and limitless joy of being. All the energy that there is and all the enthusiasm there is, all the intelligence there is and all the happiness, is at the point of our consciousness, and is accepted and does flow through, in and around us effortlessly.

Now it is the law of the being of each one of us that everything that he does shall prosper, that joy shall follow him, that everything he touches shall succeed, that goodness shall surround him, that love shall flow through him to everything he touches and healing and wholeness—that everything he touches is made whole. This is the law of each one of us, and we accept the law of our own being. We accept the realization of the light and life and power and presence of the truth at the center of our being. We accept the absoluteness of that truth and our own authority in it.

Now whatever the divine pattern of reality and eternal perfection and changeless wholeness, individual in each one of us—whatever it is, we accept it and permit it to appear at the surface, unclouded, complete, perfect, whole. Now this means we accept whatever the divine pattern is for each one of us. It is a cosmic pattern individualized in and through each one of us in a unique way. We accept that, and we know there is nothing that has ever happened in our experience to reject it. It doesn't get born; it doesn't get dead; it doesn't grow old; it doesn't change; but it makes everything change all the time—the action within the action. Now we reject every belief that in any way limits the enthusiasm for life or the zest for life or the activity of life or the degrees of age or change in the reality of life, because not one of them has any truth in it. We establish in our own consciousness and our own acceptance, and project in our own experience, that which is eternally being born from the unborn.

We know, as we look back on the belief in our past, that it has no existence, and the belief in our future has no existence, and the present has complete existence extending forward and backward and around and is completely subject to the will of the present—which will is perfect. Therefore every causation set in motion in us, around us, or through us or about us is perfect causation. Every effect produced by this perfect effect, every manifestation, is perfect manifestation. Our inward consciousness knows and comprehends and hears and understands the meaning of what we say—and the wholeness of it and the peace of it and the joy of it and the perfection of it. There is one Life, which is perfect; that is our life now, and there is no other life. Right now, there is no other life—there never was any, there doesn't seem to be any, it doesn't look as though there were any, there is no one to believe there was any, and there isn't any belief in any separation.

Now that is a good treatment—to clear the track, and according to the belief of forward and backward. I was reading something from Lao-tzu the other day in which he said, "The man who knows may be learned, the learned man may never know." Isn't this wonderful! The man who knows may be learned, the man who knows what he is talking about might be a good physicist; but there might be a good physicist who didn't know. That is the perception of all the great and the good and the wise: not to decry the so superstitious and ignorant, so unenlightened, so medieval in human history and its outlook (and it is so shocked when something comes along that is different than it is; it is like the answer of the unconscious or the subjective or the inner mind of the guy when Jesus came in and it said, "Why do you come to disturb us, O Son of David?").

Whether we call it the inertia of thought patterns as psychology does, the argument of error as Mrs. Eddy* did, or the devils talking, as the Bible does—they all mean the same thing; there aren't any devils. There is no argument of error as such, other than the monotonous repetition of accepted thought patterns, and the inertia of these patterns is like a parable of Jesus: Somebody is in want, and she goes to the judge and beats on the door in the middle of the night, and he says, "Let me alone. I am in here very comfortable and my family are all asleep in bed. Go away and come tomorrow." She just beat the door down.

This is a symbolic presentation of our approach to the thing we are talking about. She would *not* take no for an answer. We take no for an answer because we haven't had enough experience of the *yes*, so that the *no* transcends the *yes*. The apostle said, "That which I do, I would not; and that which I would, I do not. Oh miserable man that I am, who shall deliver me from the body of this death?" He is talking about the inertia of thought patterns. He is talking about the thing that he would say to me if I said, "I'll go raise the dead." He would say, "No you won't."

---

*Mary Baker Eddy, founder of Christian Science.

We are all screwed up about what we think is spiritual. We think unless you put on a long face and count your beads and say the Lord's Prayer. . . . And there was a time when there wasn't any Lord's Prayer and no beads to count. How did they get as far as the beads, and who wrote the Lord's Prayer? Whoever wrote the Lord's Prayer was smarter than the prayer, or he couldn't have said it. And you are greater than every saint and sage. Any person is, for himself, greater than all the saints that ever lived, because no one can live by proxy. You go there all alone—nobody can open the door but yourself, and no one can close it but yourself. You see, if someone could open it, someone could close it—and if you could say "no" to somebody else's "yes," there is something or somebody else besides you who could say "no" to your "yes." It is only because, as Kipling said, "Each in his separate star/ Shall draw the thing as he sees it/ For the God of things as they are" that we have freedom. This freedom must, of a necessity, include what we call bondage, but it must include bondage as freedom to be bound—there can be no bondage in itself.

This is what Lao-tzu meant when he said, "The man who knows may not be learned; the learned man may never know." Because all they are watching is a process. That is good—he is not criticizing the learned man at all. In our language, we would say, No matter what the intellect may have discovered or science may have demonstrated, all of which we believe in—no matter what psychology may have proven and philosophy taught or science demonstrated, there is still a mystical element which goes beyond this, and it is very evident that there is, or there would be no science and no scientist. The scientist is himself, we will say, the mystical element that goes beyond his science, or he couldn't use his science. The artist is the mystical element that paints the picture, and if he weren't, after he had painted it he would step into it. That is why I said in our statement of conviction, God enters into every creation, which I believe, and I believe in a sort of pan-psychism, but always more than the creation—always more. I happen to believe that everything from toadstools to archangels are just varying degrees of consciousness and intelligence manifesting in infinite variations, forever ascending, in a living universe which is sentient, from "the mind that sleeps in the mineral," to whatever the Absolute is that comprehends all things within Itself, because the universe is one system.

Somebody was trying to explain to me the other night—I am not very good at mechanics—and he was trying to explain electricity, and he said that the electricity is not really generated until you press the button. I still don't understand it. But they swore to me, at least for all practical purposes, that it really has to be called on before it exists. Whether it does or doesn't, I am always likening every law in nature to our metaphysical laws, merely because God is one, the Universe is one—and as Emerson said, "Nature has but a few laws, but she plays this familiar tune over and over again"; and the Hermetic teaching says, "As above, so beneath; as below so above"—what is true on one plane is true on all, or, as Swedenborg taught, the law of correspondences; and as Jesus said, "In my father's house are many mansions"—or Jacob's ladder, ascending and descending; or the laws of parallels of Emerson.

Now all it means is this: There isn't any science known to men but what would prove what you and I believe. If we knew how to apply it, it would never deny it. Every law in nature has a corresponding reality, working exactly like it in Mind and Spirit; it has to have, or the universe would be two systems. There cannot be a physical universe that is separated from a mental, and a mental separated from a spiritual—and the knowledge that there cannot be is the key to spiritual mind healing, consciously used. In other words, we neither materialize Spirit nor spiritualize matter; we are not using a spiritual power to make a material law work in accord with good, and we are not using a mental power to control a physical power which is out of line. These things have no existence outside our own imagination—and in saying this, we are not denying either the physical form or its mental equivalent, but really postulating the theory that the mental image in mind, and the form it takes out there, are not two different things, but one and the same—equal, identical and interchangeable—and that consciousness is superior to both because they are the action of consciousness producing a two-faced unity of temporary liquidity and temporary solidity.

That is the basis upon which spiritual mind healing may be consciously taught. Not that you are using a good power to overthrow an evil power; that is confusion. Not that you are using a big to swallow up little; that is confusion. Not that you are using heaven to cool off hell; that is confusion. Not that you are using light to overcome darkness; there is no darkness—now this is where we get stuck: *there isn't.* It is hard for us to digest the thought that we are, right now, living in a spiritual universe whose only laws are Intelligence acting as Law.

Some people would say, "What strange things you believe!" but this is exactly what Eddington said, and exactly what Jeans* said, and what modern science is beginning to accept—because you can't get away from it. Now, whether we say, In the beginning was the Word, and all things were made by the Word, and without the Word was not anything made that is made, and the Word became flesh and dwelt among us, and we beheld it—it is all the same thing. The laws of nature are Intelligence acting as Law. The laws of the human mind are Intelligence acting as Law at the level of the human mind—and there is no such thing as the human mind, but at the level of this ignorance which we call the human mind. It still is subject to law—there is no chaos in the Universe; there is no place where Law is not. If there were, there would be a place where chaos is, and if there were one place in an infinity of unity where chaos was, the whole works would blow up.

And yet we mistakenly physically try to treat any organ of the body as though it were separate from the rest of it. That is a fallacy too. You can't get a pill that will hit the liver and leave out everything else. In the Bible it says, "Awake thou that sleepest and arise from the dead, and Christ shall give thee light." Emerson said it seemed as though when we came here somebody gave us a drink too strong and we are hypnotized. And he said, once in a while we sit up and look about us but soon fall back into this stupor. It is one of the reasons why I don't believe in any of these extraordinary drugs that people are taking. I think they are good for medical experiment. I wouldn't want to arrive by any artificial effort.

In other words, only in the most intense self-awareness, independent of

---

*Sir James Jeans, English physicist, astronomer, and author.

other things, do we arrive at that which is no longer artificial. We are caught up enough now in artificiality and pretense—not conscious, not meanly, but by the very nature of things being the way they are and the hypnosis that is imposed upon us from the cradle to the grave through negation. The very key to spiritual mind healing is a consciousness that we are living in a spiritual universe now, a living universe now, and that there is no difference between mind and what mind does, because what mind does is mind doing what mind does, no matter how solid it looks; but in that reality it is liquid.

Emerson said, "We view the universe as solid fact, God as liquid law." Now, if it is true, and I don't know, that you have to press the button before the electricity or power is called upon, and it has no existence until this connection is made, then it is also true that in a sense consciously or unconsciously a demand must be made upon the universe before it will respond. That would be true too; it would have to be true. Now, when I say a demand is made upon the universe, I don't mean waving your arms and screaming at it. The demand that is probably the most potent is the most silent; it is probably the most quiet. Lao-tzu said, "Most things are possible to him who can perfectly practice inaction." "Be still and know that I am God."

But, I guess, everything is in a response to a demand. But I think most of the demand is unconscious; most of the demand is measured out by what everyone has demanded. They said of Jesus, "He breaks all of our laws, he heals people, forgives their sins, companions with sinners; he is a terrible guy." The only righteousness that they could understand was that degree of righteousness which they experienced. They were not bad people; these people weren't bad people any more than Torquemada was bad, at the Inquisition. They believed they were doing the will of God and of right to pull people's thumbnails out until they accepted the Bible instead of the sword. All these people believed they were right; "the devils also believe and tremble." Billy Graham believes he is right—probably one of the sweetest guys who ever lived, as a person; what he believes is insanity. We don't have to accept this evidence merely because a fellow is good. The insane asylum is filled with very nice people who are completely sincere.

We too are crazy from some larger viewpoint—so this isn't any criticism of the others. Probably, to someone who would know that a cancer is a thought form and know it like you and I know that ice is water—he would have this attitude toward us and say it is a thing of pain in itself. (The Chinese sage said, "O man, having the power to live, why do you die?") He would say, Dissolve it. But the human opinion is against it—the experience is against it—and we cannot deny either the experience or the human opinion. But we may affirm that which is transcendent of each and controls both because one is the other—one liquid and one apparently solid.

But there is nothing solid in the universe. Even we in our freedom do not have the freedom to destroy liberty—which is the philosophic error of Communism, and that is why it will never succeed. It is contradictory to the unity of all life individuating—completely contradictory. They may have a little concept of the unity of life in humanity; but they have lost what the unity is doing in individuating itself in differentiation without division. This is the philosophic error of Communism; it has many other errors, we think; but that is the philosophic error, and no one ever beat God at His own game, you know. "Though the mills of God grind slowly, they grind exceeding small." It is absolutely impossible for it to succeed in history.

So we are absolutists living in a world of relativity. Personally, I wish to affirm the absolutism, but I do not wish to deny the relativity for fear I will throw the baby out with the wash water—and I think too many people in our field are liable to do it. I think we have to reconcile one with the other—and will, just as soon as we know that neither the one nor the other is absolute in causation. But each would become a plaything of the gods.

Thought creates all the conditions we experience somewhere along the line, but the thinker creates his thoughts. We mess around physiologically in the physical healing and it is all right; it is good in the physical, and psychological in the mental, and they are both good. And if we can straighten them out we are going to be a lot better off. But when you and I come to give a treatment, we have to take a step up somewhere else, don't we? We have to take another step, where the reconciliation is with neither the one nor the other but with what Aurobindo calls the transcendence, which does not try to reconcile the differences, the opposites.

In other words, the heat of the sun does not try to be reconciled with the fact that an iceberg is a solid floating in a liquid and the fact that the Empire State Building could be crushed between two icebergs, because everything is the servant of what it obeys. But the heat of the sun does not try to reconcile the opposites, or the facts, of big or little, right or wrong, good or evil, heaven and hell, God and the devil, hard and easy; the sun shines, and the iceberg cannot resist it, because nonresistance is the only thing that cannot be resisted. Nonviolence is the only thing that cannot be violated—it is as simple as that; but in such degree as we step down into the violence of the resistance, we are subject to the level of the violence or the resistance. Who takes up the sword will perish by it—and in such degree as he takes it up, he will be affected by it.

Now this is one of the things Lao-tzu meant when he said that the man who knows may not be learned; the man who is learned may never know. And he is right. Whether we call it that mystical element, that spiritual perception, it doesn't matter what we call it; we do deal with the transcendence in treatment, and we should know that we do. Then we do deal with that in mind which should be transcendent of our arguments through technique; and the arguments through technique are only to reach the place where we don't have to have them.

Now, I believe in using them while you need them. I believe we have a definite technique; it can be taught; it can be used, and it will work. Because we do not teach faith healing or faith manifestation, neither do we deny it. Absolute and complete faith will do it—but there are few people that have it.

Now what is the thing that happens during this process? Last Sunday evening, we went home with some friends after we dedicated the ground for Esther Barnhart's church, and I said, "Where the golden sierras keep watch over the valley's bloom" . . . and I turned around, and you couldn't see the golden sierras or the valley's blooming; but they were there just the same—but they sure didn't appear to be. We see now as through a glass darkly. But the mountain is there, and it won't move; and when they clear up the smog, that will be there which was there when there was smog. Now whatever it is that clears up the smog will not be conscious of the smog, or it will continue to get smoggier. It will be the exact opposite to it, won't it? It will be that which neutralizes it; it will be that which transcends it, no matter how it happens—it doesn't matter. The sun makes no effort to melt the iceberg—but how you and I work to get rid of something! We don't seem to get into that place of stillness.

So one of the fellows said we hadn't ought to do any of this process, and I said no, we hadn't. "Then why do you do it?" I said, "Why do *you* do it, brother? You just jump on your little horse and race down to the cemetery and raise the corpses—or shut up." In our science you have to put up or shut up. Here it is; I believe all of it. How much can we *do*? This is what is practical. Now, we must wed the practical to the ideal, because we are transcendental realists. I would never arrive at that by denying every relativity—but I could by accepting the relativity as relativity only, not subject to itself, having no law of its own isolated from the law of all being which permits it, because it expresses something that announced it. And it would seem to me if there weren't something that had to express what announced it, there would be no freedom.

In other words, I believe bondage is freedom. I believe limitation is freedom. I believe pain is freedom. (I don't like it and never had much pain—but I don't like it.) It is all right for us to believe in the relative, because we are living in relativity. We are fourth-dimensional people in a three-dimensional world. But always the fourth dimension is pressing against us, and because we don't know it, everything looks strange. I mean, it looks as though it weren't right, out here, and we try to think of that thing which will right it, and it looks as though that thing could not be. Even the truth you and I believe in seems too good to be true, doesn't it?

Even the thought of the immediacy of its availability and the absoluteness of its action seems to be too good to be true. We are running around saying, "Well, we don't know enough yet; we are not good enough yet"; and every reason we give, no matter how legitimate why it can be, makes it so that it isn't, but it is still at the *isn't* that we point. If we can understand that the *isn't* is the *is* as the *isn't,* we shall have reconciled a pair of opposites, because there are no opposites. The Gita says you have to do away with the pair of opposites before you can enter bliss, and Jesus said 'tisn't everyone who sayeth, Lord, Lord . . . and ye cannot serve both God and Mammon—this is what they are talking about, this is what Aurobindo means when he says transcendence does not reconcile, it transmutes. You could accept the iceberg as there while you watch it melt, couldn't you? Somehow or other I think we have to get rid of the resistance that we put up rightly or wrongly, but with good intentions, even in trying to get to be good. This sounds crazy, I know; but don't accept it—you don't have to take it. The studied effort to be spiritual, the unspontaneous approach to beauty will not find very much that is beautiful. "A primrose by the river's bank a yellow primrose was to him, and nothing more."

Somehow or other you and I—I guess nobody can do it for us—have to see. I gave a treatment this morning that is to work through a whole organization, in which thousands of people are engaged. There are many departments, heads of departments, stenographers, janitors—everything that goes with a big organization; and I said to myself: This statement is in every branch of this organization; there is no difference between the person who runs some department and the one who sweeps the floor—it has to affect everything and everyone for good; it has to remove every negation, every error, and everything that causes it and every belief in it, everyway; and I think I got my mental arms around the situation enough to embrace. And if I did, it will heal the whole thing just as easy as one part of it, because there are no parts in unity. Isn't that right—and I think we don't quite realize enough the sweepingness, the all-inclusiveness of what we do.

So we are fourth-dimensional people. We are spiritual beings. We are transcendent agencies living in a dimensional world, which we will always live in somewhere, and there is nothing wrong with it or it wouldn't be here. But it will not always have to obstruct us. As long as consciousness is aware, it will produce that of which it is aware. Probably we will always have a body somewhere—we are not just going to slide off into thin air, where nobody can find us. The laws of nature will persist. But we can have one that doesn't get congested and doesn't have pain and doesn't limit us and weigh anything (it doesn't have to weigh anything); it will be just as articulate.

Now we have recognized we are fourth-dimensional beings, and let's do it without being stupid and pulling a long face and looking in the mirror to see how spiritual we look and won't read anything but the Bible—and before it was written, what did they do? And when heaven and earth as we now understand it shall be rolled up like a scroll and laid away with the things that were once thought to be real—what shall we do? And so Jesus said, "Before Abraham was, I am"; "Destroy this body and that which I am will raise up another like unto it." He was both learned and he also knew. There is no reason why we may not have both, and we should have both.

We had a very successful opening in El Monte on Sunday morning, and this is a project I would like us to work on for the next month. How many of you will work on it every day? Now do it, and do it definitely, and come to a conclusion in your own mind and say, "This is the truth"—because we got off to an awfully good start in consciousness. I have a particular interest in this, not because Ed is a nice guy, but it is the first church I have started for a long time, and I want it to be—and it is—a howling success right now.

Let's stop right now, because I want to show you how I want you to treat this thing:

We are speaking the word for a new church in El Monte, and Ed Thompson is at the head of it. Now we are setting up a church in consciousness, in El Monte at the Columbia Grade School. This address is known in mind or it couldn't be named; therefore when we say this, everything that knows anything knows where it is: it is at the point of our perception, that is all; and since time comes out of the timeless and we evolute it at will, we are evoluting it for Sunday morning. Therefore when we specify Sunday morning, time and place, we create the time that will be at that place for that purpose. That is the way it works. That is the way everything works. Consequently our treatment is for that occasion and nothing else, and it has to operate on that occasion, and it will bring every person there who can be helped by being there—we don't want to waste anyone's time. It will bring everyone there who can be best served there; it will bring everyone there who can be made whole by being there. Therefore we want to get whole ourselves, so that when people come, they can be made whole. We want to let down the doorway from wholeness that heals unwholeness, so that all the power that there is will be there Sunday morning, and all the presence and all the love and healing power and all the light and all the joy and everything that is spontaneous and happy. And children will play there in the garden of God where the eternal light shines and where there is no darkness. And they will sing.

And they will dance and they will have joy and life; and even this place that is provided will not be adequate to hold them. They shall come from north and south and east and west, and this consciousness which we now have shall operate there with these other people who understand what we are doing. We are operating it. Everyone who comes in there—the healing power of that consciousness, and this consciousness, and that occasion will flow through him into perfect Light, into perfect joy, and into perfect action, into complete gladness. "I wouldn't give a nickel for a well person who isn't glad—I would rather have a corpse that is happy." At least we will get some kick out of it. This is not a droll thing; this is not a sad thing; this is not a weary thing. This is something that sings. "There is ever a song somewhere, my dear, there is ever a song." And we must sing it.

And I would have life and animation and enthusiasm that all the energy and action and power that there is in the divinity of every person coming there shall vibrate with light and life and be bound together with love and made whole, because it *is* whole. We know that the shackles shall drop from the feet of pain, and this word being the presence and the power and the activity of the living Spirit within us, it is absolute for this occasion, and we accept it in joy, and we are grateful for the privilege of speaking it—and we love it.

Now we have a pretty good consciousness right here. Let's speak it for every church in Religious Science and every practitioner. For every word that goes out on the air or anywhere else there is healing, there is wholeness, and there is joy.

Now let's turn back to the center. The only thing we shall ever really know is the center within ourselves and its relationship to all that is. This is the Life within. We make it the law of our own being, each individually:

that everything he touches shall be made whole right now. Wherever he walks, there is the Light of heaven. Now let's not say "This is too good for me," or "I am not good enough for it." The Light is there anyway, and all we are doing is recognizing it—and it is there, and we are that, and we can't help it. So we may as well accept it and drop everything out of thought that denies it.

Everything we touch is quickened into action and into life and into joy and peace and into wholeness. Now let's accept the abundance—it belongs to the universe. Let's not name it as dollars and cents—it can be dollars and cents and houses and whatever you want it to be; but unless there is something there to take this form, there won't be any form. So we can know that everything that we do prospers. Now this includes everything. Maybe it is going home and making a pie. I don't know how they can make so many bad ones; it shows the creative genius of the human mind that it can take good material and make a bad product out of it. That is freedom too.

4.

DON'T THROW THE BABY OUT
WITH THE WASH WATER

––––––––––

Ernest Holmes felt at times that too much emphasis was placed by the student of healing on techniques and study, thus sacrificing the healing feeling. Ernest had a favorite expression: "Don't get so intellectually involved that we throw the baby out with the wash water." In December 1958, to a group of students studying to be practitioners, he expressed this idea.

You are all through with the practitioner's course now, and I have nothing new to tell you. You see, we can teach techniques for practice—that is very simple—but couldn't teach someone how to be a practitioner. That would be impossible. The techniques are of the intellect, the other is of the heart, of the feeling; and I am speaking of feeling not as an emotion—not that I think there is anything wrong with emotion—but a feeling that is deeper than emotion, and a feeling in which I personally think all emotions are generated and from which all emotions flow.

We teach, as you know, two very simple but profound fundamental facts of existence: a divine Presence and a universal Law of reaction—a divine Presence which is to each one of us an Infinite Person, and which is in each one of us what we are. I was driving home from San Diego yesterday and the thought came to me about something I think would make a very good talk, which said to me (when I use that phrase I mean *I said to myself*, because there is only one self individuated in each one of us), that the over-dwelling Presence is the indwelling Person. God in you as you is you. There is nothing else you can be. You didn't have anything to do with it. You didn't make it, and you can't change it. You didn't do anything that was good enough to earn it, and you can't do anything bad enough to destroy it.

I always say that at every funeral, because it is true. Life *is*; Life is self-existent. Nothing made God. The fundamental premise of our whole philosophy is that we live in a self-existent universe, self-sustaining, self-energizing, self-perpetuating, self-knowing, self-acting—and that the entire manifestation of Life exists for the delight of its Creator. We are not here to get saved—we are not lost. We are not here to glorify God—he isn't that much out of material. We are here to express That which is, and that is what accounts for all those inward feelings that everyone has, nebulous, incoherent at times, sometimes nearer the surface than at other times, but a steady persistency back of all things, an urge to live, to sing, to dance, to express life, to create.

That is why it is known that the life that doesn't create physically dies, and mentally dies, in order that it may get a new deal again, because of the congestion of the uncreated life which came with us—and we didn't do anything with it. Now whether it is a child making mud pies or a new Pope choosing his new Cardinals, one is not more important than the other in the sight of the Eternal. We are so accustomed to big and little, good and bad, up and down, over and across, right and wrong, sin and salvation, that it is difficult for us to believe this. You and I believe there is nothing but God, that there isn't anything else. God is the snail out here—this does not in any way lessen God; it *does* glorify the snail. We are each that incarnation of a divinity, and against each presses the insistent urge that will not let anyone alone because it is there: life and more life.

Now very few people understand the meaning of a spiritual universe, because they think, mistakenly, that the spiritual universe is philosophically and religiously a theory. They do not know that the universe we are looking at now is that universe—the universe we are in now. They are looking for an eternity when things will be all right. They do not know that they are in that eternity now. They are looking for a salvation which they already have, even though they are not using it with freedom and in joy. We happen to believe in a spiritual universe. Jesus said, "Behold, the kingdom of God is at hand." Probably most of them looked around and said, "We don't see anything." But he saw something and heard something and felt something that every practitioner in our field must see. The pure in heart shall see God. Now this should be interpreted literally, because where there is no longer any adulteration of Spirit and not-Spirit, of God and not-God, of Being and not-Being, there will be nothing left but what is, which is Being; and we believe in this Being.

There is a divine pattern of every cosmic manifestation, and an individual pattern of our own which I believe is the result of the sum total of the whole belief of the human race, our directly inherited tendencies, and what we have contributed to it, rightly or wrongly, wisely or unwisely. But it is necessary that we realize that we are living in a spiritual universe now, a universe which is a perfect God—that there is a perfect God, perfect man, and a perfect Being right now, and that we are experiencing it right now, and that everything that contradicts it is itself to be contradicted. Not necessarily vehemently, violently, nor by resistance; but it is to be contradicted, because it is not true. You see, if there is such a thing as a Science of Mind, there is a technique, a mental technique, applied to the recognition of something that exists before we recognize it or there would be no principle to demonstrate.

We have a principle to demonstrate; we know how to treat, technically, and in techniques; and now each one of you will have to learn from your own experience that which no one can teach you but yourself. The Gita says the self must raise the self by the self. And from Shakespeare: "To thine own self be true and it must follow as the night the day, thou canst not then be false to any man."

Every practitioner in our field has a secret with God, and that is his realization of the divine Presence to him, in him, through him, as him—because you and I will never awaken a corresponding realization in someone else beyond the level of that recognition, realization, and embodiment of the same thing. This is why Jesus said that if the blind lead the blind, they will both fall into the ditch. They say in modern psychology that in an analysis, if the one analyzing had an unredeemed psychic liability (we will say, hated his father) and the one being analyzed had an unknown psychic liability (he hated his father), when the analyst gets to the point where the patient should reveal to the analyst that he hated his father, he can't, and it is called an emotional bias which creates an intellectual blindspot. No different from Jesus saying that the blind shall lead the blind. Jesus was a great spiritual psychologist, because he knew what was in people.

So water will reach its own level by its own weight only in consciousness, in treatment, in realization, in recognition; and you will learn out of your own experience that the most intently—not intensely, but intently—you listen to the one, you can to the other. That is another way of saying Be still and know that I am God. God is all there is. At the center of everything, Whitman said, nestles the seed of perfection. The truth we have to demonstrate is that perfection *does* nestle at the center of everything. And as Browning said, it is loosing this imprisoned splendor.

Now experience has taught that we make our way by degrees through the techniques you have learned how to use, and they are correct—they are the best the world knows about; they are compiled from what is known by the world about this particular subject. Whether you call it affirmation and denial, it leads toward something which the mind no longer rejects, which the mind accepts; but now the mind *does* accept this, to all of those who have studied the metaphysical philosophies—not only ours, but many others. Ours is not better than the others; it is just the one we use. You have learned the technique and you know what its purpose is. Itself is not the creative agency; it is merely that which looses it. All the words in the world, unless they have meaning, will not do anything.

Now we have learned that the words must have a meaning to the one who gives them. You are not trying to hypnotize someone in a treatment, you don't even talk to them mentally. You are thinking in your own mind, making certain statements, perhaps, about someone. Anyone can stand in front of Lazarus and tell him to get up and come out of the tomb, but there had to be a man who wasn't afraid to roll away the stone. I don't look upon Jesus as different from other people, other than that he had something—a fullness, let us say. How he got it I don't know, and it doesn't matter, because if you throw all the bibles right out the window and all the saints and sages and saviours out of the other window, you will for the first time in your life be ready to deal with the only thing you shall ever know that will ever have an immediate perception of life.

Stop and think about that. That will be the first time you will say, "All right; God and I in space alone, and nobody else in view." That is what you have to do. There is nothing but God. Now with this has come to the metaphysical field the realization that Mind in action acts as Law. It is as simple as that: thought in action is Law. Don't say, "Why does it?" I don't know. How can a chicken lay an egg, or any of the other things happen? Nobody knows. This is life, and even God cannot explain God. You cannot explain God logically or emotionally or in any other way. That is why the ancients, some of them, said that whatever name you give It or Him, He is not that, because He is beyond that.

Now the practitioner who will the most persistently practice the Presence of God will be able to do the most with this technique. Why? Because he is filling it with a form, he is supplying it through his words with a form, he is filling the form with a feeling, like molten lava; and we could create all the intellectual forms forever and have nothing happen. Something has to fill what is called the spirit and letter of the law, I suppose, in the Bible. "My words fly upward, my thoughts remain below; words without thoughts cannot to heaven go." We believe the Universe is a spiritual system—that all the laws of the Universe are in Intelligence acting as Law. That is fundamental to our belief. There is nothing in the findings of modern science to contradict it. There is no logician who can disprove it. And the great and good and wise have always known it.

Now, Jesus understood it. He understood that in such degree as his word was consistent with the nature of reality, it was really proclaiming its nature through his word. "Not I but the Father who dwelleth in me; yet the Father is greater than I. But whatsoever things the son seeth the Father do, that also doeth the son, that the Father may be glorified in the son."

Now you embark on an experiment in practice; you are going to travel into a country no one ever went to before. All we can tell you is that there is such a country. There are a few little wheels that don't squeak so badly, but you have to do the traveling. Here you will be your only and sole teacher, not in the development of the techniques—although you will develop techniques—but in the use of those you have; and you will discover that there is a feeling that goes with your word. Now, I am not talking about an emotion, but a deep inward indefinable something that I don't think any-body can give to anyone else. I think when we sit with, or listen to, or read books written by, people who have this thing—we get it. You know it, you recognize it, you feel it—like a song in a crowded room. That is the impar-tation of the language of the Invisible to Itself, or, as Plotinus* said, the flight of the Alone to the Alone, or the One to the One. It is my concept of what spiritual realization means to mental technique.

Adela Rogers [St. Johns][†] had dinner with me the other night, and she was speaking about "spirituality," and I said, "Wait a minute, Adela—I don't know what you mean." She was all worked up over it—"getting spiritual"—and I told her I don't know whether I am spiritual or not. I feel like I am very close to the earth; I love the things of the earth; but I can get along without them. "Well," she said, "spirituality is that which is not materialistic or material." And I said, "There isn't any matter, Adela; matter has been dissolved in the minds of thinkers for ages, and it hasn't even a peg to hang its hat on in modern physics. There is no material universe. Therefore we don't have to contend with one! Where is a spiritual universe? Where you are looking—period." That is the end of the sentence and all of the lesson. Isn't it interesting!

Don't try to be good—you don't know what good is, and I certainly don't. They didn't think Jesus was very good. Just be yourself. Whatever is de-structive is all the evil there is, and whatever is constructive is the only good there is. This is the only measuring yard, I think, and if anything does any harm, it isn't good. We believe the universe *is* a spiritual system—not as *evolving* into one—and we believe it is *now*. And, as Emerson said, we see the universe as solid fact, but God sees it as liquid law. For, he said—and this is quite a thing to have been said over a hundred years ago—matter is

---

*Egyptian-born Roman philosopher (A.D. 205–270).
†American journalist and popular social historian.

spirit reduced to its greatest thinness, oh so thin; and now we find it is reduced to some kind of energy and a flow, and they don't know whether it is steady or intermittent—and we don't care.

The universe in which we live is a spiritual system now—everything that is in it is a manifestation of that spiritual system now. The idea back of everything is first conceived in a generic pattern and then gradually individuated where the individual steps in and takes over at the dawn of history on this planet, I suppose. That is why the poet said, "A fire, a mist a planet; crystal and a cell./ Saurian and jellyfish; then caves where cavemen dwell./ Then a sense of law and order, and a face turned from the clod./ Some call it evolution; others call it God." We believe in evolution, but we believe evolution is the unfoldment of that which was first *in*voluted. "In the beginning was the word," etc. That at the center of everything is that which is perfect, that which is God.

Now we know that a series of affirmations and denials will produce a result—that is a technique. We know that gradually the denials turn themselves into affirmations. That is better—that is recognition. We know that as the affirmations turn themselves into that indestructible state of consciousness which can no longer be analyzed, we have what we call a realization. I think a very wonderful example, if it is true—and I don't care whether it is true or not; it is good—is Jesus standing before the tomb of Lazarus. "Father, I thank thee that thou hearest me"—this is recognition. "There is Something, and I am in cooperation with It—my Partner. This is the secret that I have with God, and I know that Thou doest always hear me." No stuttering, no stammering. Here is a man who had learned that the Universe responds to him, and he knew it. It embodies everything that is both faith and understanding, in one category. Then he says, "Lazarus, come on out!" And then they had a party.

Did you ever stop to think of that? I like parties. Now, Jesus was found at parties more than anywhere else. He wasn't a doleful . . . I was going to say, Christian, but there weren't any Christians in his time; they had never been heard of—this terrible thing had not happened to the human mind. Emerson said for every "Stoic" there *is* a Stoic, but in Christendom where is the

Christian? Where is a man who would give his last shirt away? I haven't found him.

Now, we have to embody everything, and every treatment you give will be an experiment with a Principle that is absolute, with a Law that has no choice other than to respond. It is done unto you *as* you believe—good, bad, or indifferent: AS. Something bigger than you does it. It is done unto you— you do not assume the obligations of the universe. "Paul planted, Apollos watered, but God gave the increase." Emerson said it as a philosopher would say it: We are beneficiaries of the divine fact. Browning said it as a poet would say it: "'Tis Thou, God, who giveth; 'tis I who receive." Lowell said it as a poet says it: "Bubbles we earn with a whole soul's tasking, 'tis heaven alone that is given away, 'tis only God may be had for the asking." And the sooner we stop trying to work out of our sinful lives and get over our self-condemnation, the sooner we shall no longer condemn others. Only the pure in heart shall see God, and only the meek shall inherit the earth.

There isn't the slightest chance of that ever failing. Only non-resistance shall be unresisted; only nonviolence shall never be violated. This is the law of elasticity, the fluidity of the universe in which we live, where nothing clashes but the mind of men. It is where the Bible says, "Know that in the beginning God made man perfect, but man has sought out many inventions." These are the thoughts, the feelings, the tools with which you are to deal. Real spiritual mind treatment—very little understood even by those who practice it—is not exercised while we condition anything to time, to experience, to past, to present, or to the future. Spiritual mind treatment is the spontaneous proclamation of a joyful and "a jubilant and a beholding soul," in the only time he can ever know, which is in the moment he proclaims it. No two treatments can ever be alike—there is no formula for treatment. We teach things to do, but we couldn't teach anyone living how best to do them. Could you? Who could teach a nightingale to sing? Who, having captured a nightingale and cut his throat, will have captured his song? There is always that thing which is added to our intellectual attainments—and I am not decrying the intellect; God knows that common sense is the most uncommon thing in the world. But there is that which is beyond the intellect, there is that which uses the intellect, and I personally believe in practices of what I call stretching the intellect—through identification of the individual with everything in the universe . . . the running brook . . . just as Whitman did. He was one of the greatest mystics, he was one with the water, with the foam, with the prostitute and libertine. He said, "I will reject you when the rain no longer falls on you"; and Jesus said, "Where are these thine accusers?"

Now in the mind of the practitioner in our field there must come some kind of a clearance. He can only give what he has. He can only do at the level of what he has realized; and he will have to learn to speak in an affirmative language. It isn't easy. We are not always surrounded by sweet thoughts or sweet people. There is much, not to overcome, but, let us say, to overlook. I always like something Browning said: "Oh! Thou dost all things devise and fashion for the best;/ help us to see with mortal eyes, to overlook the rest." A practitioner must not be depressed by depression or elated by elation. He must not be confused by confusion. It is only as we stand above and beyond them that our word has any power over them. We do not meet resistance on the level of resistance—if we do we stay on that level. We practice a transcendence which does not deal, as the Gita says, with opposites—or as Aurobindo suggested, when he said that the transcendence does not reconcile, it transmutes. "And looking up, he said, 'Father, I thank thee'"—not looking down.

Many of the prophets of Israel and the Old Testament could never get away from seeing the valley of dry bones and the persecution of the Jews—and they still have it. It is created in their mass mind, and it will stay there till they quit it. This is nothing against them; this is cause and effect. Who is there who sees and speaks an affirmative language, who thinks affirmatively? Now, a practitioner is one whose intellect has been satisfied with the logic of his belief, because a house divided against itself cannot stand. All his intellect has been transcended by a feeling which didn't have to resort to logic.

Personally, I believe one need not contradict the other. Plotinus, whom Inge classed as the king of intellectual mystics of the ages, taught grammar and administered the estate of a number of his friends. He was a smart busi-nessman. There is no reason why we should have a faraway look—it is the pure in heart that see God, not by some fantastic fantasy of imagination which wafts one on to a psychic sea of confusion where he thinks he is talk-ing to Jesus and the rest of the saints and begins to go barefooted and lets his hair grow—that is all right; nothing wrong about it; sincere—and al-most everybody in the insane asylum is sincere too. Jesus was right here, his feet were on the ground, his head was in the clouds, he united heaven and earth only because he said, "Behold the kingdom of God is at hand." Jesus would never have united heaven and earth through theology. He would laugh at it—well, maybe not; but he had a great sense of wit when he said, "Let him who is without sin among you cast the first stone."

He didn't call them what you and I would; and when Jesus said, "Be-hold," he wasn't talking about some far-off divine event toward which the whole creation moves. He was talking about what he was looking at. He was talking about what he was seeing. He was describing what he was hearing. It wasn't just a word picture, literal—"Blessed are the pure in heart; blessed are the meek, for they shall inherit the earth." Now, Jesus inherited his earth. He wasn't a weakling. He wasn't a man beat about. Don't tell me that a man who could turn water into wine needed a winery, or to raise grapes. He didn't need a bakery; he could feed the multitude. What did he want of a bakery? He didn't need transportation; he got in the boat and immediately they were at the shore, to the annihilation of time and space as we know it—but it is true. Jesus did not need a bank account; he found money in the fish's mouth. He didn't even at the end of the trail need an undertaker, be-cause he left nothing behind to witness to the belief that anybody is dead. Isn't this terrific!

I do not have any undue superstition about Jesus, but here is something at least we should take as a pattern and identify ourselves, I don't think with the man, but with the message. This is it: "Look unto me and be ye saved."

Now this is the spiritual element in what would otherwise be just a men-tal practice; and just mental practice is no good. It is that thing you can't describe. You all know what I am talking about, and yet I haven't described it. I can't and you can't, but we know there is a language which is not madness, but it is beyond the intellect. There is a testimony that comes down to us through the ages, like art and religion—the only two institutions that the ravages of time have not devastated, and they are both intuitions of the invisible. They are the language of the soul, whether it is singing or dancing or writing, painting, sculpting, or praying. Every man's life is a prayer to the God he believes in, and the God he believes in answers every man at the level of his belief. But since we are mostly hypnotized from the cradle to the grave, our level largely unconsciously is a monotonous repetition of the thoughts of the ages. I happen to believe that just as Freud said a neurotic thought pattern will repeat itself monotonously through life, so the great patterns of human belief repeat themselves generation after generation. Once in awhile someone like Emerson or Jesus breaks down the idol of the past, sees what all are looking at but very seldom see; "primrose by the river's bank a yellow primrose was to him, and nothing more."

But Jakob Böhme* looked into a geranium and saw the Kingdom of God. You and I, that is our business. Just as they have split the physical atom and disclosed solar energy, so you and I in a certain symbolic sense must split the human mental atom, until we disclose here the radiant Son of Heaven. Don't ask anybody ever if this Son exists; don't ask anybody ever if this thing is too good to be true. Don't argue with anybody about it. This is the secret you have with God, and in the silence of your own soul something answers. It doesn't answer as a word, you know; God doesn't have vocal cords like that—it doesn't come as a man with whiskers and reveal something to you that wasn't ever revealed.

There is an ear that listens to everything we think and vibrates back to us the likeness of what we thought; but because it is attuned to the infinite harmony, the range of its listening is limitless. To Jesus, it was just as natural to raise the dead as it is for us to lie down if we feel a little tired. Turning the water into wine was just a gesture of his hand. He knew of the absolute-

---

*German mystic (1575–1624).

ness of the Law of Mind in action; he knew that the whole vast universe is a meditation of God, and that all the galaxies and all the laws and everything that govern it are individuated from the Mind that sleeps in a grain of sand, to wake to some kind of simple consciousness perhaps in a rose, a little more in an animal, and a little more in man, and on and on and on to beings as much beyond us as we are, or perhaps as Jesus himself was, beyond a tadpole—and the whole thing is a living system. And since it is Intelligence that responds to intelligence, and since its response must of a necessity be by correspondence, the Law of the Universe is to us what we are to it. The God of the Universe is more than we appear to be to It; therefore "Ever as the spiral grew, he left the old house for the new."

And don't be afraid to let something in you die, because there shall be no resurrection without a death. I am not speaking about morbidity or ceasing to be, but about hate, fear, uncertainty, just plain cussedness—everything that denies the Omnipresent Fact, the Omnipotent Power, and the beauty and the wonder of the universe in which we live, and everything that denies the overdwelling and indwelling *one* God—not two.

Now this is what practice is—it is applying mental techniques to the realization of spiritual correspondences, not visualized but felt, and tying spiritual realization through mental techniques to the Law of Mind in action, through the theory that disease, discord—everything that we deal with—is Mind in action, creating the form that causes forms objectively, to its own subjective embodiment, individually and collectively. And, as I say, we are perhaps pretty much hypnotized from the cradle to the grave, by that mass concept.

Now you engage in the practice of spiritual mind healing. I don't care whether you call it Religious Science—it doesn't matter, you know; a rose by any other name will smell as sweet, and every moment is a fresh beginning and yesterday never happened and tomorrow hasn't come. God and the universe have no history. That is why Inge said, "Eternity cannot be described by straight lines, because it is not snipped off at either end." In this moment in which you give a treatment, right now, make it complete, make it perfect, even if you have to give another one tomorrow. At any moment you may burst through that shell of fear and doubt and superstition and ignorance—the dearth of spiritual realization—and find disclosed the Son of God.

Let us identify ourselves with that Sonship, with that Presence, and with that Power, for all the power there is and all the presence there is and all the life there is is Love, the Living Spirit Almighty, and all the good there is is right here in this room. The only heaven we shall ever know is now. Behold, the kingdom of God is here. Looking long and steadfastly at the rose, we see His beauty; in the turbulence of the wind and wave, we feel His strength; in the softness of the raindrop on our face, we feel the caress of the Infinite; and in the silence of the desert, a voice speaks: "This is my beloved child." We are that.

5

CHANGE THE TRACK OF TIME

A great friend of Ernest Holmes was the journalist Cobina Wright, who wrote of "Society Doings and People." This great lady was enthralled with Ernest's beliefs, and in September 1958 she interviewed him on prayer and reported his answer in a column with her byline appearing in the *Los Angeles Herald & Express* (later known as the *Herald Examiner*). The article was dated September 25, 1958, and was entitled "How to Pray Told by Church Founder." Dr. Holmes's words follow:

We all believe in prayer, and naturally we hope our prayers will be answered. Let us ask a few simple questions: What is prayer; to what do we pray; where do we pray and how do we pray?

It is self-evident, that no matter how sublime, prayer is an act of the mind based on the belief of a Power greater than itself which responds to it. Prayer is the approach we make to this Power through our thinking and believing.

Where do we pray?

Jesus gave us the answer when He said the Kingdom of God is at hand; we already live in it. Jesus had prayed in the temple since He was a child. He had also prayed by the wayside. He found God everywhere. God is right where we are; God is always there, closer than our very breath.

But the real "where" we pray must be within ourselves. We cannot jump away from ourselves any more than we can jump away from our shadows. Our prayers are within our minds, therefore there is no place to go, as though we might find God more in one spot than another.

Sometimes we feel more peaceful and quiet in one place than another, but that does not mean there is any more of God in the desert, or on the mountain top, in a church or temple. And when we come to realize that

God is already where we are, then we can realize we could just as well pray to the indwelling God on a busy street corner as anywhere else.

How should we pray?

Jesus gave us two answers to this also, when he said, when you pray believe you HAVE and you WILL receive; and another time He said that sometimes we ask and receive not, because we do not ask rightly. Let's think this through this way: God is life; therefore if we pray for life we shall receive it, but if we pray for anything that contradicts life, we couldn't hope to change the nature of God because of our petition. In other words, we pray rightly when we go along with the nature of God, and since God is love, peace, givingness, unity—we could not hope to get results through prayer if we pray contrary to these Divine attributes.

When we pray we should believe we already have what we are asking for. This is difficult, for often we are praying for things we do not now possess. We pray for happiness when we are unhappy; for abundance when we seem destitute; for peace when we are confused; companionship when we are lonely; for health when we are full of pain and suffering. It is not easy to pray for health when we are in pain, but it is possible.

We are told to pray without ceasing, for in due time we shall reap if we faint not. Anyone who practices this over a length of time will discover his whole inward thinking passing from negation to affirmation. What if it does take time and effort? Everything worth while takes time and effort.

So having complied with these few simple demands that Life makes upon us, we may pray for anything, for ourselves or others, any purpose or cause that is good. And we should EXPECT an answer. We should live in a continual expectancy of abundance, of health, of harmony, of love and friendship—merely because we believe the Kingdom of God really is at hand, and in this Kingdom is contained everything necessary to our well-being.

December 23, 1958, three months following this interview, Dr. Holmes received verbal recognition of his article while the people were assembling for the Tuesday Invitational Group meeting. Dr. Holmes then gave the following talk.

Now let us turn to that divine center within us which is both God and man and know that we treat ourselves and we treat God simultaneously—we are in and of the same Presence and the same Power and the same Life. And we are the same Life because there is but One Life, that Life is God's, that Life is perfect, and that Life is our Life now—not bye and bye; right now, here and now. Now we are recognizing the supreme Spirit as the immediate spirit within us, we are recognizing God as the man which we are, in God, which is the only man there is—there is no other man. We are recognizing ourselves as the perfect, complete, whole, happy, divine, radiant consciousness of the living Spirit manifesting as the self. There is One Self, and One Life.

Emerson said it is easy enough in solitude to be independent, but he said the great man is he who in the midst of a crowd can keep with perfect simplicity the independence of his solitude. And that is so true.

Everything in manifestation runs on a time track which is a sequence of a particular chain of cause and effect. You and I do not destroy the law of cause and effect, but we can erase any sequence in it. It wouldn't be any different than going out in the garden and pulling up a certain plant you don't want there. That is running on a sequence of cause and effect, or its own time track, and all of this is but a parallel of the action and reaction that takes place in Mind and Spirit, because the Universe is only one system; and you will notice most of Jesus' illustrations in the Bible were likening the Kingdom of Heaven to what we know about nature, because Jesus knew that, as Emerson said, nature has but a few laws, but she plays them over and over.

All you have to do is squeeze the time track together, because the Alpha and Omega are but two ends of a circuit, and while it is true that in evolution it takes a long time for things to happen, remember this, Jesus did not raise the grapes or press them or distill the wine. He snapped his finger and said, "Turn the water into the other jar." He did something maybe science will do some day.

[George] Lamsa* was telling the ministers the other day about how they got the idea of the Virgin Birth, the Immaculate Conception—that in that time a woman was either a virgin or a widow, and it was always published when they got married whether they were a virgin or a widow, and Mary was a virgin and Joseph was espoused to Mary. That was all there was to it, and look what they have done to the story.

Now in our imagination eliminate the process, and psychically Jesus projected his physical being from one place to another. I believe he did it; there is no reason why he shouldn't have—and all evolution then is for the purpose of uncovering and making active that which was already involuted before it became evoluted. That is why the Bible says, "I am Alpha and Omega, the beginning and end," and in Genesis it says, ". . . the generation of the time when the plant was in the seed before the seed was in the ground."

Nothing could evolve that wasn't first involved, therefore the whole process of evolution in which we believe is itself subject to that which involuted evolution. "In the beginning was the Word, and Word was with God, and the Word was God. And all things were made by the Word, and without the Word was not anything made," etc. The unique thing about our practice, and it is the only field in the world in which such practice takes place, is that we start prior to involution. Every thing out here is subject to evolution, but how many people stop to think that evolution is an effect. And involution, which precedes evolution, is also an effect. Whatever involutes is spontaneous, and whatever evolutes is mechanical. "In the beginning was the Word."

Now we start prior to involution, in treatment; we start with that which is transcendent of involution, consequently it automatically controls evolution. It is very important for us to understand this, because if we subject our treatment, our prayer, our belief to what is already involuted or spoken, it will be subject to the time track that now exists of any sequence. But if we start in this process, we are servants of the thing we obey; consequently, Troward said, we must turn resolutely from anything that suggests that what we are seeking to do is subject to either the past, the present, or the

---

*Biblical scholar.

future—because the sequence of the creative cause starts with pure Intelligence and nothing else; then Intelligence in motion, which involutes; then involution in motion, which evolutes—and the only thing that is spontaneous, the only thing that has self-awareness, is the act of involution, setting the chain in motion.

Troward said we start with pure absolute Intelligence. The movement of Intelligence upon itself, which sets in motion the law of its own being, produces the manifestation of the Word. But the Word is the only thing that knows itself—all other processes are mechanical—and we start, then, with that from two motivations: to set in motion a new sequence of cause and effect, something that never happened before; or perhaps to erase an old one. It has been discovered that denial will tend to erase it, and affirmation will most certainly create a new one. But in such degree as we subject our word, our treatment, to anything that is in a process, we are making the process comply with that word and consciously or unconsciously, ignorantly or not, we are subjecting the possibility of the manifestation of this thing to the limitation of the sequence already set in motion. Therefore we have to turn away from it—and this is the difficult thing and why Jesus said, "Judge not according to appearances." Now we do it. Every scientist does it.

A friend asked if I ever talked with atheists or agnostics, and I said, there isn't any such thing. The thing that makes a person think he is one isn't that he doesn't believe in something; it is that he doesn't believe in the way people believe in something. In other words, their revolt is against theology and dogma and superstition and ignorance, and I don't blame them. And he asked what would be the main objection to believing as we believe, and I was interested he said "we," which is the first time he ever said this—and I just let it alone and said nothing. I never try to "sell" what we believe, because if we try to sell it, they won't buy it anyway, and it is only when we "do" it that someone will want to buy it. I said the materialists believe in intelligence in the universe but not in consciousness, and he asked what is the difference. I said a thing can be intelligent without being aware. The universe is governed intelligently. The materialists see the intelligence at work but they will not believe that there is a consciousness in the intelligence—a self-awareness. But it is a very peculiar thing to me, because they themselves maintain the prerogative of accepting or rejecting, and all that self-awareness is, is awareness operating at the level of self-knowingness rather than compulsion.

The Universe is governed by intelligence, but we believe that on top of intelligence there is consciousness, self-awareness—there is a perceiver as well as the act of perception, and the law set in motion by the perception. And of course this is right, because even to deny it would affirm the prerogative of not accepting it, and the moment one affirms a prerogative of conscious rejection, he has passed from the field of mechanical reaction into a field of spontaneous choice, else he couldn't do the one and not the other.

The very fact that you and I are talking is proof enough that the Universe, as I said the other day to him, contains an Infinite Awareness which we do not understand other than at the level of our own awareness, because our own awareness is It at that level—and we will never find any other God. But we will find plenty more of this One Cause. We are never going to use it up, just because we aren't going to find it someplace else—and that is the essence of the great spiritual philosophies of the ages, is the very epitome of everything we believe. It is the thing Jesus understood, perhaps better than any other single individual; but as Lamsa was telling us the other day, Jesus did nothing new. He put in a more simple language that which he had learned from childhood, which I don't doubt, but he added to it a personal element—the complement to the Mosaic law of impersonality—and made the Universe a living thing in the consciousness of every person, in the only place that he can experience anything: he experiences all things at the level of his comprehension of that which he experiences.

But it goes further than that—he partakes of the creative process of the original cause. Jesus said, "As the Father hath life within Himself, so hath he given it to the Son to have life within himself, that whatsoever things the Son seeth the Father do, that doeth the Son also, that the Father may be glorified in the Son." In other words, what Jesus was saying was, just as God, or the First cause, is Absolute Life, so your life is the same Absolute

Life (so hath He given it to the Son within Himself), and it is the same Life; it isn't apart from It, it isn't approaching It—it is It.

And again we have to realize the Ancient of Days, the Changeless, the Truth to which nothing has ever happened—because God has no history, as such. If God had a history, there is nothing you and I could do but lie right down and say, Let it happen anytime now. Therefore as Emerson said, the Ancient of Days is in the latest invention—wherever we think, the Originating Creative Intelligence that sets the Universe in place is thinking, knowing with the awareness, the same Intelligence, backed by the same Law, as it was when it spoke the nebulae into existence—because they are being spoken into existence everywhere.

Creation is going on. The Universe is a spiritual system, can't run down and can't wear out, and now that Thing is what we are at the level of our intelligence, our awareness, our consciousness. We cannot change It; we can change our own level only by stretching out our own awareness, our own consciousness, our own intellect. But we come up against new fields that sometimes baffle us because we try to get our arms around the ways and the means, not knowing that they flow out of the Cause. This is why we say we choose but we don't outline. We can't help but choose, because if we chose not to choose, we would be choosing just as much as though we chose to choose. There is no difference.

It is like people in our field who say, "Well, I don't believe in treating for money, I don't believe in being material," and I ask what they *do* treat for, and they say, "I treat to know that God's idea has everything it needs." And so I say, "What do you think you are thinking about if you want money subjectively? Why would money come instead of food?" People, including lots of us, are stupid, superstitious, and ignorant, and they can't impersonalize a Law to the extent that it knows nothing about good and bad; big and little; yesterday, today, and tomorrow; and has no history, but in the split second of our perception spontaneously flows into something that even it never did before. Because if God didn't do something right this minute in me—this talk was never given before; it can never be given again—if God didn't do something spontaneous in me, both God and I would die of impoverishment of intelligence. That is why you never give the same treatment twice. You may treat the same person twice, and you may treat the same condition twice—indeed, one should treat it until it is right, if he can—but never twice alike. It is only as there is poured into this mold which thought makes—thought is the mold, but it isn't a creative thing in itself—a feeling which now springs into existence for the first time, that it is really a creative art, and treatment certainly is a creative art.

And we have to believe, then, that this creative process is still going on in us as us, and we should expect to see something new—every minute. We should never expect the same thing to happen twice alike. We should never expect life to descend into a monotony where there would be boredom. And it is an interesting thing that psychologically it is now known that the ennui of a lack of enthusiastic interest in life is what produces most fatigue in living. This has been well worked out in psychology: They call it "tired blood," but it is mental anemia really. It is a lack of an enthusiastic interest in life.

When you see someone who doesn't have any enthusiasm—life and enthusiasm, life and action—it has nothing to do with age, nothing to do with whether you are educated, or your intellect. It has to do with the need, the irresistible need, that the creative energy in the Universe shall flow through you, because it *is* you; and if you don't give it an outlet, all you will get out of that which is freedom is a congestion. So all congestion is creative, merely for the lack of an idea of flow—all of it—and all we have to do is to unthink the congestion. Constipation doesn't know it is constipation; it doesn't know it is anything, and it doesn't know anything. It only knows what is known about it, because it *is* what is known about it. And what it is and what is known about it are not separated from each other but are equal, identical, and interchangeable, just like the energy and mass of Einstein—it is the same thing. Therefore we attack it not in the sequence of its time track, subject to the law of its being—but previous to it, to set in motion a new causation.

And so freedom flows out of the same thing that produced bondage—there is no dualism anywhere. I know people who say, "I wouldn't do anything so materialistic as treat for an automobile." *I* would. They think they are getting around God or something they are still afraid of—and Jesus said to turn away from everything that looks like it. This isn't very easy to do, because the subject it images of the picture is in our own minds, and there is no difference between the picture and the thing. I always tell people, if they want money, to treat for it. The treatment is all right provided there is nothing in it that can hurt anything—you, someone; nothing that would hurt anything or coerce anything. The moment all those elements are taken out, is it not all right for an artist to paint a sunflower instead of a rose, if he wishes to? We don't fool the mirror; we can make up faces in it, and it makes them right back, and the only way to get a new reflection is to get a new image, and the only thing that can change the image is its maker. And the only thing that can set a new sequence of involution in motion that will produce a new evolution that will produce a new situation is to start not with that which is already moving. We all do; and probably if we tune in somewhere, we help it out. But here is something we probably don't give enough thought to, it is so darned simple.

I know many people who say they will treat for substance and supply but not for money; but the subjective image is there, so that in treating for substance and supply they hope they will get some money. When they wanted wine, Jesus said This is the way to get wine; when they wanted money, he said Go and get that fish over there; when they wanted more fish, he said Cast your net there. There is nothing in the Universe that denies us anything unless that which we affirm denies the nature of the Universe in which we live, and if it does, there is nothing going to come back. If it came back, it would come back meagerly and for a very short duration of time— but that which affirms the Allness is the Allness affirming its own being. I don't think there is anything in the world that isn't all right to treat for. There might be some things that perhaps aren't worthwhile, in the light of a larger experience, but perhaps they are all right.

Is there anything big, little? The same energy that holds the Empire State Building in place holds a peanut on a table. It is an impersonal force operating upon everyone and everything: "He causeth the sun and rain to come alike to the just and unjust"; but we measure it out as good and bad, big and little, right and wrong—mostly as a projection of our own unconscious ideation, what is going on inside of ourselves.

There is a logic, a super-logic beyond all logic you and I understand—a logic not based on the sequence of cause and effect, as our logic is. No matter how perfect our logic is, if the conclusion is based on a false or untrue conclusion to begin with—a wrong premise without departing from logic and mathematics—you can fabricate the most elaborate system that seems to be true, but is rotten at the roots. That is why Emerson said—and he certainly was not referring to me; but he was referring to us as a group, not consciously—we are the advent of that thing to which he looked forward, just as Jesus was not the Avatar or Messiah; the birth of the man Jesus was never prophesied in the Old Testament. It was prophesied by the Great Prophets that the time must come when the Thing they believed in should be incarnated somewhere, as It must and is still doing.

But Emerson said, Beware when God lets loose a thinker on this planet; then everything is going to be subject to change—everything. Why is that? Because a new premise is included. But most of our logic is built on the fact-fallacy of an inadequate premise; and philosophically and spiritually and theologically that false premise is dualism—not *dualism,* but a *belief* in dualism. No matter how subtle it is—and it creeps into New Thought and Christian Science and all these things—there is no such thing as a human mind and a Divine Mind. There is no such thing as a Universe divided against Itself. There is no such thing as dualism. There is no such thing as God *and* man—there can't be. There is only What Is and the way It works. There can be nothing in the Universe ultimately but action and reaction, the action being conscious intelligence and awareness, and the reaction intelligence unconsciously operating without an awareness.

Now let's treat for next Sunday's meeting, over in El Monte, and where everyone comes to hear him* and receives the benediction of his consciousness and light of his awareness, love of his heart, intelligence of his mind,

---

*i.e., minister Ed Thompson.

and companionship of his spirit in beauty, in joy, in happiness, in wholeness, in love, wisdom—and so shall everyone in that section know about this place, because even now we are acquainting them in the only Mind that exists, which is our mind, their mind, God's Mind—there is no other mind but this Mind.

Now let's treat to get rid of this smog in L.A.—to get back beyond all the arguments, back of everything to a time we all remember when it wasn't here, knowing it doesn't have to be here now—that whatever its cause may be, it can be ascertained and neutralized—and our word must find the outlet of that purity of atmosphere, that perfection which has always been associated with this remarkable country. And our dissipation of all this smog and fog in our own mind means that it is dissipated in fact. The word finds outlet in reality.

Let's know our President's message is listened to, realization of its reality is felt. Let's make it the law of our own being that we are happy, successful. . . .

6

DYNAMICS AND ANALYSIS
OF TREATMENT

After dinner our custom was to watch several of Dr. Holmes's favorite TV shows—*Bonanza, Maverick,* and any of the people from Ernest's wide range of acquaintance making personal appearances. Following this we discussed people, I guess, for whom Ernest or I might be doing prayer work (Spiritual Mind Treatment).

I learned more in these talks than in studies, classes, and lectures. Dr. Holmes was patient and taught me that even though our work was teaching and practice, we often fell down in the practice, because we subconsciously doubted our authority to pray.

In March 1959 Dr. Holmes gave one of his finest talks to the Tuesday Group on this subject. This was four weeks following the Feb. 12th Whittier Cosmic Consciousness Experience.

Now let's talk a little about analysis in treatment. What we believe in is practical, and I am particularly interested in the dynamics of our work. We collapsed the time in this El Monte church, less than 6 months, and I presented their charter last Sunday—shortest span of time we have ever accomplished this, I believe. And in presenting their charter, I said there are two things a Religious Science church stands for, and one is the recognition of the divine Presence, which of a necessity must be personal to each one of us, since it is personalized in us. And since no two persons are alike, it must be uniquely personalized to each individual, because it is individualized in each individual *as* that individual.

One of the things I think people in philosophic abstractions fail to realize is the inevitable necessity accompanying our teaching of a universality which is indivisible and in which we live—the inevitable, axiomatic necessity that even that which is universal must be intimately personal to that which it personalizes. It is a different concept, you know, than "the human down here and the Old Man up there." Did you see *Green Pastures* last night? I sat spellbound, but I didn't like the end, where the suffering came out. That is the morbidity which the human mind hasn't yet gotten over; the human mind is drugged with the concept of suffering as a divine imposition. It is intellectually and emotionally and psychologically drugged, because there is a certain morbidity about it that it loves to indulge in—like the old woman who said you could take all the weddings you want, but there is nothing so harrying as a good funeral. And she was right.

That morbidity is very well recognized in psychology, and that is why Freud said a neurotic thought pattern repeats itself with monotonous regularity throughout life—it is always morbid. People have these neurotic thought patterns—we all have them to a degree. If they are rather serious, they desire to be alone, that they may suffer with them. They become antisocial for the purpose of sitting on their fannies and feeling bad. This is true—it is not facetious; it is absolutely true. Now it is not because the real person wants it, but because the *neurosis* wants it. Rather interesting, isn't it? So much so that in all psychiatric work one of the first things is to separate the neurosis from the neurotic. Any good psychologist will tell you that it is not the neurotic but the neurosis who is talking. Mrs. Eddy called it error making a claim, and she was right. She said to separate the belief from the believer.

It is this thing that told Jesus not to cast the devils out of the pigs, etc. At the end of *Green Pastures*, God said he has to suffer and they all have to suffer, and this is what goes back to the old theology—but the whole thing was beautiful. Now we all suffer and keep on suffering because we don't know better, but it is always the repetition of a thought pattern that doesn't belong to us—*invariably.* Suffering in and of itself can be neither person, place, nor thing—law, cause, medium or effect of itself—but it certainly sets up a big front and screams and argues, so that Jastrow* said one of the main troubles

*Joseph Jastrow, American psychologist and author.

is what he called the inertia of thought patterns, which he said actually argued as though they were entities.

The neurotic likes to be by himself, that the neurosis may endlessly repeat itself; and it is always attached to certain definite experiences which now have no relationship to the apparent objective situation that causes it, but rather uses that upon which to play its familiar tune. It is always that way, practically, and recognized.

We have the concept of a divine Presence which is personal to us. That is the basis of all religions, all life—of everything—and believe it or not it is the basis of every man's reaction to life. I don't care who he is or where he came from, what he does or what he believes, fundamentally at the root of all his concepts of life is his conscious or unconscious sense of relationship to the Universe in which he lives—whether he is at home in it and secure with it, or not. It doesn't matter who or what he is. As Emerson said, we have mistaken Jesus the man for virtue and the possibility of all men. Therefore we act endlessly as we do this week.* The whole performance of this week is foreign to my mind—I wasn't brought up in it. I could not crawl on the cross with Jesus on Friday and then crawl off it on Sunday. I just could not do it.

This whole idea of morbidity that goes with religion is based on a sense of insecurity, on a sense of not being at home in the Universe, not being wanted, needed and loved, not belonging. It is based on a completely dualistic concept philosophically, therefore it is based on a completely dualistic concept theologically (therefore a completely materialistic concept philosophically), and neither is compatible with modern physics—*neither*. You cannot reconcile very much: you can reconcile no philosophy of materialism or theology of dualism with the findings of modern science. That is why in the last 25 years, and last 10 and last 5—and it will increasingly accumulate— that is why scientific people of the last few years and of our day and who now begin to write on more than the technicalities of their science, begin to philosophize and begin, whether they know it or not, to accept the very

---

*i.e., Holy Week in the Christian liturgical calendar.

position our philosophy is based on—infinite Intelligence acting as Law, and infinite Presence acting as Person. And this will increasingly accumulate until the need of man will be met in this field.

Arthur Compton* said that science has discovered nothing to contradict the concept of a universal Mind to which men are as its offspring—and that is interesting. He said materialism was 25 years behind the times.

Now we have this first concept; and the next one is the dynamics that go with it—and I think they belong together and should be taught together, whether we call it the law of Good that is greater than we are, which it is; or whether we call it the divine Principle, as Christian Science does, which is a good enough term for it; or whether we call it the universal Subjectivity as Troward did; or call it the Soul of the Universe, as it was originally taught; or the feminine side of nature, which receives the impress of the masculine and is impregnated with it and gives birth to creation, which is the immaculate Child; or whether we go with Plotinus and say there is a phase of Mind which is a blind force not knowing, only doing—it doesn't make any difference.

Because we are not only surrounded by divine Presence, which responds to us as Person—we are surrounded by a universal Principle, which responds to us as Law; and to this concept of Law we must add the concept of creative Intelligence without self-awareness, other than the awareness of what It is doing, not even knowing why It is doing it. That is why Plotinus called it a blind force not knowing, only doing. That is why Mrs. Eddy said, "Christian Scientists, be a law unto yourselves." That is why Jesus said, "The words I speak unto you, they are Spirit and they are Life. Heaven and earth will pass away, but *they* can't."

They have all recognized the universality of a Law which acts subjectively to, maybe not a higher Principle . . . but as a self-awareness which operates in It, around It, and through It—"The Spirit moved upon the face of the deep." We just call it the Presence and the Power and the Law, and that simplifies it and contains the whole works; and it is good to keep it

---

*American physicist.

simple. We believe in the Presence which we commune with, and the Law which we definitely use, consciously and concretely and for specific purposes. There is nothing wrong with this, there is nothing materialistic about what we call demonstration. If a person in a Christian theology would say there was, he would have to refute all the works of Jesus, because he based his whole authority on *what happened*—the whole thing. Jesus asked no authority other than *what happened* when he spoke his word. They asked, "By what authority do you do this?" and he said, "See what is going on." This is authority enough.

Now we believe in both, but we believe the finite mind, which merely is our use of the infinite Mind at a finite level . . . of course there is no such thing as a finite level, you know. Someone asked the other day, what is real of this and what is unreal, and I said, we do not deal with unreality, ever. There is no such thing as *what isn't*; there just can't be. We deal only with reality, no matter what face it shows to us. We know that even in reality there is an action and reaction which by the very law of freedom could temporarily bind us until we knew the difference between bondage and freedom; because if it couldn't, we wouldn't be free. We are bound by the cords of freedom, paradoxical as it sounds. If we weren't, we would be bound. That is why Annie Besant* said, "Karma is the law that binds the ignorant but frees the wise." The same wind will blow a boat safely into the harbor or wreck it, depending on the way it is used.

Now I want to see a group of people . . . who if you almost have to beat them over the head with a club to make them do the few simple things that a group of people have to do to prove, as a group of people, what this group of people believe in. We have not exercised enough authority in our movement; and when I say that I shudder at my use of the word, because I am not talking about the authority of an organization, but the authority of something it uses. This is the new idea of authority we must introduce. It isn't my authority or yours. It is the authority of the thing we teach people, because it will never work very much other than on the basis of somebody recogniz-

---

*English theosophist.

ing its authority, will it? How can it? "My words fly upward, my thoughts remain below; my words without thoughts cannot to heaven go." The word is only a mold, a mechanical thing; the word is not a spontaneous thing, because it doesn't say itself. Therefore even the word has to be a reaction of the consciousness that generates it, doesn't it? "The words that I speak unto you, they are Spirit, they are Life." But some words are not very much alive!

At any rate, the word is a mold; but the thought, the feeling, the complete acceptance, the complete embodiment of what it does mean . . . when Jesus said, "Heaven and earth will pass away, but my words remain"—this was probably a literal statement. It seems to me if Lazarus hadn't come out of the tomb when Jesus told him to, Jesus would have had to crawl in with him and they would still be there. We cannot imagine an absolute affirmation knowing anything about even a relative denial, can we? That is why I think it is so important we realize that the human mind may not deny, even though it tries to. It may only affirm in two ways. If there were such a thing as the possibility of an absolute denial of the reality of the Universe, the Universe would be operating against Itself—do you realize that?—and science has found no energy in nature that will destroy itself. Jesus said, "If I do this by Beelzebub"—which is just a word picture, because he knew there wasn't any devil—"that wouldn't be good, because that would be a power divided against itself, and the world cannot operate that way."

Now these things we have to know; but just knowing them isn't enough. It isn't just enough for us to know God is Love—I mean it is a theory; if our arms are not around each other, how do we know God is Love? "Love only knows and comprehendeth love." Jesus said, "If you want to know about this doctrine, do it, and you will find out whether it is true; there is no other way." "Act as though I am and I will be"; "Be firm and you will be made firm"; "Believe and it shall be done," etc.

Now our conviction about the mechanics of things probably exists at the intellectual level and may exist at a feeling level; but if it exists only at intellectual level, remember this: a man with a good intellect may make a mold—and a perfect one mechanically, mathematically, with complete precision—but he wouldn't fill it with life. So in addition to that which he may mechanically do, there has to be a meaning; and there is no creative mold without a meaning—there just can't be; it is an unfertile seed.

So that feeling, I think, is something that while it will not deny the acceptance or rejection or analysis of intellect . . . the intellect may perceive, analyze, accept, reject, deny, affirm, and go through terrific performances until it builds an edifice or theoretical ladder from the earth to the skies; but it is a great question whether the intellect would ever climb the ladder, as such. *What* climbs the ladder, *whoever,* need not be repudiated by the intellect—is that clear? There is something else that goes with it. Now that something else that goes with it is really what is meant by the philosophy of mysticism, of intuition. It is a language of the feeling which, while it does not deny the intellectual conviction, sort of sweeps it up, adds warmth and color and feeling to it, which every artist will know as the difference between a technique and temperament. So the intellect may furnish a perfect technique, and I think it should—because if we have a science to teach, there is a principle involved, the way it works; it may be taught; a technique may be delivered and somebody use it, and we get a result. This I think we should never lose sight of, else there will be people running around looking kind of wild-eyed, saying, "This guy has such a terrific understanding; and when I get good enough or know enough or reach this point of exultation . . ."—you know what I mean; and such people never get anyplace in our movement. They go on year after year, and after they have been in it for 40 years go back to a practitioner for treatment of a headache.

They don't quite seem to see: "I am the guy; this is it; this is the way it works; God speaks." I chose four subjects to use in June when I will speak for Carmelita:* God's Body; God's Business; God's Friendship; and God's Voice—as simple as that; arriving at the same thing. Now whether or not we call this a mystical concept, it will make a wonderful series, I think. Emma Curtis Hopkins† is the best example of mysticism—metaphysical mysticism, as we understand it—as Plotinus is an example of intellectual mysticism, too

---

*Carmelita Trowbridge, Religious Science minister (later, independent).
†American religious metaphysician and mystic, New Thought "teacher of teachers."

difficult; and of course Eckhart and his mysticism is most beautiful of all to read. The man who wrote this knew what he was talking about, it is so darned simple.

Here is where a certain form of mysticism . . . but remember, mysticism is not mystery; mysticism is not psychism—it doesn't get hunches to sell this stock or where to drill an oil well. That is psychism, and nothing wrong with it—part of what is, part of the knowingness of the ever-present Mind that put the oil there; and it can be done. But I am talking about a transcendence, a something, a feeling that is beyond thought. It is beyond analysis, beyond the possibility of the intellect's comprehending; yet as I said last week at the close, this thing we are talking about is something which the isolated intellect can neither know nor comprehend, because it has not attached itself to the concept of a liquid universe governed by flowing laws which are intelligent—or as Emerson said, "We see the universe as solid fact; God sees it as liquid law."

It would be inexplicable to the intellect and absolutely impossible for analysis, any kind of analysis, to take mind beyond the threshold or that entrance to the thing that is not explained but must be accepted. I would like to cover that point, because a lot of people say, "After all, you are getting us to a place where you go off the deep end." This is one of the things the other psychologists harangue against Carl Jung about—they say he has gone off the deep end of mysticism. He hasn't gone off any deep end at all. He just went to a place where they couldn't follow. But the strange thing is, every scientific research in the world does the same thing, but people don't realize it, through a process of analysis, or induction and deduction . . . because induction is only a series of steps of deduction—there is no such thing as induction and deduction in reasoning, any more than there is any such thing as affirmation and denial metaphysically; they are just different steps in the same thing. I think that is why Kettering* said that every invention is an intuition, and the progress of the invention in the development of its techniques is but a series of lesser intuitions. When you follow it out, it would

*Charles Kettering, American electrical engineer and inventor.

have to be—because God cannot analyze but can only affirm. Therefore His language is yea and amen.

The mind—we will say the intellect—may conduct itself by a process to the doorway, gateway—Evelyn Underhill said there is a place in every person's mind that is this gateway—the gateway through which things inflood rather than outgo. Browning said, "It is Thou, God, Who giveth; 'tis I who receive." We are beneficiaries of the divine Fact. You and I didn't make the Universe; we may only accept It. We cannot even reject It. We may seem to; therefore it will appear to us in the form of our rejection—but it will appear in some form, from the lowest hell to highest heaven; and they are all made out of the same thing, because the lowest hell will become the highest heaven if you become harmonious there, and vice-versa.

Now the intellect may conduct the mind; they do this in science. They say, Here is a principle, it will always work this way; and they don't try to explain it. But in religion and philosophy we try to explain everything that is inexplicable. This is one of the fallacies of theology and philosophy—I don't mean all theologians or all philosophers, but these people who run around and say what God's will is or what God's purpose is, or what God said, etc., etc.

The intellect, then, may lead itself just by cold-blooded reasoning, by mathematics. Pythagoras said it is all mathematics anyway. It may lead us to the place of the divine influx, but it won't cross that threshold through analysis. It is impossible, because here we get to the fact that the chicken lays the egg and the egg comes out of the chicken and the chicken out of the egg; and there is no rationality to it at all—doesn't even make common sense. Seen this way, there can be no such thing as life, because there is nothing to support it. Look everywhere you may and see if you will discover the song of the nightingale; dissect its body, etc. You just can never capture the song. It is just there; it is self-existent. Nothing made God.

So the intellect takes us to the place of acceptance. Now we want even more than this; we want the acceptance of not just a nebulous, theoretical Universe of possibility—and I don't really mean that, because if that were so, you would be conducting yourself to a Universe inane, inactive, unproductive; and you might fall again back upon your reason, which might even help out here a little, to help save something that is wrong—because there isn't a song. We will say there cannot be any such thing as an awareness that is not aware, there is nothing as an unexpressed life, there cannot be any such thing as a knower and have nothing known—there is no such thing as a Creator without a Creation.

Therefore, having arrived at the boundless possibility of limitless self-existence—inexplicable acceptance, even by pure mathematics—the logic is that something will have to happen to get beyond the threshold: something new, something wonderful—a new Creation. And so although we do not carry that which is explicable beyond the threshold of the inexplicable, we have not arrived at a place where nothing makes sense and it is all a vacuum and a dream. We have merely taken ourselves to the place where God sings a song—that is all—whether it is in the life of invention or whatever; but we have now reached a transcendence which no longer deals with the opposite, because it transmutes.

It becomes an affirmative language, and I think this is where we try to take our treatment. But now here we are coherent; we don't blubber; we are not incoherent. There is no God who is either praised or glorified by such inanities—not any kind. A God who has to be told He is a God is no kind of God, just like any person who is wrapped up in himself is wrapped up in a very small package; and it is all the same thing.

Here we merely venture forth into the boundless, into the limitless, into the possibility which is transcendent; but it will still be coherent. Right has to still express itself, and that is why even in modern psychology people like Kunkel* speak of the "unlived life." The creativity has to go on, and where it is refused outlet, it merely piles up the energy as alienation psychologically, because the conflict is always what is between the push here and the push back there. It is always in *here*; as Horney[†] said, always here at the center there will be four things—rejection, guilt, insecurity, and anxiety.

---

*Fritz Kunkel, psychologist.
[†]Karen Horney, American psychoanalyst and author.

Now we want this dynamic thing to enter; but we would like it to *enter*: to feel noncombative, nonresistant, nonaggressive, in the sense of aggression against something that returns the aggression—"Who takes up the sword will perish by it"; might will be met with might, meanness with meanness. I got upset recently over several very little things: The first day I got fussed up over a little thing, then the next day something else happened just like it, and then another day something else just like it, and finally I said, "What's going on?!" I talked to myself about it. Emerson said imitation is suicide, over the doorway of consistency write "thou fool," and be a nonconformist— and all he was trying to do was to say, "Watch that spark in your own consciousness; you have something there—it is your only inheritance, because heaven and earth will pass away, but this thing won't. In talking to someone the other day, I said, "Let's forget that someone close to you and to me passed away and think of it in the broader viewpoint: When he arrived, the rest of us were here who were here. He got to the same place we came to, didn't he?—We all got to the same place when we got here. Find me one atom of logic that says we won't all get to the same place when we leave." If you are going to judge the future by the past, and the unknown by the known—it is as simple as that, isn't it? Browning said, "There won't any- thing be left out when God has made the pile complete." I like this kind of thinking. Seneca* said, "Keep faith with reason, for she will convert thy soul." It will also help us out in every other way.

So we go back to this place where the Universe is now going to present itself for the first time to us in a unique way. We are not going to get on the other side of that gate and never do anything again. As the Universe abhors a vacuum, it is impossible for it to be inactive; but it is active, as Lao-tzu said, with an activity that seems inactive. He said all things are possible to him who perfectly practices inactivity, or inaction. Plotinus said, "When our face is turned to the One, our work is done better even though our back is to our work." That is mysticism. The Bible says, "Look unto me and be ye saved all the ends of the earth." They are all talking about the same thing—

---

*Roman statesman, dramatist, and philosopher (4 B.C.?–A.D. 65).

because it is only when we reach this place of noncombat, nonmonopoly, where no one has anything that takes anything away from somebody. . . . So I said to myself the other day, "Three things have happened, so you are messing around and meeting one thing with another." Either we free ourselves of these things or we are bound by externalities and there is no freedom, and nothing. So I asked myself, "What goes here?" and decided I better start a direction these things can't follow, because as long as they follow, they will have a story to tell—and we might look at it till we believed it. We have to get to a point of nondualism, noncombativeness, where there is nothing even to be saved or rectified or regulated, and for the first time we will arrive at the only place that can do all this, because in this nonresistive silence is the real affirmation and real action. All things are possible to him who can perfectly practice inaction. All action will flow out of that—like all voices will come out of the stillness or silence. So let's do it.

> Now we are right here at this threshold where we are going to leave behind everything that says we can't step over. We are not going to take any of the darkness in with us, we are not going to take any troubles here, because there are no troubles this side of the gate. We are not going to take any impoverishment, fear, misunderstanding, or hurt—no patterns of antiquity that are repeating themselves over and over again just to show they have that much life. All this is behind us. This is what Jesus meant when he said, "Get thee behind me, Satan."
>
> And we know that where we now are, all joy exists, all perfection is forever. This is light, love, laughter, a song. It is peace; it is still. But here the most terrific action takes place we have ever imagined: Everything is alive; everything is awake, aware, whole; and everything is joy. Do we, then, drink from the well of salvation—the well which no man dug—and eat of the bread which no man made, and drink the wine which was not distilled—?

7

NO DIFFERENCE BETWEEN
THE PRAYER AND WHAT IT DOES

—————

We don't hold thoughts, because creativity is immutable, and you can't stop that which is continuous and everlasting. In other words you can't hold the wind in your hand.

Relax and let it happen. Our attempts to force too much defeat us. The more you strain, the harder it is.

This talk of Nov. 18th (Thanksgiving time) 1958 enforced this conviction.

I sometimes think that Dr. Holmes bounced ideas off me for my reaction. I was under the impression that he thought that if *I* needed it, everybody else did.

We are knowing the activity of the living Spirit within us, the one and only Presence, the All-Power operative now perfectly and permanently without effort, as we see it, known through us as the Law of our being or whatever we speak that word for, careless of the results because we are certain of them, with no burden or responsibility other than the knowing—knowing why we know what we know. We hold our mind to the perfect influx and outgo of absolute divine Intelligence, Law of order, Presence of peace and power, and the Essence of beauty. We know there is that within us which sees, knows, understands, and comprehends the meaning of itself, accepts it, without strain, without effort. And as we turn our thought to this church, this institution and all its branches and all the many phases of its activities, the word that goes out from it, whether written or spoken or on the air—we know that word carries with it the complete authority of itself, perfect realization of itself. Healing and wholeness go with it, and everything that every practitioner in this Movement prospers and heals instantly. Wherever this word is known, wherever it is spoken, the Law of its being is manifest in joy and harmony and love and wisdom.

Now we turn to our own consciousness—this thing which alone can, so far as we are concerned, be aware. We know it is infinitely aware; it is perfectly aware; it is permanently aware—all the Presence and all the Power there is in the Universe. Now let us establish in consciousness a church we are starting in El Monte—because this church stands for the conscious knowledge of the Presence, the power of perfection, of wholeness, of the manifestation of the living Spirit in Its own work, for God is not only in Creation, God is Creation—or else there isn't any Creation—and we are aware of this, we are establishing in our own consciousness a center to which everyone may come who needs help, who wishes to give help, a consciousness of love and beauty. We are establishing a thing of gladness and joy, and there is no weight, no burden, no heaviness, no past, no weariness connected with it. It is a song—a hymn of praise and a song of joy and a triumphant procession. It is a thing of beauty, of deep feeling, of high vision and of laughter, of the silent communion of the soul with its source, and the outpouring of the Spirit in its own Creation. Everything that we ordinarily would think, by a process of evolution shall unfold over a period of time we announce to be right now and here, in this time and this place and today. All that is ever to be, is; and it is going to be all that there is. Therefore all that there is, is what it is right now, without delay. That is good.

How many of you have ever read Emma Curtis Hopkins? You have to get the key to what she is talking about, because it sounds screwy until you find out what she is saying. But I suppose when Jesus said, "Behold the Kingdom of God is at hand," they all looked up and said, "The man is crazy!" They didn't see what he was looking at. They did look at what he was seeing. Now that is pretty good; and it is true. They were all *looking at* it, and he *saw* it. And I thought, Sunday—I was down in Mexicali; we had been in Palm Springs and drove on down there; it is the dirtiest place I have ever seen; I didn't know there was anything like it anyplace; they seem to be very happy people, more happy than we are; happiness is a different thing than we think it is; you can't buy it—and I thought to myself, where the vision is, there the Thing is.

This is the whole theme of Emma Curtis Hopkins's *High Mysticism*: Where is the vision? Are you looking at a valley of dry bones or at mountain peaks and summits of splendor and glory? Because wherever the vision is, there is the imagery that molds the circumstances under which we must live. And I got to thinking quite a bit about it, because I was waiting for some people, and I thought, "This is the way it will be while these people think this way. They are not worse off than we are and we are not better than they are. This hasn't anything to do with big or little or right or wrong or round or square. There are no comparative things in the universe—there is no God that knows God is little in one place and big in another. The Universe itself knows nothing about good and evil—it only knows that It is; and what It knows, *is*; and what *is*, It knows; and Its knowing is the isness of what is. It is the law of its propulsion and the love of its impulsion, because it is the givingness of the Infinite Self to Its self that it may experience Itself. Because if It experienced Itself without manifestation, It would remain in a dream state.

As long as there is a Creator, there will be a Creation. And as long as there is a Creation, there will be a Creator in and as and through the Creation. It will be a manifestation, but it will not be separate from what manifests. It won't be the Creator *there* and the thing *here*; and you will notice that in treatment, the treatment is the thing. The treatment is its own law, it is its own announcement, it is its own action. It is its own cause, its own effect. And it is its own whatever we call time, space, or anything in between. And the treatment contains everything that can ever come out of it—and nothing can ever come out of it that isn't in it.

That is what people do not understand about our science. When I say *our science*, it would be the same in Christian Science, Unity, and any of the New Thought or metaphysical movements. Most people think, "Well, holding thoughts is good." *The Power of Positive Thinking* has had the biggest sale of any book in modern years, and it is a very good book and has helped millions of people—but it isn't what we teach. This is no criticism. I think this man is the greatest and is doing more good than anyone else in the nonmetaphysical field. But we don't sit around holding positive thoughts. You might say God doesn't say, "I will plant corn if it doesn't rain tomorrow," because God is the corn and the tomorrow and the planting and the harvest, and it all transpires in the Mind of God—and the Omega is in the Alpha. Psychology will say, "Well, suggestion is a very good thing for people"; but it isn't what we teach—because we don't suggest anything to anybody. And someone will say, "Yes, whatever you concentrate and set your will to, you can do." This has nothing to do with what we are talking about.

We are talking about two things only, which must suppose something back of them; perception supposes a perceiver, but we are talking about the perceiver and the thing perceived as being equal, identical, and interchangeable in exactly the same sense, I suppose, as Einstein said: Energy and mass are equal, identical, and interchangeable. He *did not* say that energy operates on mass; we *do not* say that Spirit operates on matter. He did not say energy operates *in* mass. These things are what he *didn't* say; he didn't say energy operates on it or in it—he said it *is* it; and if it were not it, mass and energy could not be interchangeable, could they? If the Universe is something other than a thing of thought or a movement of Intelligence, then there is no movement of thought or Intelligence that could affect anything in It—isn't that right? Our whole theory is based on the fact that the Universe is a *living* Universe, that it is an Intelligence operating as Law, that the Law of its operation is the movement of the Intelligence within It and upon It, *as* It.

Now if we arrive at that, there will be no difference between the treatment and what it does. The treatment will be what it does, and what it does will be the treatment and the doing—and they will be equal, identical, and interchangeable; and there will be no difference except one we don't see and one we do see—but what we do see is what we don't see as the prototype of what we do see.

Now this does not exist in any field other than our own—it would be impossible. Several of us were talking last night about how anyone can describe an experience unless he has had it. It is impossible. Shakespeare said, "He jests at scars who never felt a wound." Someone said, "Love only knows and comprehendeth love." Jesus said, "If you want to know the meaning of this, do it." Our motto is "To do is to know." They are the same thing—the doing and the knowing. Now no one understands us except people who are in our field. That doesn't exclude it, because thousands of people are studying to understand it, and they will; but unless they get the key to the whole thing—that, just as Einstein says, energy and mass are equal, identical, and interchangeable, which means they are the same thing . . . one is not opposed to the other, "approaching" or "receding from" or "evolving into" or "out of." *Equal, identical,* and *interchangeable!* You can turn energy into mass and mass into energy! Now this was exactly what Quimby* taught and what Mrs. Eddy taught, who were the forerunners of the New Thought movement—and I don't care who thought what or where they got it, because Truth doesn't belong to anybody, fortunately. What do we care what the Apostles wore? It is what they knew that matters.

As Emerson said, no kernel of grain can come to us unless we plant it and harvest it—the immediate Thing in our own consciousness, because each one has to do It and be It for himself; because he is It, but he doesn't know he is It. Therefore he is like a fish swimming around in the sea looking for water because he has heard of it, and he doesn't know it is running through his gills, and that he is in it and derives his life from it. So "In Him we live and move and have our being."

I was thinking, Sunday, if all we thought about was mud flats, we would be living on mud flats. Now maybe we would be just as well off. I am not talking about the comparative degrees of social order, because I don't know that it makes any difference. There is nothing beyond happiness—and if you can be happy in a mud puddle, you are better off than you are being miserable on a throne. As someone said, a half of something is better than three-fourths of nothing, and I am sure it is true.

But, I thought, *it is certain wherever the vision is set*—because here are a

---

*Phineas Parkhurst Quimby, American inventor, religious philosopher, and mental healer.

group of people who at least, when it rains, can put a little sand in the front yard and not walk through a pool of water to get to the street. Now if this law applies, we are all in some kind of a mud puddle, aren't we? and sitting beside some kind of a stream that is stagnant. And so the comparison has nothing to do with looking down our noses and saying, "Thank God we are not as other men." I suspect that the average person there is as happy as the average person in L.A. The question is: Couldn't he be happy without the mud puddle? If he couldn't, I am all for his having it, because it is all relative anyway, and no one knows what is good and what is bad. The ones who think they know so much about it are evangelists.

Now there is nobody any more screwy than they are—because their dualism is something terrific, and the evil that goes with it; but that is their vision. Hell will never cool off until people get cooled off. Emerson said he went out into a field after a hot political meeting and nature seemed to say to him, "Why so hot, little sir?" And in one of Shakespeare's plays—I think it happened in *Romeo*—he is a little guy and says, "A little pot soon boils."

I saw there, and thought, *they are just as well off as I am; I don't think I would like it this way; they wouldn't like it the way I have it.* The comparison is not that they are socially inferior or intellectually inferior. I don't know that they are. Some of wisest people I have ever known have very little intellectual training—but they seem to know about something that the intellect is often offended by if we try to coerce it to believe. As a matter of fact, intellect, as much as we need it, we have to stretch consciously that it may become aware of that which is superior to it—even to get enlightenment.

I think there is a soul-touching and intellectual process that stretches the intellect through the imagination and feeling until it lets in more spiritual territory, which now becomes a part of the intellect. And I cannot conceive that we reach a place where chaos is and we don't have any intellect or intelligence. I don't think we push out into the Universe to the loss of identity. I think we merely take in more territory, and more, and more. "Ever as the spiral grew, he left the old house for the new."

But here is the whole theme of *Where is our vision set?* Now particularly in treatment, because we discussed this quite at length . . . and from someone who is supposed to know nothing about it, other than as a sweet "believe-it-is-so," I got some of the most profound wisdom I have ever listened to—isn't this amazing: you never can tell where you are going to learn and from whom—and an absolutism that was perfectly amazing. You never can tell what people are thinking about when you see them in ordinary life. You think probably they are pretty far from what you are—and you like to think your own exalted thoughts, which you find aren't so exalted when you come to analyze them and wonder how you got that way yourself. But it really gave me a very interesting slant on the absolutism of relativity. Because if there is an absolutism beyond relativity—which there is—we don't yet know it, and even that which we postulate as absolutism, is reached through relativity. And if the reaching out isn't the thing that it reaches—if it isn't the thing that is reached after and with—then if our hand touched it, we wouldn't recognize it; it would look unfamiliar and we would throw it in the river. We wouldn't understand it.

Now Jesus said, "Behold"; he saw what he was looking at; *they* were looking at what he saw but didn't see it: "Eyes have they but they see not." Jesus said, "Behold"; and they looked up and said, "The guy is screwy; he sees nothing, because there is nothing there, and we don't see it either. And because we don't see it, it isn't." Now his vision was tuned into something that he saw, so what he was looking at, he saw; what he was looking at, *they* looked at and did not see. That is all the difference. Where is our vision set?

Now Troward said—and he is by far the best writer in this field; about half my stuff comes from Troward; the other half came from wherever I could pick it up; what is left over I made up, because by then I knew it didn't matter who made it up, because it was all made up anyway; sort of like our discussing very elaborately this morning whether we should try onions and celery to put in the turkey dressing—Troward said: in such degree, in treatment, as we believe that our treatment is conditioned by the past, the present, or the future, we are not treating in what we might call the realm of the absolute, or let us say the realm of unconditioned causes. I like "the realm of unconditioned causes" better than "the realm of the absolute," because it means more to me. It isn't any better.

The realm of unconditioned causes: that which all of effect must come from, and upon which effect must depend, but which itself does not depend upon effect. Therefore, the effect would be the plaything of the cause. Relativity is the plaything of the absolute, in a sense. But our treatment and what it is going to do would depend on where we condition it, and we shall condition it wherever our vision is. "And he went up into a mount and when he was set, his disciples came unto him and he opened his mouth and taught them, saying Blessed are the pure in heart for they shall see God." He didn't say that other people wouldn't see. He said there is a divine vision; that no matter what it looks at, it will see through what Swedenborg called the exteriors into the interiors—through an interior awareness—and it will see God, because it will see what it is looking at; but all people will be looking at it and not see what it is looking at. Now we believe there is a vision, mental vision, which looks away from what doesn't belong, and looks at the place that does, according to where the spiritual vision is set—in the realm of unconditioned causes, then, Troward said. This is what we are dealing with. Whether or not we are aware of the fact, we are still dealing with it; and what it shall do for us will not depend upon it, because what it does for us is a reaction of what we have done, not *to* it, but *in* it.

I was explaining to a young fellow this morning—young producer at one of the studios. He was working so hard, and I said, "Larry, you don't force anything, you don't coerce anything, you don't hold any thoughts, you don't put in anything—you always take it out. Always. It is already in there." His mind was all burdened with things he has to do. He has a great responsibility, and he was making it a personal thing—he had to make things happen. Now is the time to relax, I told him; we take everything out. And he said, "Then what makes it happen?" I said, "It is like you put the acorn in the ground, that is your part. Now there is an idea involved in that; and nothing can happen to the idea but that it will grow, and nothing can stop it but its own law. It is its own evidence; the oak tree is already there. You put an idea into your mind, and it will work exactly the same way, because the Universe is one system."

"Well," he said, "then I don't have to strain"; and I said, "No, the more you strain, the harder it is going to be." There is a certain relaxation. The realm of unconditioned causes is also the realm of Einstein, I am sure—of pure energy, before the action takes place which causes it to become mass (but it can turn itself back into it).

Now suppose we had a bottle of liquid and you could turn it into a mold and it would become a human body—have all the action a human body has. But now something has endowed it with intelligence also; and then suppose, theoretically, you could turn the body back into the bottle, and as you turned it it would become liquid again. You would know that objectivity and subjectivity are equal, identical, and interchangeable; but you would know there is something beyond both. This, of course, Einstein didn't philosophize on—a something that had will, had volition, had life, had self-determination, and which discovered that energy and mass are two sides of one thing which may be liquid or solid; but when it is the one it is the other, and when it is the other it is the one.

Einstein himself stood above this with his equations, separate from the thing he was equating, in a sense—didn't he? At least let's say, he manipulated it: he turned the liquid into the form and turned the form into liquid. Quimby did the same thing a hundred or more years ago. He said that mind is matter in solution, and matter is mind in form; but he said they are the matter of Spirit. In other words, he had a third thing he postulated there, which uses mind, whether it is liquid or solid. Mrs. Eddy said disease is the image of thought that appears in the body. They are saying the same thing. Emerson said, "We see the universe as solid fact, God sees it as liquid law." This is the basis of our whole work—that consciousness establishes its own form independently of any form that is already established, but only when it has a new impulsion or idea or vision in the realm of unconditioned causes. We live in the realm of absolute cause, which is causeless, but which causes everything, within itself; whose sole and only action can be upon itself; and whose sole and only reaction can be the reaction of itself to itself, making out of itself that which it presents to itself for itself in itself.

I like always Aurobindo's* thought, as he says, "for the delight of God." I have never anywhere heard a more beautiful expression of the mystical meaning of creation: he said it exists for the delight of God. Nothing has ever satisfied me as much, because now we know that where there is an inhibition of that creative stream, all of the psychological liabilities occur which psychiatry and everything is working on. We know that.

Well, then, if we had this kind of an energy and mass and somebody to turn it back and forth . . . now it wouldn't do any good if Einstein just arrived at the equation; he said, Boys, go out and do it this way and turn it back and forth, explode it and see what happens—that is the way they got the atom bomb. Tennyson said, "appearing when the times were right"—but not a good thing for the world, as we see it now; maybe it will be. It is as good as we make it.

But Quimby understood that there is a "superior wisdom," which he called Christ, and the use of it, which he called the science of Christ. One of his whole sayings was on the nature of man and another on the science of Christ. That is where scientific Christianity comes from; because he said the relationship of this thing which holds the visible and the invisible in its hand—I am putting this in my own terms—is the relationship of something superior to both the liquid and the solid, to which the liquid and the solid are the matter of wisdom.

Both the word and what the word does are products of the thing that speaks the word. He called this a divine wisdom and a superior wisdom. He said, "I represent this man of wisdom, and I enter your opinions and I explain why they are, and I explain away the solid fact," which in this case was disease. Mrs. Eddy went way beyond him but this is very interesting on its simpler basis. He said, "I explain away the solid fact, and it liquifies; and you ask me, what is my cure, and my answer is: my explanation is my cure."

---

*Sri Aurobindo, Indian seer, poet, and nationalist.

Jesus said, Know the truth and the truth shall make you free. Psychiatry says, Bring it to the light of day. But we go way beyond that.

Jesus always operated from the absolute position of the unconditioned in the realm of unconditioned causes, without reference to the past or present or future—"Who was born blind, this man or his parents? and who did sin when he was born?" Now Jesus paid no attention to it. He didn't say, Let's discuss the theory of the Jews, or Let's discuss the theory of the Hindus. They were both good people. They knew of only two contracts—grandfather to grandson; incarnation and reincarnation. They couldn't imagine anything else. He steps right out into the emptiness of spiritual space and says, Three cheers for God! I have a new one! That is all that happened; we don't have to get sanctimonious. Jesus knew something which he called the truth, which was acquainted with freedom—I Am—and he knew it in his own consciousness and nowhere else. And that is where you and I will have to know it.

And so just as Einstein and the scientist and the physician "stand superior" to manipulate the energy and mass of their doubt, so Quimby said there is a superior intelligence that does, and will, mold and remold that part of nature which is matter as form and mind as liquid form; and matter as form is more solid than mind, and mind as liquid form is a little more juicy than matter. But they are the same thing—they are equal, identical, and interchangeable.

Now if we are living in such a universe, then we get back to the mystical concept that I started with; this is the mechanics which react to the concept. Now these mechanics will always be there, but they are always covered up and always hidden. In other words, if things work the way in which they work, that is the mechanics of the universe; and it is either Jachin or Boaz—either that one of the two pillars in front of the Temple of Solomon that stands for the law, or the other one, which stands for the word or spontaneity. Every form is liquid, every form is transparent, every form contains a light which can be seen, every form responds to the language that addresses it with a consciousness of union with it, from the lowest to the highest forms of life—from the mind that sleeps in the mineral, waves in the grass, awakes to simple consciousness in the animal and self-consciousness in man and God-consciousness in the hierarchies in which I believe. But I don't believe in them in the sense of masses that are controlling us. I am talking about the upper hierarchies of intelligence manifesting through instrumentalities which have now arrived at a perception of the meaning of intelligence—because in Jesus it automatically flowed; he saw it and therefore it was. When we see it, it will be; but see how we are conditioning everything we do. Now that means that while our treatment creates and deals with process, in a sense, all process that we add to it is inherent in the Law, and the word is superior to the Law. As Troward said, you start with Absolute Intelligence, then word, then law, then thing. But it is only up here in Absolute Intelligence that we come into the realm of unconditioned causes, because there are absolute causes and there is the Absolute as cause, and there are any number of variations of relativities that become the absolute to that which is relative to them. Right down the line.

Emerson said that we awaken with consciousness that we are on a certain step, and we know there are steps above us and below us—Jacob's ladder—which intuition perceives; so there are any number of relative causes—and any relative cause that we stop at, we make it temporarily an absolute cause to that which is relative to it. In other words, it controls it. It governs it. If we believe we are subject to planetary influences, we will become subject, not to planetary influences, but to whatever subjective and psychic belief the world has created relative to what they think it does. If we believe that there are devils, we will be subject to some kind of satanic influence, which has no existence outside of human beings, which will be commensurate with the sum total which all people believe it to be who have believed in it and still do. "The devils also fear and tremble."

If we believe that we are subject only to the law of harmony, we shall harmonize, at present, with what is the top level of what the uniform concept of harmony is. I think if we broke the bonds of the lesser, we would be like a balloon where all the ballast is thrown out. I don't happen to believe anybody would stay in this world if he got rid of all the things that keep him here. Now I am not saying whether it is desirable to come or go;

I don't know and don't care. I think we still have considerable weight around our neck—and I haven't seen anybody who has loosed it. Every bondage we subject ourselves to, we automatically in our vision subject ourselves to the mathematics of that bondage. We are tied. Jesus said of Lazarus, "Loose him and let him go." And we have to be loosed before we can go. If our thought must be in the realm of unconditioned causes, still, when it comes to treatment, our believing that there is anything other than action and thought will lead us to the diagnosis.

Now this is what they do not understand in psychosomatic medicine. I know I believe in medicine, I believe in surgery. If we could get our vision beyond all these things, we could sleep without a pill; and while we sleep with the pill, we are subject to the harm that the drug does to the human body and mind, which knocks out both body and mind.

Every form of conditioning which we give our treatment does not condition the principle; it makes the relativity of that principle equal only to the conditioning which is being imposed upon it. Now this doesn't imply that it has any bondage, or that it is caught, or that it is evil or limited. The very fact of its freedom proclaims a necessity of this thing we call its bondage to us, because that is the only way we look at it; and I think we shall have to see that bondage is freedom, else we will be struggling with another set of dualisms. Freedom *and* bondage—this cannot exist. And we shall be trying to lift our consciousness to a point of perception, not of freedom as opposed to bondage, or the destruction of bondage as opposed to freedom, but of action without restriction. Just action. This is the way it is.

Therefore every treatment must have that tint of absoluteness in it, in the mind of the one who gives it—it doesn't matter whether anybody else knows anything about it—and it is arrived at in such degree as one is able mentally and theoretically to let go of everything even that the treatment has to get rid of. That is rather interesting, isn't it? Now 90 percent of all healings and demonstrations are made through a process, a mental process of arriving at this, but I don't wish to imply that I am thinking of a divorce of the absolute from the relative—there is no such thing as a relative separate from the absolute or not proclaiming the absolute. The slightest relativity proclaims the absolute at the level of that relativity. I struggled for a number of years to knock the relativity in the head with the absolute—and the only thing that got knocked out was myself, and I realized I didn't have strength enough to fight the Universe. That nonviolence, that flexibility, that acquiescence, if you will, walks with you. "And whosoever shall compel thee to go a mile, go with him twain"—what is it that makes you walk two? That is what Jesus was talking about.

In other words, Jesus knew there was no combativeness in the Universe. He knew there is no dualism, he knew there is no something else—there is only one end. And so if our treatment is to be absolute—it is going to be absolute anyway—but if it is going to function in *the realm of unconditioned causes* (which is why I like that expression) or if it is going to transcend the condition, or change the condition, it has to rise above it to the point where it sees either the *completion* of the one or the *process* of the other one. Either one will do it. As you hold a piece of ice in your hand, it melts. The process is *holding the ice in your hand,* and there is nothing wrong with the process, because it tends to the clarification of thought into manifestation of the thing thought about.

So I have been thinking about that, even down there the last two or three days—kind of engaged my thought; and driving through the mountains and the desert, always I was trying to figure out in my mind what does *the realm of unconditioned causes* mean to me? I don't know what it means to you; you don't know what it means to me; but I do think in the interchange of thought we very frequently get it clarified, and it means more to each other. I believe very much in the psychic communion between groups and between people— that something is set up; they call it *darshan* in India: a relationship which, flowing out from the group and the individual, reaches a little higher altitude and flows back into the group and the individual, more rarified.

In other words, if anybody gave a talk to an audience and helped the audience, it would have to help him. If he gave a talk that depressed the audience, he would have to be worse off for having given it. Anyone who talks a lot about hell in his sermon will be more deeply in hell afterwards. I don't say this as condemnation. Everybody has a right to be in hell or he wouldn't have created it. But he would be more deeply immersed in it.

Now it is hard for us not to talk about morbidity, isn't it? I thought when I looked at those guys: my God, it is terrible—how can they do it? Then I thought, it is home to them, it is where they live, where the kids are playing*; they are probably happier than we are. Therefore it is to the interior of the thing and not to the exterior that we have to look—to the feeling of it. (But I did leave that place very gratefully.) And let's see if we can't do that in our own mind and awareness.

To become conscious that we are manifesting, that we are existing, we are speaking, we are thinking in the realm of unconditioned causes where reality makes a thing out of itself by becoming the thing that it makes, and that we now turn to it—"Come to me and be ye saved": that is what it means; "Looking up they beheld his face only": that is what this means; when Moses came down from the mountain his face shone: it all means the same thing—it has no reference to a physical altitude; "I will look up unto the hills from whence cometh my strength": same story as *Pilgrim's Progress*—"As he reached the top the burden fell off and rolled away": it is the mind no matter what age is perceiving—that there is an altitude of thought where the eye views the world as one vast plane and one boundless reach of sky: that is what the poet said; he is telling the same thing Jesus did and all of them, probably through intuition, inward feeling, a witness of the soul; He has never left Himself without a witness.

And we do perceive the wonder of it all, and we do accept the wonder of it all—and *all* of it, right here and right now. And so it is.

---

*i.e., Mexicali. See p. 219.

Part II

8

COSMIC CONSCIOUSNESS
EXPERIENCE: FEBRUARY 12, 1959

Dr. Holmes spoke at the Dedication of Christ Church of Religious Science, Whittier, California.

At the time, the minister was Rev. Reina Lady Smith. She also was a good friend of mine. President of the Board of Trustees of the Whittier church was William Hart, a friend of more than thirty-one years.

That evening Dr. Holmes experienced what has been accepted as a Cosmic Consciousness experience. He kept me up most of the night talking about it, telling me I must never tell anyone what we discussed.

Thanks to Reina and Bill, I was given a seat in the space over the platform where an immense immersion baptismal tank had been removed. This furnished me an ideal vantage point to look down on the platform and Dr. Holmes while he was speaking.

That night he told me he had the sensation of being at the roof of the Church looking down at himself talking. I asked him what he saw. He said, "The whole church and people there became a pool of light." When he left the podium, he stumbled momentarily as though with an effort the man on the roof was forced back into the man at the podium.

Following the address of February 12, note in particular the talks of January 27 (two weeks before this address) and February 10 (two days before the address). Both talks were given at the meetings of the Tuesday Invitational Group.

After February 12 there were three Tuesday Invitational Group talks on healing work (Feb. 24, Apr. 14, and Apr. 28). Note the vein of the talks, reflecting the Whittier Experience.

Rev. Reina and Bill Hart gave me a cassette tape of the talk after it had been transferred from the disk of the old Grey Autograph that had been used to record Dr. Holmes's talk.

["This is William Hart speaking. We are privileged to bring to you Ernest Holmes' Dedicatory Address at Christ Church of Religious Science, Whittier, California, on the night of February 12th, 1959.

"The occasion is notable because Dr. Holmes experienced the greatest illumination of his lifetime during this talk. The tension of the moment is clearly discernible in the changing quality of his voice as the talk progressed.

"There were present on the platform that evening, in addition to Dr. Holmes, Drs. William H. D. Hornaday, Mark T. Carpenter, Barclay Johnson, Reina Lady Smith (the local minister), and the local Board President, which position I then held. In the congregation were over 400 persons, with a small overflow listening to loudspeakers in the basement.

"Sitting behind Dr. Holmes, I could not see his expression during his experience, but I am told by others that his face was really radiant. When he turned from the podium to retake his seat on the platform, he appeared physically debilitated and emotionally overwrought. He quickly regained his composure, however.

"During the reception which followed the dedication, I learned from Mrs. Smith that Dr. Holmes had told her briefly of his experience but was hiding it from the congregation for fear that it might be misunderstood. As soon as the situation permitted, Doctor Holmes went home, chauffeured by his friend Dr. George Bendall. At a much later date Dr. Bendall told me that Dr. Holmes, with whom he was living at the time, kept him up a good part of the night discussing the experience.

"We apologize for the poor quality of the tape. The original recording was made on a borrowed Grey Autograph—an early stenographic device that recorded on a plastic disk. The voice was then transcribed to a home-type phonographic record and later placed on modern tape. The original recorder was concealed in the lectern which Dr. Holmes was using. He leaned often against the lectern, causing it to squeak and groan. Unfortunately, the recorder was at times more responsive to the extraneous noises than to the speaker's voice. The next voice you hear will be that of Dr. Ernest Shurtleff Holmes."]

I have the keenest personal interest in such an occasion as this, and the most impersonal interest, in that I love it personally, and I don't feel that it has anything to do with me at all, other than that it is a certain phenomenon which is taking place in my day and which I have the privilege of being some part of. Tolstoy in *War and Peace*, which is still called "the best six novels ever written," by all the writers, said that any person today who appears to do anything worthwhile, probably has the least of anyone of his age to do with it.

He is merely something—an instrumentality—that the principle of evolution probably leaves upon the shores of time to see what'll happen. If it happens, he has the opportunity of being one who appeared to help. If it doesn't happen, he and it go out on the next tide, because only that which persists in evolution—finally, that which is worthy—can remain. As Tennyson said, "So careful of the type it seems, so careless of the single life."

Our movement grows and expands very rapidly—as rapidly I think as is possible—because we would not wish to mistake its end and purpose, which is not the building of churches. It is not the dedicating of churches—it is what happens in them after they are built, and after they are dedicated. It's what happens where there are groups of people in our conviction who meet together for the only two purposes for which we exist—teaching and practice. We have many orators in our midst, such as Barclay Johnson and Bill Hornaday and others here—but that isn't enough. What happens? For, as Shakespeare said, "A man may smile, and smile and smile, and be a damned villain still."

So we could profess and confess and exclaim and proclaim that God is all there is, and no one would believe us; unless something happens when we say it.

We are a teaching and a practicing order in the Christian Faith, who believe in two great fundamental realities—the Divine Presence, personal to every living soul and uniquely personal to each and every one of us. That's the first great cornerstone. The next is a Power for Good, and the Law of Good in the Universe greater than we are, that we can use for definite and specific purposes. The first one, everyone believes in. The second proposition, probably about twenty million people in this country now believe in, somewhat. And that two hundred thousand of them really know what it is that they believe—I doubt it.

It is our endeavor, through our educational system, to teach people what this principle is, and how to use it.

And there is a growing conviction in my mind that it should and must become the endeavor of all of our leaders to exercise some kind of a discipline over their membership not as to their theology—because I'm the world's worst theologian. I don't even know who wrote the books of the Old Testament, and I'm sure I don't care. I don't know what kind of underwear the Apostles wore, but I'm sure it's worn out! and most of their other beliefs are, too. They did not have electric lights or automobiles. They didn't know how to make pancakes, and I doubt very much that they had very much understanding of what Jesus had taught them. That is not our endeavor, to convince somebody of our faith. It is to *prove* something—first of all to ourselves; then to the world—and we have no authority before the world, and should ask for none—and will have none, *ever*—I hope—other than the authority of the work that follows the word. Should we become the most prosperous organization in the world, and build temples that would make Taj Mahal jealous and blush with shame . . . we should have become the most dismal failure in the entire history of the evolution of man's concept of God. It is not at all strange that the time should have come and it happened to come in our time; and we happen to be those through whom and to whom it came. How fortunate we are!

How lucky you and I are that we are here tonight. Oh, we are indeed favored among all people on earth of all ages. Why, we have taken the banner that Jesus resigned when he said to the thief beside him, "Do not be afraid. Today shalt thou be with me in Paradise." It is quite a banner. It is with this banner that we advance, and advance from chaos and the night.

We are a teaching order, not a preaching order. We are a practicing order, not a proselyting order, and the world has waited long and too often vainly for something to happen; for some healing power of the unseen magic of the Spirit to be evidenced at the cornerstone. . . .

When I was a kid I knew people who even had oxen—it's a long time ago. I did meet somebody down at Johnnie Hefferlin's church last night and he said he admired me very much, and he said, "You are so much like another friend of mine. He is ninety-two." And I said, "Well, I'm still holding my own. And as long as I don't slip backward, everything's going to be great."

But I had something stirring inside of me—what they call a restless foe. I would like to get one thing done without getting another started that's a little bigger than the other thing, else you *are* slipping back.

You know, we haven't yet done what I believe we should do with our membership. Now we're here tonight to dedicate a church, a physical building. I think it's beautiful, I think it's wonderful. I think it's a miracle, but I know why it is here. It's here because you're here, and because Dr. Reina Smith is here; and because your consciousness and hers and Bill's and all of you wonderful people out here have cleaved together, and what happened? Power—like the weaving of a rope, where one strand will hold no weight, but united it will hold terrific weight.

We have yet to see what the multiplied consciousness of a church body can do, if they are properly trained, if they permit someone to exercise an authority over them—not of their theology for which I wouldn't give a nickel anyway, not of their private lives which are no one's business but their own, but of one thing only—there is a Law of Good. There is a Power in the Universe greater than we are and we can use it; and it will multiply its effects a thousand times, in my belief, through the united consciousness of a group.

I have had so much inward conviction about this the last year—and the members of the Ministerial Association know about it—that I know, as I know that I am here, that you, right here, under the leadership of your most inspired leader, who has balanced the human and the divine equation, so that God and man unite on earth—*you* are going to prove this. Others will.

I know that *you* will—because of what's happened here. Let me tell you this: it is the only excuse we have.

There are many wonderful religions in the world. We are not better than the others. We are not more spiritual. We are not more evolved. We are not more anything, other than this one thing: we have co-joined our consciousness with the eternal verity of the Universe, that that everlasting and eternal Father of all life, and the Mother of all creation forever begetting the Only-Begotten, is begetting Him in us, right now. And that the word of our mouth is a word of Truth in such degree as it emulates and embodies the Truth which sanctifies the word to its unique service of healing not only the sick, but the poor in heart.

We are dedicated to the concept that the pure in heart shall see God—here; that the meek will inherit the earth—now; that one with Truth is a majority; that every one of us, in the secret place of the Most High, with center on his own consciousness, has the secret with the Eternal, the Everlasting, the Almighty, and the Ineffable: God and I are One. And I see you doing this; and I see you uniting in one great hymn of praise, one great union of effort, one crescendo of song, and one enveloping light of consciousness . . . [long pause]

I see it! [longer pause]

O God . . . the veil is thin between. We do . . . mingle with the hosts of heaven.

I see it.

And I shall speak no more.

At this point, witnesses agree, Dr. Holmes seemed to stagger slightly, and he returned to his chair. The event was not disclosed nor was it committed to writing until eleven years after Dr. Holmes's death on April 7, 1960.

9.

TREATMENT CLARIFIES
THOUGHT

We start in Santa Monica next Sunday morning. I want all of you to work every day this week for the right consciousness and a full house next Sunday morning at Santa Monica. Few people realize that all in the world a treatment is is a conviction or belief you put in your own words, and that the Universe is made out of words. This is the most difficult thing we have to believe and yet it cannot be any different in our field than Einstein's concept of energy and mass being equal, identical, and interchangeable. Our whole theory is based on the concept that there is no difference between the thought and what it does, there is no difference between the thought and the form it takes. Because how could thought change a form unless form were thought as form? It just couldn't. That is the whole basis of our treatment.

Let's treat that. I'll show you how I treat it, and this is the way I would like you to treat it every day this week:

We are speaking definitely and specifically for this particular location, Santa Monica Bay Women's Club the next four Sundays, and after that right along. Certain notices have gone out; they will be in papers. People have spoken about it, telling each other about it. And we know that place will be full and running over, that every person who has received this notice whom we can benefit will be there. Every person who has been told about it who can be benefited by being there—we don't want him to come if he can't—will be there. Every person who reads about it who can be benefited by being there will be there. We know there is a consciousness of healing, a consciousness of wholeness and happiness and well-being, a consciousness of love and friendship and unity and security and peace, which everyone feels and knows and understands, because it belongs to everyone.

Now we know that as people sit there they find themselves healed of all unhappiness, of all sorrow, of all grief, of all loneliness, of all confusion, of all doubt. This word which we now speak is present and active in this group, doing and being and accomplishing and becoming exactly what is in our mind now, because we speak it for a definite place, a definite location, a definite time—the only time and place there is in the Universe which is the one we place in time, so far as we are concerned. Therefore it operates at this time; it cannot fail to operate; it is present, active, healing, renewing, vitalizing, filled with goodwill and good cheer and love, and filled with beauty and harmony. It embraces this audience in light. And that is the way it is.

Last Sunday there were about twice as many in Santa Monica as usual because of the work we had done. And last night I had a meeting of the Board of Santa Monica Trustees—and Don Fareed* is president of the Board—and they were telling me how they could feel a movement. It is interesting, isn't it? The most interesting thing in the world to me is to find some definite action taking place in what appears to be outside of us, as a result of what we are doing inside of us; and I don't see that we would have any evidence that what we are doing is real, unless something definite does happen out there. We would, I think, soon just be mumbling words without meaning. We have no evidence whatsoever that what we believe is true, outside of what it does.

As you know I am on the radio with Bill [Hornaday] twice a week for awhile on questions and answers, and I said last week, "There ain't no hell." Someone might have written back and said, "The hell there ain't!" Someone did write and said, "Dr. Holmes may think there isn't any hell, but he will find out!" Isn't it strange how difficult it is for people to give up their sa-

---

*Son of Ameen Fareed, M.D., popular and renowned psychiatrist, who frequently wrote and spoke for the Religious Science movement.

dism, and every pit of it is a projection of their own unconscious sense of guilt. If this sweet soul could cool off hell for herself, she would send me to heaven gladly. Wherever she is, she is a sweet person and she would like to save me. How strange it is that the human mind is so morbid and so afraid and so cluttered up with confusion that it doesn't think straight.

Someone told me just last night—one of the Board members, who was interested in the youth movement and having a party—that one of them said to this person, "You will either have to give me an aspirin or a treatment," and she said, "Well, I don't carry aspirin, so I can't give you that, but I carry treatments with me; so now let's all get together"—there were about sixteen girls there, about 16–17 years old—"and let's remember that treatment is clear thinking; and we will think clearly." And before they got through thinking clearly, the girl said, "Well, it is all gone!"

Now this could not happen unless whatever transpired in the consciousness of those who were working produced that effect, because we no longer suppose we sit here and pray to a God up there to do something over there. When this happens and something over there is done, it is measured out over there at the level of the acceptance and embodiment here in a field of unitary wholeness. We have a lot of practitioners in this group, and they come from different groups, many New Thought movements; and we all think exactly alike when it comes to treatment, as far as I know. We learn in treatment that the treatment is the thing. Why will a treatment do more good and become more effective at one time than another? It isn't because God listens; it isn't because we are better at one time than another. It is because there are times when we have a more complete acceptance of our own word than at another.

Therefore treatment is clarification of thought, it is clear thinking. I think it lets in more light than there was, more power, more love, more wisdom; opens a mystical doorway to a greater awareness when we treat; but it will still happen that the mechanics of it will be that the word is the thing. Now I believe this is the principal key to the whole thing. Once we admit a prayer can be answered or ever has been answered, we have admitted there is some kind of a something, whether it is God as a Parent, or Law Principle, or Presence—and I believe in the Principle and the Presence. We have admitted there is something that either acts upon our treatment or is acted upon by it in such a way that either the treatment is the thing, or the power operating upon the treatment becomes the thing—I don't know which any more than I know how an acorn becomes an oak tree. I don't know, nobody knows; it doesn't matter.

But let us suppose the treatment is the thing. I think the word I speak— "It is spirit and it is life," Jesus said; and I think he was right. Then our aim is not to speak the right word, necessarily, but *a* word that is so completely accepted that it can operate. And if its action is by reaction, and its response by correspondence, or by corresponding to our attitude toward it and in it, we must realize that there would be a mechanics and a mathematics, not in our giving the treatment, but in what happens when it is given. I believe the universe is a combination of spontaneous combustion and mathematical reaction—just another way of saying it is a divine Presence knowing, and a universal law responding at the level of the knowingness of the Presence.

We do not look upon God as a principle, but as a Presence. But I think the principle of the Law of Mind in Action is an action as mechanical as any other principle in the universe. It won't be a principle unless it is; it couldn't be. And it most certainly is a principle. Now there will then be some words. All words will have some power, some words will have more power, and some all power.

Jesus probably spoke words that had all power. He said, "Heaven and earth will pass away, but my words shall not till it is fulfilled." That was more than faith. It was more than conviction. I think to Jesus there was no difference saying that than for you and me to say the sun is shining. He didn't put any force into it; he didn't put any concentration into it; he didn't hold thoughts or will anything to happen. He didn't suddenly get good and spiritual so God could give him a drink of water. Jesus was not superstitious; as a matter of fact the ones around him were, but he wasn't. He said, This is the way it is, and he likened the operation of that law, in his parables, to different laws of nature.

So some words will have more power than other words; some words theoretically would have all power; and all words would have some power. Now we look for the word that has all power, naturally. We should; and we would find that word. There is some conviction we have to surrender to our own word. I think that is what I am trying to say, and I hope it makes sense. I never thought of it that way before.

A conviction that we have, we will say we surrender to God—but isn't that surrendering it to the way you are doing it? And therefore we would have to have a conviction intellectually—and I think inwardly that what we are doing is true. I mean, it isn't make-believe. It isn't a sad, sweet song, it isn't a hymn of praise, it isn't a supplication. These things are not wrong, but it isn't these.

But it is a reality—and such a reality in our own mind that if we were treating for the disappearance of a stomach ulcer, it shouldn't be there when we get through treating. It should be dissolved. Now the only way we can prove it, and know this can be, is the proof of it. And the proof of it could take place while everybody was looking. I had just as soon a doctor would be attending a patient of mine, and giving them an examination every day if they wanted, as not; because that has nothing to do with "water being wet." If I conceded that it did, I would limit my treatment to the doctor's opinion and be a servant of the thing we obey. It is just another field of superstition.

As a matter of fact, probably the guy needs a doctor unless I can prove that he doesn't. I don't see any sense in knocking crutches out from under somebody; I think he should throw them away *if he doesn't need them*. Because we are controversial and contentious. However I think the real way is non-controversial and noncontentious, along the theory that nonopposition is the only thing that cannot be opposed, nonresistance is the only thing that cannot be resisted, nonviolence is the only thing that cannot be violated. But we measure things from such a short distance that we don't realize that. We say Jesus was betrayed by his followers and he was crucified by the Romans and what was the sense of the love he had? Well, if a few hours of suffering is consequential in 2,000 years of adoration, the balance is all in the favor of Jesus. It always is. Though the mills of God grind slowly, they grind exceeding small. Compensation is necessary, but Jesus knew and Gandhi knew and we all know to some degree, that there is no way to gain all without first giving all. There isn't any compromise, the Universe does not bargain with us. It doesn't say, If you are good I will send you sugar candy instead of a thunder bolt. There is no bargain we make with it; it has to be met on its own terms. But these terms are not arbitrary. God is Love.

We don't have to wonder if the Universe rests on the shoulders of Love when modern psychiatry sides with us. Did you see the notices recently of how the Lutherans have stopped preaching hell? If hell cooled off for the Lutherans, that would be something. And the Pope wants the Protestants to become Catholics—what a lack of a sense of wit! Evolution is forward, not backward.

The Universe has to meet us; we have to meet it on its terms. It is demonstrated that love is superior to hate. But, you know, we will never know *how* superior until everything is surrendered that is not lovely; that is our trouble. We would like to let go of it enough to squeeze through an almost closed gate; we still like to reserve the privilege of beating the hell out of a few others. But the Universe doesn't compromise with us.

It says, If you love, you have to love John Smith. He may be a stinker, but you have to love him. You have to love Mary Lou. She is a prostitute, but you have to love her. Because the Universe is that way. But we set up our little things.

If you want to get out of hell, then nobody can ever be in it. Why do you have it for one, who is just stewing in your own juice—? Nature, Emerson said, forevermore screens herself from the profane; but when the fruit is ripe it will fall. Nature never compromises with anything or anybody, or the exact laws of science, mathematical and mechanical and inexorable and immutable; but it is now believed even in physics that the old concept of cause and effect no longer holds good. This is very significant to a metaphysician because prior to Jesus they had believed that. The Jews, Mosaic law; the Hindus, the law of reincarnation and karma, which is the fruit of action— *karma* means the fruit of action. And so they taught the law of cause and effect—an eye for an eye, and a tooth for a tooth. You have to work out everything so you don't have to come back here in your karma.

Now Jesus did not contradict either one of these assumptions. He knew better ones. He knew of the instantaneous here and the eternal now. He knew of a Universe which had no history. And I have been thinking about that: God has no history, truth has no history. *We* have a history only because we consent to it. Who said, "History is a tale that is told"? Napoleon, that is right. And that is true. And Emerson said, "History is the record of the doings of that Mind on this planet."

The thing we are dealing with has no past and no future. It only has the present—but because our present is the past rehashed and our future is the present reenacted. That is a good idea. That is in accord with the whole law of karma and the law of cause and effect of Moses; and it is also in accord with the psychology of Freud in some ways, where he said a neurotic thought pattern will repeat itself with monotonous regularity throughout life.

I had one recently—a terrific neurosis—and I didn't like it very much, and it was of no consequence; they never are. My neurosis was attached to somebody, as it generally is. I thought one day, this is a very nice person that I am unconsciously displeased with (or whatever it may be). And I thought, this is a nice guy; I don't believe any of the things about him that I believe about him. So I got to thinking in retrospect and found that what I was believing about him was something that had happened to me several times throughout my life. And so I began to call him by the name of the places where it happened, sometimes 40 years ago; and the first thing I knew, the transference of the neurosis from this particular person was to the others, and from there to nothing—because it was ridiculous. Isn't that interesting?

This is true; this is a quick analysis. This is all that can happen to any analysis and is of no consequence. But I thought then, I wonder if all unhappiness, all impoverishment, all disease is not merely a neurotic thought pattern repeating itself over and over at our expense, and mostly from the experience of the whole human race—because I don't happen to believe that I am smart enough to have thought up all the good I have had or all the evil I thought I had; and I haven't had much evil. I don't think we are good enough to create a soul or bad enough to destroy it. It is here, and we are hell-bent for heaven; but we are mostly hell-bent too much of the time—and yet we are hell-bent *in* heaven, aren't we?

Some words will have all power, all words will have some power. The word that has all power must be a word to which we have surrendered everything that contradicts it. "Who has surrendered all hate to love; who has surrendered all unloveliness to love." Sidney Lanier* said that none of the singers ever yet has wholly lived his minstrelsy. Jesus said, if you want to know about this doctrine, try it. He knew darned well that anybody who did what he did would get the same results. Heaven has no pets.

God has no chosen disciples, the universe has no history; if it did, it would have ceased to exist before it started. It is difficult for us to conceive a timeless time in which a temporary time of necessity takes place so that the timeless shall express itself—an absolute absoluteness in which a relativity may transitorily transpire, in order that the absolute shall be expressed without the relativity ever being a thing in itself; and of course all the philosophers have known this. That is why St. Augustine said that time is attention, recollection, and then dissipation.

Dean Inge† said that time is a sequence of events in a unitary wholeness. I simplified it by saying that time is a measure of any experience, but it is never a thing in itself. It couldn't be, because there is something that compresses eternity into an hour and stretches an hour into eternity. But in our treatment then we would have to surrender everything. Now this is, I think, what Jesus meant by losing your life to find it. Jesus never lost his life or he wouldn't have been resurrected, because if he were dead, he would have been dead, period; and all the wailing of seven thousand angels would never have brought him to. He wasn't dead. This is a metaphor, an expression. We would have to give up unloveliness to be loved—there isn't any question; we would have to surrender all confusion to be at peace, and this isn't easy, because our neurotic thought patterns seem to operate on their own.

I believe it must be that everything that is a negation—everything that

---

*American poet.
†William Ralph Inge, English prelate and author.

contradicts what ought to be and what has a right to be and what must be in Truth and in Reality—must, from the standpoint of that other thing, not be so. It couldn't be. Jesus said that the unreal never has been, the Real has never ceased to be; but the two are so confused. I am finding that the greatest difficulty in this thing that my brother and I are writing* is the section on Reality and Illusion. It has taken more of my time and thought than five other sections, and I haven't got it resolved yet, to put into print, because it is a very subtle thing: What is real and what isn't real.

Plotinus said that everything is as real as it is supposed to be, but that nothing, or no thing, has any self-determination. All things, he said, are indeterminate. I like this much better than the assumption that *everything we don't like* is unreal, because I have watched the convolutions of the intelligences that exist in the brains of those who preach this doctrine, and I discover that finally this particular kind of absolutism runs around denying everything it doesn't like and affirming everything it does—and God is always on its side. It is a terrific psychological attitude to assume, but I couldn't quite take it. Plotinus said that everything is as real as it is supposed to be, but that nothing has self-determination. He said, "If I were to personify God, I would say I do not argue, I contemplate; and as I contemplate, I let fall the images of my thought, and they become things." As the Hermetic teaching said, Everything on earth is a copy of what is in heaven.

Now we would have to surrender: If we are treating for abundance, we have to surrender lack. This isn't easy, because someone says, "If I hurt, I hurt; and if I haven't got a dime, I know I haven't got a dime." But here is the cold Law. Someone says, "Well God wouldn't let it be that way." Well, that *is* the way it is; it isn't any other way. God did not say—of course God never said anything—that if you stand in front of a mirror you won't cast a reflection into it. We are bound to the reflection. It is the meaning of that famous story—would you call it an allegory?—of Plato's about the caves. He tells about the slaves, or these people who are in the caves, and they can't see

---

*The Voice Celestial, Ernest Holmes and Fenwicke Holmes (Los Angeles: Science of Mind Publications, 1960).

out. All they see is their shadows, which seem to have chains, and they mistake the shadow for the substance. In other words, they are chained by the shadow of their own belief—but they *are* chained.

It would be impossible to speak a word of absolute prosperity and success while we believe in its opposite. How are we going to get around it? I suppose everybody coerces his own mind; I have to coerce mine—because you can't live in disagreement with yourself; it is psychically like trying to go two ways at once. But I do it this way: I have come to believe that the relative is the Absolute *as* the relative—very simple. Nothing has in itself or of itself to be denied—that there is absolutely no bondage as such, and that bondage is freedom—because in my system I cannot have any dualism. I never speak as an encyclical; this is just what *I* believe, and you don't have to believe it at all. Everybody has to get himself out of the doldrums, pull himself out of whatever trap he is in. I tried many years ago to arrive at it by denying everything that didn't seem good, and I found I was just denying everything I didn't like. I am not intelligent enough to pick the sheep from the goats.

So it is easier for me to say, I am bound by my own freedom, and my bondage is my freedom. But I don't like my freedom this way; therefore this thing hasn't anything to say about it. Then I remove a contention from my own mind. That helps me, because I think that in treatment there has to be flexibility. You are dealing only with yourself, and yet you have to be on pretty good terms with yourself to live. I think you have to believe in yourself. I don't think it is egotism to believe in yourself; I think it is a false assumption not to. But I believe in a self that I must get most of myself out of the way of. Can you get yourself out of the way long enough to know the truth about this? Because the truth is none of "your business." There is a truth that, known, is demonstrated; there is a word that is all power, even though all words have some power. *There would have to be a complete abandonment.*

Now I believe this is what faith has done throughout the ages. I don't care how they prayed; most people's God is grotesque, and probably ours is to a finer perception. We think we are way ahead of certain concepts, and I think we are, but there are probably concepts above ours since there are beings beyond us, as we are beyond a tadpole. I hold this as axiomatic. It has to be that way in a universe—not a universe that is expanding, but a universe in which all evolving things are expanding. Evolution is an effect and not a cause.

You never can explain anything if you put it as cause; but you can if you put it where it belongs: as an effect—as all the great have done. It is the very basis of Hindu philosophy—the divine spark that impregnates the mundane clod, containing in itself the essence of its own being and the pattern of its own performance, so that all evolution is merely the unfoldment of what was involuted. I believe in that. It is what the Bible speaks of as a pattern shown thee on the mount. It is an essential part of the Greek philosophy; but they got it through Pythagoras* via the Hermetic teaching. It came down originally from Egypt; a surprising amount of the Greek philosophy did, because Pythagoras went to Egypt and studied and traveled there.

So we would have to surrender. And I find it easier for me to say this thing—it is as real as it is supposed to be, but it hasn't any reality to itself, it is a shadow. Therefore I don't have to fight it, I don't have to argue against it; but here we have to have a complete surrender. Troward said it is not a surrender of a different kind of a power and essence; it is the surrender of the lesser to the greater, and it is only in degree—because the life of God is man; there is no other life. There is only one life. And I think this is what happened wherever prayer has been answered through faith; and plenty of it has, and so instantly that it is amazing—the most instantaneous cases of healing and manifestation the world has authentic records of. And the largest number do not come from the metaphysical field. Did you know that? They come from the field of orthodox prayer. I think we ought to gladly recognize it and intelligently analyze it; but they are very rare indeed, compared to the signs that follow the metaphysician, because he knows what he is doing.

But we must not overlook the fact that faith has produced these miraculous things, and instantly. Then we shall see that faith cooperated with the

---

*Greek philosopher and mathematician.

principle that we teach and believe in (though we don't always have the conviction); there is a sort of emotionalism that went with it. But very few people ever had it compared to the people in our field who work it out more or less axiomatically and mechanically and grind it out by hand—it is better, and something you can teach people: that the intellect and emotions surrendered; and the will, in a moment of exaltation, got enough clearance in the mind to let something happen before the subconscious reaction set in.

I remember being in New York many years ago when a Dr. Hixson was there, a healer in the Episcopal church by the laying on of hands. A man came to me and said he had a very prominent goiter and that the doctor had healed it. Then, he said, he went away and the goiter came back. Then Dr. Hixson healed it again and it went away; and then came back again. This is a very interesting thing to one who thinks: the fervor of the prayer, the conviction, the faith of a very wonderful man dissolved a form—but the image was still there, and it restored the form. But I am interested in the fact that it dissolved the form. We will say that it melted some ice but didn't change the temperature of the atmosphere, so the water froze again.

But it does give proof of the liquidity of the water, and, in that higher temperature, of the nonsolidity of that which denied the liquidity. I am talking about ice and water of course. The goiter disappeared—it made two grand disappearances and two grand reappearances, like most of our prima donnas. It finally went away and didn't come back. Here was the subjective image of the seed of the thing.

What constitutes a science of Mind is that we know these things, and we know that there is a cumulative power in treatment. It *is* cumulative. We know that it is cumulative in its effectiveness. What I am trying to say is, it will be a direct-ratio proportion mathematically and mechanically to the inward acceptance of the word. The objective manifestation will have nothing to do with it. It hasn't anything more to do with it than a piece of ice can say "I won't melt" when it is in the sun. It has nothing to say about it. The only question is, does the ice get in the sun? But we limit it, you see; and when we limit it, we change the atmosphere. We say "Maybe;

maybe—maybe I don't know enough; maybe I am not good enough; maybe this person resists, maybe I can't help this person because he doesn't believe I can."

All of this has nothing to do with it whatsoever, if our theory is correct. It only takes one person to know. And having realized that this can happen, then we have to know that it only takes one person to know. It wouldn't take a thousand. A thousand persons knowing something wouldn't make it more or less true than one person knowing it would. The truth known would have to demonstrate itself. Mrs. Eddy said that truth known is demonstrated. Jesus said, "Ye shall know the truth and the truth shall make you free."

Now we have to feel the absolute independence of what we are doing, the absolute authority of what we are doing. I don't believe words have much power unless there is authority in them. I think the authority is not an assumption, and I don't think the authority is merely an affirmation or a vehement proclamation. It is the authority of the knowledge of the way that it has to be; it is the authority of somebody who said, "I will plant this seed, and it will produce a plant." This is absolute authority.

It is the same authority as if I should say, "This is a watch." If I were to spend the rest of my life thinking up an affirmation that I do not myself deny, I couldn't think one up any more complete than to say, "This is a watch." When I say, "This is a watch," there is nothing in me to say, "Maybe it is a clock." There isn't anything in me to say, "Is it really a watch?" or to ask any other question about it. It is just a watch, and neither God nor man can make a more powerful statement. But it is simple, isn't it?

Nothing in me doubts it; I know it is a watch. I wouldn't say their or anybody's thought can influence whether this is a watch, let all the world deny it and the ages deny it. Jesus said, "Stretch forth your hand." He didn't argue with what people believe; he didn't care who believed the man was born blind because his grandfather had done something to someone. This was twaddle to him. Isn't it strange that the most powerful thing we can say or think has no psychological forced positiveness about it.

We are redeemed from fear and superstition; I just haven't got any.

Therefore we are not afraid to make the assumption of authority lest something blast us. In other words, we are not afraid of the Universe in which we live. We know the Universe has no history; it can't have. God is not growing up—that is a cinch to me. We know that there could be nothing to contradict whatever the truth is; there is not the truth and something else. This we know. There is not something plus nothing, leaving nothing equal to something. We know there must be a word that has all power. Now we must know that we can speak it, and listen to it.

So let's do it, and let's know we do surrender everything that is unreal, everything that says "it can't," or "you hadn't ought to," "you are not good enough to," "you don't know enough." We surrender everything that denies the divine Presence, the divine Reality, the universal Law of Good, the love, the fatherhood, the brotherhood, the Unity. This Unity necessitates fatherhood and brotherhood and motherhood and sonship—you and I haven't anything to do with it, but we enter into the joy of that inheritance, into the limitless calm of that universal peace, into the bliss of that eternal Light which casts no shadow; we are alive, conscious, awake. This is not the surrender of action or movement or purpose or intention, or accomplishment or the drama or joy of life, or the song of life. It is quite the reverse.

All these things exist that the one singer shall sing in us. Therefore we surrender everything that denies the song which is beyond all songs, which we sing. All of the love there is in the Universe is right here, in our experience now, right now—it is not by and by—all of the abundance, all of the glory, all the good, all the peace, all the power, all the joy and all the gratification.

Now we know that everything we do shall be prospered, made happy—no waiting, no procrastination, no deferment, no delay. This word is what we are doing; what we are doing is this word. They are inseparable. This word is the law and the thing and everything. And now we know that everything we touch shall be blessed—everything. There is nothing can go from us to any person but a blessing; nothing but life, nothing but joy, nothing but happiness. There is no morbidity, no hurt, no fear, no lack, no want, no limitation. We shall bless and heal everything we touch without even being aware of it, just like a light is light—"So let your light shine"—and we believe in that light; it is real. So everything is made whole, everything is healed that needs healing, everything is made glad and happy and bursts into a song, everything is prospered. This is the law of our lives. We will it so, we decree it so, we announce it, we surrender everything that denies it. And having isolated and surrendered everything that denies it, there is nothing left but the central fact that affirms it—that we are That. So it is.

10.

WHAT IS SPIRITUAL
MIND HEALING?

No matter how often they are told, many people do not understand the significance of spiritual mind healing nor what it is nor what it is based on. Most people think we are materializing spirit or spiritualizing matter or that we are influencing lower planes by a higher plane—and there is no such thing—or that we have suddenly gotten so spiritual that God sits up and takes notice. There is no such God, and there are no such people. I wish there were such people but know there couldn't be such a God.

I was trying to explain to a man last night that the universe as such—that the manifest universe—must exist, as Aurobindo said, for the delight of God, and that the universe as such has no purpose as theology teaches purpose. The only purpose an infinite and unobstructed Being could have would be to express Itself as what It knows Itself to be. It hasn't the purpose of saving Its own creation, because It doesn't know that Its creation is lost.

We were discussing the possibility of some great metaphysical play, something that would contain the affirmative factors, and he was telling me how difficult it is when the producer gets ready to make a picture. He said that by the time they have taken it to the Catholics and then to the Jews and then to the Protestants and they are all pleased, the "hell" is beat out of it and there is nothing left but a little sweet love story that doesn't mean anything or do anything, and he said that very few people realize what a terrible handicap this is in producing real pictures.

If we produce a religious picture the way we think about it, somebody else might not believe in it. It would be a wonderful thing if such a picture could be made. So few people understand the basis for our treatment; so few people understand what is meant if we say that we are living in a spiritual universe governed by mental law and that all substance itself, whether it is formed or formless, is merely mind in action—or, as Quimby said, matter is mind in form and mind is matter in solution—that the treatment is not a mental or spiritual thing, operating upon a physical or material something; that the apparent material and physical something is not any different from the formless part of itself—it is merely the form that that same substance takes, because thought could not affect anything other than that which was a product of mind, could it?

Whether we say with Mrs. Eddy that all is infinite Mind in manifestation, which is a pretty good way of saying it—except if she were living today, she would not be talking about a material universe, because there isn't any; nobody believes in any. Science doesn't believe in a material universe as they thought of it 75 years ago. Or whether we say with Spinoza,* "I don't say mind is one thing and matter is another, but I say they are the same thing." Or whether we say with Quimby, "Mind is matter in solution, and matter is mind in form." Or whether we say with the Bible that the invisible things of God from the foundation of the world are manifest by the visible. It doesn't make any difference.

We are really saying—or, with Einstein—energy and mass are equal, identical, and interchangeable. They are all saying that what you see and what you do not see is the same thing, except what you do not see is what you do see when you can see it. But here is the whole basis of spiritual mind treatment consciously used or scientifically used or applied definitely for a specific purpose, and this is why people who originated these ideas, like Quimby, Mrs. Eddy, and others—no one person; *all* of them—had insisted that treatment is not faith healing.

This is no denial of the benefits of faith healing, because faith healing would undoubtedly utilize the principle which may be consciously used. We

---

*Benedict de Spinoza, Dutch philosopher (1632–1677).

believe and know that a definite statement made in mind produces a specific result in a neutral field, or, as Kimball* said, this treatment or this argument logically presented to mind produces a certain result. Quimby said, "I stand as a lawyer stands to his client"; and he said, "I enter the man of opinions, so to speak, and I represent the man of wisdom, and I explain that what is wrong are his opinions manifest, because matter is mind in form and mind is matter in solution." Then he said that the thing will work like mathematics. That is where we got the idea of mathematical conclusions; it came from Quimby entirely, at least as an original concept.

And he said, "You ask what the cure is, and my answer is that my explanation is the cure." All he meant by that was, if his explanation contains an evidence in its wording that is accepted, it will produce a result. Then the other fellow [Kimball] said, this argument logically presented to mind produced this result. Now this is very interesting, because 75 to 90 percent of all healing that has ever been done in the metaphysical field has been done by a process of argument, of affirmation and denial, followed by as much realization as the person has at that time. Because no matter how much they all contradict each other in the New Thought field, they all, when it comes to practice, do the same thing exactly. And since something happens, we have to assume that there is a medium through which it happens—which is exactly like what Troward called the Universal Subjectivity.

But here again there is a very great confusion over that, because when we speak of a Universal Subjectivity and an individual subjective, we are liable to be misled into the assumption that there is an individual mind and an individual law, which isn't true at all. We are very liable to believe that the Universal Subjectivity, as people call it (or as he called it), is a thing in itself—which it never is.

Everything that bears the mark of subjectivity, the subconscious, the unconscious—the subconscious and unconscious of psychology and the subjectivity of the psychic and metaphysical field—is never a thing in itself. Is

---

*Edward A. Kimball, celebrated teacher of Christian Science.

that clear? It may look like it, it may act it, it may repeat itself with monotonous regularity, it may control the destiny of the race—which I guess it
does—but it is never a thing in itself. It is always an effect operating in a
medium which acts as though what is believed in is true.

But it is always subject to a greater truth, or to *the* Truth. Plotinus referred to it as a blind force—not knowing, only doing. Now as Troward said,
this medium, whether we call it our own subjective which has no existence,
or a Universal Subjectivity which exists as law but not as person—not as
something which can be aware of what it is doing or how to do it—acts
without even knowing that it is acting or why. Would that be clear?

People mistake the concept of law with the idea of God—and the idea of
God is no more the concept of mental law than the idea of God is the concept of electricity or gravitational force. There is so much superstition about
it all, very little clarity of thought; because the Law will always remain, as
Troward said, impersonal, plastic, neutral—but creative and intelligent,
having no mind of its own. Plotinus said the same thing. It and all creation,
he said, are indeterminate; not illusion—they are not unreal; they are as real
as they are supposed to be—but they are not self-determinate. They exist
there as an effect.

Now spiritual mind treatment consciously used, then, is a definite and
persistent and consistent attempt to think straight and logically, basing the
assumption on a concept of an undivided and indivisible spiritual Universe
here and now, and translating everything into the terms of Mind in action
as law, and conscious intelligence as directive power. There isn't a branch of
metaphysics that would escape coming under these two categories of Presence and Person, and Law and Order.

Now the Law and Order themselves are merely the way the Presence and
Person manifest. They are the way. It is a very interesting thing, because no
matter what science we may be studying or looking into—all scientific
investigation, physics and everything else—we don't deny anything it
teaches. We believe it is true if it is true: What is true is true. We just affirm
this, however—and I am sure they would too—that all science watches the

operation of the Law and the way it works and what it does; not what it is or why. Science cannot answer *what* nor *why*—only *how*—in the operation, and doesn't pretend to. Neither can we.

Now why would that be? Because there is no God who could explain to Himself, or to anything else, what God is. There is no God who could justify His own being by explanation, because that which can explain is not First Cause; it is secondary cause explaining its relationship to Primary Cause. Therefore there is no God to argue with, and no God who knows anything about an argument, and no God who argues.

Now we have to assume as the basis of everything—the whole basis— that there is such a self-existent principle of Mind and such a self-existent awareness, Presence, or consciousness as a Supreme Being or as God or as the Spirit, and that they are inexplicable; that the Law knows nothing but to do, and the Presence knows of nothing that can contradict It.

The history of the whole human race is in the operation of the Law. Whether it is true or false doesn't matter; this is where the ancients got the idea of the illusion of mind and the illusion of matter, or form, because they knew one was as great an illusion as the other. Whether or not they had our concept of their being the same thing I don't know. Sometimes I think they did, and sometimes I am not sure, but it doesn't matter; we do. But we have to see that in the operation of what Mrs. Eddy called the mortal mind, and the Bible called the carnal mind, and Troward called race suggestion, and Jung called the collective unconscious, we see not the operation of an entity in Mind but the operation of a Mind principle responding to what was, and may still be, an entity individually or collectively—and endlessly repeating the errors of the ages. And individualizing them until some individual consciously or unconsciously individualizes himself out of the law of averages that is established throughout the ages by the consensus of human opinion and experience. Does this make it any clearer?

If somebody believes that a certain planet affects him, then what everybody who ever lived thought about the effect of that planet will now affect him. But the planet itself won't be affecting him; it will be the belief about the effect of the planet. And because it will work like mathematics, everybody will say it must be true—because it does work like mathematics. Everything works like mathematics; everything in operation is operating in a field of mathematics and mechanics. And everything has color and tone, I think—definitely. And everything looks as though it were depending upon itself—and there is nothing seen or in operation that could depend upon itself. Otherwise the only creator that there would be would be a blind force. And the very fact that you and I can differentiate between heat and cold, the very fact that we can affirm or deny anything, shows that the primary cause is not a blind force. The very fact that I could deny God is proof that there is no God who could be affected by my denial.

It is the very proof of the possibility of more than one kind of experience even in the field of unitary wholeness, or what the Ancient Hindus called the period of ignorance and our theology more crudely calls sin. You know, the Christian theology is much more crude than the Hindu philosophy; but don't say I said so. It isn't as well thought out. Salvation by grace only is not as well thought out as salvation by works; but we have to combine both of them.

The period of ignorance—now this is the background of what is called Eden. In theology we have sin and salvation. And the story of the Garden of Eden is a story, and it just didn't happen this way, that is all. But here is a story to adorn a principle. Every religion has told it, and all in the world they mean is this: Whether it were planned or not—and we don't believe in divine plan—the creative principle operates in such a way that it automatically and arbitrarily supplies the evolving instrumentality with everything necessary to complete its journey. Browning called it a spark that disturbs our clod. It is called the Atman in Hinduism; it is Christ in our religion; it is an Avatar; it is a Buddha—all it means is this: it is the incarnation of the Divine in the mundane, and it is referred to in our Bible as Satan falling like a flame of fire or something, and landing on the earth, and theology interpreted it as their having had a terrible fight up there and having thrown the guy overboard—very crude theology; not very much finesse to it.

But it means the impregnation of the mundane clod by the divine spark of life—what Troward refers to in the first chapter of *Bible Mystery, Bible*

Meaning, as the period of involution which precedes evolution. Involution is a spontaneous thing, and evolution is a mathematical outworking of it, whether it takes what you and I measure as a year or what we might measure as millennium, and it is what the Old Testament in Genesis refers to as the generation of the time when the plant was in the seed before the seed was in the ground. In other words, the divine idea before it was embodied by a process of law and action and reaction was entirely spontaneous, and every seed contained it. All the poets have referred to it in one way or another; it is the foundation of all teaching of the beginning of the individuation of the Spirit. But of a necessity if this is going to produce that which will sometime—let us say in a very human way—return to it that which was given, it has to set it in motion and let it alone.

There is no such thing as mechanical spontaneity. There is a mechanics in the universe, but it is a reactive thing to that which is spontaneous, self-explosive, self-assertive, whose law operates mechanically and mathematically but itself is neither mechanics nor mathematics but is a spontaneous self-proclamation. That is why one of the oldest sayings in the world is, "Spirit is the power that knows itself." We believe absolutely in the God who is Self-Knowing, but not self-knowing as though a God said, "Here I am, but there you are over there"—but the God who knows and whose self-knowing is in us at the level of our self-knowing; and that level of our self-knowing is Its knowing in us at that level. Therefore we believe that the relative is the Absolute at the point of the relative. It is not an illusion at all. Therefore you don't have to get all messed up in higher mathematics or higher metaphysics by finally coming to the place where you have a great reality and a great illusion. There is no such thing.

Plotinus, whom Inge called the King of Intellectual Mystics of the Ages, said that everything is as real as it is supposed to be, but nothing has self-determination. Quimby said that all things are really liquid, taking enough form to express themselves; but they are really liquid, and there is no difference between the mind that formed them and the form that is what they are. And common sense will teach us that if that were not true, a thought could not dissolve a form, could it? If the form were separate from thought, if it were something different from the nature of mind, then they couldn't get together at all. Impossible.

But let's get back to this idea; it interests me very much, because Aurobindo speaks of it as the period of ignorance—the Christians call it the Fall, the sin, and salvation. Emerson—who saw beyond Christianity, because he said that we have confused Jesus with virtue in the possibility of all men; and that is quite a slice of reason—of course was familiar with all of the old teachings; that the only way individuation can spring full-orbed is to start out with the potential. Browning said, "a God though in the germ." So if there are, as I believe, beings beyond us as we are beyond a tadpole, and then beyond that: in the sequence of that evolution of being there will never be a moment that we don't know ourselves and belong to the plane on which we live; and it won't be any different than it is here, in a sense—but *more*. There won't be a loss of what we are, but always more added to it. We would have to be let alone to discover ourselves, while the compulsory and mechanical necessities of evolution, or laws, would work automatically, just as the automatic working of certain parts of our physical body has nothing to do with our thought—like the genes that, Williams says, in the fruit of the family tree are never affected by anyone but are brought to each generation in the Ark of the Covenant of God. Isn't that interesting?

Otherwise we would have destroyed all creation. If any individual or group of individuals have the power they would like to have, God help the rest of us. I am a great believer that when the fruit is ripe, it will fall; but as Emerson said, "Nature forever more screens herself from the profane." No great amount of spiritual power, in my estimation, is delivered to anyone—and I don't mean a God that withholds it and delivers it; but one just can't take it until one takes it in its own nature, and its own nature is Unity and Goodness and Truth and Beauty and Reason. Not that there is a God who withholds it; but we can't take it till we can reach it, let's say.

At any rate, we would account for the endless ages of stupidity and trouble because of ignorance; and yet we would see that this is the only way we should ever spring full-orbed into being, and we would see another thing: that God and nature, the Universe, withholds nothing from anyone—it is all delivered. This is what I interpret as the Christian theology of grace. Not grace because Jesus was a nice guy; that is weakness. Grace because the Universe is Itself an infinite givingness—It can't help it; that is Its nature— and because it is in our own experience only the one who gives all who gets all. There isn't any other prescription—that is it. As you give, you get— good measure pressed down and running over; the eternal circuits—because there is a justice without a judgment, and that justice is merely the balance and equilibrium of the Universe. It has to be there, and we suffer not because of the judgment imposed upon us but because of the judgment of ignorance. That is why Emerson said there is no sin but ignorance and no salvation but enlightenment.

Now just as every other law awaits our recognition of it, it doesn't know it is waiting. The law back of our ability to have television didn't know it was waiting until somebody discovered how to use it; it was just there, and when somebody used it, it didn't *appear*, but it *went into operation*, because that is the way it works. It doesn't seem strange to me that the time should come in the evolution of the human race when some people like we are—for this is what I think is the part we play in evolution, as well as all people who believe as we do; millions of them in the world—should come to see that spiritual law is natural law, that the Universe in which we live is a spiritual system and makes sense, that ignorance of the law excuses no one from its effect, as people say. If these things are true, why doesn't the Bible tell you so? The Bible does not give you a recipe for pancakes, much less this type of thing. Something new is emerging in the world. This is not an old philosophy warmed over, nor even the Christian faith with a little something added and warmed up. This is itself, according to the eternal verities of the Universe, taking place at all times and as entirely new things appear which were not preceded by logical parentage; and every science recognizes it—biology and horticulture and everything.

There is a principle back of all evolution which responds to the demand made upon it in the terms of the demand, good, bad, or indifferent; right or wrong as we understand it—this principle doesn't know anything about any of this. It just acts by reacting, and reacts by correspondence, exactly like a mirror; but there is infinite intelligence back of it. And so we find—someone must have understood this—"As in Adam all die, in Christ all are made alive." The original of that is, As in the first Adam we all die, so in the second Adam—which is Adam Cadmon—we all live. The second Adam is Christ, Buddha, or Atman—the same thing. All it means is that limitation dies.

I asked Adela* yesterday to write a story about the principle of the Resurrection—not necessarily the Resurrection of Jesus; just to suggest it and to say that for every death there must be a resurrection, and for every resurrection there had to have been a death of something—if it were only that you are less mean today than you were yesterday. The more mean had to die to get the less mean resurrected, didn't it? It is a principle of transcendence, forever flowing in where we let go; "nought is the squire when the King's at hand; withdraw the stars when dawns the sun's brave light"—or as somebody said, the full gods will have to come when the half gods go. But we should look back to that principle operating where whenever a demand is made upon it, it will answer in the terms of the demand made. And now some group of people have come to realize this and will perceive the meaning of the mystic who says, "Act as though I am and I will be." Jesus said it too: Believe and it will be done. And since there is now a spontaneous reaction to a mechanical actor, as far as you and I are concerned we might get a great wallop out of it or a little kick, just in experimental work. Everything isn't cut and dried and done.

I think we are laboring and belaboring and belabored and fussing, like climbing a tough hill where every time we take two steps we fall back one and half; because we are still climbing a hill. And the hill will be there as long as we see it. That is why Mrs. Hopkins said there is a group of people—she is referring to Old Testament people—who while they believed that God was all there was and had an exalted idea of God, always saw them-

*Adela Rogers St. Johns.

selves as oppressed and in the valley of dry bones having attached to a race something that doesn't belong to it. We all have done it.

But as we try to conceive that there is no otherness, there is no difference, there is no opposition—that everything that is an effect is a sequence of a cause set in motion without knowing why—we would see that ignorance is the only sin there is. We should see that no one could measure the possibility of thought, no one could say it cannot be that way; no one has ever yet disproved what I am saying—no one—by logic, reason, or experimentation—no one ever will. Insofar as anyone has tried either to prove or disprove it, they have proven it. Therefore we have every justification in the world of trying to arrive at that transcendent state of consciousness where there is no argument and no contention, no opposition and no otherness, and where our own nonresistance will dissolve everything that seems to be resistant, because nothing can resist nonresistance. Nothing—just nothing.

Two icebergs will destroy battleships, because on this level force meets with equal force—and that is a law too. But the iceberg cannot resist the heat of the sun. This is why Aurobindo said that transcendence does not reconcile, it transmutes. Isn't that interesting? Jesus said, resist not evil and it will flee from you. Gandhi taught nonviolence. And they were both right.

Now there is nothing below the level of a certain thought. (I am not talking about good sweet thoughts.) It is like all the great questions that great people have asked, announcements they have made: something in us says, Yes; and we spend the rest of our time until we know what it is. There would be at any particular level of thought (everything that is below it is subservient to it) *everything*; not *something*. It doesn't matter who believed what or how many believed which.

I was interested in something someone said last night about some very prominent Catholic woman saying, "What right does this man have to say there is no hell and that there is nothing to be afraid of? Well," she said, "we are saved from hell only by fear." We are so afraid of the Universe that we are not sure but what God will knock our teeth out if we do say "hell." We worship the devil and are afraid of evil and are bound by a rope of sand in our whole belief about limitation. I think the most logical thing in the world for

Jesus to do was to tell Lazarus to get up; and if Lazarus hadn't come out, Jesus would have crawled in.

I don't think it was strange he turned the water into wine. That is what they happened to want. There is a slow process in nature that does this; but who shall say it has to be done that way, beyond the time when somebody knows it doesn't have to be done that way—? Ignorance of the law excuses no one from its effect. Who shall say but what the very law that tramples the grapes of wrath will produce a celestial wine? And because it is too good to be true, and because it is so completely opposite to what we have believed, people will say they speak with a certain madness. They said Jesus was crazy, you know.

We are dealing with this kind of a transcendence and we may as well know it, because expectancy speeds progress—and if we don't have a conviction that "it can be," we are going to have a conviction that "probably it can't." Just as I have often said to you—and I told this fellow last night; he said it is an idea for his play—when Jesus fed the multitude, in all this throng the only person who could help him was the kid that didn't know it couldn't be done. The rest knew it couldn't be done, and why. He didn't know it couldn't be done. Jesus knew it could be done.

I always liken it in my own thought to that spontaneous thing, that child in us that never dies. We ought to carry him right along into our experience and if we think we have any wisdom—because all of our wisdom and all of our experience *he knew* before we got there. All of it. It is what Wordsworth refers to in the "Ode on Immortality" when he says that the youth is nature's priest. But, he said, "Ever more the prison walls' experience clothes him round," until finally he forgets that "celestial palace whence he came." But he further said, "In moments of calm weather though inland far we be,/ Our souls still have sight of that immortal sea/ That brought us hither, can in a moment transport us thither,/ And see the children sport upon the shore/ And hear the mighty billows rolling ever more."

As metaphysicians, then, instead of crashing round the icebergs and beating them against one another—which I think we do a lot, and everything kind of shatters—we ought to be more like the sun that shines nonresistantly, but remember: persistently. It isn't a weakness that it doesn't assert itself and scream how hot it is. It is a state of being; and we have to do that. So let's do it.

Let's treat our Santa Monica group—I want that place packed Sunday. And we know to here come the just and good and wise and those who can receive our message in joy and happiness, in recognition and with resolve to use it; and we know they are blessed by being there, and everyone who is there is healed. It is a transcendent experience for all of us. Whoever can be helped and healed is drawn there because you are saying it.

And we know we are establishing the law of our own being right here, the law of our life, that everything we touch is healed. There is a transcendence in us, there is the originating power and force and will and consciousness, the know-how. No matter what we call it, it is God, it is the real self too. Now this is the Son: nonresistant, non-argumentative, noncritical, noncondemning—this Thing which dwells forever more in the secret place within, healing and making everything whole It touches. It is our will, our desire, our acceptance that everything we touch shall spring into joy and happiness and laughter and truth and beauty.

Now let's do another thing: let's know we have great joy in life; that all heaviness and burden—the weight—falls away, as this spontaneous Thing springs into its own Self-Existence and the light of Its own truth and the love of Its own givingness, the power of its own Self-Existence. Let's see if we cannot know that without any conscious effort everything we touch is healed—every person, every situation—and that without any effort this perception continues to be with us. Now we know that there is no law of the past that limits, no belief of human mind whether we call it stars or whatever we call it—there is nothing that operates but the Truth, nor can nor ever will, and we embrace the Universe and everything in it and love it. It is beautiful, and we are perfect beings living in a perfect Universe surrounded by perfect beings and perfect situations—and we shall admit nothing else. Therefore we do not have to clash on the level of resistance.

11.

BASIC TREATMENT WORK

[Ernest read his poem of the Fable and some parts of "Illusion"]

Every religion that ever existed has taught the main ideas contained in this, and this is just the way I said it. Our Bible says, "A mist went up from the face of the earth," etc. I wanted to get your reaction because there has to be a background for this whole section on Reality and Illusion,* what is real and what isn't, without making anything absolutely unreal. I do not believe in the unreality of anything, other than the illusion of our perspective of the thing, which must have some reality, else it wouldn't be there.

Plotinus, whom Inge called the king of intellectual mystics, said everything is as real as it is supposed to be, but things in themselves have no self-determination—they are indeterminate; and I think our philosophy is very close to that. Aurobindo is very emphatic and denies much of the theory of Buddhism, which he thinks is a theory of nihilism. I was reading something of his last night where he said, in the true perspective matter is the complement of spirit and necessary to it, and is not unreal at all—and I believe this. God's world is not a world of illusion.

Bill† and I are doing questions and answers on the radio, and one last night I believe was truly an inspiration. I don't know what the questions are

---

*Ch. 7 of First Book of *The Voice Celestial*, by Ernest and Fenwicke Holmes.
†William H. D. Hornaday, Religious Science minister and close associate of Ernest Holmes.

till he asks them, and this was about two different religious beliefs—Should a Catholic and Protestant marry?—and I got something of an inspiration and said, "If people view it rightly, each would feel there is a contribution of the other and both would come to greater fulfillment from the two different heritages." And this would be right if we weren't so little in our own consciousness.

Our concept is that we live in a spiritual universe right now. God is not evolving—nothing has happened to God; but within this Thing which does not evolve, there is a continual manifestation of life and an evolution of forms, ad infinitum, forever—never more but always less; but all motion takes place within That which does not move. That has been the teaching of the Ages. It does not make movement an illusion, but it backs it up at every point by the substantiality of That which does not have to move—and this is why Lao-tzu said, "All things are possible to him who can perfectly practice inaction." That sounds silly, but it isn't. Our Bible says, "Be still and know that I am God"—because it is out of the Silence that all movement comes. It is within the Silence that all movement takes place; and it is out of the Unmanifest that manifestation comes; and the first basic principle we have to suppose is that creation, the act of creation, is merely the act of a creative Principle operating upon Itself, and out of Itself making what It creates—and what It creates is still Itself as the Creation.

The creation is not an illusion; people *do* have livers and lungs, etc. There is no illusion anywhere, and everything put in place will belong "to all the parts of one stupendous whole,/ Whose body nature is with God the soul." And our poet said, "Nothing useless is or low,/ Each thing in its place is best;/ And what seemed but idle show/ Strengthens and supports the rest."

We believe—or I believe—in everything. The child at play is not an illusion; but there is more playing than the child. I was talking to a man the other night about creating an atmosphere in a scene—he never heard of me and probably will never hear of me, but he happened to come in where we were and sat there for while—and he said, "I am more relaxed than I have been in six months; what goes on?" He said, "It has something to do with you." I said, "I am just a relaxed screwball," and he said, "Whatever it is . . ." and we got to talking, and I said, "This may sound screwy to you," and I talked good metaphysics applied to his profession. And he said, "I have known this all my life!" Isn't that interesting! He would make the most wonderful metaphysician, because his business is in making the illusive real, in making the soundless things speak, in making the silence speak, in making the unknown normal, in creating an atmosphere which everybody feels—and I understand he is one of the best in his field.

Now we don't believe anything out here is an illusion—but we don't believe anything out here makes itself; and the thing that differentiates our philosophy from all others—I don't mean only Religious Science; I mean all metaphysicians, Unity, Christian Science, Divine Science, etc.; I am talking about the modern metaphysical movement as a whole—there is a philosophy they have and teach and practice that is not understood by any other group of people living, or who ever lived; and don't ever think something new hasn't come into the world with Quimby, Mrs. Eddy, and the New Thought leaders of early times—a new philosophic thing was announced, a basis and a new practicality; because contrary to what most people believe, we do not influence anything or anybody, we do not suggest anything to anyone or anything, we do not spiritualize matter and we do not materialize spirit. And we are not using good with which to combat evil or righteousness to overcome unrighteousness or good to overcome evil or God to beat the devil over the head with a cosmic club—this is exactly what we do NOT do.

Our whole practice and theory is based on the assumption that the visible and the invisible are just as Einstein said about energy and mass: equal, identical, and interchangeable. Spinoza had said the same thing, only he said, "I don't say mind is one thing and matter is another." And when Quimby said, "Mind is matter in solution and matter is mind in form," and Mrs. Eddy said, "All is infinite Mind and its infinite manifestation," they were all saying the same thing—and the Bible says, "The invisible things of God are made known by the visible," etc.

Now it is only on the assumption that nothing moves but Intelligence that we can give a treatment. Eddington said that we can think of all the laws of nature as though they were intelligence acting as law, and Jeans* said that we can think of it as an infinite thinker thinking mathematically. We believe that while the thought is spontaneous, the way it works and what happens is a mathematical and mechanical reaction. Pythagoras saw this; he said that all is motion and number, but there is a Mover. Music can be reduced to numbers too, I believe. So can the whole universe. But remember this: you have not explained the operation of the universe when you say it can be reduced to mathematics, because mathematics does not know that mathematics is mathematics. You see, if we stopped there, we would have nothing; so this is a fallacy. The engine can be known only because there is an engineer. That is why our two great assumptions are Presence and Person, and Law and Order. And that has been held throughout the ages.

Now our whole method of technique and practice proceeds on the assumption and basis and theory that Law is Mind in action, and that wherever we create a mental state relative to anything, and identify that thing with it, that which we recognize in our statements, realize and speak into them, tends to become true as to this situation; and because it does, whatever we put into the treatment will come out of it. Say, "This is the law of elimination to whatever is discordant, whatever doesn't belong; this establishes harmony"—it will do it.

Now the next thing is *why* and *how*. Nobody knows. Don't ever try to explain the why or the how, but only the way it works. Science can watch a process of the birth of anything and say that at this stage this happens, and at that stage that happens; until finally they will have it worked out as a principle. Each day of incubation something happens to produce the chicken. But how it can happen they can't answer, or why it can happen they don't try to answer—only *the way through which* the how and the why operate to produce the what, which itself alone knows.

Someone was talking to me this morning about a case, where there are

---

*Sir James Jeans, English physicist.

several different attitudes, in settlement of something. We don't give advice; I don't have any advice to give or know what to do. But I do say that there is something that does know; and when I say that there is something that knows relative to this action, I do not create the something that knows, but I do set the stage for that which knows to now know this. According to the theory of all emergent evolution, whenever a demand is made upon the principle, it answers in the terms of the demand made. What I mean is like this:

Say you are inventing something: when you announce this thing, the creative principle, acting as law, accepts the answer and intuitively and instinctively and innately knows—without knowing that it knows—what the answer is and produces it. Now I am not talking about God the Spirit; I am talking about the Universe of Law and Order. If that were not true, Luther Burbank could not have done the things he did. He made a demand on the intelligent creativity of the soil. Neither the soil, the potato or tomato, or Luther knew what would happen—and this principle didn't know consciously what would happen and doesn't know now. But it will always have to happen, because certain combinations will produce inevitable results. That is what I mean by saying that the principle acts by reacting: it reacts to the demand made upon it by answering that demand. This is held even in academic circles—in the departments of philosophy; what they call emergent evolution.

This is why Jesus said, "The words that I speak, they are spirit and they are life." There wasn't any question in the mind of Jesus but what his word was going to become a thing in this Law, and do exactly what he implied in his own consciousness it would do: "Go, thy servant is healed"; "Turn water from one jug into another and it will be wine"; "Cast your net over here"; etc., etc. Jesus was not like some man who would go into a grocery story and want stringbeans and ask for succotash. He was the most direct, most specific person who ever lived—at least one of them. And so we are dealing with a principle which not only receives the impress of our thought and acts upon it creatively; it is a principle which knows within itself what to do. So if we say, "I want a machine that will blow holes in spaghetti," this thing will think up such a machine. It just responds by announcement.

So I said, "I don't know anything about these legal matters; but I know this: right here, there is justice; truth; no lie; no liar; no one to tell a lie or believe one; no misrepresentation." And I said to this person, "I am not treating for you to win a case. I wouldn't do that. But truth and justice will prevail. Nobody can be lied to. What more do we want than the absolute truth?" I wouldn't treat in a controversy like this for anyone; I always ask if they think I am treating for them to win a point of law. How do I know but what they are the liar? And they always say, "Oh no—it is right."

What is the principle involved here? The principle that enables us to treat from One Principle and One Substance, just because it is the unitary cause of everything—to treat for anything or all things that come out of the One Thing; and if it is necessary to have a specific something, then we will get it.

Now the whole principle and practice and possibility of the answer to prayer is the definiteness of the request, and the equal, inevitable, mathematical reaction of something mechanical to that definiteness, delineating that and not something else—because while the Universe is a unity, as Emerson said, the center is unity but the circumference is multiplicity or variation. All things come from the one thing. Philosophy has taught academically—which even psychosomatic medicine does not understand, but comes nearer to it than most forms of medicine—body-mind relations which science doesn't know, medicine doesn't know; only metaphysicians know, not that they are better but they happen to have found this out, and the answer is right here, and it follows there is no difference between the thought and the form it takes. Thoughts are literally things; they do not operate upon things; and this is possible if the Universe in which we live is a system of intelligence, a spiritual system governed by laws which are Intelligence operating mechanically as Law, always producing an inevitable result—two and two will always make four.

Some people were yakking yesterday about something, and I asked them how many people it took to convince them the world is flat. If we were depending on our thought, our willpower, our creativity, our manipulation . . . Jesus said, "Who by taking thought can add one cubit to his stature?" And yet Jesus above all is the one who turns right around and says, "Take thought." But why? "Because it is done unto you." That is the key to "Take thought" and to "Who by taking thought . . . ?" It is a paradox until we understand the subtlety of it.

"It will be done unto you." And this we must accept as the nature of the Universe in which we live. You can't explain it. Don't waste time in trying to explain it. There is more that cannot be explained than can be. Even God could not tell you what God is, because God would have to tell you what God is by comparison with what God is not. Therefore his language is "Yea" and "Amen."

It is absolutely impossible for the Ultimate to know that It is the Ultimate; it is equally impossible for It not to know—and there is a difference. We have to suppose such an absolute as Consciousness and such a reaction as Law and Order; therefore when we give a treatment, as Quimby said (he is the first one who discovered how to give a spiritual mind treatment, and everyone has followed this), the difference is in the similarity only. He said, "I stand as a lawyer stands to his client. Here is a man of opinions but there is a man of wisdom. I explain away the opinions, and you ask me what is my cure, and my answer is, my cure is my explanation." Jesus said, "You will know the truth and the truth will set you free." Quimby was proceeding on the assumption that mind is matter in solution, matter is mind in form; but he said they are both united. Put together, they constitute "the matter of a superior wisdom"—and that is very interesting.

This is completely necessary to understand because while we say that all is infinite Mind in manifestation, etc., we are supposing something that observes the similarity and interaction and polarization, because there is nothing in the whole universe but polarity between action and reaction. We have to suppose, then, that the reaction is equal and identical with the action, because it is the Omega of its own Alpha, and the one is in the other. The Old Testament says that this is the time when God "made every plant of the field before it was in the earth."

And this makes the treatment dependent upon nothing but clear thinking, logical arguments; or straight affirmations; or unexplained or unspoken realization. These are the only ways we know: Clear thinking, by affirmation and denial, as Kimball* said: This argument, logically presented to mind, produces this result; or prayer of affirmation accepted; or complete realization without argument or prayer or anything else. They will all three work. I think we tend to combine the first and the last—more or less an analysis coupled with a realization. That is about where most of us are.

But always it will be that which supplants one thought with another; and because the whole thing is in an eternal state of liquidity, that which denies the solid will affirm the liquid, and that which denies the liquid will affirm the solid; and the action and reaction will go on this way. So we fall right back upon our own state of consciousness when we give a treatment: how many people will it take to convince us the world is flat? There are not enough in the world.

But let us tell ourselves forty times that we have a bad stomach, and the stomach—which is indeterminate, hasn't any sense—would react that way. If we thought harmony enough, it would heal it. Someone says it is all nonsense. Who knows? Never let anybody kid you into thinking you don't know. Never listen to arguments that say the whole world has believed such-and-such. Always somebody has to break the sound barrier, stretch the horizon out further. This is eternal progress. We are betwixt and between that which seems so real and is as real as it is supposed to be, but which has no innate reality, no innate determination, no choice, no mind—like time, the timeless, and eternity. But they all depend on the Old Man.

We don't wave any wands. The only one we wave is compliance with the laws of nature, which work mathematically, the use of which may be inspirational and illuminative, but the reaction to which Jesus was so certain of that he said, "Heaven and earth will pass away, but my words shall not until they are fulfilled."

---

*Edward A. Kimball, celebrated teacher of Christian Science.

12.

WHAT HAPPENS WHEN
WE GIVE A TREATMENT

I wanted to discuss what happens when we give a treatment. There was a discussion the other day as to whether or not we are a Christian denomination, and I said of course we are a Christian denomination, and several said we are not; I said we are a Christian church, and they agreed to that, because we believe in and follow the teachings of Jesus, the greatest of all Jewish prophets. There were no Christians when Jesus was around; Jesus never heard of a Christian, and he would be amazed if he could come here today and see what we have done to what he said.

It was very interesting to me. As far as the world is concerned, we are a Christian denomination and we wish to be; but Mark* explained to me that we are Christian insofar as we follow the teachings of the Bible and of Jesus, but we are not Christian theologians, because we do not accept what has been attached to it by theology—much of it—and that is rational, I think. We don't believe in devils, in hell, in purgatory or limbo; we don't believe God chose some people to reveal something to, and didn't to others, because that is ridiculous. We believe in *divine patterns,* and not *divine plans.* But all of this Jesus taught together with all other great teachers.

I have been waiting for some years for something like this to come up in our movement, merely to clarify it—because I have never once imposed a

---

*Mark T. Carpenter, Religious Science minister and associate of Ernest Holmes.

personal opinion on our church movement. Whatever I believe I do not try to impose on our ministers or say, "This is what 'we' believe." In my mind we do not believe anything unless we all agree that there are certain things we do agree on. I wouldn't want to be any part of starting another closed system. But having this question come up through a ministers' meeting, now I can tell them what I believe, and they probably will say they believe it; and then we will arrive at what we believe without my imposing what I believe on what they believe, and no one will know the difference. And this is the way to get your own way, if you just have patience.

I was thinking for about two hours after dinner—thinking about treatment; because I don't believe our movement is worth a dime unless *something happens.* We are not just another group of people, nor just another religion, nor just another philosophy or science. In line with Divine Science, Christian Science, and all the other metaphysical movements, we believe in something that is added to the philosophy and the theology of what all the churches believe in. We do not disbelieve what they believe in, fundamentally. In essence they all believe about the same thing. But we do believe this: that we are living in a spiritual Universe right now. The Universe is a spiritual system; it is intelligent and governed by Intelligence. Because it is intelligent, it is a unity. Because there is nothing unlike it with which to divide it, therefore it remains a unity.

That which is a unity—whether we think of a unity small or large—because it is indivisible, it is present in its entirety at any and every point. That is what is meant by the Omnipresence of God. It really is an axiomatic and mathematical and logical proposition that whatever the original Creative Genius is, whatever God is, God is what we are—and there is no difference between the word of Truth we speak and the word of Truth God speaks, because when we speak a word of Truth, it is Truth announcing itself, and that is God. "Who hath seen me hath seen the Father." Emerson said, "Who in his integrity worships God becomes God." It cannot be otherwise.

But since God is infinite, as Troward said, It goes on ad infinitum, but with never any point of saturation, like the sequence of numbers: you never exhaust the possibility of multiplying them by themselves or adding another unit equal to the sum total of the first one.

What we have to arrive at is the significance, first of all, of the intellect— unless we have that far-reaching consciousness of fate and conviction which certainly is wonderful, but which very few people have; and the average person cannot wait, necessarily, for that transition of thought through some inward experience which lifts him, as it were, above the mundane clod to the Seventh Heaven of bliss. He has to start right where he is to go where he is going; and unless by some inward awareness or intuition we grasp the significance of spiritual things, we have to begin by some proposition that will at least acquaint the intellect with the validity of the proposition—Is it so, or is it not so? *Life is*—that is self-evident. Whatever Life is, it is. We choose to call Life by the name of God or Truth or Reality or the Supreme Intelligence or Divine Spirit or Creative Genius or Universal Mind. It doesn't matter what we call it; all these mean the same thing. Life is, or the Truth is that which is. That is the first axiom of reason or self-evident reality.

Now it is self-evident that there can only be one Life, because if there were two and they were opposed to each other, they would neutralize each other. If there appeared to be two and they were just alike, they would co-alesce; they wouldn't be two at all. That is why it says, "Hear, O Israel, Eternal the Lord thy God is one." That is why the Hindu said, "What we call matter is Atman, because there is nothing but God." Now they did not use the stupid approach that many modern metaphysicians have taken in order to arrive at the Reality: to deny everything they don't like. This is not the right way. I find that eventually they affirm everything they want to be so and deny everything they don't want to be so. Truth has nothing to do with our human opinion. I would suspect my opinion as much as I would anyone else's.

Truth is what is and not what we think. We may believe what is not so; we can only know what is so.

There is One Life, that Life is God, that Life is my life. Emerson said there is one mind common to all men, etc. They have all announced it. God is one, and there is only one of whatever It is, and this is self-evident. Well, if the One is all there is and It isn't divided, then while our imagination may not include the scope of the reference, our intellect and sense of reality can accept the fact that all of what is (now this is difficult to understand and I don't pretend to understand it, but I accept the fact; it is hard for me to understand that all of the only God there is is between my two fingers here; sounds egotistical and conceited, and it has nothing to do with either) all of the God there is is at any and every point of infinity. That is why Mrs. Eddy said It is neither beyond the point nor approaching it; It is *at* the point—and she is right. And it is why the ancients said It is that whose center is everywhere and whose circumference is nowhere.

I was thinking about these things last night. They are not new to me or to you; but I was thinking about the relationship of this to a treatment, because I had given several treatments, and I thought that one of these treatments didn't sound quite real to me—like you were talking to a void and nothing happened. It seemed like the words went into a vacuum, and it wasn't real to me; what I had said didn't sound real. Treatment is the heart of our work, and without it what have we to offer? Nothing to offer except the proof. We have something to prove, and that is the availability of Presence, of Law, of Person, and of Power—personalizing without ever being personal in the sense of a possession, because at the moment it becomes personal in the sense of a possession, everything we think we possess personally will ultimately obsess us. It is true. I don't care what it is. I am speaking of the essence of things.

This is no different from the Bible saying that we are servants to the thing we obey. Now there is nothing wrong with possession as *use*. It is rather that there can be no such thing as individual good in the Universe: where would it come from, this good that belongs to me—? I do not see where there can be an individual anything in the Universe; because if there were, then that individual something, whether blade of grass or archangel, would block the entrance of more universality into itself and could itself never evolve into more universality. The door would be closed. It is logically, mathematically, and intuitively certain that this is so. That is why Emerson said, "Cast your good on the four winds of heaven," and Whitman said, "The gift is most to the giver and comes back to him"; and Jesus said, "Give and it shall be given unto you," etc.

Now to get back to the other proposition: it is not by merit of any virtue we possess that truth is truth; we are only fortunate if we see it and understand it and accept it. And I was thinking I had given two or three treatments that sounded pretty real to me; and when I think one and it doesn't sound real, I start all over again and say it out loud. Did you ever try that? Sometimes it does something, because sometimes the thought seems nebulous. We have to treat, in situations like this, that only the truth can be known, only the truth can be revealed, and only the truth can be accepted, and only the truth can be acted upon. That will cover any case at law or any place else. We can work to know there is nothing but the truth; no one can utter anything but the truth; no one can believe anything but the truth or listen to anything but the truth or act upon anything but the truth. This we have a right to do, and it has nothing to do with our opinion. Then I said to myself, "What power is back of the word I am speaking?" Would you think anyone who has been in this sort of work as long as I have would have to get right back to "c-a-t spells cat," etc.—?

It surprises me; but believe me, I don't hesitate to do it, because I know if we jump a loop here and run around and nothing happens, there is something fundamentally wrong—and we can all get confused and make mistakes. So I said, "Get right back here. What is back of my word?" And then I said, "There is nothing back of my word. If I have a word that is ineffective, there can't be anything back of it. Nothing of conviction is going into it, and I have been merely announcing what I hoped might happen tomorrow."

Hazel* used to say to me, "Be sure your treatment is not just your desire or wistful wishing; be certain that when you are through with it, the Law and Order of the Universe is behind it and you have nothing to do with it. It is none of your business." The treatment is no good until it is that way: it is the authority of Truth and not of the one who announces it. The moment

---

*Hazel Holmes, Ernest Holmes's wife and a skillful practitioner.

it becomes the authority of the one who announces it, he is holding a thought, sending out a thought, willing something, concentrating.

At a meeting recently someone was to give a treatment, and they had so many things to do before they could give the treatment that I couldn't treat at all, and I got confused. We have something that the world is waiting for, the proof that the most simple person can do. He doesn't have to be able to read Greek or Latin; he doesn't have to arrive at the exalted place where we only see a shadow. This is it: "The words I speak, they are Spirit and they are Life." So I said, "What goes on?" And then I said, "I think probably I am sending thoughts out, and that isn't what I want to do. I am trying to make something happen, and that is not the way the Universe is organized. It cannot be." Then I thought, "It can only happen inside of me anyway—my treatment is my acceptance." The word itself, I think, is a mold. I don't think the word is a creative thing. It appears to be one; but let's say it isn't exactly that.

Jesus did not teach superstitions, he did not teach or say the things that theology said he said or taught. He said things that they interpreted to mean what he didn't. He said, "I am the way, the truth, and the life. No man cometh unto the father but by me." He is talking about Atman, Christ, Buddha, Truth, the Spiritual Man. The only mediator between God and man is Christ. This has nothing to do with Jesus. Jesus was the greatest of the Jewish prophets, a Jewish boy; Christ is the same as Buddha, the Enlightened One, the Perfect Man—the perfected man. And so I finally said, "It is none of my business, I neither know nor care anything about what happens. But this I know: nothing can be misrepresented; only the truth will be known. There isn't anything or anyone who can articulate a falsehood, or anyone to believe one; nothing to act on what isn't so—because what isn't so isn't so, and that is that." This morning the word came through that it was so.

I could not complete this treatment while I was trying to get it outside myself. This is what I discovered, and this is why I am interested in it. While I tried to make this treatment do anything or be anywhere other than where it was, it got separated from me and I didn't know whether it went anywhere or not. It is a funny, illusive thing, but a real one. And I thought, "I have taught this so long that maybe I have forgotten what it means"—and this too can be true. We can be so darned theoretical it doesn't work. And I thought again: in the present state of our existence, every layman must be a practitioner; it is no good if he isn't. I just want everyone to know there is such a thing as a treatment, there is such a thing as a Principle that reacts. They do know how to do it; what they know is the way to do it. But they may not be sure they know—and the way they know is the way it works. This is the illusive thing.

Everyone believes all things are possible to God. Almost everyone today believes theoretically in what you and I believe; most of them do—you almost never find anyone who doesn't. They may interpret it differently and have a superstition or ignorance about it, but most people believe there is Something that can do anything. But how few people, even in our own field, *know!* But the word, in my estimation, is not the essence or mold—a word without a meaning, without an acceptance in the mind of the one who utters it.

Then I started reading Aurobindo again, and it starts out by saying that we will never get anywhere while we believe in a spiritual Universe operating on a material one or a physical one, which is so true. Einstein said that energy and mass are one, and Quimby said that mind is matter in solution and matter is mind in form, but there is a superior Intelligence to which they or it are as "the matter of Spirit"—which is same thing. All these people have reduced the Universe to a fluidic something, taking a temporary form.

Did you ever read Eustace's* book on Christian Science simplified? I don't care where it comes from, it is a good book, and Truth is always Truth and doesn't belong to anyone. In this he said, we don't spiritualize matter or materialize Spirit; we are not using a spiritual power to operate on a physical one, else we shall be using some power to operate upon the inertia of a resistance. And as long as we operate upon the inertia of a resistance, we shall

---

*Herbert Eustace, teacher of Christian Science and author of *Christian Science: Its Clear, Correct Teaching.*

be resisting it—and we shall rise little higher than the contention of a struggle where opposites that are more or less equal contend or crash, like two icebergs, rather than getting some other thing up there which melts them. We are not trying to get a Spiritual Universe to operate on a physical one. We are not trying to get a word of Truth to operate on a word of un-truth. This too is dualism. We are not trying to get a good to overcome an evil. There is no evil in the Universe—you know what I mean—and if there is, where did it come from? But there is certainly a mistaken concept of what is good; the illusion is not even in the simplest fact but in our reaction to it. The earth and the sky do not meet out there—but there *is* an earth and a sky. I don't feel we have to even deny experience; you certainly do not have to deny fact to affirm a faith, because, as I read, the larger order includes everything. The greater includes the lesser.

We have to get away not only from contemplation of dualism in our sys-tem but even so far as possible from the further mental contention of ex-plaining to ourselves that since there is no dualism, our word is going to work; because in this is a subtle negation—and even in this affirmation—because the mind may only affirm, even though it does it negatively. There is no dualism in the Universe; on this we agree. There appears to be, and on this we are agreed too. We have to get to a place where appearance is not something to be contested against or fought, but merely be clarified by knowing it isn't.

The subtleness of the mind is the most illusive thing in the world, and in this very illusiveness is the key to success or failure. Someone I think quite a little of is away, distant; here is what looks like quite a proposition and has to be neutralized; and adding this all up together, I have created an adver-sary. And once you have an adversary, you have to fight with him or he will cut your throat. And this is subtle. Here is this very innocent illusiveness, probably the key to success or failure.

Troward talked about the way to know whether we are treating in the Absolute. But I don't like that expression, because it looks as though you had to go from the relative to the Absolute, which you don't—and which he didn't mean. But too many absolutists interpret it that way. Relativity is as absolute as Absoluteness, because it is Absoluteness at the point of Its own relativity, that it may express Itself; and there is no dualism in it. That is true. Plotinus said that everything is as real as it is supposed to be, but nothing has self-determination. It is quite a thing to dare, sometimes, to come honest with yourself—but how revealing it is! And that is the trouble; and we hate to look at it.

And yet until I am willing to, then I am the guy who has to live with myself all the time. So I thought, "Start all over again. None of this is any of your business. You have dragged in more things to get rid of, and while you have them, there they are." So finally I was able to get to the place where I could say, "Truth is all there is; there is nothing else. Nothing can happen but what is so; nothing can be believed in except what is so; nothing else can be acted upon; no one can articulate or act on something that isn't so, because there is no one else to speak."

So by the time I got through, I felt about 50 to 75 pounds lighter physically—because a mental burden is a physical one. There is a book which starts out by saying, "We used to think a person has to be well in order to be happy. We now know a person has to be happy in order to be well—and this is not putting the cart before the horse."

Then I thought about something else: all this wouldn't be so much to me if I didn't keep on thinking, "Why is it so?" But we cannot explain life. God couldn't tell you why God is God. There is no God who can do anything other than announce. And this is why it is that the more exalted the mysticism in the teachings of the world, the less the explanation. Jesus never explained anything; he said it is like this and like that and like something else. The greater they have been, the less they have explained and the more they have announced.

However I feel this: very few people have this mysticism, and very few people understand what they are talking about. We go through processes of reasoning to arrive at that which could not reason; but if it did, it would be reasonable. Jesus said, "I judge no man; but if I did, my judgment would be just." All of our processes of reasoning are merely methods whereby we arrive at that which knows no process and operates by announcement, involved within which announcement are the processes of the evolution of the idea which the word has involuted.

This is what Troward explains in the first chapter of *Bible Mystery, Bible Meaning*—the chapter on Involution and Evolution—and what the Bible explains in the beginning of Genesis where it says this is the generation of time when God "made every plant of the field before it was in the earth"— and it means what Browning meant when he said, "A spark disturbs our clod" and what Whitman meant when he said, "At the center of everything nestles the seed of perfection," etc. All evolution—we do not deny evolution, you know—is the logical unfoldment of involution.

Ouspensky* said that we go down a street and see a house, but traveling in this direction we only see a small part of it; someone coming from the other direction sees another part of the house. Now nothing happens to the house. If we were in a position where we could see all four sides, we would see them all at once. The other three sides were not absent merely because we couldn't see them. And Aurobindo explained the same thing where he said that whatever is going to evolute throughout eternity had to be invo- luted, and that all processes of evolution are merely the unfoldment of what is involuted. This is all a grand idea of a universal thing which they have all taught: involution and evolution—that in the original meaning, it is the divine spark impregnating the mundane clod, or Lucifer thrown over the embankments of heaven, falling to the earth like a flaming sword. It all means the Light that lighteth every man's path. It means the Light of Life impregnating this, and now It is this clod—matter is Brahma; manifesta- tion is God. Mrs. Eddy said the same thing when she said, "All is Mind and its infinite manifestation," because their whole process of treatment is based on the assumption that there is no difference between the thought and the thing—and I think that is correct.

This will hold true, then, in our treatment: that the nature of Reality is such that God didn't will it—there are no cosmic plans; God isn't going somewhere. Dean Inge said that an infinite will is a contradiction of both

*P. D. Ouspensky, Russian philosopher and writer on abstract mathematical theory.

logic and mathematics, and that is true. So the whole creative process of evolution or unfoldment is merely an effect, and it is of the nature of Reality. Therefore this is the reason why if I treat I don't convince anything but myself: there is only one Self, and It really doesn't have to be convinced. But I have to break through my intellect to the place where my whole being emotionally and intellectually may *accept*, and not even look for the evidence; because to it the word will be the evidence. "The words I speak, they are Spirit and Life."

So let's let it happen here—and know that our word is the presence and power and activity of the Living Spirit. We don't make it; it can't help it; we have nothing to do with it or to say about it—it is transcendent. We don't will it, wish it; it is so. And we know "There is that which scattereth and increaseth"; there is that gathered which is scattered; and all the power and presence there is is Light and Love, the Living Spirit Almighty—and I shall forever be. That which I am is now; what God is is now what I am. "I am that which Thou art, and Thou art that which I am," the eternal song, the living joy, stillness of peace, security of love, joy of action. I am That; and in this which I am is all life, all motion, all action, reaction, every song, every dance and wind and waves and splendor of the sunset and song of bird—and love of children, and mother pregnant with hope and father joyous in the giving and ineffable beauty, over all, in all, and through all. So it is.

13.

PRAYER MUST BE AFFIRMATIVE

There is so much that we seem to have forgotten about what we used to know about the simplicity of this thing. Did you read the article in the *Times* this morning about the Episcopal clergyman and what he had to say about prayer? That shows a tendency of the times. It is a metaphysical article; it said that prayer must be affirmative. Now from our viewpoint we get right back to what Quimby said—and everyone said that he was an infidel and charlatan; remember, this was 100 years ago, and he was the first one who ever discovered that there is such a thing as what we call affirmative prayer, and how it works, in the whole history of the world that we have any record of—he said that Jesus did his work *with understanding*; that if he were healing with faith, he would have been a humbug. Mrs. Eddy said somewhere that if we are healing by faith, we ought to get healed of faith so we can heal with understanding—not in those exact words.

I told you some time ago I knew a Methodist bishop 45 years ago who said the time would come when all Christian Science pagodas would be upside down in hell. Here is a radical departure from the concept of prayer when we consider that down here at Redlands University they discovered that the affirmative prayer, which Cherry* Parker called Prayer Therapy, is

---

*Nickname of William Parker. See William R. Parker and Elaine St. Johns, *Prayer Can Change Your Life* (Prentice-Hall, 1957).

70 percent more effective than the ordinary prayer right straight through the line, so that too arrives at a principle. The thing that Quimby and Mrs. Eddy and early New Thought teachers believed, and all of the metaphysical field that differs from the other concept of prayer, is right here. And when we inquire into it, then, and when we analyze it to see what it really means—not just on the surface—we have to accept that the prayer is its own answer in the terms of its own acceptance. We can't avoid it. Don't you think that is right? *The prayer is its own answer in the terms of its own acceptance.*

Jesus said, "It is done unto you as you believe"; therefore we have to accept that nothing can come out of the prayer unless it is put into the prayer. And yet no power is put into it. It is taken out. It is something of a paradox; but we don't put power into life—we take it out always. We don't put anything into anything. As Emerson said, "We are beneficiaries of the divine fact." Browning, putting it poetically, said, "It is Thou, God, who giveth; it is I who receive." And Jesus went around telling everybody to believe and have faith—it is done unto you as you believe—and then turns right around and says, "But who by taking thought can add one cubit to his stature?" We have to reconcile all these apparent opposites to find the kernel inside the nut that is really edible.

This is very important, because if we are going to teach a science of religion or Christianity; or applied, or practical, Christianity; if we are going to accentuate even what Parker discovered down here—to put it down in a form that all superstition is removed from; if we are going to do all this, then we are going almost to be shocked ourselves, and a little mystified, because life is a mysterious thing. I gave the best talk on prayer Sunday night; wish I had had it taken down. Nothing new—but it came together so well. It came up that if we compare the concept of Jesus as absolute intuition—and he said, "It is done unto you as you believe"—and the way we think of it as a scientific thing, in that we know what goes and how and what to expect, then we are going to have to arrive at the conclusion that nothing comes out of the prayer. Now this is the treatment, other than what we put into it; and yet what we put into it is now the power that makes it what it is. And yet it must be we who put it in.

If we didn't, one kind of prayer wouldn't be any better than another. Some very good things happened last Tuesday here, and they can't happen unless the treatment is its own answer and unless there is no difference between the treatment and what it does. And that is why it is we never try to repeat a treatment and give it twice alike. There are no formulas for treatment. Our daily meditations are not formulas; they are merely inspirational readings for the purpose of getting someone into an attitude. You will find that all Christian Science practitioners read *Science and Health* all the time. They do not read it as a formula, but to keep their mind as, we will say, in tune. It is probably a good idea. When you get so you don't have to read any meditation, you will have one more savior out of your way—you will be that much nearer the thing you are after, because, as Emerson said, "We are that much weaker for that one who marches under our banner." Isn't that interesting? These are only instrumentalities, like an automobile or something we ride is; they are not the destination. That is why Emerson said that travel is a fool's paradise.

But to get back to the essence of the thing: if a prayer is 70 percent more effective if it is an affirmation, that is the right way to pray. We are sure of that. If some affirmative prayers are much better than others—which our experience teaches us; we are sure about that—if there is no formula about a prayer which we know is true, then every prayer or treatment is a spontaneous thing or proclamation of the mind knowing it. And if all that is true, then we know that the answer to the prayer is in the prayer when it is prayed. This is what is shocking—and yet we don't put it in; we take it out. We know it as well as we know that the chicken is in the egg when you set the hen, and that the oak tree is in the acorn when you plant the acorn. But if these things are so, then we find, again, the place of what we call realization as an acceptance; but we find something else that I was never quite so clear about as I was Sunday night. Isn't that funny!

So this is a new sidelight in my own mind on the scientific angle. There were a number of university students there who belong to University of Colorado, and this guy tells me that they set up a terrible argument with him, and question everything—but they come. So I made a few answers, and one of the boys, who is an honor student, came up afterwards and said, "Would you speak at the University? I could get a very large group there." And I asked if it would be a waste of time or if they were really interested, and he said they were really interested. I finally got this insight and said, "We may view it poetically; we may view it inspirationally; we may view it intuitively; but according to experiments down at Redlands, they didn't view it any of these ways. This is what is important about it—that it did not come out of another religion; because if it had, it would have lost much of its value. It is up to us to find out what the rightness is. They took from every stratum— doctors, students, lawyers, whoever would come—and these people didn't have any great religious conviction; they just said, 'Let us experiment.'"

Quimby said that if Jesus had healed by faith, he would have been a charlatan, and that is shocking; and Mrs. Eddy said that you have to get healed of your faith before you can heal with understanding—and she was right too. And yet there is nothing wrong with faith. Faith does also comply with the condition, and would comply without understanding. But you cannot teach faith. You cannot teach consciousness. Through contact with someone who has consciousness we may gain it. That is why people read certain people, why they will go to hear certain people. Anyone who has a consciousness will impart it to the audience. Jesus said, "If these people didn't cry out, the rocks would have to." He knew that they ought to be absolutely still without noise; but terrific, titanic impact was being made between himself and people around him in the ethers of the universe, and he said, "It is no wonder they are screaming. If they didn't, the rocks would have to jump up and holler because something is happening."

Now Jesus was not a mere sentimentalist. He never departed from logic. He was as profound as Plato or Socrates—but so simple that nobody believed it; and they don't now. And you will find if you read the teachings of Jesus very carefully that he had just two things to teach: a divine Presence and a universal Law—nothing else. Everything else comes under this—all the beauty, everything; a penetrating vision to see the one, and an acceptance to do the other. "Blessed are the pure in heart, for they shall see God." Only the pure in heart can see God because Love only knows and comprehends Love. Beauty only understands Beauty. Peace knows nothing about discord. Tranquility knows nothing about confusion. Faith knows nothing about fear. Heaven knows nothing about hell. But we get right back to the basis upon which our whole practical application is organized or made. These people down here at the University didn't have any particular faith; they were a group of people who merely did what somebody told them to do. You know, it is the most difficult thing in the world to make an ordinary person understand what a treatment is—to cause him to see how simple it is, then to get him to know *This is it*, and he knows what it is, and he knows how to use it; then to get him to use it in that simple way, and then get him to accept that what he has done is right and he may expect a result. It is the most difficult thing in the world.

People will listen endlessly and endlessly to abstractions they don't understand at all and not get anywhere; and Jesus knew this and said it is like a child. But he never overlooked the profundity. He taught a divine Presence with which or whom we may commune, and that our word is the presence and power and activity of a creative cause which creates the situations it would experience out of its own know-how and its own "know-be." And its own "be" is something which nothing, neither God nor man, can explain—because if you were to personalize God and say, "Now God, how did you get to be God?" He wouldn't know what you were talking about. In other words, the Ultimate cannot explain the Inexplicable; the Ultimate *is* the Inexplicable. That is why the first axiom of rationality says that the truth is what is, and we have to assume that there is "what is," or nothing would be.

"I am that which I am, beside which there is none other"—and we have to get 150 people to believe that they know what a spiritual mind treatment is, to understand what it is, to accept *this is it*, to agree that they are good enough, know enough, and have learned enough to do it and say, "This is it," and then get them to do it. There would be a dynamic something created that never happened before—and this is what I am interested in. It seems to me that everyone in our field should be interested in this. It is so inspiring that I don't know how anyone can help being enthusiastic about it. This is the most creative act that is known to the mind of man—treatment. It is the most creative thing the mind of man can engage in—because without tools, brushes, or pigments or forms or instruments, something happens creatively, merely as a result of something you think inside yourself. You don't even do it—because "Who by taking thought can add one cubit to his stature?" But you think it, because it is done unto those who believe. And the very fact that it is done unto those who believe is added to the thought that you cannot add one cubit to your stature by thinking, and put together by the thought that belief, which is thought, does it—and we shall find again, to get back to the pinpoint of the complete abstraction, that the reason for it all is that we are dealing with Self-Existence. That is the secret, the key. But Self-Existence is not easy for us to imagine, merely because it isn't easy for us to accept the very simple fact that the whole nature of the Universe is Self-Existence, that there has to be That which makes things out of Itself by Itself becoming what It makes through the law of Its own Being, which will have to be absolute—and that God didn't make It; It *is* God. It is part of the dual nature of the Infinite. Not dual as duality but, let us say, as attributes—the beingness of the Being.

But these things that we have to accept are difficult merely because we haven't made them easy; because the scientist, strangely enough, accepts in his field what people in our field will have to learn to accept, which is the great simplicity of no longer arguing as to why or even what the principle is that they accept, because they have demonstrated that it exists.

We have to do the same thing. It is what they all do: they don't say what is energy? what is life? what is thought? what is the mind? what is the soul? Only theologians tear themselves apart over these silly questions. Emerson said everything, and they said he was an infidel. But he was smart; and people still don't know it. *It is the complete acceptance*—and it is the most difficult thing in the world about treatment. But there is nothing can deny it, nothing can stop it, nothing to say it can't be or hadn't ought to be, nothing to limit it, nothing that has to help it or boost it or support it. It is what it is because of the self-existence of the creative consciousness of the Infinite, which is the only consciousness that there is—which is our consciousness in such degree as we are aware of it. That is the way it works. Is that clear? But it is so darned simple—who among us is going to accept it?

I can say to 150 people, "You are going to come here every Sunday morning, and do this thing (not these words) every day for 10 or 15 minutes, according to the occasion." This is a project, and they actually do it. I wouldn't be surprised if some Sunday morning the roof would take off and float out over the ocean—and as Jesus said, if the people didn't scream, the rocks would have to. This is conviction. This is the thing Jesus had. He didn't say anything that was new to the world. The stuff they discovered recently and say the Essenes had said—God is in the rock and plant—Hindus had said: "Lift the rock and you will find Me, cleave the wood for there am I." All the beatitudes have been said a thousand times. The difference between Jesus and some of them was that Jesus knew what the words meant. Anybody can say to a paralyzed man, "Stretch forth your hand." But who would *expect* it to stretch forth?

There couldn't have been any difference in the mind of this man—at least it seems to me that there would have been no difference—between his saying, "Get up and walk," and the guy getting up and walking. I don't believe there was any difference. I think this is just as Einstein said—energy and mass are equal; Einstein said this same thing scientifically, did you know this? He didn't say one operates upon the other; he didn't say one influences the other. And we do not say that we spiritualize matter or materialize spirit. We say one *is* the other; they are the same. Ice is water, and water is ice; but not all water is ice, and ice is not all the water there is. There is a lot more of it. Jesus said, "Not I, but the Father who dwelleth in me; but the Father who dwelleth in me is greater than I; and yet it is This who dwelleth in me that is what I am. Whatsoever the Son seeth the Father do, that doth the son also, that the Father may be glorified in the Son," etc.

You will notice in his healing, which you and I will call his demonstration, Jesus was not beseeching or praying. Jesus communed, recognized, unified, and worked by *command*, but not by an arbitrary command—to scream an affirmation at an empty void or into a vacuum of endless space. But you know, right now as I talk about it, I could just get up and scream like hell—it is the way I feel about it. There was a guy who came Sunday, and he said, "Do you talk in Los Angeles?" and I said no. He said, "If you are ever going to give a talk, let us know and we will fly out to hear it." I thought, this guy doesn't have to fly anywhere. He has already been where he is going. He doesn't want to hear me; something happened to him, so he listened to himself, perhaps. All revelation is self-revelation. All healing is self-healing. All truth is self-truth. All the God we pray to, and the only God we *could* pray to, is the effort of the mind to discover itself, being the thing it is in search after. This is the center from which Jesus talked. It isn't conceit, because you have nothing to do with it. That is why the Gita says that the self must raise the self by self.

Now if we got the thing cornered and captured and caught where we know what it is and where it is, how stupid we are that we don't do better with it! But we get right back to that simple thing. We are not stupid; as simple as this thing is, it is the most revolutionary thought that ever came to the world—now not what I am saying—but what Jesus said, and what they all said, and what we reiterated. It is the most revolutionary thought that ever came to the world. That is why Emerson said, "Beware when God lets loose a thinker on this planet." Governments, institutions, political systems, economic systems—everything is going to change, because there is something shattering about this thing. It will level all. But believe me, when God does let loose a thinker—of course, God doesn't let loose of them; they loose themselves in God—he will speak a language so simple people will not accept it. It has to be that way—the most startling thing, intellectually and philosophically; because 90 percent of psychology as it is taught is materialistic; at least 90 percent of all theology in the world—every kind—is dualistic; and most philosophy is materialistic. It has tended to change in the last 25 years, but it is still over on the side of dualism and materialism and will be until it recognizes the similarity of the visible and invisible—energy and mass—what appears and what doesn't appear—and, in regard to our field, in practical application, until it knows what you and I are talking about. I don't claim to know it; I just know it is true. There couldn't be one bit of difference between what we say and what happens when we say it, because *what we say* is *the thing doing,* announcing itself as *the thing done,* and existing in a medium where time does not exist and space does not enclose—a medium of absolute freedom, of spontaneous combustion or self-announcement. This is the secret Jesus knew.

But he knew it in such a human way. He called one of his followers and named him after the God of thunder and lightning, because this guy got mad one day and wanted Jesus to call down anathemas on somebody who had laughed at them. Jesus was one of the funniest men who ever lived. We don't like to think this way, because we think it's sacrilegious. All these old guys came in and wanted to stone the prostitute, and Jesus had a lot of fun with them. This is real, the essence of a very subtle wit. He said, All right, you have all the answers—and being completely pure and without sin, you take her out and slit her throat. This is high wit in my estimation.

But there was that thing about Jesus—when he said, "Let it be done," there wasn't any stammering or stuttering; he didn't turn pale or shake. This was to Jesus like a child saying, "Pass the bread," knowing it will be passed. That is why he said, "If ye ask bread, will you get a stone?" Jesus knew the exactness of the Law. Jesus knew no one beseeched God. God is the bread. God is the stone too—or else there wouldn't be a stone. As we discussed the other day, the emotions of love and hate are the same energy; but being channeled differently, it becomes an emotion of love or an emotion of hate. But it is an identical energy. The only thing in the world that can make it work is what made it appear not to work; the only thing that can make it appear not to work is what makes it work; else you have dualism in the universe. We have not got a good and bad; we have not got a right and wrong; we have not got an impossible ethics and morals in the universe. We only have action and reaction, the sole nature of which action has to be in harmony and what we call love and givingness, or it would destroy itself; and since it hasn't, it is.

We don't have to argue whether God is love or not, or whether God is givingness. We don't have to argue whether this Thing is good or whether It is joy or beauty or peace—there can be no argument against It. Science knows no energy that will operate against itself. What do we argue with? And we certainly do a lot of arguing, don't we!

Our spiritual conviction is arguing with our psychological self. That is good, and it's worth an hour's talking to say, That is it. Our spiritual conviction is arguing with the psychological reaction, which is largely unconscious. Hazel* used to say that we are so marked by experience. She was the wisest person I ever knew, and she had no superstition. She used to say, "The Universe is just, without judgment." What do people mean when they have to recite the Lord's prayer, or something you or someone else wrote for a treatment? Don't they know that a treatment is an entity in itself—that what will come out of it is what goes into it, nothing more and nothing less—? It cannot be less, and it would be impossible for it to be more— because this is the measure-upper. Take a 2-gallon pail and lift up out of infinity 2 gallons of liquid: you will have just 2 gallons in the pail. That is all the pail holds.

Our psychological self contains the memory of the whole human race. I thoroughly agree with Jung's concept of the collective unconscious; it is no different than Mrs. Eddy's idea of mortal mind, and the Bible's of the carnal mind; but to make it more simple: just what everybody has always believed impinges upon all of us. We don't even know why we are Democrats or Republicans—it is mostly because we are Northerners or Southerners. We have no real rational, intelligent reason at all, do we.

There are logical reasons, yes; but if we had been born Baptists, we would be Baptists, etc. At any rate, we shouldn't compare it to our theology, because they are mostly nonsense anyway, but we should compare it to our belief and reaction to life itself. How many people in the world believe they could say to a paralyzed man, "Get up and walk" and have him do it? One man did it. Why don't people believe they can do these things? Practically everybody in the world believes there is *some* power that could do all the things Jesus did. But how many would attach themselves to that power, or it to them? Right

---

*Hazel Holmes, Ernest Holmes's wife (d. 1957).

in our own field: how many people in this room believe he or she is the one who could do it?

We are getting down to cases, and this is what we have to accept; and we cannot accept it while we believe we *have* to do it. We cannot accept it until we know we *can* do it. And here is the paradox; and this is why Jesus said, "It is done unto you as you believe"; "but who by taking thought can add a cubit to his stature?" This is what Quimby and Mrs. Eddy and the whole field have contended, and what the theological field has never known or seen or understood—and it is interesting to see the first glimmering of this faint flickering of the eyelashes looking up and saying . . . Jesus said, "Behold!" And they all looked up and said, "We don't see a thing!" But Jesus saw something; and what he saw was real and dynamic.

We can *say* that the cancer doesn't have to be there, the tumor doesn't have to be there, the poverty doesn't have to be there, the itch doesn't have to be there; but then we get into a quandary about ourselves, and our teachers say, "Look at me and die—you are not good enough yet." And all this is silly. We don't get right down and say, "Here is a guy who took them right off the campus and said, 'I am not worried and don't care about your theology; just try praying, and *believe* in your own prayer—and let's see what happens.'" A group of untrained people, raw recruits. So why don't we forever put all superstition out? Why don't we forever brush aside, and not say, we are not good enough—? Who told us we were not good enough?—What is good? A very relative term.

We put off the day; we deny that which we will have to affirm. And I will admit every claim about not being good enough, etc.—but I will still say, jump in the water and see if you won't get wet. And anyone who will pray affirmatively will get a result. But we will carry it further and say it cannot be that way unless the thought is the thing, and unless one is merely the liquid form and the other just exactly as Quimby said: mind is matter in solution, matter is mind in form; but there is a superior wisdom which uses them both. If we want to think, and not accept things on another or higher altitude of faith—which is good—then somewhere along the line faith must pass into knowledge, and knowledge into understanding, and understanding into acceptance, and acceptance into announcement. That is the way it was with Jesus. He didn't try to explain very much; he just announced it.

We have to get to a place where we say, *This is it*. Then something comes up—inertia, thought patterns, argument of error, psychic unconscious. A few idealists said there could be peace on earth. Others said, "What fools! There has always been war and always will be war." Russia doesn't want war, and certainly no other country wants war. No one wants war. But it is a psychological thing, something coming up out of the experience of the human race. And the day the consensus of human opinion would agree that there will be no more war—it just won't be there; the affirmation will have neutralized the negation. In all probability we demonstrate a harmony not too much beyond the consensus of human opinion over hundreds of years. There must be a song beyond what any human being has sung—and there is.

But the argument, inertia, spiritual awareness meeting the psychological experience of the ages meets a very worthy adversary—it is less than something and more than nothing. I read an article several years ago, called "I Saw the King of Hell," about a newspaperman and group over in Tibet somewhere where they meet once a year to demonstrate that they can overcome evil. They concentrate, and this takes the form of a gigantic man—an awful-looking thing; they conjure this thing up so everyone can see it. Then after bringing all this about—it is the personification of evil—they have to dissolve it to prove they can control evil, and they do.

Aren't we always seeing these things? Experience is arguing to us, "You can't do this or that"; and the consensus of human opinion is right there. And because someone will give up the so-called evils, and someone else endlessly prays, treats, concentrates, and something happens, we go into a still more illusive form of superstition (and I hate to say this; Emerson said, "Truth is like a cannonball") and we begin to talk about "dedication," etc.; and I believe in all this; but this isn't what makes it work. You would fall into as great an error here as if you were presenting it in a much more crude form. The guy who is drunk and the guy who is in ecstasy before an altar of his faith are the same guy using the same energy, identified with two purposes but seeking the same end, which is gratification, happiness, wholeness, security, and love. That is all anybody is after. There isn't anybody after anything else, no matter what he thinks. There is nothing else he can be after.

Let's get back, back, beyond our badness, goodness, wrong—way out there where there is nothing but space; way down there before we began to think, so there is no liability; get up where there is no noise, no confusion, no traffic, where nothing was ever done or said by ourselves, through all the ages, that alters the fact one iota: the sun still shines. Each take the name of someone and say, "This is happening; whatever is there that doesn't belong is removed, and what should be there is there." Let's know we exist in this place that time does not contain and space does not enclose. Everything we touch is made whole; the light comes through; everything has joy and responsiveness and love—and we are that thing now.

BENEDICTION

That is the best thing I have said this morning; it is a guarantee that God doesn't figure relatively, but announces absolutely. Well, let's you and me do that. That is a good place to start.

We know we are That; "I am that which Thou art." There are many requests for healing—and will each of you who made those requests think of them and the person you are working for and let's see if we can't realize that the Undivided Whole is right here, the Perfect right here, the Changeless, the All in all. And knowing that by the immutable Law of Self-Existence that which we announce must appear, the water must turn into wine because the word *wine* is used instead of *water,* what we call the healing must take place because it is merely the reaction to the word we are using. We don't put anything into it. We cannot take out all until we stop trying to put in any. It is impossible. Who put the chicken in the egg or the oak tree in the acorn? Only Life can give life. Therefore these persons whose names we have mentioned must be whole right now. We haven't anything to do with it, and it can't help it; and everything that doesn't belong must leave—it is banished; while "All that is at all/ lasts ever past recall."

So our own consciousness is lifted up to the perception of the allness of that which we are, because it is what we are. Now we know that our own consciousness is aware and alive and awake and conscious and perfect. So it is.

NOT THE END

BUT

THE BEGINNING

Volume Three

IDEAS OF POWER

INTRODUCTION

Following World War II, the people of the Free World were seeking a Living, Loving God of Hope and Freedom. In this period, and through the 1960s, the rise of healing religion was responsible for a "Golden Age" of belief. The central theme seemed to be, "Prepare us to live today, not die tomorrow."

The Rev. Billy Graham was preaching worldwide. Dr. Norman Vincent Peale, at New York's Marble Collegiate Church, was acclaimed. The Rev. Robert Russell, an Episcopalian priest, was putting healing back into the Church in Denver. Rabbi Edgar Magnin was emerging as a kindred force in Los Angeles. And Silent Unity was flourishing as never before. Many others, too numerous to identify, were similarly making their contribution.

The catalysts so largely responsible for the surge were two great emissaries of the healing message and practice: Dr. Ernest Holmes, founder of Religious Science, and Dr. William Hornaday, who was addressing thousands weekly at the Wiltern Theater in Los Angeles and later at Founder's Church of Religious Science. (Dr. Holmes had relinquished his Sunday-morning lecturing at the Beverly Theatre to Dr. Gene Emmet Clark so that he could be free to lecture in many different places.)

Dr. Hornaday was helping to establish world recognition of Religious Science by speaking and meeting with world leaders and prominent figures in England, France, Germany, Japan, the Netherlands, Switzerland, and

Africa. In the course of his celebrated tours he came to know Carl Jung, Albert Schweitzer, and several heads of state.

It was natural that when Dr. Hornaday was away, Dr. Holmes filled his pulpit and substituted for him in speaking engagements. Dr. Holmes often told me that a man with Dr. Hornaday's abilities and charisma came along once in a lifetime. The respect these two men had for each other established a perfect relationship, both professionally and personally.

The actual numerical membership of Religious Science churches may be small compared with the numbers of those in the "traditional," orthodox churches; however it is my belief that the developing Religious Science movement of the 1950s and '60s affected all religions and denominations. In fact, Ernest Holmes said publicly that "the movement of Religious Science may be erased in the sands of time, but the teaching and what it stands for will be in the minds of humanity forever."

Out of a "Golden Age," then, come the talks by Dr. Holmes gathered in this third volume of *The Ernest Holmes Papers*. Their focus, different from the previous two, helps to give a rounded picture of the man and his thought. And a bonus here is a talk given by David Fink, M.D., a renowned figure in medical circles at the time (1957), whose words lead into one of Dr. Holmes's most inspired talks.

It has been the custom of most Religious Science churches to close their services and lectures with a general spiritual mind treatment for those who had made written prayer requests and deposited them in a prayer box. Dr. Holmes observed this custom; and wherever possible, this book includes at the end of each chapter these affirmative-prayer meditations.

At such times, Dr. Holmes would often establish, for newcomers and regulars, an idea of why he was offering the treatment/meditation. He expressed it once this way:

If you ever get to that place of stillness—out of it everything comes: the uncreated creativity; the creative possibility of the individual out of the uncreated; the voice that was not spoken, yet is ready to articulate— something new and fresh, a creation that never existed and need never again be. But in the passing movements of our present fancy, the word shall become flesh and dwell among us as long as it ought to and dissolve when it is no longer necessary. "Our little systems have their day; / They have their day and cease to be: / They are but broken lights of Thee, / And Thou, O Lord, art more than they."

You and I as practitioners can throw all of our theories and all of our books and all of our previous prayers out of the window now, because they are evermore *about* it and *about* it and *about* it. They are necessary and they are fine . . . but now that divine moment is come. Emerson said, When it happens, throw out all of your theories, leave them all as Joseph left his coat in the hands of the harlot, and flee—for this is a transcendent moment; this is the moment of a new creation. . . .

George P. Bendall

1.

THE GREAT SECRET OF LIFE

In 1955 a report by Dr. William R. Parker and Elaine St. Johns was published entitled "Prayer Can Change Your Life." This report covered experiments in prayer effectiveness under laboratory conditions studying the physiological evaluations of both Petitionary Prayer on the one hand, and Affirmative Prayer with understanding of our deficiencies on the other.

Dr. Holmes said to me, "George, you had better get with this man, because he has proven scientifically what I have been teaching for 40 years." I did get in touch, and I developed a friendship with Ms. St. Johns and Dr. Parker. Elaine and I used to call Dr. Parker "The first man in the history of the world to put prayer in a test tube and prove it." This was on Dr. Holmes's mind when he spoke at the Wiltern Theatre in 1957 on August 11th, 18th, and 25th.

Now you are going to find out why this Thing* is here.

I am not tall like Bill† and George;‡ but sometimes good things come in little packages—although Shakespeare said of Romeo (who was about my size), "a little pot soon boils." And I remember Emerson saying that after having attended a political meeting or one of the old-fashioned revival meetings he would go out in the field, and Nature would seem to say to him, "Why so hot, little sir?" And I always liked that "little sir," because how little we are when we compare ourselves to What Is!

When George Bendall was giving the announcements, he was very modest saying there was a lecture each Sunday evening and not saying he is the

---

*i.e., "what this Thing is that we believe in."
†William H. D. Hornaday (1910–1992), a close associate of Ernest Holmes and pastor of Founder's Church of Religious Science.
‡George Bendall.

one who gives it. Now here is a very wonderful speaker. When he came to us months ago, I didn't know him; and I saw this tall and handsome man coming in and I wondered, Could anyone be as good-looking as this and have brains too? What a combination that would be! So I just sat down and thought I would wait and see what makes this guy tick—he *looks* all right—and he completely won my heart and admiration just by being himself: very kind, very sweet, very considerate, very dedicated, very serious in his dedication—but with something I can't live without, and that is a sense of humor. I have believed for many years hell is not a place that is hot—it is a place where no one has any wit and everything is doleful.

It is a great pleasure and privilege for me to speak for Bill and to you. This auditorium is not old to *me*; I spoke in it for ten years many years ago. But isn't it interesting that the older we grow in experience, the younger we become in spirit. That is an experience to me, and I know you feel that way. It is an intelligent person who can follow Browning and say, "Grow old along with me; / The best is yet to be, / The last of life for which the first was made. / Our times are in His hand / Who said 'A whole I planned'; / Youth shows but half—trust God, nor be afraid." I think that is a very wonderful attitude toward life.

And so I said to Bill, "I would like to do something different." I am not an orator like George and Bill; I am not good-looking like George (I don't think Bill is too terribly good-looking); I am shorter than Bill is—but I shall make no more concessions. So I said, "I don't care to follow the regular program; I would like to do something different. I would like to give an introduction—four lessons. I don't know how to preach sermons; religion is life, living. God is a presence in your own soul. Emerson said we should not say God *was* but *is*—not God *spake*, but *speaks*: the ever-present Reality.

Now it so happens the Religious Science Church is a thing of destiny. It is based on certain things that I want to talk to you about—and I certainly hope you will come all four times, because these are going to be four lessons in the fundamentals that will prepare everyone for the greatest class in spiritual mind treatment, culture, science, and religion the world has ever known, which is given once a year right here by our church. It is the greatest privilege anyone will ever have to take it; and I know you know that.

So this is sort of an introduction to that. I am interested in teaching. You see, we all believe in God—even the fool does—but not everyone understands certain things that we should know if we are going to come into an understanding of what the modern spiritual and psychological and psychosomatic outlook on life is, and put it all together. I believe everyone in this room should be a practitioner, consciously using a definite principle for a specific purpose. Now he doesn't have to be a *professional* practitioner—I don't mean that—but he should know what he believes, and why and how to use it.

So I chose these topics: first, the Great Secret; then, uniting the visible with the invisible, and how the basic principle of this thing works, and the possibilities you and I have of using it.

Bill said, "I wish you would talk about the discovery of Religious Science," and I said, "I will"; and then as I thought it over, I thought, That is silly. Bill isn't silly all the time; and I thought, That is really kind of a crazy subject, because I never claimed to discover Religious Science. I feel more like the little boy who was new in town and was looking for the post office and met the minister and said, "Could you tell me where the post office is?" And the minister said, "Well, I don't really know; I am new here myself. But," he said, "I *can* tell you how to get to Heaven"; and the little boy said, "The hell you can; you don't even know how to get to the *post office!*" You know, I have no reverence for hell, so I am not afraid to use the word. And there are times when it is a wonderful word.

I have a *great* reverence for children—because they don't know enough not to speak the truth. Jesus said, "Suffer the little children to come unto me, and forbid them not; for of such is the Kingdom of God." I have a feeling if you and I could discover that spontaneous proclamation of the child and couple it with the wisdom of adulthood, we should have much more closely discovered the Secret of Life.

I did not discover the Principle of Religious Science. I *did*, however, make a very great and wonderful contribution, and that is this: I was the first person who didn't think he had to be original. Therefore I was the most original person who ever lived—because I figured Truth does not belong to anyone; it doesn't matter who discovered it or what he believed or when.

Find out that thing that Lowell* called "the thread of the all-sustaining beauty that runs through all and doth all unite." That has been my endeavor for 50 years: to find what it is, out of all this maze and mystery, that finally delivers to you and to me what Moses and Jesus and Socrates and Aristotle and Emerson and Gandhi—all of them—were talking about.

What is our relationship to it? I found that in the Hermetic teaching. Now Hermes is rather a mythological figure, like Adam—and of course there was never any real Adam or real Eve; it is mythology, written to teach a lesson, and is all right. Never forget, the Bible was written by people like we are—some better, some worse; some more intelligent, some less; but *people*. Have no particular reverence for anything other than your own soul and the God that inhabits it. Treat the rest rather lightly but not profanely— but with flexibility; and remember, life is a comedy for him who thinks and a tragedy for him who only feels.

You must be the judge sitting in the judgment seat of your own consciousness, not judging the world but your own relationship to it. No one else can do it—no one can live by proxy. I discovered in the Hermetic teaching—1,500 years before Moses, in Egypt—practically everything that is in our Bible. Probably Moses got a lot of this from the Egyptians. I discovered practically everything that is in the philosophy of the Greeks—Socrates, Plato, Plotinus; the great line of thinkers of Greece. It is all back there, said in a different way; and I don't think that is strange. And I discovered that every one of them taught that we are living in a Spiritual Universe *now*. "Beloved, now are we the Sons of God."

And whether it is Plato or Jesus or Emerson or Buddha or Socrates or Plotinus or Hermes or any of the old guys who taught a lot of stuff—and

---

*James Russell Lowell (1819–1891), American poet and essayist.

don't be stupefied, awed by them—they were people like we are; happened once in a while to speak a truth; and we have to put all these truths together to find out what we know about God, man, our own nature, human destiny—that Thing which, whether we know it or not, we are more interested in than in anything else in the world. Every man is interested in his search after something that will make him whole.

Now whether we call it Atman or the Absolute or God or Jehovah or Our Father Which is in Heaven—what difference does it make? "A rose by any other name would smell as sweet." We cannot tell. All of these people have perceived a great Reality—this is the basis of Religious Science; there is but one Power, one Presence, one Life, one Mind, one Soul, one Spirit: they have all taught it—Christian, Pagan, Jew, Gentile; every one of them has taught it. I have no doubt that it is true. There is one Life; that Life is God; that Life *is* my life; that Life is your life; that Life is incarnated in us.

Particularly in Ancient Hindu philosophy—and basic to our philosophy, the philosophy of Emerson and Troward and modern science—is the thought that we are all in the process of evolution, unfoldment. "Ever as the spiral grew, / He left the old house for the new." "Build thee more stately mansions, O my soul, / While the swift seasons roll. / Leave thy low-vaulted past; / Let each new temple nobler than the last / Shut thee from heaven with a dome more vast, / 'Till thou at last art free." This is the cry of every soul. We are not satisfied with what has been, but only with the eternal unfoldment, the more that is to be—"that every tomorrow shall dawn with a brighter hope, and the sun shall set on the day in which beauty alone existed, and the night shall be filled with peace and the dawn with the glory of a new sunrise, whose golden beams spread themselves across the horizon of our hope to warm the valley of our despair and fertilize and irrigate the planes of our aspirations."

I have never met a single man who could not understand what we teach. People are often saying to me, "People do not understand it." I say, *"Why do they come?"* It is ridiculous. Did you know that the average person in public life and teachers of psychology, and what-have-you, in certain places are all wet?—and I mean around the head. They speak of the average mentality as being 14 years old: they are referring to *their own*. Not to you and to me. I don't believe that.

I have never spoken to an audience who couldn't understand what I was saying, if I understood it myself. But how can we expect, if *we* are confused, to deliver anything but confusion? I was taught in public speaking as a kid by the greatest teacher who ever lived: you can tell anybody anything if you know it yourself; and if they don't seem to get it, *you* are the person you have to take care of.

It is simple enough to understand the philosophy of the ages. It is simple enough to come to believe that, whatever you call It, there is only one Power in the Universe, there is only one Presence, there is only one final Law. It is Good, it is Love; we call it God. It is where we are. We are in It. Since It is present everywhere, It is in us. And It is the same God.

It is easy enough to understand and believe what the great and the good and the wise have taught: God is incarnated in *me*. There is one Life, that Life is God, that Life is my life; therefore in *me* is the Power. Now, *I* am not the Power; but *in* me is the Power—"that sets the stars in their courses and says to the wave, Thus far and no farther." *Within me.* And I didn't put It there. It is not by grace of anything I did. I didn't earn it. I was not intelligent enough to have created myself; and I don't happen to believe that I am intelligent enough to destroy myself. I believe that every person is on the pathway of an eternal progress, forever himself and never less—that we shall go on. I believe there are people beyond us in evolution as we are beyond tadpoles.

Now this isn't anything against us, nor is it complimentary to the tadpole. That is the way it is—from the mind that sleeps in the mineral, waves in the grass, wakes to simple consciousness in the animal, to self-consciousness in man, and God-Consciousness in the upper hierarchies of Heaven. Jesus taught this; Emerson taught it; Plato taught it; the ancient Egyptians taught it. It is the basic principle of ancient Hinduism. It is the very cornerstone, part of it, of science because everybody knows that everything is in a state of evolution. But you and I, I think, believe that evolution is an effect of That which is incarnated in us. There is within us that seed of Perfection, that divine Spark—we theologically call it the Incarnation and that is all right: God in me, as what I am, is myself. We are all linked up, by eternal bonds that cannot be broken, to a Power greater than we are.

Now throughout history there have been people who have demonstrated remarkable spiritual power. It did not come just to the Christian religion. I happen to have been born in the Christian faith. Some of you may have been born to the Synagogue. You don't have to leave it. Some of you may have been born Catholics or Presbyterians. There is nothing wrong with either one. We don't say that Religious Science is something you look at and drop dead. It has much to contribute to every man's religion. It is free of fear. It knows there isn't any hell, in spite of what is going on in an eastern city* describing what it looks like. How far many people have traveled beyond our perspectives! They probably have had more time.

We believe in a straight progression: there is that within me right now which some day will be so much farther along than I am, that what I am now is nothing. It has to be that way. We see right here a variation of that; therefore there is an evidence, there is a witness. "He has not left himself without a witness"; "He will not suffer His holy one to see corruption"; "awake thou that sleepest and arise from among the dead and Christ shall give thee life"; "do this according to the pattern shown thee on the mount." I do not know of any religion that hasn't taught it.

This is the genius—and it is real genius, not in me but in us—of Religious Science: we boldly started out and asked, *"Who said so?"* "The great are great to us because we are on our knees; let us arise." The only greatness you will ever find in somebody else is what you project onto him of what, on an equal level of greatness, you receive from him. How could it be otherwise? Can water reach a level higher than its own weight? It cannot.

That is why Emerson said if you go to hear a great man speak, as you come down the aisle you are giving him his greatness. You are giving it,

---

*May have reference to Sodom: "And Lot journeyed east . . . and moved his tent as far as Sodom. Now the men of Sodom were wicked, great sinners against the Lord." (Gen. 13:11–13)

because you are understanding it and responding at the same level—or perhaps on a higher level and also understanding it. *Every* man is great. "What
is so great as man?" "What is man that thou art mindful of him, or the Son
of Man that thou visitest him? For thou hast made him but a little lower
than the angels and hast crowned him with glory and honor."

You know, I found prayer has been answered throughout the ages; and
having been brought up in the Christian faith, I thought of course you pray
in the name of Jesus. Now that is fine. But if you had been a Buddhist, in a
sense it would be in the name of Buddha. The Ancient Hindus said God
cannot have a name, He is beyond all names. Perhaps it was Jehovah. "Underneath are the everlasting arms"; beneath are the girders of the Almighty.

Now if we could see Moses the great lawgiver and Jesus the great revelator of individual value, we would have the Jewish philosophy complete, and
one part wouldn't repudiate the other. It is only ignorance and superstition,
stupidity, that keeps people from getting together. How strange it seems!

We shall find that all of them have gotten the same results, and most of
them didn't get any results at all. Now why? I have said recently that with
the publication of this book which Cherry* Parker and Elaine St. Johns
wrote—and they are both good friends of mine—*Prayer Can Change Your
Life*, coming out of some psychological and philosophical department in a
university, to show the action of prayer—I said to Elaine the other day, "You
ought to follow it up with another and make it just a little more metaphysical." They have demonstrated non-denominationally out of a university. It
didn't have to come from a Religious Scientist, a Christian Scientist, a Jew,
Gentile, Catholic, or Protestant. How wonderful! Truth is beyond all this—
It is beyond everything; and "Truth crushed to earth shall rise again." "The
immortal years of God are hers, / But error wounded writhes in pain / And
dies among her worshippers."

I discovered the common denominator and made it the cornerstone of
Religious Science. Now I didn't discover the *Principle*, but the *common denominator*. That is all I ever want said about me. Anybody who thinks he

---

*Nickname of William Parker.

discovered God hasn't yet evolved to a low-grade moron. I discovered the common denominator of religious supplication, prayer, "beseechment," announcement, and modern psychological and metaphysical treatment or affirmation. And when I discovered it, of course I didn't *make* it—I discovered its relationship to all these things, put them together. This is really the only contribution I made—but it is a terrific one, because it lets down the bars and lets in the light from all these places. How little scenery we see if we only look through this small space! Let's take our hand away from the vision, that the eye may see the world as one vast plane and one boundless reach of sky.

Then, after having discovered this, I found they had *all* announced it—like Jesus saying, "It is done unto you as you believe"; Moses: "Underneath are the everlasting arms"; Moses showing in the teaching that he was taken up into a high mountain and whatever land his eye could see his foot would tread upon—"As thou seest, that thou be'st." I discovered it in every one of them; and the common denominator is so simple, it is hard to accept it—it is just belief, a feeling, *an acceptance*. That is the way it works in us.

It isn't a supplication. It isn't a crescent, a cross, a crucifix. Now these things are all wonderful—I am not arguing for or against. It is not that. It is a feeling in your own mind, right *in here*. A child may have it; a man of wisdom may possess it. Too often the man of overintellectual capacity has lost it, or, as Wordsworth said, he forgets that "celestial palace whence he came."

There is in you and in me a testimony of our own soul, a witness to our own spirit. Now it is as simple as this. The basic principle of Religious Science is free from superstition; it is free from bigotry; it doesn't think we have learned everything there is to learn; it doesn't say, "Caesar is dead and Cicero is dead and I have a strange feeling myself!" It isn't that way. There is no snootiness; there is no arrogance.

Somebody said the other day, "What do you think of what I am doing?" and I said, "I don't like your approach to an audience." He said, "Why?" I said, "You refer to your audience as 'you,' and I wouldn't go twice to hear anybody who does that. I wouldn't stay through the first talk. It is '*we*': what do 'we' know, how are *you and I* getting along? *That* is the common denominator—otherwise I cannot embrace you in my own thought. How do I know that God is Love unless my arms are around you? I don't." How do I know God is Joy unless I am joyful? How do I know God is Peace unless I am at peace? But there is something in me that *is* at peace.

The common denominator is belief. "As thou seest, that thou be'st." It is so very simple, free of all theology, free of all bigotry, free of all superstition. It doesn't say, "Go to page 10, line 9, so and so." All of these things are good; but as Emerson said, "What are they all in their high conceit / When man in the bush with God may meet?"

That is what prayer and meditation does—puts us in the right contact with the Presence and the Spirit and the Power. Now we are surrounded by, we are immersed in, there is in us, that One Life, that One Law—the One Life that animates everything, the One Law that governs everything. I happen to believe—and it is fundamental to us, and I put it there and said it is the most important thing in all of our philosophy—that we are surrounded by God. God is in us, and it is the same God—the God that is in *you* is the God that is in *me*, and that is how *I* can talk to *you*. I think that is wonderful. And the God in you will respond, and that is how *you* can talk to *me*.

We shall know each other in God, and we shall know God in each other; and as our thought of God reaches out to embrace the Universe, our arms will be around each other. There isn't half enough love. There is too much reserve; there is too much fear of being sentimental, of being misunderstood. Who cares whether or not he is misunderstood! The great and the good and the wise of the ages were misunderstood, else they would not have been great or good or wise.

There is that in you wed to the Universe, soul to Soul, mind to Mind, spirit to Spirit, and It is forevermore holding you in Its embrace—"A Love so infinite, deep, and broad / That men have renamed It and called it God."

There is a Law. The discovery of this Law, this common denominator, on the one hand, and the realization of that divine and common Presence on the other, are the two chief cornerstones of our whole edifice. And when you understand them and coordinate and polarize one with the other, and know what you are doing, you are a practitioner—whether it is professional or not. And I would that each in this vast and wonderful audience would make up his mind that no year shall pass again until he knows.

Let me tell you, there is a secret to life, and we have discovered it. There is a simplicity coordinating all philosophies and religions, and we have discovered it. There is a sweetness and a song and a joy that the light of Heaven itself shall cast its glow on the pathway of our own experience, "for Thou hast made us, Thine we are; and our hearts are restless till they rest in Thee."

Next Sunday I shall talk on the subject of the Use and Power of Faith and try to explain the principle running through all these modern metaphysical movements that makes them effective, and the simplicity of that thing. Our greatest trouble is to believe in that simplicity. Through some strange reason, too many people feel if anything is going to be deep and profound, it must be something no one can understand. Now that is not true. Jesus was the most simple man; he was as profound as Plato. I have studied both all my life.

You and I use the Mind that is God, therefore we do not put any power into our thought. We do not put any power into our treatment. We do not put any power into our faith, any more than you put energy into life. If you and I had to energize energy, where would we get the energy with which to energize energy? It is ridiculous. We may only take it out. But there is a way of doing it effectively. That is what I want to talk about next time, and I hope you will all come.

✦ AFFIRMATIVE-PRAYER MEDITATION ✦

Now we have names here of people who have asked for our help. Let us together know that everyone whose name is in here is known to the divine Intelligence that is in us right now. And we are one with them and the Law of Good that responds to them.

We are recognizing the divine Presence in them and their affairs, and we are affirming that the Presence of God is perfect and active. There is one Life, that Life is God, that Life is their life now. Whatever needs to be changed mentally or physically is changed to comply with the divine Pattern of their own perfection.

We are recognizing God. There is one Presence in them and but one Life, and they are that Life, and that Life is what they are. I am that which Thou art, eternal everlasting Good, and Thou art that which I am—sweet Presence, O sweet and beautiful Presence, inhabitating eternity, and in my soul and in everybody here. Their requests are fulfilled by the Law of Love.

Anyone who has needed help in his circumstances is inspired to do and think and act in that way which will bring wholeness and prosperity and success to every honest and legitimate endeavor.

Now as we silently bless these people, we know this blessing is real, dynamic, and powerful, far-reaching, as eternal as God. We do bless, and our love does surround; and that good will now acting as the Law of Life and the Love of God binds us together, so sweet, so beautiful, so sweet our Love. Now as we turn within, let us silently bless each other. It is so real, it is so immediate, it is so warm. We are embracing each other in love, in fellowship, not forgetting the joy and the laughter and song. "There is ever a song somewhere, my dear; there is ever a song somewhere"—and we shall sing it, and we *do* sing it.

Now may the eternal Spirit which surrounds us glorify Itself in us, because we have opened ourself to Its influx. May the Light of Heaven bathe us in joy and in fulfillment and in love. Amen.

2.

THE USE AND POWER
OF FAITH

This is our second lesson in our series of What This Thing Is We Believe In; Why We Believe in It; The Way We Think It Works; and What We Know about Using It. You remember last week we discussed a Principle of Life which is as simple as this: we live in a universal Mind and Spirit. There is one Mind and one Spirit, which is God. Now every time we think, we use this Mind; and Law is Mind in action. As Dr. [John] Haldane, the great biologist, said, the only thing that science has discovered that is creative is mind. Back of mind is consciousness, or thought. "In the beginning was the Word."

Now Religious Science I consider to be the greatest movement of modern times, or I wouldn't be here—and I don't think you would on quite as warm a day as this. The other day I asked someone, "Is this similar to hell?" Now of course, I shouldn't have asked this person; I have no reason to suppose he has ever been there. I think we have *all* been there; and when people ask me if I believe in hell, I say, "*Certainly*: I believe in the hell we are getting out of. There isn't any other."

The Universe does not insult us after it has injured us. We may be certain of that. As Emerson said, "The finite alone has wrought and suffered, the Infinite lies stretched in smiling repose." He said another thing I love: "We see the universe as solid fact, but God sees it as liquid law." That is the Law of Consciousness.

We said that consciousness—thought, something we know; feeling, thinking—is basic to everything and that we are surrounded by a divine and universal Intelligence which receives the impress of our thought and acts upon it creatively. For "Mind is the power that moulds and makes / And man is mind, and ever more he takes / The tool of thought and, shaping what he wills, / Brings forth a thousand joys, a thousand ills. / He thinks in secret and it comes to pass, / Environment is but his looking glass."

There *was* a secret to the miracles of Jesus, and we have discovered it. This "secret" Religious Science, for the first time in the history of the world, lays bare without prejudice. Now other people have known it. We are not better than other people. We are worse than everybody else in the world— but smarter. And that makes us more interesting. I wouldn't swap any one of us for ten of anybody else on earth. Why? Because, knowing nothing, we fear nothing. And that is a wonderful state to be in. Shakespeare said, "Where ignorance is bliss, 'tis folly to be wise." Very profound statement.

We know something that we are not afraid of, and we have not created a new devil to take the place of the old one, which we weren't able to sublimate but just had to dress up and call by a different name. You know, Religious Science is more than a revelation—it is THE revelation of revelations. I was talking to Dr. Barclay Johnson the other day, and I said, "You have built up such a wonderful course." (He is the head of our College. He has put together the greatest courses we have ever had.) I said to him, if I could persuade everyone in this room to take this course we would have a couple of thousand of the most emancipated people in the world; and if they knew what is offered them, they would demand it. And I am talking about *you*.

There is no other place in the world where it is given. There are no other people in the world so free from prejudice. Now I want to talk this morning on faith and the use and power of it, the ever-available law of faith and the measure of the principle of faith, and how it works, how to acquire it, how to use it, and the principle underlying it. That is enough for 13 talks right there. But we have so little time; we have to cover a lot of territory, and I want to begin by explaining something to you that some of you know but that some don't.

Within the last three months a new book* published by Prentice-Hall came on the market, written by two friends of mine, Elaine St. Johns and Dr. "Cherry" Parker of Redlands University, a wonderful man, very spiritual. Remember, one of the accusations laid against Jesus was that he appeared at feasts, turned the water into wine, multiplied the loaves and fishes, raised Lazarus from the dead, brought the boat immediately to the shore, showed them where to get money for their taxes, and resurrected himself from the dead. And they said, "No good thing can come out of Nazareth, because this man has permitted an evil woman, a prostitute, to bathe his feet." She bathed them with her tears; and I wrote: "How wondrous kind his words of love to the penitent kneeling there, / Who bathed his feet in tears of joy and dried them with her golden hair."

Here is a man, the man of the ages, who had one hand in the ever-outstretched hand of God and the other one embracing humanity. You and I will never know, no matter how high-sounding our theories are or how beautiful they sound or what they mean semantically. However, if I say to you, "I love you," you know what I mean; and if you say, "I love you too," I know what you mean; and when we embrace, we know how we feel. The semanticist may not.

That which instinctively rises from the human breast to proclaim the need of the finite heart is an utterance of the feeling of the Universe and may be considered the word of Almighty God. For the only God you and I will ever know is the One we embody. Never forget that.

Now Dr. Cherry Parker tried several years' experiments at Redlands University (nonsectarian in their faith: there would be Jews and Gentiles and Protestants and Catholics; there would be no God who ever heard there was a difference. But don't tell any of the people who haven't found it out but remain in splendid isolation and frozen emotions).

That is a good way to be—until you wake up. "Awake, thou that sleepest, and arise from the dead, and Christ shall give thee life."

Prayer Can Change Your Life.

Elaine St. Johns is the daughter of Adela Rogers St. Johns, who is like a sister to me and always was to my wife. Now, this* is the account which Elaine wrote based on the experiments of Cherry Parker. (Elaine and my brother Fenwicke are helping me to write a history of our movement. They didn't think I had sense enough to write it. And the funny part of it is, they were right.) This is based on three experiments with prayer. The first one is called Spiritual Psychological Counseling; the next one is called Ordinary Prayer, which all the world prays; and the last experiment is called Prayer Therapy, which Cherry used, and you and I believe in. Now affirmative prayer is what you and I believe in, but remember this: affirmative prayer means an affirmation the mind consciously uses for a definite purpose which it believes is accomplished as much as it can even though it hasn't seen it.

The prayer is uttered by the mind as affirmation and acceptance flowing out of consciousness of feeling and belief and faith, and it is identified with some person, place, or thing. Now he found that in the first category— psychological counseling, spiritual counseling—there were pretty good results, definite results. He found that in what I am going to call *affirmative prayer*, and he called *prayer therapy*, there were exceedingly good results— the best of all. And he found—and I am glad this came out of a university, so no one can criticize people in our field for saying it—that the poorest results came from the ordinary method of prayer as practiced by the world of theology. Now isn't this a knockout!

This is one of the most significant things ever to have happened. Here is a university without the prejudice of a particular theology (I don't criticize any theologies, because I don't think any of them needs that much attention—and I don't believe in criticizing anyway), and here is what they found impersonally among groups of people—some were ministers, some were doctors, some were this, that, or the other—over a period of two years: that the ordinary prayer that the ordinary person prays—no matter how good he is or how sincere, and no matter what his religion is, Catholic, Jew,

---

*i.e., *Prayer Can Change Your Life.*

Protestant (it is all the same—Jesus said "He is no respecter of persons; He causes His sun to shine and His rain to fall alike on the just and the unjust")—they found that the ordinary prayer got much poorer results than just good, sound psychological counseling. Isn't that terrific?

And they found the highest percentage of results came from what you and I will call *affirmative prayer* through acceptance, belief in consciousness, embodiment in thought. They applied the acceptance *to* something *for* something, identifying *this* with *that*—like saying "This word is for John Smith. As a result of this treatment [or this prayer] there will be a new activity over there. As a result of *this*, that confusion will cease." Now that is what I mean by *identification*.

The prayer has to be made *in here*; it has to be *affirmative*; it must be *accepted*; it must *identify* with something, if something is to happen, which shows we are dealing with Intelligence. Now they found also that the attitudes of forgiveness, of unselfishness, of kindness, of joy, of enthusiasm were salutary. I have made a record called "Enthusiasm Is God's Medicine." Do you know it is now known that at least three-fourths of the illness of continual fatigue, and probably most of it where there is no infection in the physical body, may be directly attributed to a lack of enthusiastic interest in life—? And I can see how that would be.

Did you ever get full of an idea and rush up to some friend and say, "Oh, listen to this," and you go on and say and say it—and then he says, "Oh yeah?" And then you wish you were dead. Your enthusiasm is knocked down; and this is psychological frustration—a lack of just plain enthusiastic interest that makes the kid sing and dance and jump up and down and scream; and you know adults *would*—but as Wordsworth said, experience closes them round until they are encased in a prison wall and they forget that celestial palace whence they came.

Isn't it too bad that people when they grow up won't still scream and holler a little and jump up and down a little and once in a while say something that they have not premeditated—to relieve the tension and let the holier ones be surprised.

Who cares!

If we could only live!

Jesus said, "I have come that you might have life, and that you might have it more abundantly." They discovered this thing in a psychological experimental laboratory in a university, just as they have discovered in another one that which can demonstrate scientifically the ongoingness of the human soul. I am so glad that it came out of a laboratory, so no one can tag it theologically.

Now that is what our work is based on—faith. But what is it? You see, there is something people don't understand: that we are dealing with mental attitudes. They don't know there are definite techniques which we teach in our College—absolutely definite. There isn't a person here who, if he will take the very short time to take that course—because the money isn't as much as you would pay to go to a series of pictures; we are nonprofit . . . if you would only do it; and I expect you will after these four talks. And if you don't, I shall forever lose not faith in humanity but in my ability to convince anybody of anything.

Here you and I have within our reach the greatest good the world has ever known. I saw it unhesitatingly—we have the most perfect teaching, the greatest technique, and the best instruction the world has ever had—to definitely and deliberately show the method and the process that is proven at Duke University and at Redlands now, and that has been the hope and aspiration of all the religious endeavors of the world.

Faith is a mental attitude. It can be consciously, definitely, and deliberately induced. You can learn how to give a scientific, effective spiritual mind treatment so there will be no question about the result for yourself and for others. This is the greatest "experiment"—the greatest experience, the greatest good, and the greatest joy that can come to the human mind.

Faith, then, must deal with a law in Nature or itself be a "nature." Now let me explain this. These talks I am giving are preliminary to the course I want you to take—because I would like these 2,000 people here, before the year is over, every one to be a practitioner. You don't have to do it professionally; but you want to practice for yourself and your family. You want betterment. You want greater happiness, more success, better health—and above everything else, the thing that intrigues me: not the "signs following," but *the fact that there is such a Power available*—the ever-available Power of Good. It is the greatest good on earth.

Now faith either *is* the law, or *follows* a law, or is *operated upon by* a law— in my estimation. Let's follow it out. Don't think it is hard to understand. Frequently people say to me, "You shouldn't try to talk in public—nobody knows what you are talking about"; and I say, "That is why I have always had such big audiences." It makes me think of a man we used to have—the most popular speaker we ever had, and the most popular speaker at UCLA. He had peculiar eccentricities, and people who knew the art of public speaking would often come to him and say, "Now if you would learn how to speak, you would be *so* effective." And he said, "I am going to when I get time; but you know, most of my life I have had to make my living speaking, and when I have enough saved up so I can learn how, I am going to do that." So far, he is still speaking.

This thing is so simple. *Faith is a mental attitude*. It isn't a new kind of underwear, or something you eat. *It is the way you think*. Faith is thought moving consciously, definitely, for a specific purpose and—if it is *real* faith— accepting the outcome of the purpose. You know just as much about this as I do. The only difference is that I am not afraid to talk about it in public. But if you knew the experience I had when I first began! Three or four days after I made an engagement to speak, I felt as though somebody was continuously kicking me in the stomach and there was no place to throw it up. It is the most awful feeling. But once I got on the platform, I forgot it. I don't know whether everybody has that or not; but it must be like seasickness.

Does a seed you plant operate upon the soil or does the soil operate upon the seed? I don't know. When they get together, something happens. So Jesus likened faith to a seed. The Word. The Bible says that in the beginning was the Word and everything was made by it, etc. Now faith is either a law in itself or it is operated upon by a law. I personally choose to think of it as being operated on by a law, even though it is a law of faith in itself. I'll tell you why.

I happen to believe that just as we are operated upon by physical forces, such as magnetism, attraction, repulsion, adhesion, cohesion, gravitational force, these are not personal things but they personalize. Now I like to feel that faith is operated upon by a principle—so that I won't feel I have to energize energy; because if I had to energize energy, I wouldn't know where I would get the energy with which to energize energy. This is one of the secrets of Jesus: nonresistance.

He said, "Who, by taking thought, can add one cubit to his stature?" and then turned right around and said, "If you believe, it is done." One explains the other. We do not make things happen; we *permit* them to. We supply the condition under which they may, shall, can, and—I believe— *must.* And I think Jesus announced it when he said, "It is done unto you *as* you believe." I happen to believe that. Therefore *I* believe. Don't accept it because *I* believe it. It will be discussed in the class.

Everything is operated upon by cosmic forces. "The Father seeketh such." "The wind bloweth where it listeth, and no man knoweth from whence it cometh nor whither it goeth, and so is everyone who is born of the kingdom." "It is done unto you as you believe." I believe that faith acts like a law because it is operated upon by a law.

Haldane,* the great modern thinker and scientist, said that all the laws in the universe operate as though they were intelligence operating mathematically as law. Eddington† said this; Jeans‡ said that we can think of life or God as an infinite Thinker thinking mathematically. That is rather interesting. There is a mathematics to our treatment—it deals with our conscious perception and our psychological reaction to it. When you give a spiritual mind treatment or pray effectively, you are alone with the Great Reality of things. Jesus said, "The Father who seeth in secret will reward you openly."

You are at the center of the Universe—the very center and core of all causation. There is nothing out here that has anything to do with what you

---

*J. B. S. Haldane (1892–1964), British scientist.
†Sir Arthur Eddington (1882–1944), English astronomer.
‡Sir James Jeans (1877–1946), English physicist.

are doing—nothing. It is to get away from the appearance, to get away from the judgment and the conviction of fact as it is now experienced to the glorious realization that, as Jesus said, "Out of these stones God can raise up seed unto Abraham"—or, *the Law can work*. Now to me this is the essence of faith.

But only a few people throughout the ages have had that sublime and divine faith, and they stand apart from the multitude and people who say that Jesus was God, and the others are favorites of God, and this one and that one God did more for. Nonsense, and more nonsense, and still more nonsense! And when they said it to Jesus, he said—out of the enlightenment of that great mind and heart and soul and intellect—"Why callest thou me good? There is none good save one, which is God." And when they sought by force to make him a ruler, he said *no*: "I have come to bear witness to that truth that makes you free. *I* have nothing to do with it." He said, "It is expedient that I go away that the Spirit within you shall now bear witness to that divine Fact—I have revealed you to yourself; I have shown you the way. Walk ye in it!" That is the very essence of Religious Science.

Destined.

Destined to heal the world—someday, sometime, somewhere, as Browning said: "In God's good time it will arrive, / As birds pursue their trackless paths; / Some way I know not when or how, / In God's good way when God has made / The pile complete . . ." and don't forget it. You and I are in the vanguard of the greatest spiritual movement the world has ever known. And out of your heart and mine and your mind and mine—trained to think, to work—shall come the force and the propulsion and the impulsion—the impulsion of Love and the propulsion of Law—that may heal the world. That is why I am interested in our classes and in our instruction.

Not everyone has that great faith. I didn't have it. But I learned there is a key, there is a secret—not a mystery. There is a way in which any living soul may consciously reproduce the monumental works of those who have that faith; "And greater things than these shall ye do." Faith understood, life understood: that is our whole teaching—to the simple, to the great, to the wise. I would just as soon explain this to the children—they know it. I would just as soon debate it with the greatest philosophers and scientists in the world. And I will never have to leave the platform—never.

The Universe is self-existent, and God comes new and fresh in the perennial springtime of every moment, bursts forth from the timeless infinite into the present incident, carrying with it the wonder, the majesty, and the might and the warmth and color of the Eternal Itself. Such is the nature of our being. Every day is a new beginning. Every day is the world made new.

Faith is a law. Now the next point, then: we talk about the principle—how should we acquire it. You and I know it is wonderful. We say, "If we had faith, if we had faith." Jesus said, "If you have faith as a grain of mustard seed, you could say to this mountain, Move." Now, after nearly 2,000 years, without prejudice, without superstition, without the claim of any special revelation or dogmatism which says, "Look at me and die": if I have made any contribution to this thing, I think I have taken the "miss" out of mystery, the dogma and intolerance and stupidity out of special revelations, and revealed at long last the simplicity of that Thing which has run like a golden thread of beauty through the great religions of the world—what Lowell called "that thread of the all-sustaining Beauty that runs through all and doth all unite."

You and I may sing a hymn of praise this morning to the creative genius of the Universe that at least this much of the blindfold has been removed, so that we are no longer hesitant to say to the least among us, to a beggar—at last having searched a lifetime for the Holy Grail or the chalice of the eternal Giver—"I behold in thee the image of Him who died on the tree." And Jesus said, "Let him who is least be greatest; he who is greatest, let him be least." There is a nonresistance that cannot be resisted, a nonviolence that cannot be violated, a prayer of faith the integrity of which is the nature of the Law of the Universe. And Jesus said, "Heaven and earth shall pass away, but my word shall not until it is fulfilled."

Now I want you to know he was talking about *you*; and *I* am talking about you; and you are listening to that Thing within *yourself* which says *Yes*—and I didn't put It there. It was there when you came in—in a few words of conversation, or the communion of spirit with Spirit as we embrace each other in the love of God or the adoration of God; "and the love of humanity shall be torchlight." Emerson said, "Take this torch and advance on chaos and the night."

Faith can be acquired by conscious, definite, deliberate methods of procedure in your own mind—so simple that a child five years old can understand it; so profound that no philosopher who ever lived can refute it; so demonstrable that no scientific mind can successfully repudiate it; so much a thing of consciousness that it carries all of our psychological reactions into a transcendence; and so human that it bears the message of love to the heart sitting alone in the darkness of human isolation, for all the world is crying for light. There is solace for the hearts longing for love—for the world is dying just for a little bit of love and to be embraced; and people are afraid of it and they misunderstand it. Emerson said, "To be great is to be misunderstood." Over the doorway of consistency I would write, "Thou Fool!" And Jesus had to take a little boy with him—just a little brat who didn't know it couldn't be done, and the man of wisdom who knew that it could. And joining their forces together, God Almighty multiplied the loaves and the fishes.

But of what use are all these things unless we use them?

What good are all these things unless we use them?? We learn things: we learn to dance, that we may dance; we learn to sing, that we may sing; we learn to write, that we may write. *We learn to have faith, that we may demonstrate it.*

The supremacy of spiritual thought-force over all apparent material resistance: I don't know of any joy on earth equal to the joy, the gratification, not of a sense of personal power—that wouldn't do it—but of the sense of the wonder of life and the miracle of life; of the sense of our partnership with the Infinite; of the sense that we may put our feet forth into what seems an apparent void, only to find them placed upon the Rock of the Ages. I do not know of any gratification that can come to the human mind or heart equal to listening in the silence and the independence and the freedom and the aloneness of one's own soul—and then someday looking out, seeing and kissing the object of our desire. What can be more wonderful?

So they proved all these things at a university, way beyond psychological counseling—there is nothing wrong with psychological counseling, I believe in it—way beyond the average prayer. There is nothing wrong with the simple, sweet, and sincere prayer. But we are talking about science and sense—pragmatic, practical things that are right down to earth: what will produce two ears of corn instead of one, how to make the hen lay more eggs or the cow give more milk; it is as practical as that.

We are going to take the time to pray. If we believe there is Something that responds, don't we want to know the best method? Don't we want to be sure that what we are doing shall be effectual? Of course we do.

⤍ AFFIRMATIVE-PRAYER MEDITATION ⤎

(In this box are contained many requests for different kinds of healing, by a great many individuals. Every person who has put his name in there is in this room. Let me tell you *what* is going to happen, and *how* it is going to happen, so we will get right busy and begin to use what I am talking about. Because somebody by the name of John Smith put his name in here saying he would like to be healed of this, or wants this or that to happen, he has already identified his desire and need with our consciousness. And because we know that desire and need is met, we are already supplying the consciousness of that Power which can meet it, and we don't have to think about him. But together, this consciousness should rise to an attitude of thought where that demonstration or answer is inevitable and necessary; and I believe it will. But I want you to know that is the way it happens as we turn within to that divine Center which is both God and Man.)

Now at long last cleared from the stupidity of dogma, cleared from the skepticism of sophistry and the rebuttal of unbelief, cleared from all of the intolerance of overintellectualism and the spiritual stupidity of thinking that there is some God who favors one beyond the other: you and I join in the simplicity of our approach, the humbleness of our faith, the gentleness of our thought, the feeling of love from our own heart that at least would say to the poor and the weak and the suffering, "It doesn't have to be that way, perhaps. Perhaps there is a good greater than you have known. 'O thou beneath life's endless load, / Whose forms are bending low, / Who totter on the weary road / With troubled step and slow: / Ask now, for glad and golden hours / Come swiftly on the wing. / Oh, rest beside the weary road / And hear the angels sing.'"

Thou infinite and indwelling Presence, forever wonderful—God of heaven and earth, Maker of the rain and the mist, the sunshine and the shadow, back of the mountain, the valley, the summit, the fish in the ocean, and a thousand million waves spilling their crest of beauty on the moonlit beach across the trackless deep. Thou Beauty—Thou infinite Beauty flowing through the life of every person whose name is here. Divine Love and Compassion—our Love that will not let us go: we are entering, for ourselves and each one of these persons, into the name and power and spirit of that which is the essence of love and gladly surrenders all it has on the altar of its conviction. Lord God of Love, Father of givingness, Impulsion forever flowing full and free, that Love which cannot be repudiated: we love; and who shall deny the privilege of that affection?

There is a sense of love and givingness in the heart and mind and soul of each one of these names whom we embrace, embrace in the warmth of our own heart, knowing their request is answered. Let wholeness come to each one. Let the eternality flow, the enthusiasm of life. All the power and energy, all the vitality that there is in the Universe shall flow uninterrupted, torrent from the source of that river which rises in eternal God. All the power that there is, all the enthusiasm and energy and action that there is in the Universe, *is* flowing through each person; and we know it.

All the peace, peace, peace—wonderful peace—and all the sweetness—oh so sweet, so very sweet, so beautiful—presses around them; wholeness, perfect circulation, perfect assimilation, perfect elimination. So shall Love come to them—Love, infinite and deep and broad—and they shall embrace the Universe and be embraced by It. There shall be no sense of isolation or loneliness. Happiness was made to be happy. "There is ever a song somewhere, my dear, and we shall sing it"; prosperity and success beyond and above everything else—the final Good. We are That which Thou art, eternal God, and we know that Thou art that which we are forevermore.

And now may the peace and the joy of Life, the song that sings, the morning star, the joy that claps its hands in the leaves, the refreshing rain from Heaven and the strength of the waves and the color of the moonbeams and the sunset, the glory of the rainbow of eternal promise and love and joy go with you forever and forevermore.

3.

THE CREATIVE POWER
OF YOUR THOUGHTS

It is very wonderful to be here again, and a wonderful thing to get this terrific audience here so early in the morning in hot weather.

This is the third in a subject which is designed to progressively arrive at certain definite conclusions. We are dealing with the creative power of Mind rather than with the creative power of our own thinking. Our own thinking utilizes a Mind principle which creatively acts upon it; therefore we tend to become like what we think.

There is a vast difference whether we say, "*I create*"—we all do create in a sense—or whether it is God, the Universe, a divine Principle, whichever you choose to call It, that creates. I do not make a rosebud—I plant a rosebush. I do not make a cucumber—I plant a seed, and something operates upon that seed. I do not create it. If I had to create even a cucumber, I would not know how to create it.

Now biology is the study of life in the human body, and all the biologies rolled into one have no more idea what life is than a jackrabbit has about mince pies; and I don't suppose a jackrabbit knows *anything* about a mince pie. All of the psychologists living, dealing with the operation of thought or emotions: there isn't one of them who knows what thought is, there isn't one of them who knows why feeling is, there isn't one of them who knows any more about what mind is than a child building little castles out of mud. It is interesting, isn't it?

Well, let's get the theologians' "dibs" in now. All the theologians in the world do not know any more about the nature of God than you and I. Remember, there are no prophets other than the wise. Every bible that was ever written was written by human beings, like we are. What I am trying to establish is that we don't know as much as we think we know. Someone has said, "I used to think I knew I knew, / But now I must confess: / The more I know I know, / I know I know the less."

Now science observes how these principles work. It studies the action and reaction of thought and emotion in the human mind; but it doesn't know what the human mind *is*. It studies the actions and reactions of life in the body; but it does not know what life *is*. Theology looks about it and speculates philosophically and idealistically on the nature of God. No doubt it is partly right; but "No man has seen God." And then they have the nerve to tell us which way we are going. This is amusing; it isn't even insulting. Such ideas can't insult anybody's intelligence, because there isn't anything there to insult it.

I must have an animosity to theology or I would never mention it. Isn't that strange! Shakespeare says, "Thou dost protest too much." It is a very interesting thing. Now physics is a study of universal energy acting everywhere. There isn't a physicist in the world who would even try to tell you what energy is. Let's take one other category, one that interests me particularly—that is, all of the creative arts. I love them above everything; they are so tied in to that which is beyond this mundane—for feeling, the creative imagination, revelation, and the inspiration. I look upon religion as one of the creative arts. Isn't that strange? Religion is the most creative thing in the world, and without it we are dead—temporarily.

No artist has ever seen beauty. He can't tell you what beauty looks like. He feels something and then he objectifies it. He paints a picture, or chisels something out of marble—an angelic figure—out of his imagination and feeling, but he never *saw* this; it is subjective. That is why we call what he does an "object" of art, meaning it is an objectification of the subjective mental state.

Here are the great realities of life, and no one has seen them. But we know a great deal about them by seeing what happens to people who hate instead of love; to people who cry instead of laugh; to people who have fear instead of faith: we are right in concluding that the nature of reality is affirmative.

If we discover that certain things that people put in the body are not good and when they don't put them in it is better, then we have a right to say, That is best. Therefore our sciences are built up pragmatically. That means *practically*, on observation—the gathering of a vast amount of data through endless experimentation, until at last modern science is able to say with complete certainty that all of these principles actually exist; but it also says with equal certainty that we must understand their laws to use them. And then their use becomes an individual thing.

Now this is the way it is with the creative power of Mind. We do not have to be superstitious to believe that we are surrounded by creative Intelligence, which receives the impress of our thought and acts upon it, always tending to bring into our experience those things which are both conscious and subjective. Now let me explain that.

We have what we call our conscious thought; we hop and skip and jump along the surface of things, as we are doing now. But there is a deeper realm of mind. It is the same mind where all our habit patterns are stored, continuously repeating themselves until, as the Apostle said, "That which I do I would not, that which I would not I do. . . . O miserable man that I am, who shall deliver me from the body of this death?"*

Now that is psychologically sound, because Sigmund Freud said that a neurotic—that means an unhappy—thought pattern will repeat itself with monotonous regularity throughout life, just like it is playing a tune. And all psychology, psychiatry, and analytical work is based on the supposition that you can uncover these thoughts but that it is not the thoughts themselves that are creative. That is what you and I must learn.

Here is where we differ from psychology—not to repudiate it; we are not among those metaphysicians who deny everything they don't like. They

*Romans 7:19, 24.

have a peculiar coercion of their own. I believe everything is as real as it is supposed to be. If a person hurts, he hurts; if he feels badly, he cries. There is want, lack, and apparent limitation in human experience, and there is no use denying it. But perhaps it doesn't need to be; perhaps it is not intended to be. It cannot be possible that life creates death. So when somebody asked Jesus what God's relationship to the dead is, he said, "He is not a God of the dead but of the living, for in His sight all are alive." That is wonderful. Just because you and I and the world have used this creative Power wrongly does not mean that *It* is wrong. Moses said, "The word is nigh unto thee, even in thine own mouth that thou shouldst know it and do it." He said that it is a blessing or a curse, according to the way we use it.

Now suppose that you and all people, while we have independent thinking and are individualizations of God or the Universe, each one a little different, are in reality all using the same Mind. There is only one Mind. Emerson said there is one Mind common to all individual men. The sixth chapter of Deuteronomy says, "Hear, O Israel: the eternal, the Lord Thy God, is one God." The Hindu says that everything that is is but a different kind of manifestation of the Only Thing that is; for He is one, undivided, indivisible, and ever present. And Einstein said that there is one law in nature, which is common to all laws. In other words, he said that there is one Law which dominates, governs, controls, synthesizes, unifies, coordinates every known law. Now this was his last pronouncement and has, to my knowledge, not been explained. *I* would understand it, anyway. But they are all saying what I am talking about.

There is only one Life. You and I do not have a mind separate from God. We have the Mind *of* God. The scripture says, "Let this mind be in you which was also in Christ Jesus." Now the word *Jesus* is a name, like John. There are probably 50,000 boys in Mexico named Jesus. *Christ* has the same meaning as *the Buddha* or *the Atman** or *the Anointed* or *the Avatar* or *the Messiah* or *the Enlightened*. It means the spiritual Principle and the divine Pres-

---

*In the sense "the innermost essence of each individual" (*Webster's Collegiate Dictionary*).

ence. Let yourself be renewed by the renewing of your mind—that is, changing your thinking, putting off your "old man"—the habit—and putting on the new man: the exalted idea which is Christ.

Now we should get these simple things in mind, because they are fundamental to our whole system of thought; and I very much want you to take our course: If you have had it, review it. If you haven't had it, let nothing stop you from taking it. It is the most valuable course in metaphysics given in the world today, anywhere, by anyone—at any time; and it is to be given morning and evening—so you can take it; and the price is very low. *Just take the time.* It will do more for you than anything that ever happened to you. But this is the foundation of it: One Mind, and we use It.

Now I want to *prove* that to you. I don't want you to believe anything just because I say so—because I have a pretty good imagination and can think up a lot of things that are not so. But I am not a conscious liar; and everybody is an unconscious liar without meaning to lie.

I do not think we should make such a claim to divinity that we forget we are human. The human proclaims the divine; and here we are, a lot of little human beings doing the best we can—laughing and crying, singing and dancing, praying and exalting; then sometimes falling into the depths of despair. Everyone does this, and the man who says he doesn't—he does. And so what? Let us accept it, nonresistantly; otherwise we shall be so inflexibly fighting life that we will get no fun out of it. You know, if the tree didn't bend a little before the wind, it would break off just like an icicle. Nature has provided a flexibility; and "He has tempered the wind to the shorn lamb." Nature is that way. Only man is inflexibile.

You watch people who have no flexibility; they have to say, "semantically speaking"—and that is stupid. We don't have to explain these things. If I say I love you, *that* is what I mean. We don't have to explain these simple things. We *feel* them. If I reach out and put my arms around you and hug you, you know this is an emotion of affection, and we don't have to say, "Is it like the affection of a cat? or a canary bird?" We *know*; because all language has come out of the *feeling* to action, and the impulse and necessity of action. You know what *I* am talking about, and I know what *you* are talking about when you talk to me. Let's keep it simple.

And let's realize this: the profound thinkers of the universe didn't know very much more about it than you and I do; but they knew a lot of words we don't know the meaning of. Always remember this. I have made it a habit for 40 years when I am reading something that looks kind of tough to understand—and yet I know it is good—and I come to a sentence that I am not familiar with . . . I don't know just what it means—so I read it out loud three or four times and listen to it aloud; and then when I think I know what it means, I lay the book down and say it out loud to myself in my own language, three or four times. You will discover in reading you do not wish to transfer the written transcript into your vocabulary; that wouldn't be you. But you want *the thought*. The man has a thought, and you want it. Then you want to put it into your own words, because then you will never forget it. I have done that for 40 years, and it is a great aid. Just say, "Now I think the guy meant this: . . ."

Now we have to put the most abstract philosophy into our own simple words, or we are never going to get it. Then we shall know and understand and assimilate and digest and be able to use what the world knows. It is like our food: we eat it, we assimilate it; it goes into the blood and tissues and bone and the marrow and becomes the physical body.

So our thoughts—what we must learn—must go into another kind of a body, which becomes the body of our thinking; and you and I must know why we believe what we do without having to explain why it is true. And don't feel embarrassed about that. There isn't anyone in the world and all science and philosophy and religion—they are the only three sources through which knowledge comes . . . all of them combined cannot tell you how you can wiggle your finger. Now isn't that silly! They cannot tell you how the nuts and potatoes and soup and apple become hearts and livers and lungs and brain cells (if any). They can't tell you. They don't know, and they don't pretend to know. All they can know is that it happens. Therefore you have to keep the channels open, because where there is circulation, assimilation, and elimination, there is health in the body and normality in the mind; and now they are learning that the mind can't do that unless it has a strong spiritual emotion.

You might say, "Well, I came here to hear about the creative power of thought"—and that is what I am talking about. If I came here to tell you how to make potatoes . . . now I can tell you how to *mash* them; if I came here to tell you how to do a painting or make lumber for building a house or create bricks—I couldn't tell you. We do not do these things. We can only be told how to put natural material together that becomes bricks. That is all we can be told. That is all anybody knows.

Now it is a funny thing: when it comes to speculative philosophy and religion, somebody rises up and says, "God has told me the whole works. Believe as I believe or go to the place that is hotter than L.A. has been recently" (but with no humidity). Wouldn't that be something? Now I treat hell and the devil very disrespectfully, because I haven't the slightest respect for either one, or for anybody's belief in either. It is all bunk. If anyone can tell me how we are going to learn to be happy by being unhappy, I want to hear about it. How are you going to keep dry by jumping in the water? It is beyond me.

The creative power of our thought—your ability to demonstrate, to give a treatment or say a prayer (I don't care what you call it) that will be effectual and produce a result—depends entirely on your knowing that you do not put anything in. You take it out. Never forget this. That is why Jesus said that the Kingdom of Heaven is like a child. "Suffer the little ones to come unto me and forbid them not, for of such is the Kingdom of Heaven." I love that. He was a man who spoke and thought as a child. Plato was no more profound, and far less simple.

Now you and I are scientific when we approach our principle just as a physicist or a biologist or a psychologist would approach his principle— impersonally saying, as Emerson said, "Naught unto me; tis Thou, God, who giveth; tis I who receive." Browning said (and Emerson said) that we are beneficiaries of the divine Fact. We are surrounded by a creative Intelligence which *does* operate upon our thought, whether we know it or not; it *does* create the body, making it sick or well; it *does* control our circumstances, making them happy or unhappy; it *can* bring any good into our lives that we can conceive rightly in cooperation with it—and it *will* and it *must*, and there won't be any question about it. Jesus said, "Heaven and earth shall pass away, but my word shall not, till all be fulfilled."

No one understands our science until he has come to see that, as the Apostle said, "I sowed, Apollos watered, but God gave the increase."* Every scientist in the world will say Amen to that. They will say, "We are using laws of Nature. Fortunately, we have discovered that they will work with invariable exactitude. We may rely upon them, because they are principles. We may learn new ways of using them. We may discover one day that what we call bondage is freedom." And I believe that. As Isaiah said, "He shall turn captivity captive."

I believe the power that makes us sick is the only power that can make us well. The power that impoverishes us is the only thing that can enrich us. If it were not so, the Universe would be a dualism and there would always be an evil contending against the Good; and God is One. "I am that I Am, beside which there is none other." I believe in absolute Unity. You and I are using the same Mind, the same Power. We wouldn't know each other if we weren't using the same Mind. But we are individuals in It, and all of It is back of each one of us. Just as you and I do not create the watermelon but may so comply with Nature that one little seed will produce half a dozen watermelons, each with a thousand seeds in it—there is a principle of multiplicity—so you and I by conscious cooperation with the laws of Mind reacting to our thinking can and will and must and do bring good or ill into our lives.

Now keep it as simple as that—because if you are so fortunate as to decide to take our course, you are going to learn how to be a practitioner. It is the greatest good that can come into anybody's life. You are not going to be taught any superstition or dogma; and you are not going to be taught that only the Religious Scientists can jump into the water and not get wet.

One provision I have made is that whenever I shuck off this mortal coil,

---

*1 Corinthians 3:6.

there isn't a thing of mine that whoever is left here can't take out and put in the ashcan the next day. Isn't that wonderful? I would not wish to perpetuate my stupidity, my ignorance, and my limitation. Someone will come along and do it better. "Ever as the spiral grew / He left the old house for the new." "Build thee more stately mansions, O my soul, / While the swift seasons roll. / Leave thy low-vaulted past; / Let each new temple, nobler than the last, / Shut thee from Heaven with a dome more vast, / Till thou at last art free, / Leaving thy outgrown shell / By life's unceasing sea."

The last word will never be spoken; *you* are the last word. *You* are the revelator. *You* are the medium and the mediator between yourself—which is John and Mary, the human Christ, the Incarnation—and God the absolute. No one shall lay a gift of God upon your altar to the glory of the Eternal but yourself, for *you* are the gift. Lowell said, "Bubbles we earn with a whole soul's casting, / Tis Heaven alone that is given away; / Tis only God may be had for the asking." "Ask no man." Ask not of me or Bill or Reg* or George; we are those struggling toward the Light. "For what was I, / An infant crying in the night, / An infant crying for the light, / And with no language but a cry."

But "the feeble hands and helpless, / Groping blindly in the darkness, / Touched God's right hand in that darkness / And are lifted up and strengthened." Be simple. You alone shall meet Him face to face in the Secret Place of the Most High, the tabernacle of the Almighty in your own soul, where God lives. This is the starting point of all creativity. *Now* your thought will be operated upon.

What is more logical than to go about it definitely, and for every negation create an affirmation—? Instead of saying, "I cannot," say, "I can; you can; he can; we can; they can; it can—God can." There is a Power that *will*—in simplicity. Then, when the other thoughts come up, deny them. It will erase them gradually. It takes time. Be patient. You are working with an absolute certainty, and you see that you don't feel obligation or responsibility.

---

*See p. 61. "Reg" refers to Reginald Armor, the earliest of Dr. Holmes's associates besides his brother Fenwicke.

You and I don't know how to make a liver. We know how to use thought that will heal a liver that looks bad. We do not know how to make a brain. We can use thought that will so stimulate the brain cells we have that they shall multiply along the line of our desire. We do not know how to create Substance. We can use thought as realization and receptivity to Substance until everywhere we turn, the supply we need for our daily things will come to us.

Couldn't we see abundance everywhere? How many leaves on the trees, how many stars—how vast is everything! And all this vastness belongs to us. It is all pouring itself through us. How much are we receiving definitely, deliberately, consciously, day by day, everywhere we look? Couldn't we see happiness, even where it looks sad—?

"Oh dry those tears, life was not made for sorrow." "There is ever a song somewhere, my dear; there's ever a song—somewhere." And love: couldn't we learn to love everybody? And someday when our arms are encircling God and the Universe and humanity, we shall know that God is Love. No one will have to tell us. No one will ever have to prove it to us. And all the abstractions and speculations of the human mind shall fall like dust; and the Light that is direct and simple shall reveal to you and to me.

There is a Power greater than we are that we use. It is so very simple; and as you study this course—and I say you would be very foolish not to—remember, one with God is a majority. We may *know* the Truth; we can only *believe* what is not so. If all the people in the world believed what is not so, and only one person knew the Truth, that one person who knew the Truth would repudiate the belief of all the rest of them. That is why Jesus said, "The words that I speak unto you, they are Spirit and they are Life."

Just as surely as tomorrow shall come and the sun again shall rise across the darkness of the horizon and spill its beauty and warmth to awaken the valleyland into fertility, human beings into warmth and color—so you and I, looking across the new horizon of a greater possibility, may walk forth and meet the living God and feel His embrace and know His Presence and may come to know at last of the infallibility of a Power that the simplest may use, as a child is held in place by gravitational force. "O living truth that shall endure / When all that seems shall suffer shock, / Rise on the rock and make us pure." May the living presence of the eternal God awaken within each one of us now the realization of peace and joy.

O Infinite Beauty, diffused and infused, spilling Itself over us and flowing through us in the majestic harmony of warmth and color and feeling: our minds are open to Thy divine influx. O infinite Sweetness beyond compare, O sweet Presence: flow through us in Joy. To You we surrender all littleness and all fear and all doubt, that the living fountain from the eternal River of Life flowing from the Mind of God shall renew our vigor, remake our strength, ennoble our being, heal our bodies and fortunes, and bring peace to the waiting heart. Thou Love that evermore embraces us: we surrender all hurt to Thee. In Thy Wisdom make us wise; in Thy Light give us light; and in Thy Joy shall we laugh as children playing on the shores of time as the great ocean of eternity evermore flows and flows into our being. Amen.

➤ AFFIRMATIVE-PRAYER MEDITATION ↢

(A great many names have been placed in this box. Some have requested healing, some perhaps love and friendship, betterment of circumstances. Now each one knows what he has asked for. Our treatment and our consciousness united, I believe, will act for each one—if he receives, without question, the good he has asked for. Don't try to see how it can be brought about; just say, "I am accepting the fulfillment of this." And remember: when you treat someone, you identify your prayer or treatment with him. It is for him. Then your whole time is spent realizing within yourself something about him—always on the supposition that I have talked about this morning: that Something acts upon your thought toward your identification. That is, I am treating: "This word is for John Smith. He lives at such-and-such a place." You forget about him. Then you form your statements to cover the need, sometimes denying what appears and affirming its opposite—it doesn't matter—until you yourself are convinced. Now Something greater than you are operates upon it. It is a law in nature. *It is a law.*)

As we turn within to that divine Presence which is both God and Man, unifying us all together in Love, the first thing we do is *realize* that Love and turn to each other and mentally embrace each other. I love you. I adore you. I surrender that part of myself which is pure Spirit to you in love. It is wonderful. And you do to me. And we are embracing each other in love—oh so sweet, so very tender, so intimate love. So shall joy come to us.

There is one infinite Peace now indwelling us and each person particularly who has put his name in this box. Now we are going to bless him. God bless him or her. Let him receive the blessing; it is real. We bless him—and everything within him is blessed, and everything that doesn't belong to him is eliminated; and everything that belongs to Perfection is manifest.

There is one Life, that Life is God, that Life is his life. It is perfect *now*, and It is manifesting in him now, right now. Let him receive it. Not from you and me, but from out of this thought, from out of this great Mind which is God, this Power which is good, this Law which is perfect. It is so, and this word shall continue and it shall prosper. Everything that this person does shall prosper. The way is made perfect and plain and straight and immediate and permanent and happy and whole and prosperous before him. All the love there is and all the friendship that there is is delivered to him. There is no resentment; he has surrendered every hate, every resentment, every doubt, and embraces the universe of wholeness. So shall Love guide him and govern him and Peace flow through him, the Light of Heaven go with him. Sweet friend in God, you are blessed and all your ways prospered. That which does not belong has fallen away, and the limbs are strengthened and the circulation is perfect. Every organ and action and function of the body proclaims the divinity, the harmony, the unity, and the perfection of Good; and you are prospered in Love now and forevermore. Amen.

And now as we go into the great joy of life, the light of the living

Spirit shall go before us, the love of the eternal God shall wrap us around, and we shall be embraced and we shall embrace. So may it be that there shall go forth from us the Light of Heaven. May every person we meet be blessed and may every situation we contact be prospered. We surrender ourselves to this—we dedicate ourselves to this—in love, in joy, and in gladness. May the eternal Spirit go with us, guiding and guarding us forevermore. Amen.

4

HOW TO ENJOY ABUNDANT
HEALTH FOR CREATIVE LIVING I

―――――――

In October 1957 Dr. Holmes was looking forward to sharing an evening lecture with David Fink, M.D. He was as well renowned a medical personality as a devoted metaphysician with a strong belief in the teachings of Dr. Holmes. They had selected a topic for the October 29th talks to a joint session of classes at the Institute of Religious Science at 6th and New Hampshire, Los Angeles. The topic for the evening was based on the idea that your attitude could make you sick or make you well.

Dr. Fink elected to speak during the first half of the evening and Dr. Holmes the closing half. They decided to label the entire evening "How to Enjoy Abundant Health for Creative Living." Dr. Holmes was particularly impressed with what Dr. Fink had to say about sacrifice. In fact he thought of it as "sacrifice without morbidity." He stressed that no psychiatrist or metaphysician would ever make anybody more whole than the psychiatrist or metaphysician himself was. The talk that follows was Dr. Fink's contribution. Chapter 5 is Dr. Holmes's.

DAVID FINK, M.D.

I can't tell you how happy it makes me to be here with you. How many of you have heard me before?

Oh, gracious, I'm with friends, then—I hope!

Of course, it puts me under some obligation to say something that you haven't heard before. I imagine you would be pretty tired of hearing me say the same old things. So I won't—except to say, by way of parenthesis: always practice relaxing your muscles, and you will feel better. Relax them at every possible opportunity; never use muscles in tension that you don't have to use.

A certain woman who was a very dear friend of mine—I loved her; she went on to a better world to my great sorrow—used to say to me, "Doctor Fink, you aren't telling me anything new. When I work, I work hard; when I sit down, I relax; and when I worry, I go to sleep." She didn't worry, and her life was an inspiration to me and to my wife. She was a wonderful woman, a wonderful mother, a wonderful friend.

Well, that is the way it goes. You can't keep them with us always, and all we can do is emulate and try to live up to the best that our friends demonstrate and expect of us.

Now I happen to be, as you know, a physician and metaphysician; and the two are not incompatible by any means. When I first came here last Saturday night, I was registering at a motel and a call came in at the desk. A young man was sick with influenza; so they wanted a doctor, and they couldn't get one on Saturday night. They asked me if I would go and see the boy—an engineer just coming in from South Dakota to work at Douglas. He had a temperature of 103 and was the kind of person who could have had very serious results from his troubles.

I felt that the surest way to get him well quick was to treat his mind. You know, I can't treat the virus—nobody can—but I could treat his mind. And he made such a remarkable recovery that anyone who was willing to open his eyes and his mind and his heart could not have failed to be impressed by the rate of recovery. And it wasn't his great constitution that got him well, but a constitution that was adopted all before he ever came on this earth.

He was helped by God; and because he was willing to believe and have faith, he got well quickly. It is so simple. You know there is, of course, a "natural" explanation for everything—a physical explanation for everything. The physical explanation is that disease processes are augmented by an adrenalurgic* reaction. It has been demonstrated in the laboratory by Hans Selye, who made experiments on poor harmless rats that weren't doing him any harm—and he found out, by these animal experiments, what Ernest Holmes has been saying all these years.

---

*This should perhaps be *adrenergic*.

At any rate, the disease reactions—the response to disease—can be augmented or decreased by attitudes, such as when this man was receptive to a religious attitude, when he was willing to believe that God would get him well, if only he didn't *try* to get well. *"Don't try to get well,"* I said; "don't worry about your troubles. You can't *help* but get well if you only let God cure you and relax. Take it easy; and remember: it is only a matter of a few hours and you will be healed." The adrenalurgic reaction ceased, and his temperature fell naturally. It is so simple. People make themselves sick with their attitudes.

Now what I am going to talk to you about tonight is how to enjoy abundant health for creative living. Abundant health, of course, is worthless in itself—completely worthless. A patient of mine, a diabetic who suffered from diabetes ever since she was 14, had made a "career" of curing herself of diabetes, and of course all she had done was make herself worse and worse. So I asked her: "What would you do if you were well? What do you want to *accomplish*?" And she told me that what she wanted to do was work in the Church of Religious Science and conduct group therapy, have discussion groups in her home, talking about metaphysics and how to improve her own understanding of life.

"Well," I said, "what is stopping you? Go ahead and do it, and let the diabetes take care of itself; take it as a matter of course. If it helps you to take insulin once a day, regard that as a minor annoyance and take it and forget it and get busy with your metaphysics and the group you are gathering, and work with Doctor Whitehead* up in Monterey. *Let's get something done.*" And she did; and her blood sugar fell. It is as simple as that.

Now what I am talking about is this: you can have abundant health if you don't search for it, if you don't seek it. Don't make abundant health your goal in life, because it will be a very elusive goal. It is like seeking happiness: you don't find happiness by seeking it; you find happiness by doing something which makes your life meaningful. Then happiness comes to you like sunshine. It comes to you from without. It just pours in on you. You *are*

---

*Carleton Whitehead, Religious Science minister.

happiness—but you mustn't seek it, any more than you must seek health. You must seek *creative living*—and you can have abundant health for creative living, if you make creative living your goal. *That* is what I want to talk about.

How can you achieve success? Why is it that some people are just naturally lucky and other people aren't? How can you be one of those lucky ones? You *can* be—you can *all* be lucky; because "good luck" is the fruit of your character. The kind of character that you develop, that you make for yourself, that you create will make your own good luck, your own abundant health for creative living.

Just what would you like to accomplish? Let's be very practical about this. This is one of the things I ask my patients: *What do you want?* One patient says, "I would like to lose weight; but every time I diet, I gain." Another patient says, "I would like financial security; but every time I try to make money or invest it, I lose money." And another person says, "I would like to have friends and be popular; but people just don't like me. I am always lonely. I just don't have any friends. There is something about me that chases people away from me, people I would have as friends." Another person says, "I feel gloomy, I feel sad, I feel blue. I want to get rid of my depressions."

Okay; these are just *some* things. Others say, "I would like to enjoy greater self-confidence." Others say, "I would like to make my marriage work; but my husband doesn't like me, and he doesn't treat me right, and I think he wants to get rid of me." Or it might be a husband who says that about his wife—he wants to make his marriage work. Another man says, "I am an alcoholic and would like to lick the alcohol habit and achieve sobriety." And of course I always say, *"Why?"* And if he would say, *"Because I want to accomplish something worthwhile,"* I would say, "You have already achieved your sobriety, my friend. Just keep your mind on wanting to accomplish something worthwhile and you will never in this wide world ever again take another alcoholic drink."

These are the things people would like to accomplish—these among the 101 other things which they think would make them happy. Each one of us has his own ideas of what would make him happy, what he would like to accomplish, what would amount in his life to creative living. And I say, *any* of these things, *all* of these things, are within your power to take. They are yours for the asking. All you have to do is to go about these projects intelligently and you can't fail.

That is what I am talking about tonight: how you can go about these projects intelligently. What makes you fail. What makes you succeed. The answer is so absurdly simple that I am sometimes ashamed to get up before an intelligent group and tell them, because it seems to me that anything so simple must surely have occurred to all of you. But I am the kind of person who has to say the obvious anyway; so if I bore you, it won't be too long.

So I am going to tell you what I think makes some people fail in achieving the happiness they seek, in achieving the success they look for—what makes them fail in achieving creative living and makes them deprive themselves of abundant health: *what makes them fail.* In one word, it is their *attitudes. Attitudes* make you fail or succeed—your *attitudes.*

Now what is an attitude? An attitude is the way you are prepared to act in any situation. The way you are prepared to act in a situation is your attitude. You may not know how you are prepared to act in this situation or that situation; but you always *are* prepared to act. And it is *knowing how* you are prepared to act that enables you to fulfill your attitudes. Now I think that is worth a little more elaboration, discussion, and clarification.

The situations in our lives are a part of a flow of life. Situations in which we live flow around us, past us, constantly. The situations are constantly changing, in states of flux, in states of constant motion. As each situation arises, we are prepared to react to that situation in one way or another. The situation within us—our interior environment—is constantly changing. Either you have eaten and are full right up to here; or else you haven't eaten, and your backbone is pressing against your stomach, you are so empty. Your interior situation is constantly changing, and your exterior situation is constantly changing, and how you are prepared to act in one situation or another will determine your happiness or your unhappiness, your success or your failure, your abundant health or your abundant lack of health.

Now *attitudes*: I think I might as well explain this a little more fully.

Let's say you are going into a department store and you expect to be waited upon. Now of course this won't happen in the great city of L.A., where all of the department stores are loaded with so many good things, and the help is so well trained, etc., etc. But if you were to go into a smaller community where the help is not so well trained, you would find that what you expect and what you get are two very different things.

If you go into the store expecting the clerk to have at his disposal an unlimited quantity of goods; if you go into that same store and expect the clerk to know the stock perfectly; if you go there expecting him to have an intuitive sense of your needs and what you can afford and what you want to buy; if you go there expecting the prices to be well within your reach for exactly what you hope to find (even if you don't know exactly what you are looking for when you go into the store)—and you meet a clerk who is indifferent; if you meet a clerk who doesn't know the stock; and if the stock itself is limited in its quantity: then you are going to be frustrated.

Your attitude is one thing, the situation is another, and frustration results. And as a result of frustration, a whole chain of events occurs within your body, including muscle tension; including your intestines going into spasms; including your glands of internal secretion pouring forth adrenalin into your system; including your rapid breathing and dry mouth; and so on and so forth. And this will give rise to a feeling of anger, or hostility.

But if you were to go into that store with a *different* attitude, saying, "I'll just go and see what happens; I'll treat whatever happens as a matter of course. I'm not under any particular obligation to buy. I'll look around and do my best, and my attitude will be one of hopeful expectancy; but it won't be one of being positive I am going to get exactly what I want when I want it, or even better than I had hoped."* If that is your attitude, then you won't

---

*This is not quite Ernest Holmes's teaching. See, for example, *The Science of Mind*, where he says, in a slightly different context, "We need only turn over to Intelligence our highest conceptions . . . and there will be delivered to us something much finer than it was possible to picture" (p. 645).

be frustrated; and furthermore, you won't be suffering from all the processes which lead to harmful emotions and disagreeable dealings. You can't change the clerk's attitudes.

Let's talk about the woman, for instance, who wanted to lose weight. What is her food attitude? Her food attitude is one of weak self-indulgence. Her food attitude is that food represents to her the love she did not receive when she was a child. And so whenever she is bored or whenever she is disappointed or whenever any disagreeable sensation or feeling or situation arises in her life, she runs to the icebox and makes herself a sandwich. And that is why it is impossible for her to lose weight with that food attitude. The food attitude is all wrong.

Another person who wants to get rid of that depression has a self-attitude that is punitive—self-punishing. That person is depressed. Why? Because he or she (and I have both he's and she's in my practice) feels guilty for things that have been done in the past. And because she is constantly feeling guilty, she feels that she is going to be punished. She is afraid of being punished. She is afraid of hellfire; and her fear of hellfire is so great that she furnishes the oil for the flame. It is that attitude, that self-attitude, punitive self-attitude—that attitude that Judas had that makes her suffer in a minor way what Judas suffered in a major way; and I think that most suicides like those of Judas arise from feelings of guilt and feelings of despair.

Now a normal attitude, a healthy attitude, a simple attitude that every physician and metaphysician would have her take would be that of trust in the infinite love of God. You know, no one could be worse than a traitor. I think a traitor is about the lowest form of life. A man whom you depend on who goes over to the enemy is pretty low; and any man who has been a traitor has the right, he might think, to feel guilty. And one of the greatest traitors in history was Saint Peter, who lived with the Lord, who saw his miracles, who had opportunities such as none of you will ever have of being in contact—physical contact—with Jesus. And yet three times he denied his Lord. Three times in a row.

What a traitor! And yet what happened? He had one saving grace: he did not lose hope; he did not despair; he did not go into a depression and say,

"Oh what a worthless worm am I!" Instead, he trusted in the infinite love of God and became the first and greatest saint—the founder of the Church, or at least the first leader of the Church of Jesus.

Now if the Lord can forgive St. Peter, who was a traitor, and take him and make him the keeper of the Keys of Heaven, why should any of us who have never had those opportunities worry about the mistakes or the sins or the evil that we have done in the past? All we have to do is be sorry and resolve not to repeat our mistakes. And as soon as a person takes that point of view—I don't care whether you call it the advice of a physician who says, "Forget it," or the advice of a metaphysician who says, "Believe in God, and God will heal you"—he is free from his depression, because he has changed his own self-attitude. He has ceased to punish himself. He has ceased to put himself in the role of the devil, roasting himself in hell, and he has put himself in the position of the angels who are lifting him up to Heaven.

Your attitudes can make you well or your attitudes can make you sick—your self-attitudes and your attitudes toward other people. The person who says, "My husband doesn't love me": we went into her case and what did we find? Her husband is the kind of person who wants a mother. He wants a *motherly* wife—the kind of a woman who will make her husband's career, her husband's happiness, and her husband's success *her* career. That is the career in life she must adopt if she is going to make her husband happy, or at least satisfied, because that is his need.

And what about her? She is a very good daughter, she is very good to her mother; and being a good daughter is more important to her than being a good wife. And then she says, "I want to make my marriage work; I want my marriage to succeed." Well, it can't succeed with that attitude, any more than the person can lose weight whose food attitude is that food is a substitute for human friendship and affection. Food is *not* a substitute. And as soon as she changes her attitude toward her husband from that of being a critical sister to that of being a devoted wife, her marriage cannot fail.

If you want to make anything succeed, you have first of all to analyze the attitudes which have given rise to the failure. If you want to get rid of your depression, I assure you: get rid of your feelings of guilt and fear of punishment and you will never feel depressed. You *can't* feel depressed. You will wake up singing. But you will never wake up singing if you keep harping on the past.

I remember one woman who badgered the life out of a priest because she ate pie on Friday and she said, "Maybe there was lard in the pie crust";* and the priest said, "Go say ten Hail Marys and God will forgive you"—which was very foolish advice on the part of the priest, I think, because it only made the woman sure she *had* committed a sin. So she said ten Hail Marys; and then she wasn't sure God had forgiven her. So she came back to the priest the next afternoon and told him the same story and the same story and the same story, until finally he said, "Go to a psychiatrist"—which was perhaps one way of saying, "Go to the devil!"

So she came to see me, naturally, and I had to give her a religious instruction—tell her that if she had eaten not *lard in pie,* but if she had eaten *the whole hog* on Friday, it would make no difference. The important thing is how did she feel about the future? How did she feel about God? Does she believe in God or doesn't she? If she believes in God, God isn't going to worry about her nibbling away at a little piece of pig. The pig was already dead. Of course, if she had bitten a live pig, it might have been different. That would have been *really* cruel!

Now all of your attitudes cluster into what they call *character traits.* You make your own "luck" with your character traits. A character trait is a cluster of attitudes that determines how you are going to behave in a more or less organized situation. Some people have the character trait of always exploiting their friends. Other people have the character trait of picking the "cards" of their past days—each card a different episode—shuffling them up, and dealing them out to their husbands at two o'clock in the morning, in different combinations. A kind of devilish solitaire I would call it.

There are a number of character traits; the character trait of a man who is trying to get something for nothing, who doesn't realize that God created this world on the theory that if you don't work, you don't eat—and he thinks

---

*Refers to the obligatory abstention by Catholics (at that time) from eating meat on Friday.

he can beat the game. And naturally he is always losing money on the horse races, and wondering why his savings are all frittered away. *Naturally*; because the character traits, which represent a whole cluster of attitudes—dependency, and desire to exploit someone, get something for nothing, etc.—the character traits which are his techniques for living (that is what a character trait is: a technique for living) are character traits that are bound to get him into trouble.

Now my thesis—I am still talking about abundant health for creative living—is that anyone who does not have abundant health for creative living should examine his character traits—his techniques for dealing with situations. Each character trait represents a cluster of attitudes—what he expects of himself, or what he expects of life. If he wants abundant health for creative living, let him examine his character traits.

Now as I said at Asilomar, one sure way—one simple way—of acquiring the right character traits is to *stop*, *look*, and *listen*. Look at the people in real life or in fiction or in biography or in autobiography who have the character trait that you would have, that you admire. Hero worship is the beginning of growth. No one can grow into a man who does not have an idea of a man's role in this world, and little boys usually acquire this notion of what it is to be a man. They acquire it from observing their fathers and other men in their immediate environment when they get to be about six or eight years old; and they become, in a way, hero-worshipers and grow up—actually grow up into manhood—not by accident but by copying the behavior of people whom they consider manly. And the same thing applies to women. The best thing that can happen to a girl is to have a mother whom she can admire, emulate, and finally leave. It is a good thing for a girl to know how to untie apron strings. The time to tie an apron string is when you go into the kitchen and not when you go into your mother's home.

It is through hero-worship, through analyzing and admiring the character traits of those whom you would emulate that you acquire the character traits which enable you to grow into abundant health and creative living.

Now there are five steps to abundant health in creative living, and I am going to give them to you. First of all, there is *the goal*. The goal represents your visualization of the situation that will satisfy your needs. You have to visualize the goal first, whatever it may be—a happy marriage, a wealth of friends, a more spiritual life—thousands of goals, each one of which represents your needs; and of course every rounded person has more than one goal. You might want good taste in interior decorating. Whatever your goal is, you visualize that. That is number one.

Number two: you have to visualize yourself as the kind of person who has the character traits that make for the kind of success that you want. We will call that *vision*. Seeing yourself, thinking of yourself, as a different kind of person—as the kind of person whom you aspire to be.

Goal first. Vision second.

Number three: *repetition*. Constantly keep in mind the goal and the vision—the goal you are trying to achieve, and the vision of yourself as the kind of person who is fit to achieve that goal.

The fourth you might not like. The fourth step is *sacrifice*. My friends, there is nothing in this world in the way of abundant health for creative living that can be achieved without sacrifice. Sacrifice is as real, as fundamental, as religious, as medical, as scientific, as this table and as God Himself. One of the earliest stories of the primitive Hebrews began with the thought of sacrifice. I think it was Abraham who was asked to sacrifice his own son to God and showed his willingness to give up the thing he loved the most. And then God gave him a substitute to sacrifice in its place.

There is nothing in religion that means a thing that does not involve sacrifice. I have often heard these social workers say, "Give till it hurts." I wouldn't take anything from a man who gave till it hurt. I would be too proud. I say, "Give until it feels good." Give until it feels good. If you do not lose your whole self in something, you will never gain anything. It is only the person who dedicates himself to something more worthwhile than himself who achieves his own self. The essence of success is sacrifice, if you want abundant health for creative living.

Health is like one of those plans they had during the Depression: $30 every Thursday, or something like that. The idea was that every Thursday, everybody was to be given $30 in scrip, and it was to be dated; and if it wasn't spent within one week, the money was no good. Well, your health is that way too: if you don't spend it, you can't buy anything with it; it is "dated." So the essence of creative living is sacrifice. You have to give up a hundred things to achieve one thing.

You know, the compass is a circle, and they divided it into 360 because they used to think the year had 360 days. So every compass point points to one degree in 360. And if you go in any single direction, following your compass, you are giving up the opportunity of going in 359 different directions. You have to make up your mind to give up what you don't want and really don't care about in order to get what you *do* want and you *do* care about.

And that goes for the woman who wants to lose weight; for the man who wants greater economic security; for the person who wants friends and to be popular; for the person who wants to feel free from fear; right to the person who wants to get rid of this depression: she has to give up a *pleasure.* The woman who wants to be free from depression has to give up the pleasure of feeling guilty. She has to quit enjoying punishing someone, including—and particularly—herself directly, and everyone around her indirectly; for she spreads unhappiness the way she might spread a bad odor. But if she would love herself, feel that she has God within herself, and if she would give up this notion that she is adequate to judge herself, that she knows more about God than God does: if she would give up that pride, she would give up her depression and she would be happy.

And now the fifth thing. In order to change your character traits in the direction of better health for more creative living, you have to have a *goal;* you have to see yourself as the person who is fit to achieve that goal; you have to constantly keep it in mind by continuous *repetition,* such as you find in the magazine *Science of Mind*—repetition, daily repetition; *sacrifice,* give up, that which doesn't count for that which does. And then finally, number five—is *faith.* Faith. *Expect results.*

(And incidentally, in the form of repetition I forgot to mention that I include prayer. Prayer and repetition are practically synonymous. Constantly feel the presence of God through prayer.)

Faith is the last step. *You expect results.* Good results come to the man who expects them. No one ever catches the train who thinks he is going to miss the train and feels, "Well, there is no use going to the station; I will miss it anyway." That man will never, never, *never* board the train.

But the man who says, "Why sure; I have an hour. It only takes 45 minutes to get there. Let's go!"—that man will be on the train when the conductor gives the engineer the highball. *Expect results.* Now others have done it. As I say, you are all intelligent people, and perhaps you knew all this before I started to talk. I don't know. But it seems so simple, it seems so direct, it seems so obvious that it embarrassed me, in a way, to get up here like a little boy reciting the multiplication table before a group of mathematicians. If others have done it, *you* can do it; your friends can do it.

So perhaps if you do know all these things, you will forgive me. I have organized them, perhaps, for you—have told you how to achieve abundant health for creative living and organized it for you; and perhaps you can pass the good word on to your friends and show them how they too can enjoy abundant health for creative living, by changing their character traits to achieve the things they want to achieve. And they can do it by having a definite *goal*; by *seeing* themselves as the kind of person who deserves to achieve that goal; by *repeating* the goal constantly (and by prayer, prayer, prayer); by *sacrifice* of everything that is not essential to the achievement of that goal; and by having *faith* in results.

Now Ernest Holmes said he was going to talk right away, and so I am going to give you time to get some air and relax, and you will be more receptive to what my dear friend Ernest Holmes has to tell you.

5

HOW TO ENJOY ABUNDANT
HEALTH FOR CREATIVE LIVING II

The most difficult thing in the world is to talk the way Doctor Fink has just talked to us—simplicity. I have often thought of it in reading the words of Jesus and of Plato, who taught pretty much the same thing. But Plato is so profound, you don't know what he is talking about; and Jesus is so simple, no one realized that his simplicity exposed his profundity—because they both taught only two or three very simple facts.

The first of these is that we are living in a spiritual Universe now, in which an infinite Intelligence eternally lives, equally distributed throughout time and space, impersonal to everyone until It is personalized in and through that person; and that of a necessity there are prototypes, archetypes, or ideas, or spiritual patterns in the invisible for everything that is in the visible; and that naturally we are tied into this pattern.

But when the things that David told us about happen, we don't untie the pattern, but we untie *ourselves* from it to a certain degree, and that whether it is by prayer, medication, or surgery or psychiatry or spiritual mind treatment. All in the world we do is what Emerson referred to when he said to get your bloated nothingness out of the way of the divine circuit to restore that which in itself needs no restoration; God isn't sick or poor or miserable or unhappy. And I was particularly delighted at his idea of sacrifice without morbidity—not sacrifice from the standpoint of sin and salvation, the fall and the redemption. It is like washing a window so you can see through it.

It is like getting rid of what *doesn't* belong in order that what *does* belong shall be evident; or "loosing" that "imprisoned splendor." It is letting go and letting God, really. And I thought also of something I discovered when I was a kid, about ten years old. We were brought up without any fear; we were not taught there is a hell or a devil or any of this damned nonsense (that is all it is). Someone says, "You shouldn't speak that way about it." I *like* to speak that way about it; that keeps me from being frustrated too. But the harm that a wrong perspective of God has done would make countless angels weep. Therefore I always say, "I thank the God that is, that the God that is believed in, *isn't.*" If He were, it would be terrible.

But I discovered then, in a retired minister (I didn't know what he was until 30 years after that), that he had no condemnation for anything or anyone. And I used to wonder about it. I used to take his hand and walk down through the countryside, and I always felt close to Something that was different from anything else that I had ever contacted. It is very vivid in my memory now. It was at least 30 years ago and maybe 40, because I am approaching the age of what they call the "Ancient of Days."

I know now what David told us—I have known for years—that in the Universe in which we live (this is my way of saying it) we did not create ourselves, we didn't put the mountains up there, we didn't put each other here. This is what happened to Job. He told God he had done everything that a good guy should do, and he told God over and over again what a good guy he was. And finally God said, "Well, you are a very wonderful man, Job; but where were you when I planted the North Star and sent the wind blowing? I just don't remember seeing you around." This is when Job fell flat on his face, for at last this got him. He had gotten in the way of "the divine circuit." His self-righteousness was a condemnation; because we don't have to be either condemned *or* righteous.

As Emerson said, when virtue is self-conscious, it is vicious. Just try to spend a whole day with someone who knows he is good; and if you have never thought of murder before, you will contemplate it before night. There is nothing you can do with them—and murder is against the law.

This Universe in which we live we did not make, nor did we create ourselves; but we seem to have the privilege of a freedom, Tolstoy said in *War and Peace*—we have "freedom within the laws of inevitabilities." In other words, our freedom cannot infringe the nature of the Universe. When everybody believed the world was flat, the only thing that was flattened was their experience—because the world was round. But they did, and we all do, project into the universe of Reality the illusion or delusion or false conclusion or confusion of our own minds and look at it and sometimes worship it as God, sometimes fear it as destiny, sometimes shudder as though it were the imposition of some cosmic energy or force which is malevolent— because we worship our evil more than we do our good.

Somebody said to me one day, relative to a certain evangelist whose name is unknown, but a very good man who located Hell under Manhattan Island (and I was so glad is wasn't Hollywood, because I had so often said it *was*)— he said to me, "Don't you believe in Hell?" and I said, "No." And he said, "Well, this man describes it"; and I said, "He has traveled a great deal more than I have; it is probably perfectly all right: he has just been places and seen things." Which made me think of the little busboy who was attending a banquet given by the Travelers Club, and this man who had been a world traveler was speaking, saying how he had fished in the seven seas and shot polar bear in the arctic and hunted out on the veldt and done this and that— and everyone naturally was enthusiastic and quite overcome by his greatness, where he had been and what he had seen. And this little busboy pulls his coat and says, "Mister, did you ever have the D.T.'s?" and he said, "Certainly not!" And the kid said, "You ain't been nowhere and you ain't seen nothin'!" So it is all relative.

Here is the Universe in which we live, which we did not create; but by some Power that shapes our ends, "rough hew them though we may," we have this freedom within the laws of inevitabilities. As David has said, we can make ourselves unhappy, impoverished, and everything else—because this is our freedom. And therefore our freedom makes our bondage possible. And if it were not possible to have the bondage, we would be automatons and could not have the freedom. It is one of those abstractions that we must not lose sight of, because if we could keep that in mind until we see through it, we should understand the nonviolence of Gandhi and the nonresistance of

Jesus in a fluidic Universe which Emerson said we see as a solid fact but God views as liquid law.

And so we have that freedom—not to change the Universe, and not really to change the intrinsic nature of each other, nor really to change the intrinsic nature of *ourselves*; but to go with the tide of cosmic affairs or resist it— and in doing it, project our reaction in a universe of Reality until to us it becomes, as some of the ancients called it, Maya, the world of illusion. It isn't exactly illusion; it is *delusion*. It is not a thing in itself. And I discovered after all these years what this retired preacher knew and I felt. He no longer condemned himself; and because he didn't, it was impossible for him to project his condemnation on the Universe or on others. And there is no other condemnation.

Now there are two incidents in the Bible . . . of course, I don't believe the Bible literally. I don't think there ever was an Adam and an Eve. There was a Moses; but I don't think there was a Garden of Eden or a serpent that talked, or anything like that. This is a symbolism. And God came "walking in the garden in the cool of the day" to talk with Adam and Eve; and Adam looked down and saw he didn't have on any pants, so he jumped behind a cactus, and God said, "Adam, where art thou?" and Adam said, "I have hid, God." And God said; "This is funny; we have always been friends. How come?" "Well," Adam said, "you know, God, I discovered I am naked."

Now this is what the play is written for: God said, "Who told thee that thou art naked?" This, to me, is one of the greatest things in the Bible. *Who told thee that thou art naked? Who* told us we were such terrible people, born in sin and conceived in iniquity—and if we are fortunate enough to live for 60 years without dying, or unfortunate enough to live beyond that, it is going to be tough, and after that the deluge. *Who?* This is a concoction of an unconscious sense of guilt being rejected by the Universe and not accepted by It. And I will tell you a good little metaphysical practice to go along with what David has said; I've told it to many people who have a sense of condemnation, because we seem to be born with it out of the collective mind: "Thou, God, approvest of me." *God within me approves of me.*

Any statement that will release the tension of the condemnation without fighting it—in a nonresistant way, in a way that can restore the natural flow . . . and again, in the New Testament John the Baptist is preaching and some poor guy comes along and throws himself face down in the dirt and says, "Sir, what shall I do to escape the wrath to come?" And John looks at him and says, "Look here, guy, get up! I didn't come to tell you what to do to escape the wrath that is to come; I came to tell you that the Kingdom of God is at hand." Now there is a vast difference.

Our theology says the Kingdom of God *is* at hand, that we shall never know any God outside the confines of that only thing which can know anything, whether you call it your conscience or your mind or your awareness— I don't care. It is that thing without which you wouldn't be here; and when it is withdrawn, nothing is left; and what *appears* to be left begins to disintegrate in a split second. The *integrating* factor is "the pearl of great price for which a man will sell everything he has in order that he may possess it": your *self*. Angela Morgan* said, "That inner self that never tires, / Fed by the deep, eternal fires, / Angel and guardian at the gate, / Master of death and king of fate."

I am supposed to be tying religion and psychology together. I know nothing about psychology and very little about religion. Psychology is something there is too much known about which isn't true; religion is something too much is taught about that is false. And yet we need both, because we cannot live without either. One is our perspective of the Cosmos in which we live, and our relationship to what we think is either an overdwelling or an indwelling God. We happen to believe the overdwelling and indwelling God is one God—"The highest God and the innermost God is one God," the mystics say. I put it in a more comprehensive way by saying that God as man in man *is* man—because whatever this Thing is that we call God, It is not an old man with whiskers combing his beard and sending thunderbolts to the Baptists and blessings to the Methodists. There is no such a being, fortunately.

But the Universe is packed full of an equally distributed, undivided, cos-

---

*New Thought writer and poet.

mically whole, continually integrated Something that Browning speaks of as "the alive, the awake, and the aware." You find that in the closing of *Saul*, where David has awakened Saul from his apathy and his melancholia as he sings to him: "O Saul, a hand like this hand shall open the gates of new life to thee; see the Christ stand," and the Christ is the Avatar or the Messiah or the Buddha or the Atman—it is all the same thing: the Son, the Sonship of the Universe. And now *Saul* says, "He slowly resumes his own motions and attitudes. Kingly he is, is Saul; he remembers in glory ere error had bent the broad brow from the daily communion." And then Saul steals quietly out on the desert, and he feels himself surrounded by the alive, the awake, and the aware; and everything speaks to him . . . the stars . . . and then everything sinks to rest and peace. It is the dramatization that Browning gives to the awakening within us of what he called "that spark that disturbs our clod."

Now the Universe in which we live we didn't make; and we will never change it, fortunately. The Ancient of Days is "the same yesterday, today, and forever." But out of Its eternal Being there is an everlasting flow of a forever becoming—"Ever as the spiral grew, / He left the old house for the new." Involuted in that which we are is the seed which gives rise to that which is evoluting out of it, which we shall become. And I was thinking about it the other night and wrote, "The fruit of evolution is in the seed of involution." In our Bible it says—in Genesis—"These are the generations when the plant was made before the seed was in the ground."*

We do not change anything but our reactions to a Universe which acts by some magic of Its own, some mirror, some looking glass—"For life is a mirror of king and slave, / Tis just what you are and do; / Then give to the world the best that you have, / And the best will come back to you." Here is the magic mirror of mind, of consciousness or experience or environment—it doesn't matter what we call it—which reflects back to us that which we reflect into it. Mistaking the effect for a cause, we worship the effect, stand in awe of it, not knowing that we are holding it in place by some divine

---

*This is a conflation of Genesis 1:11 (or 12) and 2:4, 5.

Power which we are not aware of. I call it *divine* because I happen to believe there is nothing but God—in the struggle, in the mistake, in the answer: it is all some of the movement of the original Satchitananda, or divine Bliss.

I happen to believe that everything in the Universe in manifestation exists for the delight of God—not for the glory, as though God were to be glorified; not for our salvation, as though we were lost. All of this is nonsense. It is the babbling of an infant in thought. The Universe exists for the delight of its Creator, that It shall behold Itself in Its own works, know Its beauty in that which is beautiful—and in us, I believe, behold Its beloved Son in whom It is well pleased.

And always there is some reverberation from this shoreless sea of timeless movement underneath which there is absolute silence and stillness. Something I wrote wound up by saying, "Hid within all things evolved, / In silence, beauty, wisdom, will / Is that which makes the cycle move, / Unmoved, immovable, and still." It follows the concept of the Gita and of our Bible and everybody's bible I know about (and I think I have read most of them) that there is involuted, or we are impregnated with, or there is incarnated in us, or however it got there I don't know—there is something in us, an impulsion, a necessity to live, to sing, to dance, to laugh, to love, to come to fruition, and to love creatively. And that life which does not create, or is not lived creatively, creates a surplus of action, now held in the prison within us, beating against the walls of our consciousness for expression.

This is the nature, I think, of the inner conflict—it certainly is very much like that—and the tension and the frustration of the unlived life, and our misinterpretation of the objectification in which we cast the images of our own despair. And we little know something that was illustrated in something I read of a man who had a terrible dream, and he looked up and some awful figure was leaning over his bed, and he was frightened; and he said, "What are you going to do with me?" And the terrible figure leered at him and said, "I am not going to do anything to you; what are *you* going to do to *me?* I am *your* dream, you know." Isn't that terrific? I would like to have made it up!

I was going to say, "back of Dave's simplicity," and that is awful—back of *the doctor's exquisite simplicity,* which is a profundity, it has taken a lifetime of experience and application to come here and tell us the simple things he did. Because *you don't get it out of a book.* It is *in* a man; and then he sits down and as best he can records, as best he may, something that he feels. But words are so inadequate; and it is only when what he feels breathes the words that articulate what is being felt, that the man delivers himself to us and we get what he means. There is no deliverance unless a speaker delivers *himself*—everything that he is. He can talk about love all he wants to—"Isn't it grand? God is Love." But unless his arms are around his audience *literally* as far as they can be *symbolically*—because he loves them—he is not going to get anywhere.

The poet said, "If I had the time to learn from you / How much more comfort my words could do, / And I told you then of my sudden will / To kiss your feet when I did you ill; / If the tears back of the coldness feigned / Could flow, and the wrong be quite explained: / Brothers the souls of us all would chime /—If we had the time." Now this is my religion. It, too, is as simple as David's psychology. It is tied back into the concept of a cosmic Presence incarnated in everything—the bird and the stone and the running brook and the stars and the wind and the wave, the perspiration in the armpits of the laborer.* Whitman said that the prostitute and the libertine, the child sucking at the fountain of Nature from its mother's breast, the man drunk in the gutter, the ascetic, the recluse, and the one in simple adoration all say, "My Lord and my God"; and we shall never find God if we exclude any of these.

You cannot break the Universe into fragments and discover a unitary wholeness in causation, back of some of which might be an illusion and some of which might be real. Bondage is made of freedom, or there is no freedom; unhappiness is made of the possibility of being happy; and Hell will not cool off until we get to Heaven—it is impossible, because the Universe tolerates no otherness, no difference, no fragmentary representation. Everything from the smallest atom to the sidereal universe is forever singing

---

*Imagery drawn from *Leaves of Grass,* by Walt Whitman.

a song of the Cosmos, forever proclaiming the presence of That which is complete. We feel it by some subtle mystical, inner sense, and I doubt not that all of our trouble, just as Doctor Fink has said, is a result of our frustrations, which inhibit its flow—because everything is in a flow in the Universe; it is a liquidity; it is what is always called, or likened to, water—the primordial substance from which the mundane universe emanated. It is just a symbol.

Now then: if these things are true, and if what David said is true—and I do not doubt that they are true—there is only one little guy that we really have to work with, isn't there? "God and I in space alone, / And nobody else in view; / 'And where are the people, God,' I said, / And the dead whom once I knew?' / 'There are no people,' the great God said; / 'No earth beneath or sky o'erhead. / There is nothing at all but you.'" Now this isn't solecism. This is true. Every reaction we have to life is the reaction of what we are to the life with which we must live—the people with whom we are associated. What do we see? What do we hear? What is our reaction? "Well," we might say, "what has all this to do with religion?" Well, religion is a life. You know, people can pray until they get so frustrated they are crazy—because unless the prayer looses a frustration, it will just make it worse. I guess I should take this back; but it is true.

I happen to know someone who is one of the most brilliant women in America—was having lunch with her not long ago—and she was cussing things out pretty much in general. And I said, "This is a strange thing to me; why do you suppose it is that you have so much self-condemnation?" She was just about to crown me with the sugar bowl; she said, "I do *not* have condemnation for myself!" I said, "This is all you have talked about. You are projecting yourself. You are like a person who has stopped drinking coffee and says, 'Nobody else shall ever drink coffee again; it is wrong—because *I* have stopped.'" I said, "Way back in your mind you have the most terrific sense of having been cast out of Heaven as most anybody I know of." She said, "This is hard to believe." "But," I said, "this is true. Thou dost protest too loudly.' "

Now *we* are the only guy who has to come clean; and I don't believe we will ever do it until we get better acquainted with whatever this Thing is that we call God—whatever this Thing is that we call ourselves. It won't be through *a false egotism*; it will be *a certain egoism* in the sense that we shall have to respect the fact that, as Emerson said, if God hadn't had need of you, He wouldn't have put you here. You are an organ of the Infinite.

I think we have every right to intelligently recognize whether we say we are Sons of the living God or whatever we choose to call It. We are the offspring of a Universe that at least saw fit to give birth to us—and I don't believe God makes any mistakes; there can be no mistakes in the divine Plan. (*We* have plenty of them!)

I think a certain amount of meditation, prayer, contemplation reaches that Secret Place of the Most High. Believe me, I tried it last week because I felt I had some things I had to get straightened up, and I went away for six days all by myself and I talked to myself on an average of ten hours a day—because I knew I needed it—and it happened.

Now *what* happened? There is nothing that *could* have happened other than that the frustration was removed long enough for some Light to come through. "There is a Light that lighteth every man's path"; there is a Silence at the center of every person that speaks; there is a Word that is heard; there is a Presence that is felt; there is a Power that flows; and a Peace. It comes out of some eternal Stillness—so still that the Silence becomes articulate. Now I know it; because whenever I get where I think I need that, that is what I do. Now what happens? I think in a sense it is like boring a tunnel until it hits the reservoir and a clearance is made and out gushes the water, as Moses struck the rock with a rod. Because the water is always there. "He has not left Himself without a witness."

Now we practice the Science of Mind, spiritual mind healing, and we believe in it. We are the first group of metaphysicians who have ever deliberately set about, as I did 30 years ago,* to build a bridge between metaphysics, science, philosophy, religion, medicine, psychology, and psychiatry. I

---

*i.e., 1927. This marks the formal beginnings of Religious Science. But Ernest Holmes had been working on his "bridge" long before that.

have been at it for 30 years, and I hope it won't take another 30 years. We are well on the way. It shouldn't have to happen that way, because the world is going to need every good that is at its disposal. Therefore you become practitioners.

To feel that disease or poverty is some terrible evil or some awful thing imposed on us, or to lay too much stress on our own error . . . the psychiatrist has a little more charity than most religionists: he knows it is the neurosis talking and not the neurotic, and he separates the belief from the believer. We have to separate what is human from the divine, and we have to have confidence enough to believe that we are a witness to some infinite Beauty. But how shall we be a witness to that which we have not witnessed? How shall we speak that which we have not heard? How shall we know that which we have not seen, and how shall we think that which we have not conceived? We shall not.

Most of your practice won't be with what objectively it looks as though it were about; not even the people. It will be with *yourself*; because all they are going to get from you is *yourself.* They can't get anything else. As Theodore Reik[*] said in his book *Listening with the Third Ear*: there is a third ear that must listen, and an artistry about psychiatric analytical work; and if a person doesn't listen with a third ear and doesn't have that intuition developed, he will not do very much with his patients.

It is an understanding heart, a seeing eye; it is a something that feels back through all this apparent ugliness, this strange confusion, as Riley[†] said, "in that mad race where none achieve," and finds in itself that which it may now uncover in another. And believe me, such people heal those around them without any thought at all. Something is transmitted. As Whittier[‡] said, "The healing of the seamless dress / Is but by our beds of pain; / We touch Him in life's strong embrace, / And we are whole again."

No psychiatrist and no metaphysician is ever going to make anybody else

---

[*](1888–1969), Austrian-American psychoanalyst and author.
[†]James Whitcomb Riley (1849–1916), American poet.
[‡]John Greenleaf Whittier (1807–1892), American poet.

any more whole than he is himself. It is impossible. If the blind lead the blind, they will both fall into the ditch. It is something that David has learned and that field is beginning to learn, and it will hook onto religion some day—but, we shall hope, a religion without superstition; because religion with superstition is better than none, but it isn't as good as it could be.

Religion is a life—a feeling we have to the Universe. It is a way of thinking and acting. It is a secret we have with each other. It is something that reveals us to each other in love, in purity—and I am not speaking of purity in the ethical sense; I am speaking of the *pure sacrifice,* where the reality stands out—where we have nothing to sell and do not wish to buy anything; and where we live a life which I believe no one can tell us much about, other than to say, "This is the Way." I believe everyone will have to find the most of it; that is why we never give formulas. David didn't give a formula. He said, "Practice this kind of a thing and that kind of a thing." Because why? Every time you give a treatment, every time you pray, every time you talk about something, you never do the same thing twice alike.

You know, if a river is the same river it was yesterday, and stays so, and you should drink from it, in a few days it would poison you. It is only in the movement and the flow, from the mountaintops of your inspiration and adoration, that there is an imbibing that is cosmic. And so we can never do the same thing twice alike, or pray the same prayer. That is why there are no formulas. Something new, something spontaneous, something in my estimation that never happened in all the Universe before happens every time somebody takes a picture. Or as Emerson said, "The Ancient of Days is in the latest invention." It is *here.* He said we should say, not God *spake,* but *speaks;* not God *was,* but *is.* This *is* the beloved Son, which Son you are.

And so we tie this whole thing back into a sort of mystical—not mysterious—sense of our relationship to Something which is very beautiful, Something which is very still inside of us. Emerson said of the Lady of the Lake: "She is calm and, whatsoever storms assail the sea, and when the tempest rolls, hath power to walk the waters like our Lord."

Now there are people who wouldn't understand what we are talking about—would think we are crazy and all that. They said that about Socrates and Jesus—not that I am likening myself to them; but what they discovered is what we are in search of. And if as great a man as Socrates could laugh while Plato was crying and say, "Plato thinks *this* is Socrates"; and if Jesus could say, "It is expedient that I go away in order that the Spirit of Truth may bear witness to the Fact I have taught you"; and if he can say to the thief on the cross beside him, "Today shalt thou be with me in paradise"; and if we companion with the great and the good and commune with their thoughts through their written words until we enter into a psychic consciousness that isn't written at all, in my estimation (I am sure of it; that is why we read great literature, that is why we listen to great music: it is what *wasn't* recorded that is suggested by what *was*; and I believe it is transcendent) . . . if these great people could do this, so can we—you and I—with a humility that is not false, a simplicity that is direct, a claim upon the Universe where the soul makes its great claim on God that is not arrogance.

I don't think we should be afraid. I think the beginning of wisdom is not the fear of God but the knowledge, the love, the worship, the adoration, the sense of a divine Presence. As Emerson said, "How wonderful is the thought of God peopling the lonely places with His presence." And it is only when we become lonely enough that That which is Alone in us gropes out and finds the Alone in other things, and the loneliness is gone.

Alone to the Alone, the One to the One, the Only to the Only. We shall never successfully practice our Science unless we do spend much time seeking that Thing within us which is beyond fear, beyond isolation, beyond separation, beyond good and evil, beyond what theology teaches—that simplicity, that childlikeness which is not child*ish* but is child*like*: this is the essence of religion; "But what am I?; / An infant crying in the night; / An infant crying for the light; / And with no language but a cry." "But the feeble hands and helpless, / Groping blindly in the darkness, / Touched God's right hand in that darkness / And are lifted up and strengthened."

This no living soul can do for you nor for me. But hid deep within the soul, hid deep within the silence, hid in the beauty of Nature, is That which speaks. And the bush burns, and the ground becomes hallowed and the spot sacred; and That is you, and That is myself. That is each other; That is the whole world. And if the materialists shall scoff at it, we are not concerned; if someone shall criticize it, we are not dismayed; if someone shall say such things are not—we shall not listen. There is a testimony of the soul, there is an inward awareness, which you shall discover. And then you shall meet God in yourself.

6.

THIS THING CALLED LIFE

———

In March 1958 Dr. Ernest Holmes went to Florida to speak in Fort Lauderdale, St. Petersburg, Orlando, and Miami. The last talk of this series was given in Miami on March 26th. He selected the title of his favorite book, *This Thing Called Life*, as his topic for the evening.

This brief series of talks will come to a close tonight. I have so much enjoyed being here and talking with you. I never talk *to* people or *at* people. Our work is a sort of counseling together to try to find out what it is we believe, why we believe it, whether or not we think it makes sense, and whether it will work. For we have no platitudes, we have no formulas, and we have no sweet sayings. If we did, I wouldn't be here. Nor would anybody else. Religious Science in essence is not anything new in the world. In *action* it *is* new. It's a putting together the highlights of the thoughts of the ages and seeing what they add up to; and it is an attempt also to use these thoughts and embody their meaning for life. It's a life—it's a *living*—based upon the best that the world knows.

It's been very wonderful, the response we've had these two weeks here—Ft. Lauderdale, St. Petersburg, and Orlando. I don't know where all the people came from. It shows what a great vitality must exist in the idea that you and I believe in. It also shows that the world is ready for something perhaps a little different—not necessarily better, but different. The world is certainly waiting for some sign, I happen to believe (it's only my opinion), whether or not it knows or recognizes the fact—the world is waiting for definite and concrete evidence of the reality of the hope that springs perennial in the human breast. For whether or not we know or are aware of the fact, every man's life individually, and therefore all men's lives collectively, are, in the last analysis, more influenced by their thoughts of God or their belief in some supreme Power than anything else.

Now that will include every religion. This is why religion and art are the two oldest institutions in the world, and the only two institutions that have come down through the ages and not been destroyed by pestilence, tidal wave, time, revolution, or the forming and dissolution of empires. Always these two institutions have stood as though they were silent watchers over the evolution of humanity. And religion and art are intuitive perceptions of the nature of the Universe in which we live. They are a feeling toward and for the invisible.

And so I chose the subject "This Thing Called Life." I wrote a book, *This Thing Called Life,* which is one of the biggest sellers that ever appeared in this field. I deliberately chose to call it "This Thing Called Life" rather than "Jehovah" or "Buddha" or "Allah" or "the Absolute." As I was thinking of a name, a friend of mine said, "I have a title for you, but I don't think I want to give it to you." I said, "What is it?" and he said, "This Thing Called Life." I said "You don't have to give it to me—I have already taken it!"—a very wonderful title, because it calls the unknown *Life*: This Thing Called *Life*.

Now life is the thing that eludes us. All the biologists in the world do not know what life is; all the psychologists do not know what the mind is. They are merely among the watchers of the action of either an unknown Guest or an unknown Host, and no one knows exactly which—that Thing which we call God, which animates everything and makes everything what it is, and without which nothing would be. I chose to call it "This Thing Called Life" because I wanted to keep the theological connotation or implication away from it.

I discovered a very charming cousin of mine here in your very wonderful, very beautiful city, and she asked me the difference between religion and theology. I told her religion is our faith in God; theology is the dogma that grows up around it that finally people come to believe is so because people believed in it. But religion itself is native to the soul. A person without a religion is not wide awake intellectually, emotionally, or spiritually.

Religion is essential to the mind, because it is impossible for any person to feel that he must single-handed and alone combat the Universe. There is a gravitational force that's holding this watch in place, this desk, this building, and the whole universe, and we do not have to help it. It is something that operates automatically. We work so hard, Jesus said, "for the meat that perisheth," and we struggle so hard to do things by pushing and pulling and shoving and hauling, as Lowell said:

> Bubbles we earn with a whole soul's tasking;
> 'Tis heaven alone that is given away,
> 'Tis only God may be had for the asking.

Now Life exists. Nothing is more certain. Life is intelligent; It responds to us. We happen to believe It's a spiritual Presence, everywhere equally distributed, and within us and around us, and everywhere else. Life—call It God, call It anything you want to: there is Something present with us and in us, out of whose essence all things are made, within whose creative imagination all things are formed, and by whose inexorable and immutable laws all things are held in place. This is self-evident. Here we are, and we couldn't be here if these things were not true.

This Thing called Life—now what has it to do with the human personality? This Thing called Life *is* the human personality. Just as we have not seen God, we have not seen each other. We think that we have seen each other, but we haven't. We have seen the objective manifestation of something that's impelled and propelled by an invisible awareness which is the real self. Angela Morgan said:

> That inner self you have not known,
> Looking on flesh and blood alone—
> That inner self that never tires,
> Fed by the deep eternal fires,
> Angel and guardian at the gate,
> Master of death and king of fate.

Now there *is* such a self—there isn't any question about it. There is the self that no one has ever plumbed. The more deeply psychology plumbs what it calls the unconscious, or some of the deeper aspects of this self, the more it finds it still has not reached. There is always more. The Bible speaks of it as a river whose source no man has seen.

There is a flowing into each one of us, in my estimation, a unique presentation of the Universe itself; and every man is a center in a Consciousness which is Itself universal or cosmic, all-encompassing, endless, forever expansive. We are all in the process of an eternal evolution, destined to be ever more and never less ourselves. Every man is in the pathway of unfoldment. That there must be endless entities, beings, beyond us as we are beyond tadpoles, I am completely convinced.

Now this is something that we ought to believe in and realize, because what we think about we become; what we believe and accept becomes a part of our being. Our consciousness and its awareness constitute the only absolutely solid, sole, evidence of being there is; because if you were to take consciousness away, there would be nothing left. That this consciousness of yours and mine extends out or in—or perhaps both out *and* in—to some limitless infinitude, I do not know. How else are you going to account for a man like Mahatma Gandhi in modern times, a Buddha in his time, or Moses or Jesus or any of the other great spiritual geniuses? Gandhi would sit there, and a million persons who couldn't possibly hear his voice (and didn't have to; it didn't matter whether he spoke or not) became enraptured as they gradually merged into the influence of whatever we may call it; they call it *darshan* in India. It means that this thing is established between people, as whatever it is in one and whatever it is in the other meet in a third place in space. I have always known that it happens between an audience and a speaker. It's one of the first things I ever discovered. It is the consciousness of the audience and the consciousness of the speaker meeting, and then flowing back into each other, and adding something greater than either one could have done of himself or itself.

Now that some spiritual awareness, some interior awareness, some transcendent something emanated from Gandhi and Jesus and many others there is no question at all. As a matter of fact, this influence is exercised on all planes—material, mental, physical, spiritual, esthetic, artistic—and we feel people, we feel atmospheres. We little realize what they are. As Emerson said, "What you are speaks so loudly I cannot hear what you are saying." Shakespeare said, "My words fly up, my thoughts remain below: / Words without thoughts, never to Heaven go." Here is something that you cannot measure. I do not know what it is. Loosely, let us call it the personality, the ego, individuality, the Thing Itself, that which Life is in us; because I believe there is only one Life Principle. God is One. "Hear, O Israel: the Eternal, the Lord thy God is one God." I believe that there is only one Spirit in the Universe. "There is one mind common to all men," Emerson said.

I happen to believe that we live by the Spirit of God, we think because the mind of God is in us, and we expand because we expand from the finite into the Infinite. You cannot contract the Infinite, you *can* expand the finite. We may all expand more and more and yet more, and I believe forever, here and then somewhere else. I have no worry about shucking off this mortal coil. Someone said to me the other day, "You certainly don't believe everybody goes to the same place, do you?" Fortunately, God is taking care of that. I said I would ask him one thing and he could answer it. I said, "Did we all arrive at the same place when we got here?" and he said, "Yes." I said, "You've answered your own question."

There is no reason in the world why you and I should be soul-savers—because, believe me, my friends: if I am lost, there is no one else who will know where to find me. Now that is nothing against the Miamians; if we were in Los Angeles I'd say the same thing. *There is nothing lost.* But certain things in our mental and spiritual anatomy at times seem slightly misplaced. We can almost lose hope. But Truth will rise again. There is a side of us which lies open to the Infinite; then as it comes down and flows through us, it influences people—not because we try to make it; we don't want it to, in that sense.

We do not teach how to influence people, how to get rich, how to have one of those dominating personalities. That is very silly. There are lots of people who actually believe that there is someone who *can* teach them.

There is no such thing. Every man is an institution in his own right, and "Every institution is the length and shadow of somebody's thought," Emerson said. Every person is already equipped with everything he can need or he wouldn't be here. God never makes mistakes; and so I happen to believe that right back of me and right back of you, and within us, there is a unique individualization of Eternity itself, of the whole Thing. No two persons are alike. As Emerson said, "Imitation is suicide."

Now suppose there were at the center of the being of each one of us a clear channel to the Infinite, which is forever pouring out through us in a unique way, because it never does two things alike, nor does it ever repeat itself. Somewhere at the center of our being, should we properly use it, would be that thing we would all like to be, which is certain to be happy and well and prosperous, successful; it is certain to be established in peace, to experience joy, to know life; it is certain, if it is understood and permitted and cultivated, to bless everything that it touches. This would be our influence on our environment; it wouldn't be an influence that dominates people, or controls them, but it would be an influence that would irresistibly bring back from most people a very great affection, a very great love. People are lonely, you know.

One of the greatest needs in the world is to heal the loneliness of the human mind; people feel very much alone and are unhappy and insecure. Now I can't imagine any person being lonely very long who could come to comprehend the meaning of the divine presence of the living, creative Spirit incarnated in himself and one with all other people, because if he consciously practiced this, he would have more friends than he would have time for, objectively. In other words, his inward awareness automatically would attract to him that which is like that awareness.

Anyone who truly loves people will be loved by people. Anyone who has healed himself of the hurt of life will find countless numbers of people gathering around him that they may be healed too, as Whittier said: "The healing of the seamless vest / Is by our beds of pain. / We touch him in life's throng and press, / And we are whole again." Now I know there are a lot of people who study to influence people and make friends, and be superduper salesmen. That is not the way the Universe is organized. Who told God how to be God? Who told the nightingale how to sing? Who told the chicken how to lay an egg?

You know, the story of Job in the old Testament is an example of this. He was a good man; but it seemed as though there were great visitations of misfortune upon him. He lost everything he had—his family and his horses and his cattle; and he had three friends and a wife who comforted him, or tried to, and they told him he had probably been bad, and he said he thought he had been good and done everything. Finally, he had to discharge his three counselors (Job's comforters). Then Mama Job says, "Well, Papa, there is nothing left but to curse God and to die." He said, "I think you are wrong. There is an integrity in me, and in my integrity shall I see God." Now this is just a story and it is a good one.

And Job told God he'd done everything: he hadn't muzzled the oxen when they threshed the grain, and he'd left grain in the fields for the gleaners; he had given his tithes to the temple and much more; he had entertained his friends and the alien within his gates, he had been good to his family, he had worshiped God; and so he was complaining and sort of setting himself up as the only cause that there was.

So in the argument God finally said, "Well, Job, you have done very well, and I have watched you, and I have admired you; but there are some things you don't happen to be aware of. Where were you when I set the stars in their course and started the North Wind? I just don't remember seeing you around, Job." And for the first time Job realized—and this is the meaning of the story—that you and I take it out. We don't put it in; *we take it out*. It's already there. So he falls down and says, "I see now how it is: I have interfered with the divine operation of the cosmic Law." And it was then that everything was restored to him, as it would have to be.

This is a story, written by a man with a very dramatic, creative imagination, to teach a cosmic truth as he saw it.

You and I do not hold things in place; we are operated upon—not only by physical laws that are cosmic, like gravitational force, fractional repulsion, cohesion. *All* the laws and forces of Nature act upon us. We are acted upon by great mental and spiritual laws in the same way, and the final law of our whole being is the law of our acceptance or rejection of Life itself. Do we or do we not believe? Are we alone buffeted by fate? Are we persecuted by the vicissitudes of fortune? Have both God and man denied us the right to be happy? So many entertain this psychological and emotional attitude and blame everybody for everything.

And so we have to reverse this, come to an inner awareness. And there is no final psychological or physiological or psychosomatic clearance until spiritual realization changes the imagery of our imagination, that in its place it may react on the body and the environment, which are but reflections cast into the mirror of some medium that acts like a reflector to bring back to the thinker the objectification of his thoughts.

Now there is no willpower, none of this terrific thing. If a person can love enough, he will be loved; there won't be any question about it. If he has entered a state of peace in his own mind, people will feel peaceful around him and want to be there. If he sees that he is one with the great human race, he will have more friends than he can attend to. But even though this should be a hope in his mind, an anguish, a longing covertly expressed, even expressed in the Holy of Holies through prayer and supplication, and he himself did not believe his own entreaty: it would be as though it had not been heard; and this is something people don't understand. They say, "Why has God done this to me?" "Why has life done this to me?"

It is very difficult for any of us to understand that the nature of the Universe is such whether we like it or do not like it; that until we affirmatively comply with Its affirmation, even Its affirmation shall appear to us as a negation, by the same word in reverse, just as heat will burn us, cook our food, explode and burn down the building, or warm our hands and feet— just as perhaps the electrical energy that toasts the Pope's bread is the one that will kill a criminal that is being electrocuted. The great forces of nature are impartial and impersonal.

Now it so happens in our philosophy of this Thing called Life, we believe that we are one with all the Power there is. We are not that Power; we are one with It. We are one with all the Life there is. We are not that Life; It is what we are. We are a cast of the only Mind and the only creative Imagination there is. It's all here, and we have to believe it, because if we don't believe it, we believe it *isn't*. Therefore there must be an acceptance.

There's a big difference in the attitude, when I get up in the morning, if I say it's a bad day, it's a tough day, etc.—or if I say, "Good morning, God!" *That's* quite a different attitude—the attitude of a child. "The sun is lovely; thank you, God. I'm glad to be alive!" There's a very great difference how we start the day. One may say, "I wonder what rascal I'll meet, and I wonder who is going to do me in today." Now this is an attitude, and it's anybody's privilege to assume it. But there must be a government of Law in the Universe. Browning said, "All's love and yet all's law." And he was right. Then another may say, "This is the day God has made. I'm going to be glad in it. I live and exist on the threshold of opportunity. Every person I meet shall be blessed and helped; and there is a deep and abiding peace in me which shall be transmitted to everyone I meet." What a difference in these attitudes!

And now we know what mental attitudes do. They brush off on people. Personality brushes off like feathers, and everybody feels it. If we are psychically antagonistic, everyone feels it, and they feel ruffled up. They don't know why, but if we shake their hands they would like to shove us away. But if there is the all-embracing heart, even as they shake our hand with one hand, they try to get the other hand around us. It's irresistible. Now, this doesn't happen by chance. It isn't just saying, "Jesus loves me, this I know, for the Bible tells me so." That's sweet, but *this* ain't *that*.

There's something very dynamic about this, something terrific. There's something that works with mathematical accuracy and immutable certainty. Nothing can change it. It is a law in the Universe. Because we all live in the One Mind, we all live in the One Power and the One Presence. If we learn to see in each other that which we would like to be, we shall much quicker become that which we would like to be—because a house divided against itself cannot stand.

There's no such thing as my having the slightest little bit of salvation. (I hate to use the word because I don't believe in it; we're not lost. But you know what I mean.) We can't have the slightest little bit at all. The Universe will have no exclusions. Over the doorway of the Kingdom of Holiness has indelibly been imprinted the word *Others,* always. Why is that? Because each one of us is a center in the consciousness of the Whole and in the consciousness of each other. And remember this: the life that includes the most is the biggest.

So we would like to have wonderful personalities. People say, "Can't somebody come and give us a class on the development of personality?" If you know anyone who can give you a class on how to lay an egg, that's grand, and you settle with him; and I'll bet anything if it hatches, it's a rotten egg. It won't hatch. It just isn't that way. If it were that way, then a man who could hold thoughts the hardest without getting crosseyed, and the man who could concentrate the most without getting a headache, would govern everybody else. History proves the reverse. Only the lovers of humanity have been loved by it.

But we measure things by a pretty short distance, don't we? Too short, in fact. Here in eternal Existence we can measure them only by the long reach and the great out-sweep of time. It already has a way of finally dissipating everything that is negative and bringing forward the great affirmations, because that's the way It lives. It's the way God says, "I am; and that also I am, beside which there is none other."

Now this thing works automatically. A life that really loves people will be loved. But it's got to be *real.* It can't be done as a trick—even a metaphysical one—and it can't be done as a sweet affirmation, saying, "I love you, even though you are a stinker." It isn't that way at all. Love only knows and comprehendeth love. It is true. It is all-inclusive, and in such degree as that happens to one's own soul, he will be embraced by humanity. I know it. Very, very few people have ever had as much love as I have had, and I love people, good, bad and indifferent—because we are all indifferent anyway. We're all partly good and we're all partly—not *bad,* but just a little *loose* here and there, this way and that way; and that's all right. It's the set of the sail and not the gale that we must pay attention to.

We all have an inward longing, an irresistible desire to embrace the Universe, and so often we are afraid of it. Don't be afraid of that. It is only the one who abandons himself to the genius of this Thing called Life that could ever hope to have that Thing articulate itself through him. What is It but that Thing that wrote every song, and dances every dance; what is It but that Artist who painted every picture. And that is why the poet said, "When earth's last picture is painted / And the views are twisted and dried, / And the oldest color is faded / And the youngest critic has died— / We shall rest."

Now it so happens, in my belief, that each one of us is an institution in the Universe—unique, entirely new, will never be reproduced. But don't we sit around saying, "I don't know. I haven't got it. I haven't the looks, the talent, the brains or spiritual equipment"—? And in our field they say, "I don't have enough understanding, and I'm not spiritual enough." It's all nonsense; it's all a part of that strange unconscious self-condemnation that man seems to bedevil himself with through life.

I have never known a man, and never shall, who, having cleared himself first of this condemnation of his own being, will ever judge another. It's only a projection. It's why Jesus said, "Judge not that ye be not judged, for with what judgment ye judge, ye shall be judged, and with what measure ye mete, it shall be measured to you again." That's not a platitude. All Jesus was saying, if he had said it in another way, would be this: "Water will reach its own level by its own weight"; and you don't force it. Let someone get a clearance in his own mind from ugliness, and everything shall be beautiful to him.

I had a funeral not long ago, because of a mutual friend. I did not know the people or this elderly lady who had passed on, didn't see any members of the family. I sat there while the song was being sung, and I thought, "Now look here, something in me knows about this person. There is some part of me that always knew her and embraced her." So when I got up to talk, I didn't talk much about immortality. All I could talk about was *beauty*, and I did it for 20 minutes. So after it was over, two sons came to me and said, "Oh, that was terrific!" I said, "Let me ask you something: was your mother an artist?" and one of them said, "No, not in the ordinary sense; but her whole life was a work of art and a thing of beauty, and had you known her all her life, you could not have said it any better."

What was the thing I felt? It is what she was, it's the memory left behind, it's the feeling that these things go through life with us, and people feel them and they know them and they will embrace or reject us according to whether or not we are embracing or rejecting the Universe itself. And suppose we include joy and beauty and love and faith—all of these attitudes are contagious.

I read not long ago in a popular magazine about a man who got on a streetcar and was whistling and having a wonderful time on his way to work. He sat down beside somebody and had to be there for half an hour, but before the half hour was over he wished he could go out and kill himself. This man beside him was in a very melancholy and almost desperate emotional state, and this just transmitted itself to him. He couldn't understand why he felt that way. There is something about us that rubs off, definitely.

We looked at the picture of Lowell Thomas[*] and his son, their travel to Tibet last summer; and here always the prayers and prayer wheel, praying, praying, appeasing the devils and evil influences, the hills and bad spirits of the canyons, and exorcising the spirits of the water before they could cross the flowing river where the water is very swift. How silly; yet is that any different from what we do in our theology? We think that is very crude, don't we? Yet it isn't one bit more crude than what 90 percent of the people do, each in his own language. And that's all wrong.

What kind of a God are we proclaiming, what kind of This Thing Called Life? Seems to me we should be filled with joy and happiness. Dare to be yourself; you have nothing else. That thing which the Infinite and Almighty has endowed each one of us with we have rejected because it is so simple, so unassuming. "How could it be me? It must be some great character, some great figure in history; it must be some saviour, some Christ or Buddha." No, *they* did it for *themselves*; and they did well. Therefore they become great wayshowers—not saviours.

Nothing can save us but ourselves; nothing can bring peace and quiet but

---

*(1892–1981), American traveler, journalist, and author.

our own consciousness; nothing can bless the world, so far as you and I are concerned, but you and I. God has already blessed it, and if it were not so, we would all be living by proxy. The greatest thing that can happen to any living soul is finally to learn to take himself for better or worse; to say, "I am this that I am—good, bad, or indifferent. From this point, I must go forward." "Sun across its course may go, / The Ancient river still may flow, / And I am still *I am*."

And, as one thinks long and deeply, silently within himself, and listens, something happens to him. There is a witness to the soul—irrefutable, irrevocable, absolutely certain. The only prophetic thing that can ever happen to you and to me, is not to read—just read—what others have done, but somehow or other, taking that as an example, to do the same thing.

Now we would like this dynamic personality.

We've got it. But we aren't using it—that's all.

We would like this creative something. *We have it.* But we're not using it.

The key to the Kingdom of God was locked in the Secret Place of the Most High, in the heart of every living soul before ever time began. It's predetermined, it's predestined. It's written in the constitution and nature of the Universe that you and I and everyone else is the beloved Son, and as Eckhart said, "God is forever begetting His Only-Begotten, and He is begetting Him in me now." What a wonderful possibility!

When at long last we have laid down the burden and the struggle and the doubt and the fear and the uncertainty and the questioning "Where shall I go, and what shall I do, to be saved?" at last some sweet clarion call as from the pipe of Pan shall cause the Sun to stand still. "Sweet, sweet, O Pan—piercing sweet"; by the river is that clarion call blown by your own lips echoing evermore, "This is my beloved Son"; "I am that which Thou art, Thou art that which I am." Wonderful the ears that can hear the message of the saints and sages who proclaim not unto us but unto Thee. Enlightened is the one who at long last, sitting in the silence of his own soul, shall no longer be afraid to say, "Good morning, God!"

7.

THE POWER OF AN IDEA

Dr. Holmes repeated many times that "thoughts are things." He stressed *the power of an idea*. The preceding Miami talk was still in his thinking when he returned to Los Angeles in April 1958, and on Sunday the 27th he delivered this talk on the Power of an Idea at the Wiltern Theater. For what these two talks contained—indeed, for their very strong content—I labeled this entire volume of *The Ernest Holmes Papers* "Ideas of Power."

In the scripture reading George* read this morning, it says, "In the beginning was the Word, and the Word was with God, and the Word was God. And all things were made by the Word; and without the Word was not anything made that was made. And the Word became flesh and dwelt among us, and we beheld It." The Bible and all bibles—because ours is one of many—all start with the proposition that there is one Life, one Mind, one Intelligence, one Law, and that everything proceeds from this One, and everything lives in this One. Everything lives by It.

Dr. Bill† is back in New York with the Guru of India.‡ He is to the Hindu world what the Pope is to the Christian world: countless millions of people look to him as their spiritual guide. This is the first time in a thousand years that a man in his office has ever left India. He became very fond of Bill when he was here. He is one of the great spiritual lights of the world. It is a very great honor for Bill and for us that he should insist on seeing Bill before he embarks for India, nor could we have a better ambassador than Dr. Bill. We are very proud he had this invitation, is on this mission, and our thought

---

*George Bendall.
†William Hornaday.
‡Sri Shankaracharya Bharati Krishna Tirtha of Puri, India—senior head of the Swami Order.

and word and love are with him, as his are with us; and we shall struggle along and do the best we can. Bill is a great ambassador anywhere.

"In the beginning was the Word." All the bibles of the world teach that everything in Creation is a result of the divine Spirit—God, Jehovah, Brahma, the Absolute, the Reality; doesn't matter what you call It—operating upon Itself, and out of this Self making that which still is Itself. "Who hath seen me hath seen the Father." This is the very foundation of our philosophy: God is all there is.

When we use the word *God*, we mean the Cause, the invisible Intelligence, the Divinity, that omnipresent Knowingness; Spirit, Life, Truth, Reality—that is what we mean by God. And when we say that God is everywhere, we mean that God is in us, in each other, in this flower, in the interspaces of the universe. *There is nothing but God*. Anything that denies this divine Presence is an illusion. It is a false conclusion.

God is all there is. "I am that I am beside which there is none other." There is God, Spirit, Life and nothing out of which to make everything.* Therefore everything is God, and God in manifestation. And though I read lately, much to my surprise but not horror, that Hell has recently been moved from New York to San Francisco, I still don't believe in it. A state of consciousness has traveled across the country and, I would say, a doleful one.

Everything is made up of an idea. Our ideas are either false or else they are true. The false idea has never created the truth, and the true idea has never been disturbed by the false. Or, as the Bhagavad Gita says (and that is the book, next to the New Testament, which is read the most in the world, and has been for hundreds of years; it is the book Gandhi read every day; a universal Truth), the Truth has never ceased to be, the Real has never ceased to be; the unreal never has been.

It is our philosophy that if we scrape away the debris—that which contradicts the divine Presence—we shall find a Divinity concealed in every-

---

*This thought is expressed more fully in Dr. Holmes's *The Science of Mind*: "There is Spirit—or this Invisible Cause—and nothing, out of which all things are to be made. Now, Spirit plus nothing leaves Spirit only. Hence there is One Original Cause and nothing, out of which we are made. In other words, we are made from this Thing" (p. 36).

thing, every person, everywhere, all the time. It is our belief that in such degree as we may individually and collectively perceive this Divinity, It will appear. "Act as though I am, and I will be."

There is Something in everything and in every person that responds to this recognition, this penetration, this beholding in each other truth, beauty, love, reason, gladness, joy; responds to seeing It in our environment. And to see It in our surroundings is to call It forth as though we recognized Something which knew Its own name. "Look unto me and be ye saved, all the ends of the earth."

It is our belief—that is why we are here—that every man is "a God though in the germ." That is what Browning meant in "Rabbi Ben Ezra" where he said, "I shall thereupon / Take rest, ere I be gone / On my adventure brave and new, / Fearless and unperplexed / When I wage battle next, / What weapons to select, / What armour to endue. / Fool! All that is, at all, / Lasts forever, past recall; / Earth changes, but thy soul and God stand sure: / What entered into thee / That was, is, and shall be: / Time's wheel runs back or stops: Potter and clay endure." There is nothing but God. God is infinite Intelligence. The Word of God, the Thought of God, the Idea of God is the *Action* of God. As St. Augustine said, it was very evident that the creative Word was the contemplation of God—He didn't use crowbars or levers—and every scripture tells us that Creation is the result of the contemplation of the Self-knowingness of God.

Now by contemplation we mean that with which God is identified. For instance, we want to think about peace: it is an idea to begin with, it is a thought; we say "peace" and we begin to get a little more peaceful. We meditate upon the idea of peace; we get into the idea of peace, a deeper sense of peace; we identify ourselves with peace: "I am that which Thou art"— peace within my soul; "Thou art that which I am"—infinite peace within me. There is nothing but peace. Now *this* is identifying with peace!

And as we do, we think the idea "peace." Plato said everything is made up of divine ideas—that is what he meant: the thoughts of God; "In the beginning was the Word." God thought Creation into existence and is still thinking it into existence in you and in me. The creative Energy and Intelligence that speaks the planets into their spheres of rotation and revolution is the same Intelligence that digests our food and enables us to read the morning paper—if we can find anything in it.

"In the beginning was the Word"; and *this* is the beginning, because you never can step into the same river twice. The only thing that is permanent is change, but within it is that which identifies it. Now that is true. It is also true that that which we contemplate and identify ourselves with we will attract to us; we shall be attracted to it. Now that is one of our troubles, theoretically. All of us should be well, happy, prosperous, radiant, filled with joy and enthusiasm.

I talked to a woman the other day and she said, "I have this certain physical trouble"—which included a wrong blood pressure and wrong lots of things—"and yet the doctor says there is no reason why I should have to have it: I ought to be well." I talked to her awhile and treated her—and I said, "I'll tell you your trouble, my dear; and you don't have to accept it." I said, "Your trouble is a lack of an enthusiastic interest in life—and of giving yourself to some form of expression which expresses you."

"Well," she said, "it's a funny thing, but that is what my doctor told me." She said, "What shall I do?" and I asked, "What *did* you do?" She said, "I used to play the piano all the time, teaching." So I said, "Get out your old piano and begin to play it." She said, "I couldn't teach any more"; and I said, "How do you know you can't?" She made all kinds of excuses: fingers too stiff, can't play any more, etc.

I said, "You have stopped living but not dropped dead. Life and action are the same thing. It is now known in medicine and accepted that where there is this continued ennui and lack of physical vitality, even when there is no real particular infection or reason for illness, any doctor will tell you the illness is because people lack an enthusiastic zest for life. The child has gone out of them—the wonder, the merriment, the joy."

"And he took a child and stood him in their midst and said, Suffer the little children to come unto me and forbid them not, for of such is the Kingdom of God." You and I have to return to the kid state, some part of us; not juvenile delinquency; but we have to get back to where the kid was and grow up all over again differently. This sourness and this bitterness and unenthusiasm for life—it can happen when you are 9, 19, 29, and doesn't have to happen when you are 100. It all depends. "In the beginning was the Word."

Now an idea which persists will take form. Someone said, "A man who seeks one thing in life, and *but one*, may hope to achieve it before life is done." Ideas are realities; but if that is true and our ideas are mixed, part happy and part unhappy, we will draw some happiness and some unhappiness. The law of attraction and repulsion works with mathematical invariableness, with absolute immutability, with exactness. Whatsoever a man thinks—that will happen to him. If it had to be *created* it would happen!

Therefore if we see part of the time that everything is good, part of the time it isn't, we suffer the dualism of good and evil. There is no such thing as good and evil in the Universe; there is no dualism or duality in it. *There is nothing but God.* But because of the creative power of our thought, even that which is good can appear to us as evil. One man's meat is another man's poison.

They criticized Jesus because they said he was evil. He didn't criticize them, because he knew everything is in a process of evolution. We belong to a philosophy which believes that there is nothing but God and that each one of us represents the Eternal. We sputter and spit and fuss around, throw brickbats at each other. I said to one of our leaders the other day, "Isn't it funny; all of us spend about half our time denying what we believe, sort of arguing with each other—not meanly—and the rest of the time we spend praying everything will come together good. If we split the difference, there wouldn't be much left, would there? That is the trouble with us: sometimes hot, sometimes cold." One of the poets said, "None of the singers ever yet has fully lived his minstrelsy"; and Jesus said, "If you want to know of this doctrine, try it." Love only knows and comprehendeth love. Who knows what might happen to an individual, a human, who knew nothing but love?

I tried a very interesting experiment recently when I was in Florida. (I didn't want to go—there were other things I wanted to do—but I had promised; so I went and spoke in four cities in Florida, where I am not known.) I thought to myself, What can I do for somebody whom I do not know? And we had big crowds everywhere I went; they all seemed so much like our own people. And I said, Well, I shall demonstrate to myself that I love these people. God is Love, and I love people anyway. It is only my business if love is transmitted. What is everything else? And I did it: every place I went, strangers came up to me and said, "It must be the most wonderful thing in the world to be loved by so many people!" Isn't that something?

"Who loses his life will find it." We have to surrender the opposite, the negation, if everything is made by the Word. And an idea shall prevail, persistently held—not like holding thoughts; not that way. Sort of good-natured flexibility. There is no dualism; Hell is cooled off; the Devil is dead. Someone will say, "You are a fool." But *who* gets fooled?!

So they crucified Jesus. We say, "Oh, the agony of the cross, the betrayal!" What is three days in eternity? And no human being has ever been loved the way Jesus has been loved. He wasn't crucified at all—he had a few hours of exquisite triumph, that is all. And in the exaltation of that ecstasy, he said two things that flow across the pages of history like a beacon light—and should have destroyed what is false in every theology: "Father, forgive them, for they know not what they do." And to the thief, "Today shalt thou be with me in paradise."

So they killed Socrates, the father of philosophy—and as he was dying, he laughed because Plato was crying, and he said to his other followers, "Plato thinks that *this* is Socrates, that they will kill him; and I said, 'They will have to catch me first.' I shall stay where I am." He was never caught. What were the few moments of the trial? Who is the man who changed the intellectual history of the human race?

So they shot Abraham Lincoln, the most beloved of all Americans. So Gandhi was killed; and the last thing he did was to make their sign of forgiveness. He knew. These have been the great and good and wise. No: we measure things with too small a measure; the infinite ocean is beside us, and we dip it up with a thimble.

Who is there among us who remains true to an idea for one hour, one day, one week, one month, one year, one life . . . ? I believe everything is made up out of thought. I believe there is nothing but the action and reaction of the Intelligence of the Universe, giving birth to all of Its laws, which work with mathematical certainty. That is right along the line with modern science: the infinite Thinker thinking mathematically. God is Love thinking lovingly; Goodness, Truth, and Beauty. I love beauty and cannot live without it. I would starve without it. Because there is more than physical starvation: there is esthetic starvation, there is starvation for lack of a thought of love.

Physical starvation is very simple; it only takes a few weeks. The other might go on for a lifetime—of fear, of the impoverishment and lack of living the creative life, till the joy has gone out of everything, everything sours, and we are no longer "jubilant and beholding souls, with nimble hands and running feet" to look up and laugh in the face of the Universe, and say, "Hello, God!" When that has gone out, we are temporarily dead. But never can we quite lose that Thing which is implanted—that Spark which we may desecrate but never quite lose. So we are living in the possibility of limitless abundance.

Now I happen to believe we are playing around with the most terrific idea the world has ever known. I believe Religious Science is the religion of the future. I don't think it is any of my business or yours—it is bigger than we are. I believe we ought to prove to the world that here is a group of people who demonstrate every step they take. I am taking definite steps in my own thought now to formulate some plan for the working out of that which I think will be better done throughout all our churches next year, because they all are tolerant enough to try what I suggest.

"These signs shall follow them that believe." Belief is an idea, a thought, an acceptance. But how can we both believe and not believe? Therefore we are confused. Everyone should be successful. I don't mean have a million dollars. I don't have much but have everything I need. I wouldn't want to just give my time to making money. If I didn't have it, I would give all my time to it. I think everybody should live well—*everybody*. We are just missing something. We *have* it, but we *miss* it. We hold it in our hand, but it falls away from us. We embrace it in our desire but do not embody it in our thoughts. We are a house divided against itself. We *ought* to be well, we *ought* to be prosperous, we *ought* to be happy. You and I, as we meet people—there should be a healing power emanating from us which will heal them without our even knowing it.

This is what we believe, this is what we must prove: *the power of acceptance.* Someone will say, "I don't know enough." *No one* knows enough. There isn't anyone living who knows how you can think or breathe or how your blood can circulate or how a bird can sing—there is no one living; and all the science and art and philosophy and wit and theology of man cannot tell you how a ham sandwich can become brains or blood or fingernails. They just don't know. All they can do is watch and tabulate the actions and reactions of an invisible guest or ghost or whatever it may be. That is all they know, all you know, all I know.

Therefore you and I know just as much—and more—about our science than any physicist. We know infinitely more about the human mind than all the psychologists put together, because all they studied is the abnormal mind—and about the *normal* mind they know very little if anything. I have the greatest respect for doctors and surgery and everything—but there isn't a surgeon in the world knows how your blood can circulate. He knows there are certain things that have to happen that it may; if there are obstructions, it can't—and he tries to remove them. That is all any of us can do.

You and I know just as much about the Science of Mind as is known, in its field, about the science of electricity. Just exactly. Now stop ignorantly and stupidly denying your own capacity. *We must not do it.* Don't undersell yourself before the court of the Almighty. If God saw fit to make you and me, we *belong*, and we are *needed*, and God Himself would be incomplete without us—or He never would have made us. Now this calls for persistency of an idea: you can heal everybody you touch, you can bring joy and gladness and love and rationality to every environment, by just knowing you can—that silent invisible flow; "flow, sweet river, flow"—but we cannot do it until we first have admitted it and accepted it.

I want to see the time—and expect to see it—when everyone who comes into one of our meetings who needs healing will go out well. It ought to be that way; it is wrong if it isn't that way. We haven't put the thing together right if we don't do it. We are not to be blamed; it isn't our fault: we just haven't done it. And we should not criticize ourselves for not having done it. All the wealth of the world cannot compensate for this. There is nothing the world can give us in exchange for the coin of the eternal Kingdom of the everlasting God. Jesus didn't need a baker: he could multiply the loaves and fishes; he didn't need a banker: he could find money in the fish's mouth. Why don't *we?*

We haven't quite remained true enough to an idea, merely because we didn't *know* or couldn't bring ourselves to *believe.* Maybe we are a little over-modest spiritually. Now we ought to be modest intellectually and physically and humanly. But spiritually we don't have to be modest. What God Almighty did must be pretty good. We don't have to be ashamed that we are alive. We are not worms of the dust or unworthy creatures to be snatched from the mouth of a burning abyss. That is all nonsense. We are not weaklings. "Who hath told thee that thou art naked?"

There isn't anybody going to tell me that I am outcast from the Kingdom of God; for when I look up and see the glory of Heaven and the beauty and warmth and color of the evening sunset, look across the horizon and see the golden glow of approaching day and the sun spilling its warmth through the chariots of fire across the hilltops to awaken the valley, nurture it, and bring joy to it—I don't think I am so unworthy. Maybe the physical, the intellectual is; maybe I'm stupid; but I believe I can reach down and find a grandeur there, a simplicity; and I do spend much time all alone in the middle of the night—any time, hours upon hours sometimes—and I can feel it, and I know it, and it is as real as this, and as solid; and it belongs to everybody.

And I thought last night, I better go to bed, because the time changes.* And I said, No; I want to sit here a while longer. I want to see what happens; I want to invite whatever this Thing is that made me, to flow through me. I want to open myself to It. This is the Lover of the soul—that part that makes whole, without which we are but a makeshift that camouflages or

---

*i.e., the clock would be advanced an hour for Daylight Saving Time.

counterfeits. Just a tiny speck of that divine Possibility already incarnated within us.

You and I are the chosen people of the ages (because *we* choose *It, It* chooses *us* automatically), without fear, believing that we are worthy; but with true humility, as an artist feels humble before the beauty of things even in the "exaltation of his beholding soul." "O beauty," he feels, "engulf me; O warmth and color, flow through me." So Kipling said: when this happens, "No one shall work for money, and no one shall work for fame, / But each for the joy of the working, and each, in his separate star, / Shall draw the Thing as he sees It for the God of Things as They are."

That is the way it is. "Shouting and tumult cease, / The captains and kings depart. / Still stands thine ancient sacrifice / And humble and a contrite heart." Sure, we are humble before God, great beauty, the terrific impact of the Cosmos upon our soul. But we are proud without arrogance, we are exalted without conceit in the face of men. We have a destiny to perform; we are here for a purpose, individually and collectively, to prove before the world that He has not left Himself without a witness.

This is a beginning. Yesterday is past, tomorrow is not here, today salvation presses itself against us. The Chinese sage said, "O man: having the power to live, why will ye die?" And Jesus said, "O Jerusalem, thou that stonest the prophets, how often would I have gathered thee together, even as a hen doth gather her chickens, but thou wouldst not."

God always would. Let us make up our minds that we are that chosen people—because *we* chose *It.* There shall no longer be evil in our sight; the eternal Good shall be alone without being lonely. The Infinite shall embrace us and God Himself go forth anew into His own Creation—because you and I believe; and looking up and seeing that which seems to deny our belief, we *still* believe. "Believest thou that I am able to do this?" "Yea, Lord, I believe." "Then be it done unto you as you believe." For all the world is made of belief; all the world awaits the dawn of a new spiritual renaissance. And everything in the Universe is hushed and the holy temple of the living Presence.

Dear God, we come. Amen.

→ AFFIRMATIVE-PRAYER MEDITATION ←

(We have this box with all the names, and every name is known to the One Mind, which is our mind too. Therefore we know and we answer and fulfill the needs of every person who has requested, whether it be healing or a betterment of life and circumstance. And with whoever asks for whatever good he or she needs we affirm the presence of that good, the elimination of everything that denies it. We identify this person with that good and know that this word going forth shall not return unto us or them void, but it does accomplish and it is accomplishing and we bless it and bless each here and now.)

Now may the eternal light of the living Spirit which is God—that silent, invisible, but ever-present Partner and Host whom we recognize— may this Living Presence be so real to us that It shall radiate, heal, and bless and help. Eternal Spirit within us, bring the joy of Your Presence, the love of your givingness, the abundance of your Wealth, the perfection of your Wholeness, and the joy of your Soul into our lives, that we shall sing and dance in the sunlight of eternal Truth, forevermore. Amen.

8.

HOW TO CLAIM YOUR FREEDOM

Dr. Holmes in his early days had been a "Play Reader" in the northeastern part of the United States. In those days of the early 1900s, small communities looked forward to the appearance of a good "Play Reader." The Reader sat on a stage with nothing on it but his stool and a stand to hold the Reading. The Reader read with feeling all the parts of the play.

These early experiences stayed with Dr. Holmes all his life. He always objected to too much furniture and flowers or too many people on his lecture platform. Somehow when he spoke from a theater platform, he created a deep person-to-person bond with his audience. I was there with him many times and have selected some of his memorable talks at the Wiltern Theater. These have been released at one time or another since then in sterilized or predigested form—but we have them here just about verbatim.

It is a great privilege to be here and take Bill's* place while he and his family are having a vacation.

I have arranged my talks in a series of lessons: I am not an orator; I am a teacher. I have just spent part of the last two weeks lecturing in New York at the INTA† Congress. I was invited to speak in nearly every country in the world, and practically all the states. We really have the best and clearest metaphysical teaching on earth. There is no question about it in my mind.

There is no question in my mind but what we are the next greatest religion of the future—because the religion of the future will be a combination: it will come from science, from philosophy, and from religion. It will come as science becomes less and less materialistic, which it is now doing; when

---

*William H. D. Hornaday.
†The International New Thought Alliance.

philosophy stops being dualistic, as though there were a material and a spiritual universe—or just a material; and when theology gets over its superstition. When I lost Hell, I lost the greatest asset I had: there is nowhere to send people who disagree with me; and that is bad. I miss it more than any of my infantile possessions; but I couldn't carry it along into adulthood—because the place cooled off long ago.

Now we bring together these great things; and I want to show you in the next three Sundays something I think it is very necessary for us to know: how to help yourself and others; how to prosper yourself and others; and how to make yourself and others happy. We believe in a practical religion. It has to be practical, something people can use.

I had the privilege of going last Sunday morning to hear Norman Vincent Peale.* His place is so crowded, but we called up Saturday and they very kindly reserved seats. His talk could have been given right here. It is just as metaphysical as any we give; and he truly is a great man and recognizes the principles we believe in and teaches them. Being still in the "Church," he is bound to be a little restricted. But he is less restricted than any man I have ever heard from the pulpit. Well, that isn't saying much, because it is the first time I've been to church in 25 years; so I don't know anything about it.

He is a very generous man. I went down front; he turned to a large group of people and said, "This is a man from whom I have gotten so much." Only a man who has arrived dares to say these things. Little people are so little that they hate even to lose their *littleness*—because it is all they have left. But a man like this, who encompasses a larger picture, isn't afraid to admit there is someone else in the world.

I want to talk this morning on How to Help Yourself and Others in Freedom—how to be free. What do we mean by being free? Being free does not mean doing just as we please, because no one can do just as he pleases

---

*Pastor of New York's Marble Collegiate Church and author of *The Power of Positive Thinking* and other books. Dr. Peale, on this as on numerous other occasions, acknowledged Dr. Holmes as having exerted a significant influence on his thought.

and get away with it. The truth that makes us free, enabling us to claim our freedom, must of necessity be a truth that does not deny the Unity of Good. Our freedom cannot be at the expense of others. We do have a freedom to love and be loved; but a woman does not have the freedom to pick out some man, whether he is married or single, and treat that he will fall in love with her. And she had better not try it!

We have a freedom to express all there is, but no freedom to rob some-one else. Not the slightest. I believe each one of us is an individualized God. That is quite a claim to make! We are individual infinites. I'll tell you why I think so; I don't want to believe anything just because it pleases me. That would be silly. We are really scientific, intelligent, philosophic, deep thinkers—but spontaneous human beings: we are not afraid of life. The greatest background I have had was that I was brought up in an atmosphere where fear was not known and superstition was not taught, but reverence and adoration and worshipfulness were generated. No meal was ever said without prayer; everyone prayed at night. But there was no fear. I was grown up before I knew people actually believed there was a devil and a hell and had a fear of God and the Universe in which they lived. It must be a terrible thing.

But we can be free of superstition and free of fear—but we must not be "free of ignorance": *we are thinkers*. Seneca* said, "Keep faith with reason, for she will convert thy soul." You and I are individualized centers in God. No two persons are like; no two thumbprints are alike; therefore I feel we will never be reproduced. That is why Emerson said, "Take yourself for better or for worse. Imitation is suicide." Now since God is One, there is only one God, only one of whatever It is. Life is one, since God is one. God is not cut in two, as though part of God were here and part of God were someplace else. All of God is everywhere, just as all the mathematics there is, all the harmony there is, all the abstract beauty there is, all the gravitational force that there is, is everywhere.

Gravitational force will hold a peanut on the piano or the Empire State

---

*Lucius Annaeus Seneca (4 B.C.?–A.D. 65), Roman statesman, philosopher, and dramatist.

Building in place—it doesn't know anything about big or little or hard or easy. You and I are surrounded by a Presence which is God the Spirit, and a Power which is God the Law, and these are the two great realities. The Presence we may talk to, and It will answer: there is a communion. The Power is like every other law in the Universe: It obeys, It follows, our word; It does unto us as we believe. And that is why affirmative prayer works. It is a statement: *there is a Power greater than we are, and we can use It consciously.*

But we could not use that Power to destroy that Power or to destroy God or ourselves. Therefore we can use that Power in Its greater sense only as we use It in love, in givingness, in peace, in joy, and only as we use It constructively. I believe all the Power there is in the Universe is delivered to each one of us for his individual use. Now that is quite a thing to say.

I was teaching a class in New York the other day, and I said, "We do not teach that we have power. We teach that Power *is*, and we use It. We do not say that this person is a natural healer, or is any kind of healer, or has a healing power, any more than we would say that this man has electricity or that he has mathematics. He doesn't *have* gravitational force; he is *in* it, and it operates upon him. He has the freedom in gravitational force to move about; we have the freedom in the Law of Good, which is creative, to be or do anything that belongs to the natural Law of the Universe, way beyond anything you and I could think of.

I believe the time will come when they will multiply the loaves and fishes scientifically. Jesus never did anything that can't be done, you know. He only did what *can* be done. What *can't* be done, never was done by anyone. Even Jesus never broke the laws of the Universe. He understood how to comply with them.

He transported himself from place to place at will without using a conveyance. Doctor Rhine* at Duke University has scientifically demonstrated in the last 25 years that we can reproduce the activities of the five

---

*J. B. Rhine (1895–1980), American psychologist, founder and director of the Institute of Parapsychology at Durham, N.C.

senses without using the organs of sense. Now that is something! He has proven we can think without using the brain. He has demonstrated that without using the physical body or brain we can exist and continue and be conscious. That is a scientific demonstration of immortality, right now. Job said, "In my flesh shall I see God." That is terrific—coming out of a psychological laboratory of a major university.

Now Jesus multiplied loaves and fishes, raised the dead and healed the sick, brought the boat immediately to the shore, did all kinds of things we call miracles. But there are no miracles in God's Life. God is the same yesterday, today, and tomorrow, and never departs from His own Being. Jesus understood something which he referred to as the truth that shall make us free. He said there is a Truth, and "the truth shall make you free."

Now that Truth would have to be something we *know*—not something we *do*. You and I cannot create the Truth. That thing which makes us free and happy and prosperous is something that everybody has but very few people use, because very few people believe in it. And even the ones who believe: very few of them use it scientifically, accurately, and with absolute certainty of result.

Now we want *results. We want them!* I *want* to see the time, and I *expect* to see the time, and I am *going* to see the time—because definite steps are being taken, and motion under my direction to prove—that everyone who comes into our audiences will be healed. I don't think it is any of their business: I don't think what they believe has anything to do with it. You might not believe you would get wet if you got in the water; but if you got in the water, you would be wet.

The laws of Nature are no respecter of persons. There is a Power greater than we are; there is a freedom beyond anything you and I have ever experienced. And the world is waiting for some person and some group of persons who, without superstition or saying, "Look at me and die," will have something that can be delivered to the sinner as well as the saint—because there is so little difference between a sinner and a saint that I always get them confused (and generally have more fun with the sinners).

I believe life is *Living*. I was at the convention* for eight days. I spoke lots of times but had time to see two of the best shows I have ever seen, go to three parties, to prayer meetings twice, and a banquet once. I think that is living it up. Life is not a continual prayer meeting. Like the little boy who told his grandmother that if she ever went to a circus, she would never go to a prayer meeting again.

As a matter of fact, a prayer meeting should be the most exciting thing we could go to. It should become the most exhilarating experience we could have. It should unleash all the creative ability and imagination we have, because at a prayer meeting where people who believe get together, such a power ought to be loosed that an angel chorus would sing. There should be a light, like "the light that lighteth every man's path," that everyone would be aware of. There should be a sense of a deep and abiding peace and stillness. I said the other day something I have learned by experience: every person will be alone until he is not lonely. Every person will listen to the silence until it speaks. Every person will be compelled to look at darkness until he sees a light. And every man will lie in his own grave until he resurrects himself. And that is true.

You and I have the power; but what do we do with it? Surely a prayer meeting—right here, this, today—should be the most interesting thing that ever happened to you or to me! We should come to see today—with a dynamic, creative imagination and a deep inward feeling and conviction—that we have been playing around the edge of a stupendous Possibility. The ancient Chinese sage said, "O man, having the power to live, why will ye die?"

I thought yesterday (nine hours on a plane coming home; it is such a terrific thing to have breakfast in New York and supper at home at night), "Time is not, and space is not"—but experience is. And I thought: What are you telling these sweet people tomorrow who will take an hour out to come and listen to you? This little tiny ego: will you get your big feet out of the way? And I said, Probably not; because we have to maintain a good-natured flexibility, even with ourselves, to get along in life. I prayed several

---

*i.e., the INTA Annual Congress (1958).

hours, and I thought: If just this much revelation of the Self to the self can come, then we will all be glad. I'll be glad because you cannot give without receiving; you'll be glad because you cannot receive without giving. Everything moves in a cycle or circle; and "With what measure ye mete, it shall be measured to you again."

Now there is a Power greater than we are, and we can use it. It is creative—It can do anything—and It responds to our belief in It; but our belief in It has to be a belief that It is *now* operating and that It *has* operated. Someone will say this calls for faith. *All life* calls for faith. I thought the other day, if you and I had the same faith that an electrician has, we would be better metaphysicians. Religious people do not have the faith that scientists have. When scientists have demonstrated a principle, there is no longer any question in their mind.

There is a Power that responds to our consciousness exactly the way we think, like a mirror; and if I say—no matter what it looks like—"I am surrounded by love and by friendship; I *am* love, I *am* friendship; I give and I receive and I believe it, and this is true *now*," the machinery and the mechanism of the universal Law of Cause and Effect is set in motion to make it come true, and nothing can destroy it unless I do, myself; nothing can neutralize it. I know there are people who say, "Well, you have to have a great spiritual understanding." *I* haven't met them,* and I stopped looking for them 35 years ago. "There are no prophets other than the wise."

If a person comes to me now and says, "I have it all; I know it all." I say, "All right, go out there; there is a paralyzed man: tell him to get up and walk." In our business, you have to put up or shut up, and that is good enough for me. All the professions of faith make no difference. Unless action follows, "methinks the lady doth protest too loudly," as Shakespeare said.

We follow a scientific—that is, a sure—method. We now know, as they have demonstrated down at the University in Redlands, that a prayer—we call it a treatment—is an affirmation of acceptance. Now why is it? Because you have to plant a seed before it can grow; that is all. Why does God make

---

*i.e., people with the "great spiritual understanding."

it so you have to plant the garden before you can get a garden? Just because that is the way it works. Why do you have to move a thing from place to place so gravity will hold it? Just because you have to.

Now there are certain things in the Universe that have to be accepted. We didn't make them; we can't change them. I don't think God made them—I think that is the way God is. Therefore it is said that God's language is "yea and amen."* We have to live an affirmative life, and that is that; and it isn't because God hates us or is trying to test us. All this theory that we are here to be tested to see if we are worthy to endure is just so much nonsense. We are here for the delight of whatever It was that created us— just as our whole life exists for the expression of our soul. What else could it be for? Life is made to live, a song is made to sing, and a dance to dance. We have to be glad; we have to be happy.

Now we have a *freedom* for all these things that belong to the nature of God. We have freedom to love. What is to stop me from loving you? Nothing but myself. It wouldn't be any of my business whether you loved me; but if I loved you enough, you would. What is to stop me from being glad? It won't hurt anybody. It won't save anybody for me to be sad. Jesus said, "And I, if I be lifted up"—not dragged down—"will draw all men to me." There is nothing to keep me from being glad. Nothing. What is to keep me from having peace of mind? Someone says, "There is so much confusion in the world that I can't have peace of mind." There has *always* been confusion in the world, and there *will* be in the world as long as I live; therefore shall I be confused? *No!* I want peace of mind. I can't live without it.

I had to go away the last two weeks every day sometimes for a couple of hours to do what I call "putting myself back into myself." I met so many people and talked to so many people.† I have to have equilibrium and joy and peace of mind and balance and poise inside of me or else I get dragged apart, or something. I don't know what happens, but it isn't good. It isn't good for anybody either; you can shatter anything. Walt Whitman said he

---

*2 Cor. 1:20.
†i.e., at the INTA Congress.

liked to take time to loaf and invite his soul, and we all ought to take time to loaf and invite our soul.

Here is the cause of all creation; here in you and in me is the possibility of all joy; here is the freedom we have been looking for—and we shall never find it outside. Never. Therefore if I love enough, I shall be loved. I never experienced so much love in my life as I have in the last two weeks—but I went prepared for it. I treated myself to know I loved everyone I would meet; and so many people said to me, "Isn't it wonderful to be loved the way you are?" And I said, "Well, I love people, that is all."

Love and you shall be loved. But we separate two or three people and say we love *them*; or love must come to us from this or that person. This is not love we are after. Nothing wrong about it; but there is nothing can keep me from loving everyone. Nothing. I have this freedom. Do I have an equal freedom to hate everyone? *No.* I'll tell you why. Emerson said, "Nature forevermore screens herself from the profane."

Menninger* wrote a book called *Love Against Hate*: love is a principle in nature; hate is chaos. We can hate until it poisons us, destroys the liver, creates inaction, and kills us. Then we may get a fresh start, and that is all that death is—not to the soul, which lives forever. Browning said a man may desecrate that part, but he cannot lose it. So you see, I do not have an *equal freedom* to hate; I have the *possibility* of hating for a short time.

The more I hate, the worse I'll be; the more I love, the better I'll be: that is my freedom. That is why Tolstoy said we have freedom within the laws of inevitability, by which he meant we have freedom to be lined up with the laws of God. But how could we have freedom to destroy this Universe? The great fallacy of communism, fundamentally, is that in the name of liberty it is destroying freedom, and in the name of unity it is trying to create uniformity. [Robotization and uniformity:] neither one of these things exists in nature. That is why it cannot stand. The trouble isn't economic or political— that is bad enough for us; we wouldn't like it—but fundamentally it is denying two of the great propositions in the universe: [first, that there is freedom,

---

*Karl Menninger, American psychiatrist.

not robotization; second,] that there is unity but not uniformity—that all nature tends to individualize everything, and the common denominator is in Spirit and not in a monotonous repetition of likeness (which is a great fallacy). Fundamentally, that is why it cannot exist beyond a certain time— I don't know how long; but it can't.*

We have the freedom to be happy. Now why aren't we? A few people we permit to rob us of our happiness. We say, unless love comes through them, we won't get it. Then we are always projecting our inadequacy or morbidity, fear. And every time they think of us, they don't like us—because they can't; because they are getting the vibration of our relationship.

Everything works with mathematical accuracy. Love everybody. Be glad. "There is ever a song somewhere, my dear." Let's sing it. We have the freedom to be happy; we have the freedom to be at peace, to be poised, to be calm. Now we all "know" these things. Everybody says, "Well, I follow you; I believe in what you say; that is right; *but look at all the other things!*"

Do we have a freedom to be well? Do we have a freedom to be prosperous? I think we do. I think freedom includes all these things. It is now known that the vast majority of disease—way above 75 percent—is emotional in its nature. That doesn't mean it is unreal. It's silly, to me, for people to say that sickness isn't sickness—of course it is; or poverty isn't poverty—of course it is. But that doesn't mean it *has* to be. I believe we have the freedom to be happy, to be well, and to be prosperous. Why shouldn't we, in a Universe the nature of which is so extravagantly abundant and so abundantly extravagant?

We have the freedom to be happy. I don't think there is anything worthwhile without happiness. If a person isn't happy, what is worthwhile? We *ought* to be happy. But how are we going to be well, happy, prosperous unless we believe in some fundamental things that we can prove, and prove them right here and now—not in the by-and-by, not when we have shucked off this mortal coil. *Right now.* Whatever is true, is true *now. This* is the time;

---

*The reference, again, is to communism. Dr. Holmes's words proved to be prophetic long before most were prepared to accept their validity. See also *Holmes Papers*, vol. 2, p. 175.

we are the people; *this* is the day; *you and I* are the ones; *here* is the place. *Right now.*

We have to make up our mind, and it isn't going to be easy always. Emerson said it is easy enough in solitude to do all these things; but, he said, the great man is he who in the midst of the crowd shall keep with perfect simplicity the independence of his solitude. How true that is! We don't want to retire from life or go away from living; we want to live right here where it is. It isn't so bad. It is pretty good, I think. *People* are pretty good too. Love is the thing that reveals the goodness of people—the kindness, compassion, tenderness, sympathy. We are a little afraid of it. I think the greatest ovation I ever received in my life was night before last, and I didn't speak over seven minutes; but it ended on the right kind of a note—of beauty, of sympathy, of love, of unity, and of togetherness. And then I said: "I love you all." I have never received such an ovation in my life.

Now New York people are like Los Angeles people. We are all alike. People respond. Aren't we just a little bit afraid of it? Some big, strong man thinks he wouldn't want to be sentimental. Some sweet woman thinks she wouldn't want to be misunderstood. To be misunderstood is not bad. I have been misunderstood all my life, and I hope I always shall be—because I would like to keep a little ahead always of this humdrum, monotonous, silly sense that people have. Emerson said, "Over the doorway of consistency I would write, Thou Fool."

We want to be spontaneous, we want to have joy, we want to have love, we want to have prosperity, we want to have health. These are things I want to discuss with you in the next few weeks. We *can* have them; they belong to us; but "Each, in his separate star, / Shall draw the Thing as he sees It / For the God of Things as They are." You don't have to go outside yourself to demonstrate all these things. Your prayer is just as good as mine: it is God that makes the prayer and God that answers it. That is why it can't be a petition. It is an affirmation. And that is why Emerson said, "Prayer is the proclamation of a jubilant and a beholding soul."

Let's see during this next week before we come together to discuss how to do all these things (next Sunday morning in our first great lesson)—let's train our minds this week to be affirmative. Let's get up in the morning and say, "I am going to live and I am going to be happy today. I am going to receive joy and life and love and laughter from everyone, and I am going to give them to everyone; and everyone shall be divine to me. This is the day that God has made, and I shall be glad in it." And let us give thanks every night and know that we shall sleep in peace and wake in joy and live in a consciousness of Good.

Let's see if you and I this week cannot get just a little bit better acquainted with the Guy inside of us. He is wonderful. He is terrific. He has talked to me so much these last three weeks, more than ever in my life—up in the Adirondacks and down in that teeming city. This is no stranger. This is no alien. Speak to Him, then, for He hears; and "spirit with Spirit shall meet; / Closer is He than breathing, / Nearer than hands and feet." I don't care if somebody thinks I am over-religious or sentimental. I am so religious that it *doesn't* hurt! I am so religious that it *helps*! But I wouldn't give a nickel for all the theology that was ever written.

Who told all these guys what is the possibility of my soul? Who shall tell me when that divine moment comes? Emerson said, "Leave all of your theories as Joseph left his coat in the hands of the harlot, and flee. To you alone shall come the wonder and the majesty and the power and the might and the exquisite sweetness of communion with the Ineffable, the beauty of the divine Presence, the glory of the eternal Light, and the peace of your own soul."

⇥ AFFIRMATIVE-PRAYER MEDITATION ⇤

(We have lots of people who have asked for help, and let's start right out with the belief that we *can* help them; and after we have treated them, I would like to spend a few minutes doing what I call "stretching the mind." The intellect may analyze, dissect, accept, or reject; but there is an intuitional faculty back of the intellect that knows more than the intellect. We do not all grab it right up like that. Therefore we have to train the intellect to reach a place where it receives this greater illumination. And that is what I mean by stretching the mind.

(I'll show you exactly what I mean. If it doesn't seem like much to you, forget it—it won't hurt my feelings; but it seems terrific to me. It is merely a practice of identifying ourselves with a larger life. This was the genius of Walt Whitman; it is what is called by Bucke* "illumination of cosmic consciousness": the intellect identifies itself with the Spirit until it makes possible a greater influx of the Spirit into the intellect.

(But first of all, let us know that everyone who has asked for help, whose name appears here in this box, now does receive that for which he has asked. And if he is here in this room, as he probably is, let him or her know that right now we are affirming the presence of the good desired. We are denying any substantial reality to that which does not belong. We are establishing him in our own consciousness in the Kingdom of God, which is an ever-present Reality here and now. As we sit here, we expect everything that does not belong to dissolve as mist before the light of the sun, as snow would melt in the heat of the sun.)

There is one Life, that Life is God, that Life is his life or her life— each one who has made a request; and as we sit here, that Life, that Light, is manifesting Itself. And how wonderful it is to know that we do affirm It, we do accept It without effort; and we do rejoice that it is so— as it must be.

Silently the miracle of life transpires, silently this Good takes form, and we accept it.

(And now for a few moments let us practice together what I call "stretching the mind." Maybe you have never done it or thought of it, but it doesn't matter. It is a process whereby one identifies himself with a larger good after this fashion—he speaks in the first person pretty much:)

There is one Life, that Life is God, that Life is my life now. "I am that which Thou art, Thou art that which I am." I am one with all the beauty of life; I am one with the strength of the wind and the wave, the glory of

---

*Richard M. Bucke (1837–1902), Canadian psychoanalyst and author of *Cosmic Consciousness*.

the sunset, the beauty of the sunrise. I am one with the song of the birds; I am one with the mother holding her child; I am one with the babe drinking from the fountain of life. I am that which Thou art, eternal Spirit forever blessed; Thou art that which I am, perfect Presence, divine expanding within me. I am one with the vast throng in the busy street, one with the silence and solitude of Nature and the strength of the mountain and the peace of the desert. I am one with the rain and the snow and the clouds in the sky, the life in the ocean. I am one with the lover, one with the beloved. All are encompassed within me—for now what we are doing is identifying ourselves with the eternal living Presence within which all things are. We are one with That; That is what we are. "I am that which Thou art, Thou art that which I am," eternal Presence forever blessed, eternal Peace within me. "O living Truth that shall endure when all that seems shall suffer shock"—"Before Abraham was, I am"—forever I shall be, encompassing planets and universes and time and space and the heart of God. I am that which Thou art, O living Presence; Thou art that which I am—eternal in the now, in the here, and in this moment. It is so.

Now may the light of the eternal God be with us. May that light go before us, surround us, penetrate us. May the love of God and of each other encompass and enfold us, and eternal peace abide with us forevermore.

9.

HOW TO HELP
YOURSELF AND OTHERS

It is a great joy to be here this morning in Bill Hornaday's place while he is taking a vacation and much deserved rest. I want to express my appreciation for this magnificent audience. It is really terrific to have an audience like this in the middle of the summer, and very flattering. If my head turned easily, my neck would be broken right now—and I certainly appreciate it. I worked last night for an hour and again this morning treating just to know I would say something that would compensate you for coming. It would be terrible to come in here and hear nothing, wouldn't it? Something that we can take home with us: I know that *I* shall greatly benefit, and I want *you* to.

We find we are in the midst of a building campaign,* and I know you have been down and seen part of the building. It seems slow, but it takes a long time; and Paul Williams, our architect, tells me it is going to be the most beautiful building on the Pacific Coast. It is going to have the finest organ this side of the Salt Lake Tabernacle organ. You all want to take part in it, and we all want you to; and there are pledge cards, or you can call me up or someone. Let's all give all we can to this building fund—it is a great

---

*For Founder's Church of Religious Science, Los Angeles.

privilege. We are forerunners in a campaign of spiritual freedom, intellectual integrity, and emotional stability in a spiritual world.

It is our privilege to take part in a new spiritual renaissance—I wouldn't be here if I didn't believe it—and to do something for future ages. All of you who have given your pledges, please be sure they are kept up in payment, and add to them; and you others make new ones; and let's see what we can do during this month. We want another $125,000; we have $275,000. Our goal is $400,000. Let's raise it to that this month, so when Bill comes back he will be even gladder than he was when he left.

Also, your pledge gifts can be mailed to Church Headquarters. So please look at our building down there and realize what a terrific thing we are doing for the world. And remember this: our whole endeavor rests on demonstration. We have no other authority. We ask for none other. That is why I am talking on How to Prosper Yourself and Others next week, How to Make Yourself and Others Happy the following week, and How to Help Yourself and Others today. Our work rests on demonstration. We have to put up or shut up. And those are difficult things to do. Somebody said three things have to be done in making a speech: stand up, speak up, and shut up. The last is probably the most important. We have heard lots of people who stood up and spoke up but forgot to shut up. Well, I have to shut up at exactly 15 minutes past 11. I have no choice. Otherwise, I would probably talk till 12.

Religious Science is a new thing in the world because it is not dogmatic. We have people who believe in reincarnation and people who do not believe in it. We have every sort and condition of spiritual endeavor here. We are a melting pot, in a sense, for people who are seeking a new spiritual freedom without losing the old values. We are the greatest experiment in spiritual life of modern times. A man whose name I won't mention—he is wealthy, well known, connected with the University of Southern California for many, many years—told me he considered we are conducting the greatest spiritual experiment since the dawn of Christianity. Now this man is considered one of the most intelligent, highly respected men in the educational life of the United States, head of a great institution.

Now I believe that is true. Why? Because we are not dogmatic. I am not

a prophet. We haven't any saints. I don't know about Reg and George.*
"Saint Reginald" and "Saint George" would sound all right; but "Saint
Ernie" would sound awful—and if they ever do that to me, I'll haunt them
if I'm dead, and have them arrested if I am living. "Saint Ernie" would be
awful. "Saint George" might not be so bad—he is the one who slew the
dragon. There has been a dragon in every spiritual culture and it stands for
that which binds us to duality.

Religious Science hasn't very many dogmas: *it believes in God.* You will
find, out in front, on a slip—if you haven't got it—*What We Believe.* I wrote
it 30 years ago, and I want you to read it and study it and think about it. It
is what you and I believe in, I guess. God is all there is; there isn't anything
else. God is the dancer, the singer; there is one Singer, one Dancer, one
Writer, one Mind—but each one of us individualizes all of God. It is a terrific but simple concept. The only God you will ever know you will discover
within yourself. That doesn't mean that you are God. God is what I am, but
I am not God, thank God!

But what *am* I made of *but* God? He is over all, in all, and through all.
Now there are two fundamental things you and I believe, as I understand
it. God is a divine Presence inhabiting eternity, and indwelling our own
heart. I love that thought. The other day, I put my arms around somebody
of whom I am very fond, and I said, "I think a lot of you." And then I said
to myself quietly, "This symbolizes to me that my arms are around the
world, around everyone I know and everyone I meet, whether I know him
or not." Wouldn't that be the meaning of "underneath are the everlasting
arms," beneath are the girders of the Almighty—?

There is something about you and me that is cosmic, universal, stretches
over time and space; let us learn to think better of ourselves. You know, you
don't have to be conceited or get a big head to say, "God made me, and God
cannot make mistakes. No matter what it looks like, God did not make a
mistake when He made me." *He didn't.* God cannot err. The Universe is
never defamed. The laws of God cannot be broken.

---

*Reginald Armor and George Bendall, close associates of Dr. Holmes.

Now Jesus understood this. The great claim that his soul made on God was that "God is what I am, where I am, as I am, right here and right now—behold, the Kingdom of God is at hand. There is one Life, that Life is God, that Life is my life now—perfect, complete." You and I believe in it. There is no evil entity in the Universe. We all experience evil and negation, but there is no entity of evil. The more we can turn to the Good, the less evil will be apparent or real in our experience.

God is a divine Presence in our heart, enabling us to think and know and will and do and recognize each other in God, to behold in each other the living Presence. How wonderful to look upon humanity and say, "I behold in thee the image of Him who died on the tree." It is wonderful. Love is the lodestone of life. Love is the only emotional security that is known to the mind of man. Love is the basis of everything, the divine Givingness. There is no security without it.

We believe we are surrounded by Love. Now we also believe we are surrounded by a Law—this is the next important thing—of Mind in action: something that acts creatively upon our thinking, always tending to produce it in form and project it in our experience the way we think it; "As a man thinketh in his heart, so is he." These are the two great pillars of our conviction. They have been believed in since time immemorial. The Law and the Love, the Presence and the Power. These are the tools we work with to help ourselves and others.

Now this means, in the simplest form, that you and I have the Power within us now—right now, right this morning, right here, just as we are. We haven't got to get converted, we haven't got to confess our sins. We haven't time for that. We haven't got to get somebody to save us; because if we are lost, nobody would know where to look for us. That would be a waste of time. You are your only saviour. Jesus knew this. "Why callest thou me good? There is none good save one." "It is expedient that I go away."

Now you and I have to wake up to the fact that the true Saviour, the true Redeemer, the Thing that all the great have told about—*we are*. "I am that which I am." We will never find salvation outside ourselves. You know it as well as I do. If you and I didn't know it, we wouldn't be here; we would be somewhere where they think that they can hitch their wagon to a star and be wafted off to the Elysian fields without any cooperation with the laws of their being. That cannot be. Fortunately, the Law of our own life is resident within us, arbiters of our own fate: freedom without license.

We are surrounded by an intelligent creative Principle which operates upon our thought. Now that is the reason why some prayers are answered and some are not. Every prayer is answered in such degree as it accepts its own answer, and that is why down here at Redlands University they have discovered that the affirmative prayer is the only prayer that makes any material difference—70 percent above the others. Well, we will accept that. It is why Jesus said, "When ye pray, believe that ye have."

Now we are bringing this stuff right down to something we can consciously practice and use to help ourselves and others. You can do it just as well as I can. Anyone can do it. We are surrounded by a creative Intelligence that operates upon our thought, always acting to bring into our experience that which is like our thinking. We can what we call *treat*. Now what do we mean by *treat*? We mean that we think something, say something, articulate something affirmatively by accepting that it is now accomplished, and identify what we say with ourselves or with some person, place, or thing.

Now let's analyze that a little, because this is a lesson. What we want to do is be taught. There is no use being taught unless *we* do it. A Chinese sage said, "O man, having the power to live, why will ye die?" I said to George Bendall this morning at breakfast, "If I take this salt shaker and move it over here, I have changed its position in gravitational force. I pick it up again and put it over there. But *I* don't make it stay down here; *I* don't make it stay down there. I lift it from here and put it there, and it is acted upon by a force." He said, "Of course."

I said, "George, how many people does it take to lift the thing over and put it down and convince gravitational force that it will hold it in place?" He said, "Just one." I said, "All right. How many people does it take to have a prayer answered, an affirmation accepted, or to make a treatment effective?" He said, "Just one." "Well, I said, that is one of the things I want to tell this wonderful audience this morning: one with God is a majority." I thought last night, when I was treating for this occasion—because I believe in treating for everything; I know it works—I thought to myself, I want a few simple things to more completely convince myself: how many people does it take to plant a rosebush so that the law of growth and productivity and creativity will make it bloom? Just one. One with God is a majority.

Now we are going to have to know this; because otherwise we will always be looking for saints and saviours "over there," and we shall rush from one to another. Someone back East said to me there was a very wonderful man doing some wonderful things, and he was going to be here and there; and I said, "Now this is grand, this is perfect; but he can only reveal you to yourself. If you have to rush today from one kind of a saviour to another, and tomorrow to another one, looking wild-eyed—you are not going to get anywhere."

Get still; get quiet; still the turmoil of the outer sense. Be still and *know*: YOU are the one you have been looking for. You are going to have to do it before you can make a good treatment. Why? Because we either affirm or deny. We either believe in our own word or else we don't. Who can make us believe in our own word? Nobody but ourselves.

Now another thing I wanted to be sure and mention to you: a treatment must be independent of the person who gives it. Now this is important. When I go out and plant a garden, I walk away and leave it, and I know something is going to make it grow. Its growth—the law of its being, that which is going to react to it out of the Universe now—is independent even of myself, though I planted it. I was the gardener only. We speak of "making" a garden. We *plant* one. *Nature* makes the garden; "God gives the increase."

Now this is necessary to know, because we get so all tied up and get our great big feet and our little egos in the way and think we have to do so much. Let me tell you: the person who uses this Principle the most effectively is the one who is the most deeply inwardly convinced of a simplicity and an integrity of the Universe, and that he is the one who can do it. No conceit about it: he can *plant* the garden; the garden is independent of him. All right.

He can plant it for someone else. He can go over in the other guy's yard and plant the seeds if he has asked him to; he has identified the creativity with that man's garden. That is all the difference there is between helping yourself and others.

Now we would like to do this. Every man wants to help himself. We believe he ought to be well, happy, prosperous. We have no superstition about it. We believe anything that will help him is good, whether it is a pill or a prayer. We are not confused about that. All instrumentalities belong to God. The Gita says, "All paths of worship lead to Me—all shrines to Me alone belong." Don't be confused.

Now another thing. People say, "I am not good enough." I have lived a long, long time, yet I feel younger than I did 40 years ago because then I thought I was pretty responsible for everything and now I know I am not. It is a great relief to be able to set the Universe down and let it roll. It is a terrific thing. Takes a long time to learn it, too. I haven't found anybody who is "good enough" yet, and as long as a quarter of a century ago I stopped looking for them, because most of the ones who thought they were good were so uninteresting to me (I wouldn't say *stupid*).

You are plenty good enough, because God made you. What you have to ask yourself is not "Am I good enough?" Rather, "Is my thinking constructive enough? Do I love enough? Do I give enough? Am I happy enough? Am I kind enough?" These are the evaluations that are spiritual—not if you are "good enough." Of course you are good enough; and if anybody ever tells you that you are not, remember this: he is but projecting his own unconscious sense of guilt onto you and trying to hang it on your ears. Don't take it. Feel sorry for him. Shakespeare said, "Methinks the lady doth protest too loudly."

So you are good enough. Then you are *spiritual enough.* I don't know how spiritual "spiritual" is. How more spiritual can you be than to believe that God is all there is and to love and adore God and talk to God and know you live in God and God lives in you—? I don't think you have to worry about that. God is all there is. You can't change it, and I didn't make it; we can only accept it. It is a simplicity. *God is all there is.*

Then "Do I know enough?" This is a bad one. "Must I take another class to get that sacred Lost Word?" Nonsense! There isn't enough in all that to even make a decent dish of pea soup. *Of course* you know enough. If you know how to think, you know enough. If you know how to believe there is something greater than you are, you know enough. The whole question is: do you *do* it?—and do you *believe now* that your word is in prayer or in the Law of Mind in action or is a seed of thought planted in the Absolute and that it must bear fruit? The only difference between Jesus and others was that he said, "Heaven and earth will pass away, but my word shall not."

Now remember this: *you* are the person; *this* is the place; *now* is the occasion; *right here* is the time; the word is in *your own mouth*; you are *good enough*; you *know enough*; you are *spiritual enough*.

The next thought is: "*How* do I do it?" Not by concentration. I am not criticizing concentration—I don't know anything about it. I do know it is wonderful. Where does a mathematician concentrate the law of mathematics? He doesn't. He *uses* it. Forget concentration. When you plant a seed you do not concentrate any creativity. You plant a seed!

Do you "hold thoughts"? Of course not. You let go of them. Do you *will* anything to happen? If you and I and all of us willed—until we dropped dead from exhaustion—that the world would be flat, it wouldn't flatten out a thing but our own heads. *Nothing.* We have to comply with the laws of Nature. Every scientist does; and we are scientists when it comes to using this Law.

All you do is to affirm and believe in your own affirmation. What do you convince? is next. Now remember these steps—they are very important: You *affirm* it; and the next thing is, after doing that, you must *let go* of it, kind of forget it—even though you return again to it the same day or the next day; but drop it. Now this, perhaps, is the most difficult of all things. This is where we have to have faith. But we are not having faith in a forlorn hope, but in a Law of Cause of Effect that we know exists. Here is where self-training comes in.

I said to myself the other day—because something didn't happen that I thought ought to happen, and at first I was disappointed—"Now look here, little guy!" ("Why so hot, little sir?" Emerson said.) "You just forget it! If that was the way for it to happen—it will!" Do not for one moment permit yourself to doubt what you are doing: *faith is acceptance, in the assurance of a Law that is now proven to exist*—and it *will* work. "I will work, saith the Lord, and who shall hinder me?"

You and I have that faith, but we use it negatively. We don't say that we have to think up an affirmation; every time you speak, you affirm, even though it be negatively. We must believe that *this is it*, and that it is going to work. Now every scientist has to have this kind of faith; he has learned that this thing works; and if you and I knew—just as we know that if we plant a garden it will grow, that when we plant a seed, it will "take"—we would have faith. And that is the way it works.

Next we must identify our word. Now that is simple enough: I write a letter and address it to somebody and send it to them—to their name and street number, city, state, and country—and then I throw it in the mailbox. I don't give it a thought. When you give a treatment, you say, "Now this is for myself," or think, "This is for myself"; or if it is for somebody else, you merely speak his name, or think it, and say, "This is for him [or her]." Now that is what I mean by identifying your treatment with some person, place, or thing.

If it is for some situation that needs harmonizing, you say, "This word is for this situation in this home [or this office]. There is harmony, there is unity, there is love, there is cooperation. This word removes every sense of confusion and doubt, uncertainty, antagonism, resistance, or resentment [whatever has to be eliminated]." You put it in the form of your own words and announce that it isn't there. This sounds funny, because it *is* there; but you take a little piece of ice and hold it in the heat of your hand, and it will melt, become liquid: there are no opposites to God—there is only one Power in the Universe, and in such degree as it is used constructively, it will take precedence over everything else. Where is the darkness when the light shines? "And the light shineth in darkness; and the darkness comprehended it not." That is, it had no power.

You are the person; *here* is the place; *today* is the time; *this* is the moment; the word is in *your own mouth*. It is an affirmative word. You speak it and believe it and identify it with what you want to happen and then let go of it, no matter who you are working for.

Now the next thing I would like very much to make plain—very much: do not, please, wait till you know more, get more spiritual, get a bigger understanding—and feel more weak in the stomach! *Please do not wait.* The garden that isn't planted won't grow; the seed that is not sown will not flourish. The word that is not spoken cannot act; the prayer that is not said and accepted cannot be answered.

Next, experiment with it. I think this is one of the most important things—to experiment with what you know. Take two or three people and work for them every day as well as yourself. You can't hurt anybody; and it will help you. Take time to affirm whatever you think, and don't be afraid to deny what appears—it has an eraser; it rubs it out like rubbing wrong numbers off a blackboard—and affirm for this person everything until you sort of relax and say, "Isn't it wonderful! This is the truth about him. There is peace and harmony and joy. There is success and everything that belongs—'all this and heaven too.' This word is for him and for myself and my family"; and build up a case remembering this.

I would like to put it this way: it is as though a universal Ear were listening to what you say and reacting upon it according to the realization of the logic. Now I want to make this plain. There is a universal Intelligence that reacts to our word creatively—there isn't any doubt about it—and it is all-powerful. God the Spirit is more than that, but this is God the Law. It is what you are using; this is the Principle of the Science of Mind and of every other metaphysical movement no matter what it calls itself. It has to be that way.

Therefore your argument, if you have one, is within yourself to convince yourself. Sometimes you will find yourself saying, "Now the truth about this person is that there is perfect circulation, perfect assimilation, and perfect elimination. There is no stagnation." You will make that flat denial. Why? To straighten out your own mind. But the Principle back of it is—and listen to this—*a mental and spiritual argument logically presented to mind.* This is the method that has healed and helped 90 percent of all people who were ever helped in the last hundred years by all the movements. They all use it, remember. An argument which contains more affirmation and denial, logically presented to mind, will produce a result which is resident in the conclusion of the argument. Is that clear? It is so terrifically important; but *the argument takes place in your own mind.*

This is a lesson on how to give a treatment, you know, and *you* are the fellow who is going to do it. You are going to do it this week. Now if you do this, you are going to get a great wallop out of it—and I am not afraid to use the word *wallop* in spiritual things: we don't have to sit around and look sweet and sad and anemic in order to believe in God. That is terrible. I like sort of a lusty, husky faith in the Infinite. Whoever told us we had to become emaciated to worship? Nonsense! Riley* said, "As it is given me to perceive, / I most certainly believe / That when a man's glad, plumb through, / God's pleased with him, same as you."

There is a laughter of God—let's laugh it. There is a song of the Universe—let's sing it. There is a hymn of praise—let's praise it. There is a joy, a beauty; there is a deep, abiding peace; let's experience it. Right now, today. If you believe what I say—you are a good practitioner. If you use it, you will produce splendid results—and that is the next thing: to prove it to yourself; and after perhaps long years of waiting, coming back to the only Center there is, a God of Heaven and earth—YOU—YOU—simple *you*, simple *me*; unimportant, apparently without much influence in the world—it doesn't matter—but in the integrity of our own souls, in the communion of our own spirit, in the exaltation of our own consciousness, we may yet prove to the world that God is in His Heaven, *now.*

You are that Heaven. What a wonderful experience! What great joy should accompany everything that we do—an expectancy, love. Love everything, praise everything, recognize all things, believe all things, accept all things; and "To thine own self be true, and it shall follow as the night the day, thou canst not then be false to any man."

---

*James Whitcomb Riley (1849–1916), American poet.

→ AFFIRMATIVE-PRAYER MEDITATION ←

(Now we have time for a treatment. We have in this box the names of those who have asked for help. Next Sunday I would like to talk to you on How to Prosper Yourself and Others. There *is* such a law. It is not telling you how to make money or get rich—I don't know or care anything about that; but there is a Law that will bring to us everything that makes life worthwhile and happy and prosperous—if we want to use it. It is very simple; we can understand it. It *will* work. And may I thank you for your great kindness. I know we are every day thinking love for Bill Hornaday during his vacation and knowing that every good thing is coming to him and to his wonderful family. We love and appreciate him very much.)

Now let us turn within and treat ourselves first, recognizing that we are divine centers in the Mind of God. Here within us is the living Presence. Here within us is the perfect Peace, the eternal Joy, the everlasting Good, the all-conquering Love—and we have absolute faith in it, and we know our word is the Presence and the Power and the Activity of the Living Spirit; and we know that every person in this room and every person who has made a request in this chest belongs to God, lives in perfection. Whatever doesn't belong to him is eliminated; whatever is true is revealed. The divine and perfect Pattern of his own being is manifest silently, simply—simply, but with certainty. Everything that doesn't belong to God's good Man *is* eliminated—and we know it and he knows it; and we expect it and accept the authority of this word in joy. Everything that he does will prosper, because of all the power there is—Love, the living Spirit Almighty. Every request is accepted and manifest now.

Now as we turn to That deep within our own soul and mind and consciousness, registering each in his own name—the Name of the beloved Son of the eternal God, the Presence and Power of the Infinite, the Will of Good, the Givingness of Spirit, the Peace and that Light that lighteth every man's path—we accept the glory of the Kingdom of Good, now and forever and forever. It is so.

And now, living Spirit; and now, divine Intelligence and Light that lighteth every man's path: we go forth in joy to greet the eternal dawn, the everlasting radiance of the countenance of the living Spirit. And the love of God goes with us and ". . . makes its store / To a soul that was starving / . . . in darkness before." So shall our light and love envelop every person we meet and sing a song, a hymn. And God bless us and keep us forever.

10.

HOW TO MAKE YOURSELF
AND OTHERS HAPPY

I would like to talk about our Church and the new building. We are building the first Christian church that is absolutely free from dogma and superstition, that has a very high intellectual level but does not overlook the spiritual and the level of feeling. I would laugh myself to death if I thought *I* had anything to do with it. These things happen, and they are bigger than you and myself. It is happening to us. We are the forerunners of a new aspect.

We are a Christian denomination. Someone said we didn't believe in Jesus; of course we believe in Jesus—and we believe in Buddha too; we believe in Socrates; we believe in Abraham Lincoln! And more than everything else, we believe in our own soul—the only immediate testimony you and I will ever have that we exist or that God exists or that Jesus showed us a way. We believe in every Wayshower.

We are the first Christian denomination to be free from superstition, dualism, and dogma. We are taking part in building an international monument to Truth*—that is all you have to say to anyone. So let us support that, and let us do it with love and great joy.

---

*This probably refers to the construction of Founder's Church of Religious Science in Los Angeles.

You know, Religious Science is not something I invented. I didn't make it up. I put a few flourishes to it—but it is the outcome of the thought and the feeling of the Ages and the great minds of many denominations and religions. It embraces all of them—Buddhism, Mohammedanism, Hinduism, Zoroastrianism, Taoism, Confucianism, Judaism, and all of the different sects of the Christian faith, of which there are about 250 in America, just as there are several hundred, in India, of the Hindus. It embraces the affirmative part of all of them and comes up with the idea that the Universe is chock full of God; "In Him we live and move and have our being." Each one of us is an outlet to God and an inlet to God. As Emerson said, you are dear to the Heart of the Universe, and if God hadn't had need of you, He would not have put you here.

Now what is the reason for our being? I'm only going to tell you what I think, and if you don't like it, just quietly walk out—don't disturb anyone around you; and if you do like it, just try to think with me about it. Why is Creation? I'm going to tell you what I think: I think it exists for the delight of God. What else can it exist for? Someone will say you are here to get saved. I don't happen to think we are lost, and I know darned well if I *am* lost, there isn't anybody in the world that will know where to look for me. Claptrap, jargon, nonsense, asininity, and confusion—that is all I can think about it right now.

The Universe exists not for us to save our souls—they are not lost, believe me; nor because the Devil has got us: there isn't any Devil, there isn't any Hell. Somebody said, this morning, "Have you heard from Bill?"* and I said, "Yes." And they said, "Where is he?" and I said, "Just a little south of Hell"—because he is way down there in the tropics. But of course that is just a word picture. There is no Hell, no Devil, no Purgatory; there is no Limbo. This is all nonsense made up by minds who are either vicious or ignorant. But it doesn't add up to anything. It is not sane.

There is a Law of Cause and Effect that beats us up when we beat life up, and will beat the living stuffing out of us until we get tired of it and have

---

*William H. D. Hornaday, close associate of Dr. Holmes.

had enough and act in accord with the laws of harmony which are fundamental to the nature of God and the Universe in which you and I live. That
is why Jesus said, "They that take the sword shall perish with the sword";
"Give, and it shall be given unto you." And Emerson said, "If the red slayer
think he slays, / Or if the slain think he is slain, / They know not well the
subtle ways / I keep, and pass, and turn again." That is, the Law always
moves in a circle.

The Universe must exist for the "glory" of God, in a sense, but really for
the Self-expression of God and the delight of God. You and I are born out
of It, and we are born out of a divine urge that creates. "The wind bloweth
where it listeth, and thou . . . canst not tell whence it cometh, and whither
it goeth: so is every one that is born of the Spirit," Jesus said. God is the
Spirit; the Spirit seeks; there is a pressure against everything to express life.
The dog must bark, the cat must have kittens, the hen must lay eggs, the
artist must paint (no matter how terrible it looks), the singer must sing, the
dancer must dance: everything must express life. We are born to create, and
we can't help it. Why is that? Because God is in us, the great Creator.

Now in psychology they call this the Id and the Libido. It doesn't matter
what it is called. *Libido* means an emotional craving back of all things for
self-expression, the repression of which leads to psychoneurosis. You may
wonder what this has to do with the subject. I am leading up to the subject,
and if I don't get to it, it will be too bad. But there is no use choosing a subject unless you can prove there is a principle governing it. My subject is How
to Be Happy and Make Others Happy—and, I might add, without wistful
wishing or idle dreaming or psychological withdrawing from the realities of
life. There is a Law governing these things, and we must understand It, and
then we can use It.

We can't help but create. A person who doesn't love something, a person
who isn't happy, a person who isn't loved and doesn't make others happy,
and others don't make him happy, is unexpressed. Something about him
is born and died and going around inside him like a corpse which he is
carrying—and we all carry too many of them. There is something unexpressed, and he isn't yet awake and alive and aware of the great realities of

life. That is why we miss those whom we love: they open a channel to us. But back of it all, what is happening? God made us out of Himself. Why? There wasn't anything else God *could* make! *God is all there is.* God and nothing, God plus nothing, leaves nothing but God. "We are born of eternal day / And made in the image of God, / To traverse a heavenly way." We have to love; we have to be loved; we can't be happy without love—we can't be happy without security.

Now there is a pressure against everybody to live, to dance, to sing—and I know, because part of my activity for 45 years is to take people's hair down and see what they look like; I mean their reality: dealing with people where they live. They are all just alike; *we* are all just alike—except each is an individualization, a unique representation. But our emotions, our thoughts, our feelings, our longings, our needs, the needs of the human being: he must love and be loved; he must be happy and make others happy, because he can't be happy unless he does; and back of it all there is the great urge to live.

Now this is back of all modern psychology and psychiatry, and there has been a difference of opinion as to what is the nature of that urge. The original instigators of what is now pretty much modern psychiatry and modern psychology—the three main ones—had three different viewpoints, as you all know. With Freud, it was biological love. With Adler, it was the will to power and personality, and the expression of the Ego. With Jung, it was (and is) that we all represent, dynamically, the history of the whole human race. It is rather a broad-gauged presentation but pretty true coverage. They all have a little different idea, and personally I accept all three.

There is a desire to love and be happy, to give, to receive; back of it all, a necessity to create. Consequently it is known in psychology that the life that does not express the love and joy and receive it buries a lot of its necessary creativity. It can't help it. It is the uncreated life, the uncreative life. We all have more or less of that.

Now it is known definitely that at the back of 85 percent of our physical troubles, *all* of our unhappiness (I think), at least 85 percent of our accidents, and I believe pretty much everything else—I have just told you what has been proven—there is a repression in us: the great creative urge has been sat upon or hasn't found fulfillment, and so it raises all kinds of troubles. It is said that 85 percent of all diseases are because of this—not just by metaphysicians like we are, but by doctors, psychiatrists, psychologists, people who have made a study of it; and there isn't any question but what they are right. Now we *want* to be happy, we are *born* to be happy, we *ought* to be happy, we *should* be happy—but our nature is such that each one of us is an individual creative center in a universal Law of Wholeness and Completion.

There is nothing wrong with God. *We* may be wrong; *we* may suffer (we do); *we* may be impoverished (we are); *we* may be unhappy (we get that way). But we are born to be happy, to be abundantly supplied with every good thing, to have fun in living, to consciously unite with the divine Power that is around us and within us, and to grow and expand forever. "Ever as the spiral grew, / He left the old house for the new"—and we are all Hell-bent for Heaven, whether we believe it or not; and we'll all get there.

Sam Walter Foss* said, "Let the howlers howl / And the growlers growl / And the scowlers scowl, / And let the rough gang go it. / But behind the night / There is plenty of light / And the world is all right, / And I know it." And Jesus said, "Fear not, little flock; it is your Father's good pleasure to give you the kingdom."

Now each one of us is a center in creativity. We want to be happy and we want to make others happy. We don't quite know what is the most important thing. I wish to mention this morning one of the most important things any one of us can learn. (If you don't believe it, please do not reject it, think it over, if it takes you six months.) Would it seem possible to you or to me that the reaction to us of people we meet is unconsciously invited by us, unconsciously drawn to us, by an immutable Law, and held there until we loose it ourselves—? This is the only obsession and the only devils there are. *We* are the obsessing entity, and *we* are the only devil we will ever meet. I don't believe in a Devil, but sometimes I believe in a lot of them. I say I don't believe in any hell we are going to, but I am constrained sometimes to believe in the one we are getting out of. "If I make my bed in hell, behold,

---

*(1858–1911), American editor and humorist.

thou art there. . . . If I say, Surely the darkness shall cover me, even the night shall be light about me." "Yea, though I walk through the valley of the shadow of death, I will fear no evil, for thou art with me." This we must never forget.

The divine Center, the living Presence, That which you and I did not put there—we didn't have sense enough; we don't quite realize it *is* there. Therefore we live incompletely; but always pressing against the gateway of our consciousness, seeking admission, is That which forevermore sings the song of Its own wholeness, forevermore embraces us. O Love that will not let me go! I believe in It: God is Love.

We are all sensitive. Now the more sensitive you are, the more you pay for it until you are redeemed. Then the better off you are; everything has its price. The more hurt a person gets, the more he can give—the worse he can suffer, and the better off he can be when he learns how to use it. The atomic bomb is very destructive; but that energy "cryptic in Nature, which it has caught like fire from heaven," will some day be the energy that runs all the machinery in the world, shoves every boat across the ocean, every train, every airplane, lifts the water of the sea and distills it as pure as a mountain spring. That is what is going to happen to this cryptic energy, this fire caught from Heaven. But it *could* destroy the world. Let's not be afraid of forces merely because they have been destructively used.

The most destructive force you and I have—and the most constructive— is our own unconscious emotional and thinking and feeling state. Now I am just like you are, and you are just like I am. We are not different—we laugh and cry, we suffer, we get over it, we get tired, we get rested, we fall down and pick ourselves up, we get all messed up and then try to straighten it out. And if it weren't for the goodness of God, we wouldn't last ten minutes, because we haven't that kind of sense. We are all unconsciously trying to commit suicide.

I had a friend once whose husband killed himself; and some person who lacked divine Wisdom, and God knows was without intelligence, said, "He went to a special place reserved for suicides"; and she came in tearing her hair. She said, "What can I do?" and I said, "Sit down, sister, till I beat some sense into your head. Didn't you know that we *all* commit suicide?" And she said, "How is that?" "Well," I said, "some of us eat too much, some of us drink too much, some smoke too much—and some are just too damned mean to live." Wasn't that terrible? But she is a smart woman, and I beat some plain, common sense into her head, and she went out knowing there was no particular hell with a special rack upon which her beloved husband was roasting. And I said, "We *all* do it sooner or later—because *all* death, so-called, is unnatural. So forget it. Who are we to question the goodness of God, the integrity of the Universe, or the immutable laws of our own being—?"

It is like Walt Whitman, who was kind of lazy like I am—I find lazy people live longer and take it easier; he said, "I loaf and invite my soul." I wonder if you and I do enough loafing. There is a divine Something inside us, of that I am sure. Wouldn't it be terrific—kind of tragic at first, and finally kind of comical, and the most dynamic thing we ever discovered—if we would say, "There is no law but my own soul shall set it under the one great Law of all life." If I am sensitive, if I have lost the object of my love temporarily, yes—I'll cry.* Tears are made to be shed. I'm not afraid of tears, and I think it is a silly person who says he doesn't have to shed them and never feels badly. It isn't true. He is just lying to cover up a great truth, and that will never get him anywhere. This is not daydreaming or escaping from reality.

We are the most realistic people who ever lived on earth. It is a *transcendental* realism, however. We believe in the transcendence. Now we want love, we want happiness. How, if what I am saying is true—that everything goes out in a circle—if I sit here unhappy, hating everybody, saying the world is against me, which all may be true in appearance—how am I going to draw anything *but* that? I discovered years ago to my own satisfaction that in dream analysis, in psychiatry and psychology—and in a few years it will be proven to be true—the interpretation of dreams is not on a scientific basis at all; because what *is* on a scientific basis—two and two will make

---

*This may be an allusion to Dr. Holmes's loss of his wife, Hazel, in May of the preceding year.

four wherever you find them; sugar will be sweet whether it is in a sugar bowl or a dust pan—isn't true of these things, because unconsciously the analyst induces a state, subjectively in his patient, which is like his own conviction so he can interpret his dream. He doesn't know it, but he is planting it there.

The mind unconsciously pictures things and projects them—and says, "Nobody likes me; I am not attractive; nobody loves me; I haven't got what it takes." Now everybody who meets us, meets us psychically—that is, subjectively. He meets us on three levels,* and we can't help it; that is the way we are made. I had a doctor call me up the other day to tell me about a patient, and he said, "Ernest, I know what you believe; but this guy needs certain medical care." And I said, "Wait a minute; I am nobody's fool, and I don't believe I can think a thought that will keep somebody from bleeding if I cut his throat"; and he said, "You're a doll!"—just like that. And I said, "Give me the diagnosis and I'll work *with* you: I *do* believe." And he said, "I do, too." And that is right.

When this thing is put together, it is going to do terrific things. Now whether we know it or not, we live on three planes: man is spirit, soul, and body—or pneuma, psyche, and soma. These are taken from the Greek. *Pneuma* means spirit; *psyche* means mind; and *soma* means body. We meet people on all three planes—spiritual, mental (including psychic), and physical—and we can't help it, because that is the way we are. If there is in us a spiritual transcendence, if there is a universal concept, people will feel it, but they won't know *what* they feel—and that doesn't matter; but they *will* feel it. If there is in us a deep love for everyone—even though, say, it is oversentimental—they will like it. If consciously or unconsciously we are embracing the world, they will know they are included. If we are hurt and sensitive, it will repel people from us.

Now this is why it is. You know and I know in our own experience. We know, by watching others, how terribly sensitive people suffer and seem to repel the very thing they so greatly desire. This is all in accord with the

---

*See below.

Law. It is the Law that binds the ignorant but frees the wise—like every other law in nature: it binds the ignorant but frees the wise. Moses said that the Law is in your own mouth—a blessing or a curse. The person who is so afraid that people will hurt him and then says all kinds of crazy things, because he is embarrassed, is trying to get somebody to do it. The very effort subjectively flows through the psychic receptivity of the recipient and returns to him with the same unconscious sense of repulsion.

If I am afraid that people won't like me ever, they can't. I have planted in them the dream about me that I am interpreting through them. That is why I spoke about the interpretation of dreams. I know I will be contradicted, but I don't care. I know the time is coming when even in psychiatry and psychology they will say there is only one universal Subjectivity and we use It. There is no such thing as an individual mind at all—there is a *Mind principle*, and we use It. There is a Spirit, and we live by It; and a Law which governs everything, and each one of us has his awareness in It, reacting back to him—because the Universe is one system. This I know.

Now it is mathematically certain to be true: if you are sensitive, if you are hurt, if you are unhappy, you cannot make other people happy, because all that can project from you is sensitiveness, hurt, and unhappiness. It is impossible. Therefore we must rise above it; but we must have a reason for doing so. If I know, and I am 100 percent certain, that every rebuff I get from life is an unconscious reaction of something I have put into my own law, I shall at least for the first time say, "Thank God I now have a key. And no matter how long it takes, I shall arrive!" I know of no other system of thought that teaches it—not in our field or similar fields. Yet Jesus taught it. "Give, and it shall be given unto you." Laugh, and people will laugh with you. Now it is going to be a pretty tough thing. The Truth is not easy always to follow.

I must follow it, though—because I was born as sensitive as anybody ever was—so sensitive that I had a sore throat all the time. I had it swabbed out and out and everything done to it, and it didn't do any good. But after I got over my sensitiveness, I didn't have it. Sensitiveness is morbid—creates "morbid secretions." I know what it means to be hurt by life; no one knows any better. I have seen the time—and when I was quite young—when I was so hurt I would go to a show because I was alone in a big city, and would have to get up and walk up and down the street to keep from getting so depressed that I thought I would go crazy. Isn't that terrible?

But we are all just alike in these things, and it is nothing to be ashamed of. We don't have to be ashamed if we have a hairlip, you know; we don't have to be ashamed if we have blue eyes. Our psychological confusions are not our fault, they are just things that are happening to us that we must learn about, and they must be corrected—because we *must* be happy; we are *born* to be happy. Now don't worry about making other people happy. If you are happy, you can give what you have got, and if you are not, you can't.

What right do we have to believe that we ought to be happy? We believe in God; we believe in the destiny of the human soul; we believe in the transcendent Presence within us. I caught myself spontaneously saying the other day—I guess it is from the Bible—"I was with You before the world was."* Now I am talking to God without thinking about it, right out loud—in the bathroom—and I said, "I was with You before the world was; I was with *You* before the mountains were made or the sea was formed or the universe was created.† 'The sun across its course may go, / The ancient river still may flow—/ I am and still I am.' I was with You, God, in the beginning—except there wasn't any beginning, just a picture. And what You have made, You know what to do with." I was working on a problem I didn't see the answer to—and I said, "*You* who make all things in me, make *this*; let it be so."

We must start right here: I must be happy. I must find a reason for being happy. I must know that while there appear to be, out there, things that make me unhappy, fortunately I can change them—because finally there shall come to me no kernel of good but the grain I have raised myself, and ground, and baked into the loaf of the bread of Life which I shall eat and share with you. If this were not so, we would be checkerboards, a game of chance, and all life would be a tragedy. And this we cannot attribute to the infinite and ineffable God.

---

*See John 17:5.
†See Proverbs 8:23–30.

I accept, but it is tough; it is hard. It is realistic. Can a man lift himself by his bootstraps? He can, if he understands what he is doing. Conscious, definite treatment *will* work—coming to see I am one with the Whole Thing; I love everybody; I give to everybody; I am happy; I sing. There is no sadness to the soul. There is something in you and in me that is transcendent of tragedy and sorrow and grief and loss—Power perennially springing from the innermost recesses of that unborn Reality which is evermore being born in us today. This is the glory of our work; this is the power of what we do; this is the Presence of the living Spirit we adore; this is the song we sing. "O living Truth that shall endure / When all that seems shall suffer shock, / Arise on the rock and make me pure."

We have our message to the individual first—to you, to me: Beloved, you are that Thing which you seek; you are that Thing which you long for. The great and the good and the gracious God exists in you. "Act as though I am" and consciously dissolve those thoughts and feelings and fears; and look out. As Emerson said, "The universe remains to the heart unhurt; the finite alone has wrought and suffered, the Infinite lies stretched in smiling repose." I can say with sincerity, and I believe with certainty, there is an immutable Law of God that can make you happy and make me happy. And because we are happy, people around us will be happy; because we love, they will love us; because we embrace, they will embrace us. To surrender to the dignity of that Law, to the love of that Presence, to the glory and joy of that Being and no longer be afraid of the Universe in which we live . . . "Fear not, little flock, it is your Father's good pleasure to give you the Kingdom."

Let us enter in and possess that Promised Land. Someone might say, "I don't know enough, I am not good enough." I have *told* you enough; and if you are not good enough, neither you nor I can help it. But you *are*! God didn't make a mistake when he made you. You are an exalted being. You are the graciousness of the living God; you are the incarnation and embodiment of the living Spirit; you are the joy of God, you are the delight of God, you are the song of God. But *you* didn't make it, and *you* can't change it. And anyone who will sing a song will hear it come back from a thousand other voices; anyone who will love enough will be loved; anyone who will be happy enough will make happiness, and make others happy. He can't help it.

If It were out *there*; if I had to wait for the vicissitudes of fortune, good or ill; then It would be a reed shaken by the wind. But if there is an integrity within me, shall I not have the patience and courage and fortitude at long last to look up into the face of the eternal Life in which I live, and say, "God, I thank you, that *I* gave birth to every trouble I ever had and every sadness and every fear"—? I know what tears are as well as you—because if I didn't, I should be in the clutch of extraneous forces from which there would be no escape. But the soul is free and the Spirit is boundless. "Thou hast made us—Thine we are." I was with Thee before ever the world was born, or the mountains or the sea or the sky, and I will be with Thee when the belief in a material universe shall be rolled up like a scroll and laid away in the archives of men's memory.

I am that which Thou art, O living Truth. I am that which Thou art. So the key is here. Should we not be enthusiastic? Should we not be joyful, even though we are still burdened with our previous mistakes? And at long last—too long!—I have counted my seven times over and over; but seven times one are seven. The dreary monotony, the hopeless anguish, the sleepless nights, the tears that were shed and unshed, the cry of the heart—why? How long, O God? And then the answer, as a sun rises across a new horizon, as the birds sing, as the laughter of children comes to the years and the hope and the heart: "I was with thee before the world was—in love, in joy; and My world shall be joy and love." Lord God of Heaven and Earth, my God forevermore. Amen.

⇀ AFFIRMATIVE-PRAYER MEDITATION ↽

(Now we have a lot of names in here; different people want different things to happen in their experience. Each person who has put his name in here knows what he wants to happen. He will specialize what we are believing; that is, he will identify himself with the result of his desire, as though it were already accomplished. Now this is following the pattern of Jesus, who said, "When you pray, believe you have it." The experiments they made at Redlands, and all metaphysical work which is an affirmation made in the present: it now is this way; it has been proven and demonstrated this is the way to do it: "When ye pray, believe you have it, and you shall receive."

(So the persons will believe; and you and I, working with them and for them in our own consciousness, will know that each and every name that appears here represents the living Presence of the eternal God, the embodiment of the living Spirit, the perfect Life.)

There is one Life, It is God, It is this person's life now, whoever it may be. He is under the government of That; he is directed, guided. Everything this man does shall prosper. He knows what to do and how to do it and receives the impulsion to do whatever he ought to. There isn't a thing about his activity that he doesn't know. Any person he ought to meet, he will; any information he ought to receive, he will receive. New ideas, new thoughts, new things, new friendships, new situations, new conditions are coming to him, flowing joyously. His mind receives them; he is glad.

There is no past, no sin, no condemnation; there is no judgment: we are wiping that out. God has not made any mistakes in him—he is all right, and he knows it. "In joy shall he drink from the well of salvation." Joy and love and friendship shall accompany him—that is all that goes out, that is all that comes back. He is guided; he is prospered: everything he does shall prosper. It is prospering now, multiplying. He gives and he receives and he is blessed.

And for every person who has asked for a physical healing, let us know his body is a divine Pattern: God has made it. "Thou hast made us; Thine we are." And in this moment our recognition of the Presence of the living Spirit makes whole and new every organ, every action, and every function of his body, circulation, assimilation, elimination—it is a body of divine ideals and ideas and truths and realities. It is in harmony with the infinite Pattern which has created and sustains it. This word is the law of elimination to everything that contradicts that.

And now shall love and joy and gladness and the longing of the heart and companionship of life fulfill the aspiration and feeling, and meet the needs of the daily life. There is nothing wrong with us; we were born to be whole and happy. And now as we silently bless this person, he is indeed blessed; and as we turn to the great heart of Love in and around us and recognize the divine nature of our own being and consciously unify ourselves with the living Spirit, we thank God. And as we look at each other, we behold there the living Presence, love and friendship, and joy forever and forevermore.

11.

YOU ARE A SPIRITUAL
BROADCASTING STATION

Our subject this morning is "You Are, or Might Become, a Spiritual Broadcasting Station."* Now this is either true or it isn't true; and if it is true, it is one of the most startling facts the human mind can conceive relative to human relations, whether we know it or not or believe it or not: that we are automatically broadcasting, sending out influence, thought, feeling—something that on its plane is tangible. Then this is one of the most remarkable things we could consider; because somewhere in the aura— that is, in the extent of this atmosphere which surrounds us and is created by us without our knowing it—exists sickness and health (most of it), poverty and wealth, love and friendship. And because I am long-winded, the second half of this talk will be given next Sunday morning.

You just can't give this sort of thing in 30 minutes—because we *teach* something. We don't preach; we *teach*. We have no "healers" in our movement and no prophets. "There are no prophets other than the wise." No one has a healing power, any more than someone has electricity. He can have an upset liver, but he cannot *have* a healing power: he *uses* one. Who has gravitational force? He has a freedom in a field of gravitational force.

---

*See "You Are a Spiritual Broadcasting Station," pp. 270–75 of Dr. Holmes's book *Living the Science of Mind*, for a different treatment of this subject.

Now if you and I are spiritual broadcasting stations, then this broadcast is automatic and unconscious most of the time: we don't even know it is there, but it is working. "And seeing the multitudes, he went up into a mountain; and when he was set, his disciples came unto him; and he opened his mouth, and taught them, saying, . . . Blessed are the pure in heart: for they shall see God." This is the beginning of the Sermon on the Mount and the Beatitudes—the greatest spiritual discourse, probably, the world has ever received.

A *mount* stands for a consciousness of transfiguration—a high estate of consciousness. I take it that "Blessed are the pure in heart: for they shall see God" must mean that there is a certain attitude of thought, of mind in consciousness where the divine Presence is revealed to us in the things we look at and in the people we contact. Jesus must have meant this. He didn't mean we would see what the artists have depicted as an old man with long whiskers, sending thunderbolts to the Methodists and sugar candies to the Baptists, etc. There is no God, fortunately, who knows anything about our little idiosyncrasies and our puny efforts toward salvation. Someone said they were sorry they brought someone to hear me the other Sunday because his friends were Baptists. Now I used to be a Baptist, and they are nice people; and no one need be ashamed that he is a Baptist. And if he has been baptised, he needn't be ashamed of the rite—it is beautiful and very sweet. But if he thinks there is any salvation in being ducked, he is screwy.

I always say, "I thank the God that *is*, that the God that is believed in, *isn't*." "Blessed are the pure in heart: for they shall see God." Where will they see God? In each other; everywhere: in the tree, in the burning bush. They shall hear Him in the song of the birds, in children at play. They shall really see God wherever they look, wherever their vision is set. "As thou seest, / That thou be'st; / As thou beholdest, man, / That too become thou must: / God if thou seest God, / Dust, if thou seest dust."

Who has had vision enough to look for God, try to see God everywhere, stayed with it long enough? Only the man who has done that could deny what Jesus affirmed; and the man who *has* done it, *won't* deny it. And the people who haven't done it, don't know anything about it; and we shouldn't be worried if they think we are kind of screwy. So what! Who should worry what anyone thinks, if we have demonstrated to ourselves something that makes life more complete—?

Now we are broadcasting stations. Do you remember a woman came up back of Jesus and touched the hem of his garment and was immediately made whole; and he turned around and said, "I perceive that power has gone out of me . . . your faith has made you whole."

Vincent Sheean in a book called *Lead Kindly Light*—which is a story of the life of Gandhi, whom he knew—says that when Gandhi sat with even 2 or 3 million people, farther out than you could see—a sea of faces, an ocean of people—there was established between him and these people what they called *Darshan*. It is something that communicates itself between the audience and the speaker, and the speaker and the audience. I have always felt it; I can tell when it begins to happen with an audience. I have always thought of it as a kind of triangle—I don't know why; but *here* the speaker is, *there* the audience is, and something else is formed *up here* which flows back to each one, accentuated and multiplied. I am sure every speaker feels it and every audience does: a communication is established.

Now down here at the university where Dr. Parker* teaches in the Department of Psychology and Philosophy, they established that you can bless plants, as you know, or curse them or tell them they are good or no good; and they will respond—and at a distance. This is not something that happened in the corner of the earth that couldn't be demonstrated. It is so! It has been known for a long time that there are people who could take this watch, and could see George† in the watch crystal—and they had never seen him before. Now he wouldn't really be in there; it is like people looking into a crystal ball: there isn't anything in the crystal ball, you know; but they use it as an instrumentality. *They would see him.*

It is called *psychometry*. It is in the realm of the psychic sciences. A brick that was in the house of Julius Caesar—they would describe the house; and

---

*William Parker, co-author of *Prayer Can Change Your Life*.
†George Bendall, close associate of Dr. Holmes.

if they are clairvoyant, they might see people going back and forth; and if they are clairaudient, they might hear their voices of 2,000 years ago. It is possible for anyone under a certain psychic condition to "remember" anything that ever happened to anyone who ever lived, if they tune into the vibration of that person's consciousness as it then was, because nothing has happened to it as it now is; because time has no existence in this medium.

All these things are true, because they have been demonstrated and demonstrated over and over again. We are all emitting some kind of an atmosphere. You have often gone into a home and sat down and wished you weren't there—you feel irritated and fidgety and want to scream. *I* have, and I don't scream very much—and then other places you say, "I would like to sit down here!" I met a woman the other day who is about six feet tall, and someone asked how I liked her, and I said, "She is the kind of person I feel I could sit in her lap and be rocked to sleep." She is that motherly type. Someone else ruffles us and we think, How did *you* get in here?!

This is the real thing. The aura is the mental atmosphere around us. You can even see it: sometimes it is light and sometimes it is dark. It varies. When a person is angry, it is like flashes of lightning. It can be heavy or light. Now we are all familiar with these things; but everyone didn't know it is possible to see these things and hear them; but it is. So we are all broadcasting something. I read not too long ago in *Pageant Magazine* or some popular one about a man who gets up feeling very happy and jolly, gets in a streetcar to go somewhere, sits down beside somebody, and begins to feel morose and unhappy and sad and wishes he were dead—and he discovers this other man is in a very depressed state. He sits in the atmosphere of depression. That is a broadcast.

These things are not imaginary. But you know, they are so startling, so dramatic, so fraught with intense meaning that if we really quite understood what it would be like, we should naturally want to broadcast that which is good and true and beautiful. You know, if everybody gets to believe in a new-fangled kind of disease, most everybody gets it. Doctors know this. This is no criticism of doctors: they know it better than you and I. We cooperate with physicians. I often ask a doctor, if I am treating anyone, to give me a diagnosis and tell me what ought to happen for the patient to be better so I can treat that it *will* happen. I have no superstitions; I don't believe in any devil or hell, etc., or future punishment. There is no God who is going to add insult to injury. I just kind of believe in God and nothing else.

I think we are living in a Spiritual Universe governed by mental laws, or Intelligence acting as Law; and I think each one of us is surrounded by the atmosphere or aura of his own thinking and his own background. Way back in there, as Carl Jung says, is the whole world. That is the mortal mind or carnal mind or collective mind—doesn't matter what you call it; and we are all attracting or repelling, according to the atmosphere; and we are all broadcasting this atmosphere.

There are people who are so self-conscious, so self-critical, so effacing of themselves that even in company you can feel a sense of rejection around them. You know these things as well as I do. It isn't conscious: they didn't plan it that way; God knows they didn't want it that way. There are people who are so lonely you can feel their loneliness. There are people so impoverished you can almost smell the odor of poverty. Please don't think I am screwy. These things are true. They are amazing. But it would *have* to be that way, because the Universe in which we live is that way. God is an infinite Mind.

I think we all live in an infinite Mind, and our thoughts go into It and surround us, and then they attract or repel; but they are always influencing everything they touch. Now we know that everything has an atmosphere. It isn't going to be very long before they can take a splinter out of this podium (whatever they call it) and send it to London and they will take a picture of this podium. They will tune the camera into the vibration that is going around the world from everything and returning—because all energy returns to its source with the speed of light; and that would be 7½ times in a second. The camera would tune into this particular object because the splinter from this object would tune it into *it*. Then all they would have to do is take a picture in that vibration and they would have this podium.

Don't think this is funny. They are almost doing it now—and doing things that are proving this principle: just with a drop of your blood, taking a picture of the internal organs and the soft tissue. I have seen it done. And sometimes when I mention this, people say, "Don't say such things, Ernest; people will think you are crazy"; and I say, "Isn't that grand! What difference does that make? *I have seen it done!*"

The Universe is a little different than we think it is; but the practical result of this thing is terrific. It means that whether you and I know it or not, whenever anyone thinks about us, they are not exactly tuned into our innermost life, but they *are* tuned into the periphery of that which extends itself, no matter where they are on earth; and this explains most clairvoyance. I am not denying clairvoyance—because it is true. Now don't laugh; this is true, and I have seen it—and I don't drink very much! (But if I did, it would not be anybody's business.)

You see, we are not reformers; and do you know *why* we are not reformers? Because we never got *ourselves* reformed. And anybody who *gets* himself reformed won't try to reform anybody else—because he will be free. Someone has said, "Life is a comedy to him who thinks, a tragedy to him who feels." I am not a reformer; so I don't even know how to tell you how to pray. Emerson said, "When that divine moment comes, leave all of your theories as Joseph left his coat in the hands of the harlot, and flee." No one can tell me what is right for *me. I* know. And even if what I "know" as right is *wrong*: it is "right" for me when I *think* it is right; and I will have to suffer by it until I *get* it right; else I would be an automaton.

At any rate, whether we believe it or not, every time anyone thinks of us, he tunes in to some part of us, he tunes into what we are broadcasting. He can't help it. Now this is true from the farthermost ends of the earth—because of this subtle emanation, whatever it may be; *I* don't know. I read not too long ago some very eminent scientist said a brick is different than we thought it was. He said there is a flow through this brick and an emanation from it around the world like the speed of light, and back to it. It is more than a *solid fact*: it is a *fluidic emanation.* How much more so this is in the realm of Mind!

Now we would like to feel—*I* would—that everyone we touch is made happy and whole. I tried a very interesting experiment last February when I went back to Florida. I had spoken a couple of times in Miami, but I spoke in four cities this time. I had never been in them and didn't know the people. The only thing I treated for all day on the way there was that I loved these people. I don't *know* them, but I *love* them—because I think love is the only security there is in the Universe. There is nothing worthwhile without it; and with it, a person can live—even if he has nothing else. We *must* have love, and for *everybody*. I'll bet I had a hundred people say to me, "It must be wonderful to be loved the way you are!" I never treated anybody would love me. I treated *I* would love *them*. But you see, the thing goes out on a circuit and it comes back on a circuit. "Give, and unto you it shall be given; good measure, pressed down, and shaken together, and running over, shall men press it into your hands."

Now antagonism is broadcast; overcritical attitudes are broadcast; coldness, disdain are broadcast. We feel these people, shake hands with people only to embrace them in our thought or push them away from us mentally. You do it and I do it and everyone does it. We can't help it. I know we would all like to be a blessing to everything we touch; we should like to bring peace and joy to every situation; we should like to bring encouragement and love and confidence and security and sympathy and compassion. We should like to broadcast it—so that everyone who thinks of me will think, He is a wonderful guy. What is wrong with that? I'd rather have someone think I am a wonderful guy than that I am what some people get called who are not wonderful guys.

What is wrong in wanting people to like you? I don't see anything wrong; I don't think it is a bloated ego. What are we here for? There is nothing wrong with the ego; it is what we have done *to* it and *with* it. It is a very valuable thing, and if we didn't have it, we wouldn't be here; there wouldn't be "anybody at home."

There is no God who is trying to curse us. We don't think half well enough of ourselves. You are the most wonderful thing you will ever meet, and I am the most wonderful thing I'll ever meet—but I do amuse myself; and I like that, too—and we are the only person we are ever going to have to live with throughout eternity; and we are going to attract or repel according to what we are. Of course, we ought to find out how to broadcast that which is worthwhile.

Now it is very simple. We have to love, if we are going to broadcast love. We can't hate and broadcast love any more than this harp will broadcast the piano. Kind after kind—everything reproduces its own kind always. That is the way Nature is. Now when the woman came up and touched Jesus and was healed, it was because there was such a consciousness of wholeness within him, and of givingness and of love, that the moment she entered it she felt it. It operated through her and healed her.

No one knows yet what would happen right in an audience like this if enough people knew it was going to happen. It would break down all resistance, dissolve all apparent solidness, and heal, I believe, everyone—and beyond that bring joy and comfort and assurance and love to the saddened heart. That is what we all need. It is nice to have money when you need it, nice to be free from pain; but it is more wonderful to have no fear and no uncertainty and have confidence in the Universe and love for each other and a depth of feeling that will not be disturbed. Tennyson said of the Lady of the Lake, symbolizing a state of consciousness, "She is calm, whatsoever storms assail the sea, and when the tempest rolls, has power to walk the waters like our Lord." "And Jesus stilled the waves."

Now we want to broadcast this. *I* do. I'd like to know that if I pass through a situation, it is healed; if I am in a group of people, I love them and they love me and we embrace each other. I'd like to know that everybody who thinks of me feels a newness of life. That isn't ego. We are all inlets to God, Emerson said, and may become outlets. God made us inlets; we will have to make ourselves outlets.

How wonderful it would be to feel we silently bless everyone we touch and everyone who thinks of us! There is so much in what you and I believe and understand that I have said to George several times and others around me: we are playing around on the fringe of the great miracle of Life. We are on the shores of an infinite Ocean. Sometimes we feel the spray in our face, the waves lapping our feet; but how seldom do we plunge beneath Its depth!

We ought to broadcast beauty. I am a great lover and almost worshipful adorer of beauty—the harmony, the symmetry. I love to see people who do the best they can with whatever it is they have. I don't think a woman is conceited because she gets her face lifted and dresses the best she can; I think she is silly if she *doesn't* look the best she can—or a man too. Why do we want to pull a long face, as though we said to the world, "Look at me and drop dead." This terrific morbidity, this awful condemnation, is a load that must be lifted; it is a weight on the brow of progress; it saddens the heart. And whoever is so stupid as to believe it is imposed upon us—all we have to do is say, "Screwy! Forget it!"—he has a God I don't believe in.

But God comes in the still small voice, in the silent sanctuary of the heart, in the love we bear to each other—"love so infinite, deep, and broad / That men have renamed it and called it God." And I'd rather sit beside a person who loves than sit in the companionship of kings. As Emerson said, if we haven't it, "something writes 'Thou Fool' across the forehead of the king." And the simplest may have it. Almost all children have it. Practically all animals have it—and they smell the scent of fear and attack, because we are afraid of them; they smell fear and attack us in self-protection. That is how it was the lions did not harm Daniel.

Love is a coverage, joy is a grace, peace is a depth of the soul; and there is a song in the heart, even if you haven't any voice to sing it. A mute could sing it. There is an interior awareness which comprehends and embraces all things. We don't have to wonder whether the thing shall come back to us on "the eternal circuits of God." It *will*. We do not have to wonder whether it shall go out. It *must*. We don't have to wonder whether other people sense it. They cannot help it; they *do*; and they react to it. And we are the broadcasting station.

I have broadcast so much in my life; and I know I do some little thing here to myself, somebody hears it, and out there they get what is "in here." It is so with life. Wherever we go, we are met by the return circuit of our own broadcast. Wherever we are, we must drink of the cup we have handed to our fellow men. Whatever we have loved shall love us, whatever we have cursed shall curse us—because the Universe is just, without judgment, without malice. How wonderful to think you and I—unknown to the world (that doesn't matter); uncrowned, unhonored, and unsung (that does not matter)—have within us the possibility of the limitless reaches of Reality!

Just a different kind of a broadcasting station: singing day and night, it never stops; dancing night and day, it never stops; loving, living, giving, receiving, light-bearing—for there is a Light that lighteth every man's path, and you are that Light, and I am that Light; and in that Light there is no darkness. Wonderful! We are the broadcasting station and we are the announcer, and the world is the receiver: some kind of an infinite wave more subtle than the waves of the ether that transmit the messages of TV and radio broadcasting. Instant and subtle, automatically success or failure, love or hate, joy or grief, Heaven or Hell—whatever it is that we would be.

I know you would rather bless everything you touch. "Bless the Lord, O my soul, and all that is within me, bless His holy name." How simple! Joy: there is a joy which each of us may have. Peace: "Peace I leave with you, my peace I give unto you; not as the world giveth, give I unto you. Let not your heart be troubled, neither let it be afraid." "Ye believe in God, believe also in me. In my Father's house are many mansions; if it were not so, I would have told you." That simple trust, that childlike faith, that everlasting peace—something deep welling up within our nature forevermore pro-claiming the celestial day and time of eternal dawn. Love, and the world will love you; they will make an exception to you. Howsoever foolish, they will feel it. They know. Bring gladness from the heart, and the world will seek you out. But weep, and you weep alone.

This lesson everyone must learn. Within *me*: the adequate Cause, the eternal Presence, the everlasting day—little me, humble me, unpretentious me. O Lord God of Heaven and earth, we are grateful that that which was brought at earliest dawn shall re-sing itself in our heart, and in joy go forth to bless the world.

⇥ AFFIRMATIVE-PRAYER MEDITATION ⇤

(Now we have a very sweet duty to perform, and that is to use our con-sciousness on behalf of whoever has put his or her name, for whatever need they may have, in this box in faith and in confidence—with a little longing, perhaps, and a little apprehension and fear, perhaps; I don't know; but as we return to the God within us, we are broadcasting to the God within everyone whose name is here.)

"Listen, God!" (God is speaking to God, and God is answering to God—in this celestial conversation and communion—that every person whose name is here shall be blessed and *is* blessed, beloved of His Spirit.) "We are recognizing Your presence in him, in every organ and action and function of his body, that it shall be whole. It *is* whole." (We are talking to God, the God of wholeness—never had anything wrong with Him and never will; the God who never made a mistake, cannot, and will not; living Truth.)

We are blessing every person here in health and in joy; let him know the Spirit within him performs the miracle of life. And here upon the altar of our conviction we lay down every doubt and uncertainty and behold His face only, shining as an eternal light. Blessed are the pure in heart, for they *do* see God: we see Him in each one here. Divine guidance is telling everyone here what to do; and if he has a problem, let it be solved. Divine Intelligence knows all things and does all things. Let joy come to him, and Love and Truth and Beauty, and the Light of Heaven light his pathway—as It shall.

Now let each think deep within himself, say to the eternal Presence, "I am that which Thou art, Thou art that which I am, eternal God. All the joy and all the peace there is, and all the energy and action and enthusiasm and creativity there is, is in me—because God is here." Each is saying to himself, "I am one with infinite calm; I am one with all the Power and Joy of the Universe; I am one with the wind and wave and mountain and the desert and my neighbor, children at play, and birds aloft winging their way across the blue of the sky, the sunset and the sunrise, and all things. 'I am that which Thou art, Thou art that which I am' forever and forevermore. Amen."

And now eternal God, everlasting Father, giver and keeper of life, to whom is glory and power and dominion both now and forevermore: we rest in Thee. Amen.

12

LOVE: THE LAW THAT
ATTRACTS FRIENDS

Next Sunday we start a series on How to Use the Power Greater Than We Are. There *is* a Power greater than we are, and we can use It. We know It is there and know how to use It. Anyone in our day and age who is not availing himself of the opportunity of using It is missing something. There is a spiritual Presence we may enjoy, and a Law of Mind in action we may use that is actual and real and works.

We base all of our authority not on anything *I said*, but on what *you do*. I don't care what *I* said, because—much of it I would like to forget. I base any authority of what I said on what you right here *do* with what I said. We have no other authority, ask for none other, need none other, and want no other. They asked Jesus one time: "By what authority do you do it?" And he said, "How do *you* do it? But I'll show you. I'll tell this man to arise, take up his bed, and walk." Now unless there are signs following our conviction, we have no authority. We are just mumbling empty words to ourselves; might be wistful wishing, idle daydreaming, or a monotonous repetition of un-meaningful prayers. *Jesus was very explicit.*

There are two outstanding things about the life of Jesus. First of all, he forgave people their sins and said there is nothing in the Universe that holds anything against you. I have a bad sense of humor sometimes. I wonder what would happen if Jesus were here and listened to the anathemas that are directed to people in his name. It would be very interesting and makes me think of a story that was written by one of our great writers. A carload of people were suddenly shuffled out of this sphere into another one. It was another type of civilization, didn't belong to this world. One of these people was a reformer, and he found that everybody in this other world was naked; so he immediately started a reform. Now these people were very far advanced in civilization, and they didn't beat his brains out. They quietly took him to their psychiatric ward to see why he had such a dirty mind. *They* didn't! That will apply in this world too. (Guess I better begin to pray.)

Let's think of it: what accusations we project at others in criticism are merely unredeemed territories of our own inward morbidities. Today we are going to talk on love and friendship. The Bible says, "Who knows not love knows not God; for God is love." It says, "Though I speak with the tongues of men and of angels, and have not love, I am as sounding brass, or a tinkling cymbal." Browning said, "O heart, O blood that freezes, blood that burns—earth's returns for whole centuries of folly, noise, and sin: shut them in with their triumphs and their glories and the rest. Love is best."

Two of our modern psychiatrists, one of them associated with Dr. Peale,* have written books—one called *Love against Hate*, in which he proves that love is a principle in the Universe, the other called *Love or Perish*. Now this leads us to suppose that God is Love: whatever the impulsion of the Universe is, it is love, beneficence; it is kindness, it is compassion; it is sweetness, truth, beauty—friendly toward us. Now we know, psychologically, that the very first need of man is to love and be loved. We know this; there is no guesswork about it. *They* say it a different way: they say the first law of the libido is it must have an object, and the second law is the ego must not be rejected. That is psychology and psychological terminology. All it means is that everybody has to love, and the love has to be returned or we are not happy.

It is a simple proposition: everyone must love and be loved or he won't be fulfilled or happy. Therefore it is believed that love looses the greatest energy in the Universe—the greatest spiritual energy—and without love there

---

*Norman Vincent Peale, clergyman and author of *The Power of Positive Thinking*.

is a certain part of life that does not come to fulfillment. This is real; it is dynamic; it isn't just a sweet sentimentality. If I wish to bring the world to the brink of a place where it is entirely possible for it to annihilate itself: wouldn't that be a travesty, irony of fate? I don't think it is going to; and if it does, it will be all right with me, because we are all going to shuck off this mortal coil some time, and I don't see that it makes any great difference when.

Love didn't do that. Who do we remember in history? Alexander the Great, who at the age of around 30 was so dissatisfied that there were no new things to conquer—? Do you remember Caesar, Hannibal, Napoleon— except that they are dark spots on the pages of history?

No. We remember Jesus and Buddha and Socrates. We remember the great lovers of the human race. Isn't that interesting! Instinctively, then, love seeks its own, and there is no fulfillment without it. Consequently, emotionally, psychologically—and actually in reality—love is the only final security on earth. Now I am not saying this as just a sweet little guy who says, "Look at me and die." I am not doing that. This is *true*. I must accept it because it is a scientific fact. But we knew it before science proved it. Love is the only final security in the Universe; love is the greatest healing power in the Universe, and the only thing that binds people together in a community of Spirit. Therefore love is pretty important in our lives. We cannot pass it off with an idle gesture and say, "The sentimental fool!"

Love is the only security. It is the healing Power, it is the great Reality— "a love so infinite, deep, and broad / That men have renamed it and called it God." Now psychiatry, science, medicine, experience, the intuition of the poet, and the application of our Principle tell us this. Let's accept it and see what we can do about it.

Love—just plain love; liking everybody. We are so constituted that real love is real only in such degree as it is universal. I am not talking just about a love that says, "God bless me and my wife, my son John and his wife, we four and no more." That isn't love—it is selfishness; establish the fact philosophically and scientifically, because then it will be a spiritual fact. In other words, we want to know *what is so*. Now we do know: we have to love, and we have to be loved. We must feel wanted, needed, and loved. We must have friendship. We must have our arms around each other.

Some people will say this is silly, this is sentimental. That's all right. I have watched the world twirl around quite a while, and I have observed it pretty carefully, and in nearly half a century I have counseled with so many thousands; and I'll say this: I have never yet seen a person who is unsentimental, who hasn't that compassion and that kind of fulfillment—I don't care how smart he is; he might be very intellectual in his attainment.

I have never seen one single one of them that seemed very far removed from a stone image. I could hug any person here and love it, but I could not embrace a stone image—it is too unrelenting and doesn't respond. There is something in animals that knows whether you like them or not. I have never had a dog even snap or growl at me, because I love them. I never have had trouble getting along with children. Someone said yesterday that where they were going to rent a place they were asked if there were children. I said, "If it were me, I would love it if there were a dozen kids on each side of the apartment; I would love to hear them yell. There is something about it that makes me feel good inside."

Psychologically, that means this is regression and I am returning to the days of my youth. That is going to be good. You know, the Bible says if one man in a thousand shall go forth and teach man his uprightness, he shall return unto the days of his youth and his flesh shall become as a little child.* I have never seen anybody terrifically happy who is too prosaic—and remember this: as much as we admire and believe in modern science, which has given us all the comforts of life (and clothes for men that are so uncomfortable for this time of year it ought to be against the law to wear them), one of the things modern science has done is *exclusion*; and all exclusiveness shuts out more than it shuts in. A child knows whether you love him; he feels the confidence of love. I had a child brought to me a couple of weeks ago, about 7 years old. There was a pretty tough situation in the home, and

---

*Job 33:23–25.

they said, "Shall we bring the child?" and I said, "All right"; and after a few moments I said, "Let the child go out." After I had talked to the adults, finally I said, "You get out and let me talk to the child." He comes over and climbs up in my lap and begins to pat me. He doesn't do that to them: he is afraid of them.

I read where a Sunday School teacher said to a class, "Why did not the lions destroy Daniel?" and they all had an answer; but one little boy said, "I know! They were not afraid of Daniel!" Isn't that putting it in reverse? Everyone else would have said *Daniel* was not afraid of *them*, which is also true. Somebody has written a little book called *The Scent of Fear*, in which it says that the animal attacks us because it smells the odor of fear emanating from our physical being but originating in our emotional reaction. It is a thing of thought, as everything else is.

Love is the lodestone of life. We want friends: I am not trying to tell you how to influence people; that is not the way it is done. You *just don't antagonize people*; that is the way it is done; and they like you. We don't say, "I want this person to be my friend." Now there are certain handicaps (we are "fearfully and wonderfully made"). One of our troubles is we sometimes get to like people so well, and get so afraid that the affection may not be returned, that we become so self-conscious that we are not even normal with them and everything hurts our feelings. We magnify everything and call *criticism* something that is just a *comment*. Therefore to truly love and be loved, we must heal ourselves of fear, of sensitivity—because I happen to believe that most of that sensitive reaction from others we are unconsciously planting there. We have to become whole ourselves. We have to dwell on the thought of love and friendship.

I think in the background of our thoughts should always be "I love you. I love you." One of my closest friends happens to be a professional person, and every time she calls up, when she gets through she says, "I love you." And I say, "I love you too." That is the way it ought to be. Why are we so afraid of a little sentimentality? Who cares what "they" think?! You know, I have met so many people, from presidents down to paupers and from intellectual geniuses to morons, and I have never met "them" or seen one of "them" who are referred to as in "What will 'they' think?" or "What will 'people' say?" I have never met one of these persons in my life. It is a fictitious assumption.

I was talking to some people at a little party, and one of the men said, "I don't like to drink"; and I said, "Why *do* you?" And he said, "What do you think—when you go to a party and *everyone* drinks!" And I said, "No one will condemn you if you refuse it; you are only condemning yourself. Don't feel self-conscious about *anything* you do. Don't be afraid of life; don't be afraid of people, or of anything. 'Perfect love casteth out fear': it is the only security there is." And I said, "If you think rightly, everyone you know will make an exception to you. They do to me. You are the only great person you are ever going to meet; so start in with not having self-love but self-appreciation. I believe your real ego is the only mediary between you and the Absolute that you will ever discover and that it is your spiritual guide and double and the most terrific and wonderful thing anyone ever thought of. Socrates called it his *daemon.*[*]

I know it is there in everyone. We have to stop being afraid of life and of people; we have to have a decent respect for ourselves. There is a spiritual self: it dominates everything when we let it. There is apparently a pressure against everything—to sing, to dance, to love, and to appreciate, and to join with people; and people are sore and hungry for love—and we all are—so that I think we ought to embrace the whole world in our thought and feeling. I do it definitely and consciously every day—try to stretch my imagination. I thought, if I was too busy for everything else, still I would want to take a few minutes to do this every day before I go to bed at night or, sometimes, when I wake up in the morning; it doesn't matter when.

I call it stretching the mind, stretching the intellect, and I just let go and think of a few people I think a great deal of, and I embrace them in my own consciousness; and then I go out, and out, and finally in my imagination I try to get my arms around the world and kind of squeeze it, kind of press it to me. Somebody may say, "You sentimental fool!"; but I would just as soon

---

*From the Greek, *daimon*: a power or spirit; genius.

be a sentimental fool. I have met so many fools who are unsentimental and didn't even get any kick out of it. So if we are all going to be fools, let's have sense enough to be *happy* fools.

I am not afraid of the greatest sentiment, the eternal God and the everlasting Spirit instilled as the high motivating Power of man—and without it, the blind shall be leading the blind; and without love, the world can destroy itself. It is the only wholeness that there is.

Now I am not thinking of love as sacrifice and duty. Those who do things out of duty had just as well not do them—they are bloodless wretches. We don't do anything for duty. Supply the word *duty* with *privilege* and *spontaneity*. You don't love your children and your friends because it is a *duty*—you love them because you are not whole until you do. It seems to me it starts with the self: not selfish love but self-realization, self-appreciation. You are the most wonderful thing you will ever meet.

Someone might say this is terrible—*God* is the most wonderful. But Jesus had the courage to say, "Who hath seen me hath seen the Father. . . . Believe that I am in the Father, and the Father in me; or else believe me for the very works' sake." "Whatsoever things the Son seeth the Father do, that doeth the Son also." . . . "that the Father may be glorified in the Son." "The Father hath delivered all things unto the Son." Don't be afraid to *claim*. This is what I call the great claim that your soul makes on God. It is the greatest claim you and I can ever make—that at long last we shall say, "Thank God that I now realize that God is what I am!"

Now this is not selfishness, because very soon we discover we have to include more territory. If I am one with God, so are you; therefore in that Unity which we have and are and enjoy, we have to embrace each other or we are not fulfilling our own nature. If I am one with God and you are one with God, we are each one with God in one field; and until we are one with each other, there isn't the complete delivery of God. This is why Emerson said, "Nature forevermore screens herself from the profane."

Isn't it terrible if a person feels lonely and alone, and lacking in friendship and love, which every person should have! I am a great believer that people who are at *any* age should seek companionship. It isn't silly if a man and woman 80 or 90 get married: it is *sensible*. It just shows that what I am saying is true: love is the lodestone of life—companionship, a feeling of belonging, wanting and needing each other. There is nothing wrong with it; we are wrong if we *don't* seek it. But we discover that we have to take in more territory.

And isn't it wonderful if you can say to somebody who is alone:

Just you begin to think of yourself, first of all, as one in God. Make it simple. *God is all there is.* God is an infinite Presence, a divine Person, a universal Responsiveness: you can talk to God; Something will answer. We don't call God an abstraction or mathematical principle: God is a *Presence*, full of warmth and color and light and awareness—and alive. And awake. There *is* Something in the Universe. And then say, "I am one with This; It is one with me; It is what I am. I am one with all people: every person is my friend. I enjoy the love and friendship; I give the love and friendship and feel one"—just this simple way. Don't try to make it hard; don't say the 23rd Psalm!

All the disciples were great men; but we never met them, and we *have* met *each other*. We will get more out of each other than we will out of Moses. He did well for his day, but behold: we—just little funny you and myself— can look at each other and laugh at each other and embrace each other and love each other; and unless we do, that which is the essence of love will not be delivered.

Every place that we withhold it, we shut out the essence. And where we turn to; where we think we want it from a dearly beloved; we are always unsatisfied. It is back of every jealousy, every domestic problem. You can counsel with them and pray *with* them and *for* them—I believe in all of it, particularly praying *on* them—*but* when all is said and done, the proposition is personal, the problem is personal, and it is so very simple that only child-like words will explain it.

"And he took a little child and said, 'God is like this.'" And they said the children were disturbing him, and he said, "No, suffer the little children to

come unto me and forbid them not, for of such is the Kingdom of God."
And the wisest man who ever lived—the greatest revelator of spiritual Truth
who ever lived*—said, "Don't be afraid to be a child."

As I have said to you before, the poet said: "Turn backward, turn backward, O Time in thy flight / And make me a child again, just for tonight."
"Heart weary of building and spoiling, / And spoiling and building again. /
And I long for the dear old river, / Where I idled my youth away; / For a
dreamer lives forever, / And a toiler dies in a day."

Keep it simple. It is not psychological regression. It is spiritual progress
to live in the enthusiastic expectation of a child, in the love and wonder of a
youth or a maiden, in the mature judgment of one who has lived longer; but
through it all flowing is the eternal river whose source no man knows, because it flows from the heart of eternal love, friendship, compassion, appreciation. You can't do it unless you forgive yourself and everybody else. There
is no hurt in love. "Perfect love casts out all fear"; there is nothing else left.
There is no doubt in perfect love. So: to get over our sensitiveness and fear
that people won't like us (which keeps them from it); to be without criticism
in our minds (which irritates people whether anything is said or not); to
flow along with life; to love and be nonresistant.

Now as I say, there are people who say this is silly. I've watched it, I've
met them all—they have all been in my office, over and over again—and I
have seen no person healed unless there came a time when he knew the
Universe had no judgment against him or he against anyone else: he returned to the simple basis of the givingness of the Self, the recognition of
the divine Presence in everything. If you and I want a friend, Emerson said,
we must be one. We must love the world and be grateful and thank God for
it; and we shall be happy because we shall be fulfilled. And that which we
thought we did not have will be there in manifestation. This is not just a
dream. Back of it there is a Law of Cause and Effect. Emerson called it "the
High Chancellor of God," and Jesus said, "Heaven and earth will pass away,
but my words shall not . . . till all be fulfilled."

---

*This continues the reference to Jesus.

Think of the joy of it: that at last the harshness, the fear, the criticism, the doubt, the uncertainty . . . we may be fooled by a few people, but I'd rather be fooled by a few people than to completely fool myself about all people. I would rather believe in the instinctive integrity of the average person than to doubt it; and if we miss once in a while and don't ring the bell, think of the bells we *have* rung. And the Spirit isn't dried up and ossified and petrified. You go into an atmosphere where there is nothing but love, and the food will digest; there will be very little trouble or headaches; most diseases will automatically flow away as though they never belonged—because love is the only complete mental sanitation that there is. Just love. Just love.

And it is so simple and so dynamic. The practice of it also is simple. All truths are simple. There are only a few great fundamental laws in the Universe. Life gives; we must receive it. To fulfill the receipt of our gift, we must give it. That which goes out will come back multiplied and must go out again, and again and again. High motivating power, the deep spiritual inner awareness—that for which the heart longs and the mind yearns and the soul speaks—the Spirit already possesses.

O Love that will not let us go! And let's practice that love and that friendship, asking no man, "Is it intellectually sound? Can science prove it?" Science is an observer of the phenomena of nature, and that is all. They can kill the nightingale and not capture the song. Psychiatry is the Thing without a soul; and I believe it. But you and I are warm, colorful, pulsating human beings; the eternal Heart beats in our breast; even the Mind of God cries out through a great sage and says, "Come unto me all ye that labor and are heavy laden and I will give you rest. Take my yoke upon you, and learn of me; for I am meek and lowly in spirit. For my yoke is easy and my burden is light and ye shall find rest unto your souls."

O God, Thou who dost inhabit eternity and dwell in the innermost sanctuary of our hearts, we open our consciousness to the revelation and embrace of the Universe. O Love, as we receive, we give and we bless the gift; and we would know eternal sweetness, ineffable beauty. Thou God, who is Love: it is our desire that every person we touch shall be healed, every situation we enter shall be made whole. We would that our presence shall bring joy and peace; and so it shall. And so it is. Amen.

Let's give as we never gave before in our lives. The eternal Giver gives through us, and we give of ourselves and make it soar to a soul that is starving in darkness. Amen.

→ AFFIRMATIVE-PRAYER MEDITATION ←

(Now we have the names of people in this box, and they are going to believe with us that each one is attached to a divine and spiritual Pattern of his real Self.)

The inner Self, the Spiritual Self, the God Self exists here and now and is flowing through every organ and action and function of his physical being. And we rejoice in this and we permit it to be so; and he expects it to be so because it *is* so.

We know that every person who has asked for direction, wise counsel, receives it; everyone who has asked for greater success in life, or love, receives it. With him we accept the gift of Heaven from the God of Love and Peace and Joy. And so it is.

Now as we turn to that divine Presence which is both God and Man, we receive the beneficence of His love, the outflowing of His Spirit. And as we turn to each other, we bless each other and make the God of Love be—and abide—with us forevermore. Amen.

13.

HOW TO USE A POWER
GREATER THAN YOU ARE

Good morning. I love you very much; and I guess you guessed that. I understand it has been real warm in Los Angeles. We have been in Monterey, and it has been wonderful and cool and a very wonderful convention. I was particularly impressed with the young people's work. One of my age likes to companion with people of the same age, so I spent a lot of time with these kids, and they are terrific. They had a healing peace meeting, and we were all so much impressed. It was a terrific thing, this consciousness, this knowing that the Universe in which we live is a little different than it looks.

Won't all of you take your program home and every day look at that building* and call it wonderful, praise it, and bless it, and know that when it is built, people are coming from all over the world and they are going to be healed and blessed; and that everything necessary to the most beautiful idea of a building is already there. I wish you would do that every day until it is completed. It will be wonderful. The architect, Paul Williams, is a good metaphysician.

I think this audience is wonderful. I watched, and everyone comes smiling; and as they came in, I mentally hugged them, because I like people so much. And I thought, How wonderful! What a tribute to the Truth! And I

------

*The prospective Founder's Church of Religious Science in Los Angeles.

said, "Maybe they all came to hear me; and if they did, then God is good to me." And *you* are good to me, and I love it and appreciate it.

Now we are talking on How to Use a Power Greater Than You Are. We are talking about a spiritual Power everybody can use, if he believes in it and uses it. First of all, we say you could use a Power greater than you are spiritually; and someone will say, "Oh, what nonsense!" But let them stop to think a moment. Every time you plant a garden, you use a Power greater than you are. No one living knows how to make an oak tree. There isn't anyone living knows how an egg gets into a hen or how a chicken gets out of the egg; or how the chicken gets in the egg or how the egg gets out of the hen. All the scientific minds—and I believe completely in science—do not know how you can eat cheese and crackers and everything else.

We are three-dimensional people living in a four-dimensional world. They have proven at Duke University, in ESP, that we can reproduce the activities of the five physical senses without using the organs of the senses. They have proven we can think without the brain. (It will prove very helpful to many of us, I am sure.) They have proven theoretically that you can get along without this body and still be you.

No one has ever seen some other person. We *feel* him. No one ever saw love or life or truth or beauty. Yet they are there. We are three-dimensional beings living in a four-dimensional world which governs the three dimensions. In the hen somewhere is the egg, in the egg somewhere is the chicken. We do not have to try to explain the inexplicable. That is why Jesus said that the Kingdom of Heaven is like a child: "Suffer the little children to come unto me and forbid them not, for of such is the Kingdom of Heaven." A *childlike* mind doesn't mean *childish*—just simple, *child-like*, and believing.

There is a Power in the Universe greater than we are. There is an Intelligence acting as Law that receives the impress of our thoughts as we think them. It is creative, and It always tends to create for us the conditions we think about and accept; and if we wish to help someone else, when we identify the person we wish to help with what we call our treatment or meditation, it will be for that person.

Somebody might say, "I don't believe it." Well, I don't care; it is none of my business. Somebody might say, "It is ridiculous!" That doesn't bother me any. The first steam-driven boat that crossed the Atlantic carried on it a scientific treatise on why it couldn't be done. We don't have to worry about whether somebody believes it. Who cares? Our only concern should be do we *know* what *we* believe. Are we *certain* of what we believe; can we *prove* what we believe, *demonstrate* it. And we *can*. And that is that.

Now I don't think it should seem strange. Somebody might say, "Why didn't the Bible tell us about it?" Maybe it did and maybe it didn't. Why didn't the Bible tell us about automobiles? Because it just didn't. You don't have to say it had to be in the Bible to be correct; very little we have nowadays was in the Bible. Somebody might have said, "If God had intended it to be that way, He would have revealed it some way." God didn't reveal *anything* until we were ready to take it. Look at modern science. Somebody thinks about it, specializes on it, dwells on it mentally until finally he discovers the secret. The secret of prayer we are going to talk about next week—they have proven it in Redlands in a university.

It has nothing to do with whether you are a Catholic, or a Protestant, or a Christian Scientist, or even a Religious Scientist. Whatever this thing is, it is no respecter of persons. It likes everybody. Everybody can go and climb up in the lap of God and whisper in His ear and get patted on his head and hear Him say, "You are My nice little boy"; and I believe that. God is personal to everyone who personifies God; God is as good to us as we are good to God; God is as colorful as we are colorful. God, infinite Peace, delivers that Peace to us at the level that we gain peace, and Love only knows and comprehendeth love.

If anyone who thinks he has love in his life knew how to surrender himself to Love, he would be the most amazed person in the world; and if somebody else says it isn't true, he wouldn't even know they are talking! *There is a Power greater than you are, and you can use It.* I can't explain why It is there—why is life?—nobody can. I do not believe that Power knows any more about Christians than It does Jews, or Jews than It does Gentiles; It knows nothing about our little idiosyncrasies, thank God. Tennyson said, "Our little systems have their day; / They have their day and cease to be; / They are but broken lights of Thee, / And Thou, O Lord, art more than they."

You see? Simple, childlike minds, having faith, believing, accepting that there is a Power greater than we are and that we can use it—for what purpose? Every purpose. People sometimes say to me, "Well, is it spiritual to pray for, or use the power for, material things?" There is no such thing as a material universe. Science has long ago dissolved a material universe (as though there were a universe separate from the Truth that governs it and moulds it). There isn't anybody today who believes in that kind of a material universe.

There is a Power greater than we are, and everything that is visible is hitched to It—an invisible Pattern, a divine Pattern. All things come forth from It, and all things return again to It; and we are in It, and It responds directly to us personally at the level of our conviction that It is responding. And somebody might say, "Why doesn't It *force* it on us?" It doesn't force anything on anyone. We might say, "Why doesn't the garden grow carrots when we planted the beets?" When you plant a beet seed, the ground will say "beets," and when you plant a potato, it will say "potatoes." It will not say, "I don't like beets or potatoes." It's kind after kind. Someone will say, "Well, is it good to use the spiritual for our human needs?" I don't see anything wrong with it; we are trying all the time. Now I have friends who are good, honest vegetarians—yet they wear leather shoes. Shakespeare said, "Consistency is a jewel seldom worn"; and I have often facetiously said, "You won't eat meat, yet you wear leather shoes. Do you find it easier on the animal to skin it alive?" It is like the man who was so kind he didn't want to hurt a dog when he cut its tail off, so he cut it off a joint at a time.

Does the Universe want us to have *succotash*? Does it say, "I refuse to grow *lemons*"? Of course not. We have been so afraid of God, thinking we are made to suffer here so we will suffer less hereafter—or more—that we are all screwed up in our simple ideas about our relationship to the Infinite. Isn't it funny that we do not have a more close and intimate sense of relationship that there couldn't be any God in the Universe that withheld anything from us—? But there are certain laws we have to obey when we use the laws of

Nature, and it is the same in the spiritual world as it is in the physical—because the spiritual just reproduces the physical on a higher level. The laws work just the same.

For instance, there is a law of attraction and repulsion in Mind; it works just like attraction and repulsion in physics; it always tends to bring to us that which is like our own thinking. All energy returns to its source. Einstein even has said that time, light, and space bend back upon themselves. Therefore our word tends to come back to us. "Whatsoever things are lovely and of good report—*think* on *these* things," the Bible says. "As a man thinketh in his heart, so is he." "Believe and it shall be done unto you."

There is a Principle that responds to us: this is the secret. There is a mathematical mental Principle that responds creatively to us at the level of our own consciousness. To the pure in heart all will be pure. To the ones who see that everything is wrong, everything will be wrong. To the ones who criticize everyone and everybody, they will always find something to criticize, and they will gradually get so mean that their best friends will walk away from them after they get tired listening to it.

But we know what it is: they are trying to justify themselves—they are afraid of themselves, they don't believe in themselves, they have a sense of guilt and rejection and an anxiety and insecurity within themselves; therefore they are sick. In this sense, we should be sorry for them; but there is no reason why you and I should have to spend a whole day with somebody who is mean. *I* won't. I just don't like it. I like beauty and laughter and song and dancing and fun. There is no reason to suppose that God is some sad creature sending thunderbolts to Methodists and candy to Baptists. I believe one is as good as the other, and a heretic is as good as someone who is not a heretic—but he might (or might not) have missed something; it doesn't matter. The Universe loves all of us; It is impartial. That is why Jesus said, "He causes His sun and rain to come alike on the just and on the unjust."

Yes, there is nothing in nature or in God that withholds our good from us. Jesus said, "I am come that ye might have life and that ye might have it more abundantly"; so that's that. There is nothing in the Universe that keeps us waiting until we get saved. I understand there are certain people who are saved. I haven't met them. I understand there are certain people who are not saved. I haven't met them either. I never met "them" that you hear so much about. Where are "they"? *Who* are "they"? People come and say, "Ernest—you shouldn't do this; they don't like it!" And I always say, "*Who* don't like it?" "They." And I say, "Bring one of 'them' to me and I will explain why I am such a nice guy." But if "they" are so elusive, we can never get a hold of them.

I am not afraid of "them." Not at all.

Every man has to do the best he can. "To thine own self be true; and it shall follow as the night the day, thou canst not then be false to any man." You and I believe in a Power greater than we are. We believe It is Good; we believe It is Love; we believe It is Truth; we believe It is Beauty; we believe It responds to us; and we believe if we maintain a certain mental attitude of thought, It will automatically bring to us those things that make life happy. And we believe life ought to be happy. There is no "weeping God"—of this I am sure.

Emerson said, when his beloved son died, for two years he wept and sorrowed and grieved, until out of the weeping and the sorrow and the grief he learned how empty it was, how useless. And that is true. It seems as though Life, acting as Law, is quite impersonal.

You and I believe in something so stupendous and yet so simple. Its simplicity is what eludes us. If I can get all the thoughts out of my mind that say to me "I am hurt; I am sensitive; my friends hurt me" without being mean about it, without being arrogant (signs that we are protesting too loudly and fighting back), and if it is *real*: finally nothing in the Universe will hurt me, and finally I shall not any longer be led into situations where people will even wish to—and they can't.

This Thing is personal to you and to me, just as is all that God has and is and all the laws of the Universe. Isn't all of the law of electricity at the point where any electrician uses it? Isn't all the law of mathematics and higher calculus right at the fingertips of the mathematician when he is using a pen or pencil? Isn't all the harmony there is flowing through the one who sings, and all the beauty through the artist? *All* of it—? Well, of course! All of gravity is holding everything in place, as though all of gravity devoted its entire time to holding a peanut right there, if I put it there.

Now this is terrific. Someone said, "Go not thou in search of Him / But to thy self repair. / Wait thou within the silence dim, / And thou shalt find Him there." God we meet in ourselves and in each other and in Nature and everywhere. But how can we meet a God of love if we are looking at a life of hate? It isn't that way! And *Love* is not withholding. How can we meet a God of abundance if we are looking at impoverishment? Now I am not saying it is easy—but I do say it is *simple*. I say it is *very* simple. How can we look at, or see, or experience, a God or a life of harmony if we are always in discord?

But do you know, there is a certain psychological morbidity about all of us. I have known men and women who really love each other who periodically kick each other's teeth out so they can make up again. This is very common. It is one of the morbid traits of the human mind. And in that background is the idea that we suffer all this world and then go to a good place after; but those who disagree with us: the elevator goes down—way down!

That isn't so. The Universe comes fresh, new, clean, beautiful, lovely, exuberant, "exhilarant," majestic, dynamic, omnipotent to each one of us every moment of our time—That which is the original creative Energy and Force and Intelligence; That which is alive with life and aflame with love, right at the point of our listening, right at the point of our seeing, right at the point of our hearing. "Eyes have they but they see not, ears have they but they hear not, tongues have they"—but they speak no language of infinite Harmony and Peace.

Now this is the way it is. We didn't make it that way, but thank God that *is* the way it is, and thank God that each one of us has access to the infinite and ineffable All. We have to believe this. Someone may say, "*I* can't believe it." Then I am sorry; I wish you could. *I* think It is true. Someone may say, "It is ridiculous." Well, I'm sorry you think it is ridiculous; I wish you thought it was as simple as planting sunflower seeds and getting sunflowers. Did you ever hear of any creative soil that, when you plant sunflower seeds, will give you potatoes? Jesus understood this. Kind for kind. Somebody might say, "I want to be unhappy and have happiness come to me." I'm sorry: it isn't that way. You jump over a cliff, you are going to fall; and gravitational force isn't mean because it gets you there. And the trouble isn't the falling, anyway; it is the *landing*—quick, when you land! That is really where the disaster starts: at the bottom of the cliff.

You see, when we get to spiritual things, we get kind of woozy. We don't expect the laws of Nature to disobey themselves to please the naturalist. No one does. Somehow it is a peculiar thing: when we come to mental, psychological, and spiritual things, we expect the whole order of the Universe to reverse itself and chaos and confusion to take the place of law and order. But it doesn't.

It is fundamental to this whole thing that we must learn to affirm what we desire; we must learn to enthusiastically expect these things we desire. And as we advance in demonstration of this most fascinating of all sciences . . . because it is a science, the Science of Mind—just as much a science as the science of electricity. After a while we are going to learn what Parker* and these people down here proved: that the prayer works, no matter how simple, no matter whether Jew or Gentile prayed it—a boy right off the football field; they didn't care. They said, If it works, it works; and if it doesn't, it doesn't; and if it *does*, it is a principle; and if it is a principle, it *will*. And it did. Isn't that wonderful—the Affirmative Prayer I want to talk about next week. *Everybody* can pray.

Everybody can pray an affirmative prayer; so don't be afraid as to whether or not this Power greater than you are is going to operate for you. *It can't help it*. It acts by reflection. Now we will imagine there is a mirror back there; it isn't a mirror: it is really a camouflage—a pretense, but pretty. I hold up my hand and see my fingers mirrored down there. Now suppose we go down there—let's say that it *is* a mirror—and try to scratch it out of the mirror, or rub it out: you can't do it. It is there just the same.

Suppose, then, I finally discover it is my hand that makes the reflection,

---

*Dr. William Parker, researching the power of prayer at Redlands University.

and I say, "But I can't move my hand!" That is the position we are in now: we believe in the reflection. But I gradually find if I withdraw my hand and put something else out there, *that* is reflected. Then I am on the pathway to the greatest discovery of my life: that you don't have to change the *reflection*. That is the outside condition—it didn't make itself. All you have to do is change the imagery, which didn't make itself. *You* made it, and *I* made it, and *we* are the creators and arbiters of fate. There is no law under the one great Law of Life but our own soul shall set it, as it obeys that great Law of Life.

Then you have to experiment with it. No use in our coming every Sunday and talking about these wonderful things and doing nothing about them. Work it during the week. Make yourself *let* it work the only way it *can* work, and that is to *convince yourself*.

Now the next thing to remember is this: you and I carry around the thought-habit patterns of the ages (this is well known in psychology), endlessly repeating them. "Man is born to be unhappy, to be sick and poor and to get dead," and some say to go up and some say to go down (I believe, *to go over into a broader territory*, and, I believe, *never to come back*; but it doesn't matter). We are here now, and the things our ancestors believed, be they right or wrong, operate through us—so much so that when somebody first said the world was round, they said he was crazy. When somebody first announced gravitational force, they said *he* was crazy. When somebody first announced the blood circulated, they said *he* was crazy. And the Spanish Inquisition was based on a theology which was sincere but believed it had to put on the rack those who disagreed with it. Galileo was made to recant, but I understand when he got up from his knees he said, "The darned thing is true just the same!" He knew it didn't matter what the other gentlemen had in mind. They were ecclesiastical sadists.

You in the integrity of your own mind, in the simplicity of your own thought, in the directness and childlikeness of your own heart. That is why Jesus said, "If you ask your parent for a fish, will he give you a stone, or for an egg a scorpion? How much more shall your heavenly Father give you those things which are good." This is the way the heavenly Father gives it: through the

Law of asking and receiving—the Law of the Power greater than we are receiving the impress of our thoughts and acting upon it.

Since we all carry these deep-rooted thought patterns, they are automatically projecting perhaps a destiny we do not like, and we say, "Can that be the result of my own thought?" Not the result of your own personal thought, I don't believe—but the result of the sum total of *all* thinking, operating through all of us. I don't like to pick out myself or someone else and say, "Oh well, Nature is beating you up because you are no good." I don't believe in that. We are all struggling for the Light. "But what am I? / An infant crying in the night; / An infant crying for the light; / And with no language but a cry." "But the feeble hands and helpless, / Groping blindly in the darkness, / Touched God's right hand in that darkness / And are lifted up and strengthened."

You may be sure of this: there is an integrity to your soul such as you will find nowhere else in the Universe. Here you will meet life; here you will decide; and here you may neutralize the thought patterns of the ages by simply denying them—and saying something greater than that (and I believe in it): "There is a Power greater than I am, and I accept It." And no matter what the mistakes are, the Universe holds nothing against us, ever. "He took my book all stained and spotted, / And gave me a new one, all unblotted, / And into my sad eyes smiled, / 'Do better now, my child,' / Should not the judge of all the earth do that?"

Shall not the Giver of all life eternally give? Shall not That which is Love forever hold us in Its embrace? Now at last we have learned our cooperation with It as we have in every other thing in life—because even Love acts as Law. Our part is really to wipe the slate of the past clean from fear and doubt and unloveliness and write a song on it and draw children playing on the shore, happy, naked, and unafraid; and then to know that *we* are that child, *we* are that person, *we* are that beloved of the Eternal God—we in the simplicity of our integrity, in the childlikeness even of our ignorance, because we are all ignorant. Each may say to himself, "The Eternal God is my refuge; underneath are the everlasting arms."

You will prove it all alone to yourself, my sweet and beloved friends; each will have to prove it to himself and for himself. Others can heal us and cure us and help us—that is good. But the *long* healing, the *deep* healing—that which shall be with us from now on, thank God—each can and must do for himself; and then he knows something new happens to him. He lives in a different universe. He is no longer afraid of the present nor morbid over the past, nor insecure over the future; but looking up and out, he sees God's divinely intended Man, God's beautiful Creation, and the strength of the hills are his and the beauty of the early morning sunrise and the softness of the sunset, the cool river in which he plunges—all around there is infinite and ineffable Beauty; and he knows that he is the beloved of God.

⇥ AFFIRMATIVE-PRAYER MEDITATION ⇤

(Now we are going to practice what we have been talking about. There are many names in this box; most of these people are in this audience or they have asked for someone. There is someone here who knows what each of these requests is—personal for someone else. Will you, then, as the rest of us think about this, believe that it is now done. Always accept the affirmative, but don't work too hard at it. I mean don't say, "It is done" questioningly. You see, when we get all worked up about it, we don't believe it and we are trying to scream down the negation. Resist not evil and it will flee from you.)

So we turn within and we are speaking about the name of all who have asked for physical healing. God is within each one of them—perfect Life is in each one of them—a divine Pattern of perfection is within each one of them. Every organ and every action and every function of this physical body is governed by divine Intelligence in each one of them; there is perfect circulation, perfect assimilation, and perfect elimination. There is one Life, that Life is perfect, that Life is their life. All the enthusiasm that there is, all the energy and action that there is in the Universe, is flowing through them. They sleep in peace and wake in joy and live in a consciousness of God, of good, of wholeness. Our word is the law of elimination to everything that denies this. We affirm that perfection, we announce their perfection; we rejoice in it and we are glad. We know our word goes on until all is accomplished.

(Now everyone who has asked for betterment in circumstances or guidance knows his name or the one he has asked for. Let him believe he has received what he has asked for; and you and I will know, and we are so happy to announce, that he is governed and guided and directed by divine Intelligence.)

Everyone here who has asked for that shall always know what to do and how to do it and where to go and how to get there. He shall be surrounded by love and friendship. And there is nothing in him that can deny good, abundance, plenty—everything that makes life worthwhile—better than he has ever asked for, more than he can think about, beyond the range of his present knowledge. That good is coming to him which he shall be compelled to recognize, see, and act upon. If it is necessary for him to make decisions, he will. He will act wherever he is supposed to act, he will do whatever he ought to do. Back of it all we feel drawing to him everything that is good and worthwhile.

Now we say for all of us here—each one of us says to himself and to each other—we are the beloved of God. No arrogance in this. Very simple. We live—therefore we must be the beloved of God; and we are recognizing that divine Presence as joy, as infinite peace, as beauty, as perfect health, as love and friendship; and we are saying the doorway of opportunity stands wide open before us. It has nothing to do with our education or color or age or our creed or our doctrine. All of these things are swept aside.

We are the beloved of God. We are that which Thou art, Thou art that which we are; and in the Secret Place of our heart—in the Secret Place of the Most High—we commingle with the Eternal; and it is our desire, and we shall accept it individually and as a group, that every person we meet shall be glad. Wherever our shadow is cast shall healing take place; everything we look at we shall embrace and love. We desire to heal every situation we contact, whether we are aware of it or not. And it is so. "Beloved, now are we the Sons of God."

Now may the eternal light of Heaven guide your pathway and mine; may the everlasting Love and Peace and Joy of Life be and abide with us, and may we so live and so give that everything we touch shall commingle with us in the divine offering of Life to Itself, in the joy of the living, and in a peace which is perfect. Amen.

14

THE PRAYER THAT
GETS RESULTS

Good morning. I want to thank you again for being here, so many of you in the summer—it is a great tribute to the new idea which comes to the world through the name of Religious Science, which I think is the next great spiritual impulsion. I think in the next 25 years there will be thousands of Religious Science churches throughout the world. It is inevitable. It is the greatest intellectual and spiritual freedom that has ever come to the world since the time of Christ. It has terrific simplicity. I do appreciate your being here, more than I can tell you, or how much I love you. I have had people tell me my Sunday morning service was not dignified. I'm glad and like it this way when people clap. We don't have to be afraid to say, "Praise God!" because we believe there is no hell. We ought to scream it louder.

Our subject this morning is "The Prayer That Gets Results." All prayers probably have some effect; some prayers must have a *complete* effect. Jesus, was, in a certain sense, in his time a Reform Jew. He said, "When ye pray, believe that you have, and you will receive." I met a couple of kids out here this morning, each of them 16; they are of a different race; but there is only one race in my mind, and that is the human race—we all belong to it, just like there is only one God—and I embrace everyone alike and love everyone exactly alike. What God has made alike, we cannot separate.

One of these boys said he was going to be an engineer, the other said he wanted to play football. Perhaps neither one of those kids ever heard what I am going to talk about; probably I will never see either one of them again; but listen, guys, and use it and prove it to yourself, because if you use it the way I am going to talk about, it will work: affirmative prayer. They discovered, as you will see in this book—*Prayer Can Change Your Life*ˣ—at Redlands University, that when people prayed affirmatively, as it is done now, they got 70 percent better results than by the ordinary prayer, no matter how fervent.

Now you will find *why* in *this* little book that only costs $1.00; but you ought to have both of them. I like the book out of a university that comes to us and says, "We, without respect of creed, color, education have proven they can pray affirmatively and get results." But they have not explained *why*, and I am going to explain why this morning. They have *proven* it: that is the most valuable piece of spiritual information, in my estimation, that ever came from a university in the entire history of the educational development of the world—a university, impartial, impersonal. They didn't ask, "What church do you belong to?" or "Do you belong to any?" They just said, "Come and let's try it"—and that is good. And they found a 70 percent better result when you pray affirmatively. You and I want to know *why*.

I will tell you why, I think, and it is very simple. You see, if prayer is answered at all—and it is—then theoretically all prayers ought to be answered. There is no God who loves one type of religionist better than another, and I don't believe there is a God who knows one race or creed is better than another, or a Jew better than a Gentile; I don't think there is any God worried about our little idiosyncrasies. Tennyson said "Our little systems have their day; / They have their day and cease to be; / They are but broken lights of Thee, / While Thou, O God, art more than they." Jesus answered it when he said, "When ye pray, BELIEVE THAT YOU HAVE." In other words, what Jesus said—what the modern metaphysical movements have proved, what they have proved in the last few years in the Redlands University, and what you and I have already accepted but may not know well

---

ˣBy William Parker and Elaine St. Johns.

enough or I wouldn't be talking about it—is that prayers that are answered are prayers that are affirmative and are accepted by the one praying.

I am going back in October to visit a school for boys that is independently run, where these boys from the age of 10 to 18 are taught to pray for what the school needs—and they make what we call demonstrations. They are taught to pray and believe it, and all get together and pray. Not long ago they prayed for a gym and someone came along and built it for them.

There is a definite record of a man who had a school in Boston years ago called The Cullis, I believe. He was so advanced in the technique of prayer that he always prayed alone for what he wanted, and he wouldn't let people be in his employ who doubted. He said if they doubted God for 15 minutes, they couldn't be there. I am afraid if we disposed of everybody who doubted God for 15 minutes we would be left in "splendid isolation." But this man got results.

He was going to the harbor at Halifax one time—this isn't a weird fish story, this is true and on record—and there was a heavy fog, and he told the captain, "I will have to go below and pray," and he did. And when he came back on deck, the fog had cleared away and the captain said, "This is a miracle and can't happen—but it did!"

We must believe there is a Power greater than we are, to begin with. Whether you call it God or divine Principle—I don't care what you call it. There is Something around us that receives the impress of our thought and reacts to it the way we think it. Mrs. Wilcox* said, "For life is a mirror of king and slave, / Tis just what you are and do; / Then give to the world the best that you have, / And the best will come back to you."

Now there is a divine Principle, a divine Intelligence, a universal Mind, a "universal Subjectivity," as Troward† called it. It doesn't matter what you call it—we are surrounded by some kind of a Law of Mind. Now God is

---

*Ella Wheeler Wilcox (1850–1919), American journalist and poet, student of Emma Curtis Hopkins.
†Thomas Troward (1847–1916), English jurist, metaphysician, and author.

beyond this Law, just as an electrician is beyond electricity. We are surrounded by a divine Presence and a universal Law.

I am talking about the Law right now. It receives the impress of our thought; it is creative, it is intelligent, it acts upon it and tends to bring back into our experience that which we affirm in it. But remember this: if you can sit down once in a while and pray affirmatively and get a result, then what is happening *all* the time we think? Isn't that some kind of a prayer? If I say, "My poor head, my poor heart"—isn't that a prayer?

Now affirmative prayer—prayer that gets results—is one that believes in itself. We are surrounded by a Principle, a Law, an Intelligence, a Mind, a Creativity that receives the impress of our thoughts. I met this very sweet person in Florida last February—woman about 60—and I thought she looked so vital and rather pretty. She said, "I want to tell you something: a year ago I was a hopeless cripple, arthritic, could hardly walk, hands were knotted, every joint in my body ached"; and I said, "What happened?" "Well," she said, "I tried everything—even your practitioners—and didn't get much help"; and I said, "How did you do it?" She said, "I did it myself"; and I asked, "What did you do?" She said, "I just made up my mind there is an intelligent Principle everywhere and It flows through me and I can talk to It, and I began to praise It and began to tell every joint in my body what I wanted it to do and how wonderful I thought it was." And she said, "*This* is what happened!"

David Seabury,* the most popular lecturer on psychology—a friend of mine—told me that many years ago he had so much trouble with his stomach that it was terrible, and he tried the same thing: he began to talk to Intelligence there and told what he wanted It to do, and he got all over it. Now this is merely to show there is an intelligent Principle that runs through everything; and in experimenting, we ought to try everything and see what works. One of the prophets in the Old Testament said, "Try me herewith,

---

*(1885–1960), psychologist; son of Julius and Annetta (nee Seabury) Dresser, students and partisans of P. P. Quimby, mental healer and the "Father of New Thought."

saith the Lord, and see if I will not open to you the windows of Heaven and pour out such a blessing you will not be able to receive it."

There is an Intelligence that responds to us; but everything we think is some kind of a prayer, isn't it? We say, "I will sit down and meditate," and that is good; but unless in doing it we change our thought, there is no use doing it. There is no use sitting down for ten minutes and saying, "I am surrounded by prosperity; everything I do shall prosper," and the rest of the 24 hours saying "Nothing is any good." These are the moments when we center our thinking; we learn to accept. First of all, remember there is a Power greater than we are which reacts, a Principle that responds. It has now been proven—not only in religious experience in modern metaphysical movements such as ours (they are built up on this). That is why you are here—because something new is happening in the world, and this is it.

There is Something that responds. Now we have established this. Don't be impatient because of Its utmost simplicity; let's grasp It. But let's get the basis sound, and let's get it mathematical. We are thinking centers in a universal Mind that receives the impress of our thought and acts upon it, and reacts to it according to our affirmation. If this can be proven in a university, it certainly should be better proven in the church, where they already believe in these powers. If this is so, we have established a Principle. Now they didn't do this at the university. They pointed to a *fact*. I said to Elaine,* I hope the next book you write, you will establish a *Principle*, and I would like to talk with you about it.

What they have done proves the truth of what I am talking about. It is the most feasible explanation as to why any prayers were ever answered. You see, it didn't matter what their religion was. If they prayed believing, they got a result. Since we know this, let's do it consciously and definitely and knowing what we are doing. There is a Principle that returns to us, therefore It responds by corresponding or reflection. This is why Jesus said, "When ye pray, believe that it is done."

---

*Elaine St. Johns, co-author of *Prayer Can Change Your Life*.

Now that is the simple basis: there is a Power that responds creatively—It can't help it—and apparently It responds mathematically. The whole Universe seems to operate mathematically, because It is the Cosmos—It is intelligent. Therefore we personally and individually should be able to decide what the response is going to be. That is the next thing we have to establish. Sometimes people say to me, "I read a great tirade in a magazine lately where people more orthodox than we said it was a shame the way people were coming to our movements—not only Religious Science, but all the New Thought movements—because they were promised so much."

We believe Heaven is *now*; God is *now*. There will never be a day in eternity better than the day in which you and I are living, or any different. It is a continuity. Without criticizing them, let us say that what they hope to get later, we would like to have now and keep later. We do not wish to deny others the privilege of entering into Heaven some day and enjoying these things which now they do not have. I merely say we believe it ought to be possible to have them now and keep them. There is nothing wrong with it.

Now it was not difficult for Jesus to pray effectively. It was not hard for this man to pray so he always got an answer, because he wouldn't keep any man close to him who doubted for 15 minutes. He said, "I cannot have anyone so close to me who doubts God." I don't care how orthodox he was—he had cleared his mind so he knew God would answer him, and that was that. After that is established—a Power greater than we are—It responds by corresponding. We approach It affirmatively; and when we pray, we say, "*It is so.*" "When ye pray, believe that ye have." This is fulfilling it.

Now the next thing I want to consider is the *degree* of fulfillment; because even in our field we find some people are better practitioners than others. I don't mean they are better people; I don't mean they are more sincere. But they have what we call a greater consciousness. I measure everything in our work with a measuring rod of *consciousness* and nothing else; that is, the inner feeling and acceptance of a person. The inner mental reaction.

I have seen kids who had this consciousness; old people; young people. It has nothing to do with race, color, creed; nothing to do with intellectual attainment; nothing to do with your I.Q. as it is measured in schools. It has to do only with—*Do you have the capacity to believe?* and *Are you using your belief at a certain level of consciousness?* I think this is important.

I do know that in our field certain people do better than others. Some people treat more effectually for some things. I have known people who were better at physical healings and others who were better at finances or affairs. The only reason is in their own mind. I have noticed, and this should be revealing, that if people have had a very good background of success before they come into our work, it is easier for them to succeed, because they are merely applying what they already have to a new medium. It is like a salesman. A man who is a good salesman will be a good salesman with whatever he sells as soon as he learns the nature of his product.

It is like a good religion: everyone is just as "fervent"; but some might be better in consciousness, religiously. It doesn't matter what they believe outside; it is what they do to themselves inside that we are talking about. We are merely a group of people who happen to understand there is a Principle governing this, and this is the way it works, and we have a technique for using it. Use it this way, and you will get a result; and *everybody* in our field should get a result.

I have noticed that the people who have the greatest awareness of God can pray most effectively—but they still have to pray affirmatively. They pray effectually, but they pray affirmatively. For instance, you take a man who has a great consciousness of peace. He isn't afraid of anything; his calm trust of God is complete. He knows the Universe is not against him, It is for him. And he is working for, treating for, or praying for a discordant condition where there is very little peace. Hasn't he got more peace as a background for his affirmation than someone who is confused? That is all I mean. *He has.* His prayer will be more effective, even though it will still follow the law of *all* prayer: it is done unto you as you believe. You have to believe first. Action and reaction.

Now just because it *is* action and reaction, certain actions will produce certain reactions. The higher the action, the higher the reaction. One thing I thank God for in life more than anything else: I have never had to go through much fear in my life. I have gone through trouble, chagrin, sadness;

not much pain and almost no fear, because my mother brought us up without fear but very religious—that is, we read the Bible every day, said Grace at every meal, got down on our knees and said family prayers at night. But we were Congregationalists; and they are very liberal. She didn't want us to be scared to death; and I was grown up and away from home before I knew grown-up, adult people actually believed in a hell and a devil; and I don't know *now* how they can—because I haven't the mental equivalent. I was brought up that way, and that is a great heritage. And it is worth more than millions of dollars.

Someone who isn't afraid ought to be able to heal somebody who is, and following the same Principle. Therefore I say, this is the prayer that is bound to be answered, it seems to me. This is only my opinion, and I want you to try it. I do not know any more about these things than you do—I just am not afraid to get up and talk about them. It is a habit.

Very simple things you and I believe—very simple, fundamental things. We are spiritual beings in a spiritual Universe governed by laws of Intelligence. The Law of Mind in action is the final law of the Universe. Modern science is beginning to accept it; it has to be that way. Therefore Something responds. Now we don't need to worry about this. It will happen. Consequently, we are praising our environment. Are we saying, "O you wonderful heart, you perfect head, you good feet"? We *are* saying, "Life is for me and not against me. Everywhere I go things will be made perfect before me"— what you and I call a treatment; what are we treating in our own minds. You don't argue with God, you don't make Law be Law. It *is* Law; God *is* God. "I am the Lord, beside which there is none other."

Now the next thing in doing it is to keep from denying what we affirm; and this, I think, is tough. No one ever heard me say this is easy; I say it is *simple*. I don't think it is *easy* to control your thinking. A child can understand it—and I think kids use it better. I got such a thrill out of the kids at Asilomar: there is a lot they don't have to unlearn. They accept it as natural, they use it, they believe it—and it works. It is no respecter of persons. That is why Jesus said, "Suffer the little children to come unto me and forbid them not, for of such is the Kingdom of Heaven. And verily I say unto you, their angel faces do forevermore behold the face of My Father which is in Heaven."

And Heaven is within. Some prayers will be more effective than others; but all prayers, to be effective at all, must be affirmative. We must accept the answer to our own prayer; and when we understand why, we will—you will and I will. Therefore we don't worry about it any more.

I believe love is the greatest healing motivating power in the Universe, because love is givingness. I don't think you will have a good effectual prayer or preacher or practitioner or human being without great love. It is the only thing that unbinds the captive, penetrates the prison wall of obscurity, and sets the captive free from the prison of his own creation and his own undoing. Well, we have to *do* it; this is not an idle dream. I want those two boys to do it. They are young, only 16, and I'll probably never see them again; but I want them to do it. Because they haven't learned yet how "terrible" everything is; they haven't become disillusioned with life. They are full of hope, ambition, expectation, enthusiasm, zest.

You and I have to return to that same place and throw out all these things we have accumulated throughout the years of unbelief—get right back again to that simple spot in our own heart. It is normal to have faith, it is natural to believe in God, it is right to love people, it is good to praise everything— because hidden in everything there is a seed of Perfection. There is a divine creative Intelligence in the center of everything, from a blade of grass to an archangel. There is Something that responds to us everywhere we go.

A person who will take time enough to believe there is a Life within him that lighteth everyman's path with Light, the path of thousands . . . one who embraces everyone in his own mind will be embraced by all. Here is a law absolutely inviolate. Last and not least, the great experiment is in our own mind. Who shall hinder? Who shall say to us no? Here in the integrity of our own souls, in the simplicity of our own hearts, you and I can prove what the ages have longed for, lived for, and prayed for: that at last, though we did not know it and the world did not suspect it, Divinity has temporarily clothed itself in humanity.

One Heart beats in the Universe in perfect rhythm. One Mind thinks through us. One Law executes Itself in and around us. Heaven lies close about us—so close, so near, so sweet, so ineffable. O living Truth, O Beauty so perfect, O Love that cannot let us go—the Light that lighteth every man's path; let every thought of fear or doubt or misunderstanding flee from us forevermore. Lord God of Heaven and earth, within and around us: we accept, we believe, we announce; for we are that which Thou art, and Thou art that which we are. And right now we announce that the Kingdom of God is with us. Amen.

I wrote those words as an adaptation of the Lord's Prayer. It says, "Thou doest forgive us as we forgive. / The Kingdom will come when all that live / Thy will have done." In the Bible it says, "Thy kingdom come, thy will be done on earth as it is in heaven"—one of the old teachings which go way back to the Hermetic teaching, which said, "As above, so beneath; as below, so above." What is true on one plane is true on all—the within and the without—and it is really saying that the Kingdom of God on earth will come when, through a realization of God within, the *will* of that Kingdom is done. "And forgive us our debts *as* we forgive our debtors" is another statement of cause and effect, the mirror of life. "It is done unto you as you believe." "Thou forgivest our debts as others we free," this says. It is the only way it could be, because there is your action and reaction again.

Will you please practice these things. The theory is wonderful and sweet—and it is true. You will have to prove it. Just make every prayer affirmative. Say, "*This is the way it is*," and try to feel the reality of it; and then when you give your treatment, forget it. It is in the Law of Mind in action, though you do it every day. Gradually you will see how it works; you will be amazed at what happens, and it will all be so simple.

➜ AFFIRMATIVE-PRAYER MEDITATION ⬅

(Now let's do it for a good many people, who have put their names in the box, wishing help. We are going to help them now. It is a privilege.)

They are going to accept the help, they are going to affirm with us that there is one Life, that Life is God, that Life is their life right now, that Life circulates through them. There is perfect circulation, assimilation, elimination. They are spiritual beings right now. All the Power there is and all the Presence there is is flowing through them. There is only one heart in the Universe; It has perfect rhythm. There is only circulation represented in the bloodstream. In this One Life there is nothing but Good, and we know there is perfect elimination of everything that does not belong. Let us enjoy the perfect health of these people, knowing that through what we are doing now whatever seems to be wrong will be removed. And whoever asked for guidance will receive it. Divine Guidance belongs to everyone.

15.

GOD AND
YOUR PERSONALITY

It has been a great privilege and pleasure to speak to you these ten weeks. Next Sunday, Bill* will be back. A Chinese philosopher once said, "O man, having the power to live, why will ye die?" Isn't it strange this make-believe that we go through that we are so intelligent, and so on—when all we have to do is *be ourselves*, and then we will be great; because God made us great. Anything that gets us away from greatness is merely a stumbling over our own feet. "The great are great to us only because we are on our knees. Let us arise."

Thank you for the wonderful support you have given me these past weeks, the wonderful attendance—this wonderful crowd here this warm morning. It is a sign we are interested in something dynamic and vital, and we are interested together, and we are building a great monument† to the greatest truth the world has ever known. I would like you to know that you are taking part in building that which symbolizes the most liberated spiritual thought since Jesus graced this planet with his presence.

---

*William Hornaday.
†This probably is a reference to the building of Founder's Church of Religious Science, in Los Angeles. The "edifice" referred to in the fifth paragraph is unmistakably Founder's.

Jesus was a simple man who taught the greatest truth the world has ever known. He did not claim to be a messiah. He said, "Why callest thou me good? There is none good save one, which is God." When they mistook him for what he taught, he said, "It is expedient that I go away, that the Spirit of Truth shall awaken in you the meaning of what I have been telling you." Ever since then, the people have taken the teaching and surrounded it with high walls, which have closed out a great deal more landscape than they closed in. Whoever puts a high wall around his small estate will cut out the greater horizon.

It is a very interesting thing to me, because while I started this movement, I have no personal feeling about it at all. It is great and it is good and it is wise, because it depends upon the Wisdom of the ages. We have no Prophets. We are the most normal and natural spiritual group of people who ever lived, because we are not afraid of God or the Universe or each other or the future or destiny. We know that we are in the keeping of an Intelligence beyond ours; that to err is human, to forgive is divine; that "the finite alone has wrought and suffered, the Infinite lies stretched in smiling repose."

I would like to say to you this morning that every dollar you give to this edifice—and you should all give something—you are giving to the greatest spiritual cause the world has ever known since Jesus was here, and to the cause which he magnified. The individual life, sensing its personal relationship to the Universal, will give and bless that gift. The Bible says, "What is man that Thou art mindful of him, or the Son of Man that Thou visitest him; for Thou hast made him but little lower than the angels and hast crowned him with glory and honor."

Our theosophical friends refer to the Mind that sleeps in the mineral, waves in the grass and vegetable, wakes to simple consciousness in the animal, self-consciousness in man, and to Cosmic Conscious in the upper hierarchies—which means there are gradations of unfoldment or evolution from the lowest to the highest. Just as there are beings below us in awareness, there must be beings beyond us in awareness, forever. "Ever as the spiral grew, he left the old house for the new."

Our subject this morning is God and Your Personality, and I would like to spend a few minutes in a rather abstract discussion; so please don't be bored with it. I did not make it up. I happen to believe in it. All the deepest thinkers who have ever lived have believed in it. It is simply this: the Universe is a spiritual system which you and I accept. It is a system governed by laws of Intelligence. Intelligence acts as Law. That is what is back of our treatment. We are all in a process of evolution or unfoldment. There is incarnated in every person and in every thing the image of God, the nature of God, the possibility of God.

Jesus said, "I say that ye are Gods and every one of you sons of the most High." This is the great claim that Jesus made on the Universe. "Who hath seen me, hath seen the Father"; yet "the Father is greater than I." "Believe I am in the Father, and the Father in me; or else believe me for the very works' sake." He claimed that if we could see into the center of things, we should see God. "And seeing the multitude, he went up into the mount. And when he was set, his disciples came unto him, and he opened his mouth and taught them, saying, 'Blessed are the pure in heart for they shall see God.'" He meant *right here*, *right now*, this morning. As we look at each other, there would be a spiritual penetration which would see back of the camouflage, back of everything that appears, to the divine Center of our being, which is God, and God incarnated in each one of us in a unique way.

The central teaching of the ages around which even Christian theology revolves, but most theologians do not know it (and many of them do and believe it is true) is that God is incarnated within each one of us. We had nothing to do with it; that is the way it is. That is the nature of the Universe—and, uniquely, of each one of us; and we are asleep.

But as we gradually wake up, we wake up to what already exists in the Mind of God. And because we wake up to it, it appears to us—"As thou seest, that thou be'st." That is our whole philosophy, it is the philosophy of Jesus, Plato, Socrates, of all the deep spiritual thinkers. But it has a practical application, it has a utilitarian purpose. Jesus said, "It is not I but the Father who dwelleth in me, He doeth the works"; and yet he did not hesitate to say,

"I am the authority of God. My word is the Presence and the Power and the Activity of the Living Spirit; and what I am, ye are also."

"Whatsoever things the Son seeth the Father do, that doeth the Son also, that the Father may be glorified in the Son." Now the teaching is that God, the creative Spirit, incarnates and then lets us alone. Everything in Nature proves this, everything in evolution does, everything in the advance of science. Solomon did not know about an automobile. David, who by the way had the first orchestra and wrote the music for it himself and directed it— David was a great man. But he didn't know anything about modern appliances or electricity. Now all these things existed and waited for somebody to recognize them. Wouldn't it be funny if that were true of *our own nature*? That would be funny indeed! I wrote somewhere: "O *within* all things; *around*; / Brahma, Light of Life divine, / Shatter all our days of dreaming, / Absorb our being into Thine. / Let the mind awake to Brahma / That it no more separate be, / That the life that seemed divided / Be not lost but found in Thee."

Every man has a direct inlet to God. Every man is God as that man. That is the thing I want to think about in this discussion. I don't want you to think I thought all these things up. I believe them. They are true. All the great major religious origins have followed them—all of them. The Greeks taught them in mythology; in all their many Gods and all the things that seemed pluralism, was this one central thought; Emerson refers to it when he says, "There is one mind common to all individual men." You and I do not have a mind separate from God. We do not have a body separate from the Universe. There is one Mind, and we use It; one Spirit in which we live and by which we live; and one Law, which responds creatively to us as we think.

Someone was saying just last night they didn't believe much in treatment because they didn't want to be influenced. I said, "You don't know anything about what you are talking about; you don't understand this philosophy at all. No one influences anybody in our philosophy; no one treats anyone personally in treatment. He is merely referring to the spiritual nature of the individual, which is perfect."

There is inside you and inside me a Perfect Man—I don't know what he looks like. Whitman said, "At the center of everything nestles the seed of perfection." The Bible says, "Awake thou that sleepest and arise from the dead, and Christ shall give thee life." Browning refers to it as a spark which a man may desecrate but never quite lose. Emerson said it seems as though when we entered this world we had taken a drink too strong for us: "We are gods on a debauch." Now they have all said it. And you and I happen to believe in it. God in us—the Living Spirit. We do not believe we are lost souls, some going up and some going down. If there is weather hotter than this, I don't want to go to it; and moreover, I am not going.

"Heaven is lost for an idea of harmony." Many of us are in hell often and will stay there till we get out; and nothing seems to extricate us but ourselves. We have to choose to do it. Every man is "a god though in the germ."

What is this personality? I believe back of this personality, this objective and mental entity, there is a spiritual double. Now let's not get confused. I am not talking about a dual personality, or a split personality. I am just saying I happen to believe that deep within myself and yourself there is another self, of which *this* self is a lower extension, a lesser extension. I believe there is a pattern of perfection in us, for us, about us, with us, around us, through us that we didn't put there. In the beginning God made man perfect, but "man has sought out many inventions."

I happen to believe you and I are spiritual beings on the pathway of an eternal progress, with certainty before us, around us, through us, behind us, and in us—and that, as Browning said, "I shall arrive as birds pursue their trackless path." We are going to get there. We are hell-bent for heaven. We can't help it. You and I do not believe in lost souls or any of this theological nonsense whatsoever. We are liberated from the fear and the superstition of the ages, and I wouldn't be here if I didn't know that. Nor would you. It is so. But it means perhaps more than even we have ever thought.

I often think to myself. I love to just sit and think—and did, yesterday, for several hours. Sometimes I *just sit*, of course, and that is even more relaxing. I was thinking, What a stupendous thing to try to tell anybody! Only to an audience such as ours could I even talk about it; other people would say that we are crazy to say that each one of us is a divine being right now and a perfect being right now and an exalted being right now: it doesn't *look* that way. I understand that; but it *is* that way. "Thou hast made us; Thine we are; and our hearts are restless till they find repose in Thee." The poet* said, "Out of the night that covers me, / Black as the Pit from pole to pole, / I thank whatever Gods there be / For my unconquerable soul. / It matters not how strait the gate, / How charged with punishments the scroll, / I am the master of my fate, / I am the captain of my soul."

Jesus said, "Destroy this body and I will raise up another like unto it"; and when they told him they had power to destroy him, he just laughed at them. Then he said, "There is a truth which, if you know it, will free you." That truth, if it is going to free us, must be an interior thing. We arrive at it by a perception of the relationship of this immediate self to the Universe, to God, and to each other.

We need never be afraid that the knowledge of the Truth will produce a psychological or emotional instability; it is only a knowledge of spiritual Truth that will produce a mental *stability*. Nothing else can. We are so tied up with, and so tied into, and so much a part of, the Universe in which we live that we cannot separate ourselves from it. But we have freedom, choice, and volition; and while we deny this, it is but partly revealed. "Now we see as through a glass darkly, but then face to face. Now we see in part; then shall we know even as we are known."

You see, we are already known by God—by the Spirit—as the spiritual entity which we are. Now wouldn't it be amazing if you and I were the potential of all the power, all the energy, all the action, all the will, all the volition that there is in the Universe—all the endless manifestations and all the Beauty and Peace and Power—? I believe this is true. There is a self not revealed—"That inner self that never tires, / Fed by the deep eternal fires, / Angel and guardian at the gate, / Master of death and king of fate." That is you and that is me. "Oh!" but we say; "this *myself*? No such exalted being can have anything to do with me! I am weak! I am sinful!"

---

*William Savage Landor (1775–1864), in "Invictus."

All of this is true about every one of us. But there is another self; there is an inner self. There is a spiritual—I don't know that you would call it "double," but *extension*: there is a spiritual—Socrates called it his *Daemon*. By that he meant his real Spirit, his Self. It is the Thing with which, or in whom, Jesus was in continual connection. He called it the Father within him. "Our Father which art in Heaven, hallowed be Thy name": Jesus was not praying to an external God, but to a divine inner Presence which he knew to be the universal side of himself. We are all universal. This is what is back of all extrasensory perception, which has nothing to do with sending out thoughts; it is the immediate perception of the soul in a field of unitary wholeness, whose center is everywhere and whose circumference is nowhere.

We deal with one Mind, one Spirit, one Man, and one Universe—but each man a unique individualization of all that there is. "Speak to him, then, for he hears. / And spirit with Spirit shall meet. / Closer is He than breathing, / Nearer than hands and feet."

This is what all great composers, artists, creative people listen to. They may not know it; they may doubt it. It doesn't matter: that is what they listen to. That is what directs them. That is what is back of all creativity: the original Creator *in me*. That is why Emerson said that the mind that wrote history is the mind that must read it; that it can be interpreted only from the standpoint of this mind. This mind is God, the one Mind common to all men. That is why he said the Ancient of Days is in the latest invention; why Kipling said, "There are other ears behind these ears"; and Jesus said, "Who hath seen me hath seen God."

Jesus, Walt Whitman, and Emerson, so far as I know, were the three greatest individualists that ever lived. There is no conceit in this individualization. I mean there is nothing psychologically "smart" about you or me because God made us. We haven't anything to brag about or write home about because God made each one of us different. We need not be afraid to affirm our divine Inheritance; we *ought* to affirm It. But while we deny It, It does not appear. There is That within each one of us, which could not but overcome every adverse situation, whatever it may be, could not but rise triumphant, while we are in this world, to a more complete dominion, a greater happiness, a deeper joy, a higher exaltation, a more complete inward peace that is perfect.

Now this is the meaning of our personality. It isn't this little funny-looking thing. That is all right; I love it; I love all of the things it does. They are silly, but what difference does that make? We don't need to be afraid of being silly. Watch children play; watch puppies and lambs and dogs and kittens: all Nature is glad—but man pulls a long face and is sad, merely because he is not acquainted with himself. We ought to believe in this. It is the basis of everything we do without conceit, without arrogance. "Who hath seen me hath seen the Father," or God. Without any psychological inflation at all, why couldn't we say, "Wonderful me!" The ancients taught their disciples to say, "Wonderful me! I am that which Thou art, Thou art that which I am."

You know, the whole purpose, the whole aim of man is to discover himself. Medicine does not pretend to heal anyone. All they do is to permit Something that *does* heal *to* heal—and that is good, and I believe in it. Surgery does not do anything other than aid Nature. Psychiatry doesn't pretend to create an Ego; it merely removes what denies the realization, and when that is removed—the psychological and physiological obstructions— That which is already perfect assumes Its own prerogatives and comes forth as Lazarus came forth from the grave. We are dead psychologically and physiologically—but not spiritually. We are only half alive physically and mentally—but we are never incomplete spiritually.

There is a Perfect Man back of our psychological and physiological ego. If we want a brilliant personality, we have to be aware of this Man. It isn't that we want to influence people. That is of no importance to me. I wouldn't cross the street to influence anybody or convince anybody or sell anybody anything—because "a man convinced against his will is of the same opinion still." But I can say this: any person who will listen long and deeply to that divine Reality within himself will become aware of It, and he will gradually be directed by It. And he will know—and nothing can dissuade him of this one sublime, supreme fact—that "there is more to a man than is contained between his head and his bootstraps"; that he is an immortal being, on the pathway of eternal self-expression; that there is no final question about the safety or validity of his soul. "Look unto me, and be ye saved, all the ends of the earth."

And every man who believes that God in him is what he is, without conceit, now calls on that divine Presence: "Be what I am!" Loose It; let It go; open the doors of the prison of the Self and free this imprisoned Splendor. And whether it is selling shoes or polishing automobiles or racing horses or singing a song or writing a hymn: they are all the same thing. Let the unwise try to divide the indivisible—don't *you* ever try to do it!

God is in the child at play. "Bless children playing on the shore, / To them belong the Pipes of Pan. / The song of sea, the surf's uproar. . . ." Children; but *we* are afraid to make this great claim on God. Everyone says we are sinners and displease God. Remember this: the Universe exists for the delight of God, and *you* are the delight of God. Why not accept it? There is no arrogance in it. Every song that was ever written was written by the one Mind, slightly differentiated in the uniqueness of the individual writer. If we could keep our minds open to that, we would have divine Direction. Now think of the difference in living with yourself if you think you are poor, weak, sick, a lost soul, nobody loves you, you hate everybody, and nothing is good. That is an unfortunate attitude, and it is encouraged because people say, "Well, we *ought* to do this."

You cannot get conceited if you are dealing with God. "Thine is the kingdom and the power and the glory for ever and ever. Amen." No, you can't be conceited if you say, "God made me and I'll have to accept what God has done. God never makes mistakes. I shall have to accept that somewhere hid within the depths of myself is the God-intended Man. I shall have to accept the fact that as I recognize Him, He will recognize me; as I permit Him to take over, He will know what to do." This is the God that Jesus prayed to: our Father in our Heaven—my Father in my Heaven, your Father in your Heaven—the eternal God. "O Living Truth that shall endure / When all that seems shall suffer shock, / Arise . . . on the rock, / And make us pure."

The Man that God sees—and "as thou seest, that thou be'st"—the man that God knows: shall we know something different? Don't try to develop such a dynamic personality that people fall dead when they look at you. A man said to me one day, "I have something way ahead of your stuff"; and I said, "Thank God; it is bound to happen." I said, "What can you do?" He said, "I can go down the street and look at a man in the back of the neck and he will turn around." And I said, "*Who* does *what* to *which*?! What is all this nonsense?" We are not trying to develop one of these dynamic personalities that breathe fire. Such people bore me into insensibility. They are "children crying in the night and with no language but a cry."

However if somebody ever walks the streets of Los Angeles knowing what Jesus knew about himself, the paralyzed people will get up and follow him gladly. If anyone knows anything about the Light that is at the center of his being, it will light the pathway of everybody he touches. If anyone knows anything about the Love that is all-embracing, his arms will be around everyone in the world. It is all nonsense to say God is Love unless our arms are around people. It is all nonsense to say God is Peace unless there is a peace in our own consciousness that brings calm to everything. It is nonsense to say God is giving unless our hands are open that we may scatter on the four winds of Heaven the last atom of good we have ever received. It is all nonsense to say the Universe holds us in Its loving embrace while we dislike one single soul. As Emerson says, "It writes 'Thou Fool' on the forehead of a king."

We don't have to develop this terrific personality that knocks them over and with just a look slays them. Not at all. But we have to get rid of our denunciation of ourselves, of our renunciation of ourselves, and our denunciation of others, and begin to live as though this were the divine Man. "I am that which Thou art, Thou art that which I am." There is a perfect Man, my dear, at the center of your own being. There is a song ready to be sung; there is an oval form ready to be sculpted into a magnificent deity, uniquely presented; and "There is a God goes with it and makes it soar / To a soul that was starving in darkness before."

You are that Light and *you* are that Love and *you* are that Redeemer. You are that Messiah; you are the only saviour you will ever discover in all your travels. This is the secret Socrates and Emerson and Plato and Jesus and Whitman wrested from the Universe. This is the Secret of the Ages, the Lost Word, the Key to the realization of the Kingdom of Heaven, the entering of the Fifth Kingdom of our evolution and this is what happens: just as when you look in a mirror physically you see a physical image, there is another kind of mirror—more creative—in Life, which is a Mirror of Mind; and as we behold ourselves in It, It beholds Itself in us. And beyond that is the eternal Presence, ever pressing, gently urging, weakly calling, forever embracing.

We are in the arms of a Tenderness, we are in the atmosphere of a Sweetness, we are in the presence of a Light far beyond our dreaming. And in that Light there is no darkness; and as we take time to practice this Presence, feel the depths of this Peace, see the magnificence of this Light and this Life in each other, something awakens in us and, in its turn, within those we meet and the environment which we habitate. And gradually we are lifted from the lower rung of our own elevation in this earth, our own evolution on this earth; and we shall live here and now in the Kingdom of God.

"Beloved, now are we the sons of God." Let us live as though this sonship were real. Somehow out of that which appears as darkness, out of that which appears as isolation, fear, and doubt, and the wasted years, and the dissolution of life—like a Phoenix rising from the ashes of a dead self, some glorious form shall emerge and we shall sing, "Holy, Holy, Holy, Lord God Almighty; Holy, Holy, Holy, Lord God within me."

O Living Presence, O Eternal Sweetness, ineffable Beauty: we recognize Thy Presence, our souls enveloped by Thee, O Living Truth, Rock of our Salvation, O All-Embracing arms of the Infinite Sweetness and Tenderness. Our Father in our Heaven, may our love reach embracing each other and the world, that forevermore we shall sing Holy, Holy, Holy, Lord God Almighty; Holy, Holy, Holy, Lord God within me.

AFFIRMATIVE-PRAYER MEDITATION

(We have names here in this box of those wishing help and we hold them in our own consciousness for a few moments.)

Let's do that, knowing that each name in here and each one who put his name in here does the same thing and he receives it. He is the divine Man we have been talking about. That divine Man is recognized and realized, and manifests now. There is a divine Pattern of his physical body forever in the Mind of God, perfect. There is success and happiness and joy in everything he does. We receive for him, and know for him, and he expects for himself, guidance, perfect healing, perfect Love, perfect Wisdom. And so it is.

Now as we turn to that divine Presence which is both God and Man, we recognize our being in each other—in the infinite pattern of eternal Perfection—and it is our will to bring life and joy to everyone we meet. And the eternal Spirit goes with us, and we with It, now and forevermore. Amen.

If you enjoyed this book, visit

www.tarcherbooks.com

and sign up for Tarcher's e-newsletter to receive
special offers, giveaway promotions, and
information on hot upcoming releases.

TARCHER
PENGUIN

Great Lives Begin with Great Ideas

Connect with the Tarcher Community

• • •

Stay in touch with favorite authors!
Enter weekly contests!
Read exclusive excerpts!
Voice your opinions!

Follow us

 Tarcher Books

 @TarcherBooks

If you would like to place a bulk order
of this book, call 1-800-847-5515.